[WITHDRAWN

SUICIDE, INDIVIDUAL AND SOCIETY

Toyomasa Fusé, Ph.D.

SUICIDE, INDIVIDUAL AND SOCIETY

Toyomasa Fusé, Ph.D.

Canadian Scholars' Press   Toronto   1997

Suicide, Individual and Society
Toyomasa Fusé, Ph.D.

First published in 1997 by
Canadian Scholars' Press Inc.
180 Bloor Street West, Ste. 402
Toronto, Ontario
M5S 2V6

Canadian Cataloguing in Publication Data

Fuse, Toyomasa
 To be or not to be : suicide, individual and society

Includes bibliographical references and index.
ISBN 1-55130-108-3

1. Suicide. I. Title.

HV6545.F87 1997   362.2'8   C96-932134-1

Page layout and cover design by Brad Horning

This book is dedicated to

Lois, Megumi and Kenji

"So we may have life and have it more abundantly."

"To be, or not to be, that is the question:
Whether 'tis nobler in the mind to suffer
The slings and arrows of outrageous fortune,
Or to take arms against a sea of troubles,
And by opposing, end them. To die; to sleep,
No more; and by a sleep to say we end
The heart-ache and the thousand natural shocks
That flesh is heir to..."

Hamlet, William Shakespeare

Contents

Preface

Derived from Latin—"sui" (itself, himself, herself) and "cide" (to cut, to kill)—suicide refers to a voluntary, intentional, self-inflicted death. It has been a source of human tragedy and rich drama in theatre, literature and films for centuries in literate human civilizations and cultures. In the past 100 years or so, it has been receiving much deserved attention and research from social, behavioural and medical scientists.

Humans are born to die; no one can deny or evade this destiny. It is the unavoidable human condition. It is generally believed that there is a universal human instinct for preservation of one's life—to prolong one's life on this earth at any cost with whatever means available. Yet, some people rebel against their natural life expectancy by deliberately and intentionally killing themselves.

According to Freud, as will be explained later in the present volume, human beings are endowed with a desire to live (which he called *eros* or life impulse) as well as a wish to die—a wish to be reduced to the original state of nothingness (which was called *thanatos* or death impulse). According to this hypothesis, suicide is a dramatic and extreme expression of the death impulse that may evoke the death wish which lies dormant deep in the unconsciousness of every human. Suicide, according to this hypothesis, may make all of us become aware, either clearly or vaguely, of the very existence of the death impulse that drives us to nothingness (i.e., death). Freud called the whole rationale and process for the drive to ultimate extinction the Nirvana principle (taken from Hinduism and Buddhism, referring to ultimate liberation and enlightenment through the extinction of the body, worldly cravings and desires). Perhaps this might explain the secret of anxiety, discomfort and, paradoxically, extraordinary interest in suicide shown by many individuals. At any rate, no one is neutral or indifferent to suicide.

The present author still vividly remembers as a student the tremendous intellectual excitement aroused by the extraordinary work of Emile Durkheim (to be discussed in great detail later in the book). In his truly original and seminal work on suicide, Durkheim, more than anyone else of his time, showed compelling evidence for the close interrelationships between suicide and society. He demonstrated, for instance, that suicide rates as a collective and social phenomenon differed from society to society, and from one social group to another, the fact of which suggested to him some characteristics of social groups to which one belonged; furthermore, he demonstrated brilliantly and compellingly that, despite obvious individual differences in suicide motives, there were some discernible and persistent characteristics in suicide rates among various social groups, leading Durkheim to hypothesize supra- and extra-individual factors in the phenomenon of suicide. Central to his approach to suicide was his belief that suicide must be understood as a social phenomenon in the context of the social groups, culture and society to which one belonged. Herein lies the reason for the title of the present volume: for the author had decided, as a student, to continue the study of suicide in a cross-cultural perspective as originally inspired by this extraordinarily creative founder of modern sociology.

Suicidology today, however, has gone beyond the insights and approaches of Durkheim; it has evolved into a genuinely multidisciplinary science which incorporates the methodology and findings of psychology, medicine, psychiatry, neurobiology and even ethics. It is the central objective of the present author, therefore, to shed light on many aspects of suicide behaviour in interdisciplinary and cross-cultural perspectives, incorporating the important research findings of these disciplines in a synthetic and integrated manner. The inclusion of interdisciplinary and cross-cultural orientations and data throughout the present volume reflects the fundamental belief of the present author that suicide behaviour as a *human social action* must be understood in a close interplay between various human sciences as well as in the context of an interaction between the individual and society.

The present volume consists of seven chapters. In Chapter 1, the etymology of "suicide" is discussed in several Indo-European languages and in Japanese, revealing some interesting differences in the meanings attached to the etymology of the word. Such differences suggest deep-seated, religio-moral values in Judaeo-Christian countries in Europe and North America on one hand, and a non-Christian country such as Japan on the other. Then, the field of suicidology is defined and introduced as being composed of three major domains: epidemiology, which aims at examining the distribution and rates of suicide around the world in socio-demographic variables; theories, which attempt to probe the possible reasons for suicide in terms of sociological, psychological and biological perspectives; and praxis, which involves activities in prevention, intervention and postvention of suicide. The present book has been designed to fully explore the basic aspects of these three principal areas of present-day suicidology. Also in the latter half of this introductory chapter a brief history of social thought on suicide in Europe and North America from ancient times to the present is presented together with a discussion of the major research activities, past and present, in suicidology.

Chapter 2 deals with the epidemiology of suicide around the world. But the detailed discussion of epidemiology is preceded by a "Suicide Knowledge Test," which the reader is encouraged to take in order to test his or her current level of knowledge about various aspects of suicide epidemiology. Though the correct answers for these questions are given at the end of the test, the present book is organized in such a way that the reader will come to fully understand various aspects of suicidology as exemplified in these questions. Following the Suicide Knowledge Test, an overview of basic world trends in suicide rates is given; it is then followed by a detailed discussion of the reliability of suicide statistics (both pros and cons) and a brief and critical discussion of how death by suicide is certified and what criteria are being used by certifying officials around the world.

In Chapter 3, the longest chapter in the present volume, there is a detailed discussion of the theories of suicide from the three major disciplines that have historically informed on suicide research: sociology, psychology and biology. It must be parenthetically mentioned that usually every available book on suicidology pays a passing and much too brief homage to Emile Durkheim and his monumental work. As a necessary corrective to such a situation, a detailed discussion of Durkheim's theory has been presented. In addition to Durkheim, some other seminal sociological ideas such as the "social action" theory of Max Weber are also discussed, which have been germaine to the modern, sociological-phenomenological theories of Jack Douglas and Jean Baeschler. The latter two sociologists— the former an American and the latter a Frenchman—have argued that suicide must be understood in the context of what death meant to the deceased. Their approach to suicide tried to remove the stigma of psychopathology from self-inflicted death. To Douglas and Baeschler, suicide is more often than not a "logical response to an existential problem." Their emphasis on the importance of the inner meanings to death *à la* Weber has led to the appreciation and importance of suicide notes and psychological autopsies in the past two decades even among sociologists who have shunned suicide notes but have traditionally concentrated more on collective suicide rates than individual case studies. Thus, the "social action" theory of Max Weber, Jack Douglas and Jean Baeschler has been building a bridge between sociology and psychology. Following these sociological theories, the discussion moves to an examination of one of the most important theories of medical psychology—the theory of Sigmund Freud. Freud's ideas on "object loss" as a precursor to depression and grieving have laid the foundation for the present-day approach to grief and bereavement, depression and postvention. After the discussion of Freudian theory, a brief introduction is made to the theories of Karl Menninger, Edwin Shneidman, Norman Farberow and Aaron Beck, all of whom have much informed the field of suicidology with their ideas on suicidality, crisis management and the role of hopelessness in the etiology of suicide. Then, a discussion of biological theories ensues, introducing the reader to the contributions made by neurobiology (such as the role and function of amino-acid based serotonin in the alleged etiology of suicide) and genetic factors as revealed in family risk, twin and adoption studies. Such biological theories have gained enormous attention and ascendancy in contemporary suicidology in the past two decades. Finally, the author's own synthetic model is introduced as an attempt to understand suicide behaviour in its total and holistic dimension.

Chapters 4, 5, and 6 present ongoing research in modern suicidology that may shed light on various aspects of suicide behaviour. Chapter 4 discusses the increasingly evident relationship between diagnosable mental illness and suicide. Thus, a fairly comprehensive discussion on one of the most important accompanying aspects of suicidality— depression—is discussed in terms of its assumed relationship to suicide, together with a discussion on the cross-cultural dimension of depression.

For the benefit of the average reader, the author introduces some basic criteria and assessment tools for mental illness as well as some controversies surrounding the difficulties in diagnosing and determining mental illness.

In Chapter 5, the author presents one of his own cross-cultural research on "*seppuku*" (also known as "*hara-kiri*" in the West)—ritual self-disembowelment in Japan—as a case study in suicide and culture. *Seppuku* has been a time-honoured practice of self-inflicted death in Japan among the samurai and among military officers in modern Japan. A revised and much expanded version of the author's earlier study, published in *Social Psychiatry*, the discussion of *seppuku* demonstrates that it is little related to mental illness and other forms of psychopathology, as it has been positively sanctioned for centuries as a normative and honourable way of death in Japan. As such it is a necessary corrective to the Euro-American tendency to equate suicide too readily with mental illness and psychopathology. The concept of *seppuku*, as independent from psychopathology and mental illness, may no longer be so alien to the West either; the theories of Jean Baeschler and Jack Douglas, as discussed in Chapter 3, try to understand suicide primarily as a "logical response to an existential problem." Recent trends in the West towards affirming the "right to die" and "dying with dignity" reflect a shift in thinking from psychopathology to ethical and legal questions, suggesting the ascendancy of a concept similar to that of *seppuku*.

In Chapter 6, the discussion focuses on the question of physician suicide. Some researchers have argued that doctors kill themselves at a rate higher than the general population, whereas some others have insisted that the physician rate of suicide does not exceed that of the general population of a similar age. A comprehensive survey and careful re-examination of all available data renders some tentative conclusions on this controversial question. There is also an analysis of two particular questions on physician suicide that have consistently emerged in most studies: gender and medical speciality.

The last chapter, Chapter 7, presents many aspects of suicide in terms of crisis management. The focus of the discussion is on three dimensions of crisis management: prevention, intervention and postvention. In terms of prevention, a focus has been centred on the origin, philosophy and development of telephone crisis lines, which have been in the forefront of suicide prevention since the 1950s. It has been pointed out that the emergence of the lay-centred telephone helpline is one of the most remarkable phenomena in the history of mental health. Then the discussion moves to reviewing the nature and type of crisis intervention currently available and practised by the medical, non-medical and synthetic models. The discussion of suicide as a human crisis also includes some practical guidelines for detecting the clues and warning signs of suicide, basic information on misconceptions and myths about suicide, and do's and don'ts in dealing with the suicidal. Finally, the chapter concludes with the discussion of postvention—the question of dealing with the surviving family. This last chapter is much more focussed on the practical aspects of suicide management, drawing considerably not only on the author's past research and field work in more than 40 countries but also on his own involvement as a volunteer in one of the crisis centres in Toronto.

In the Epilogue, the author presents a highly personal view on the question of why suicide should be prevented and intervened. This final postscript is a shorter and abridged version of the author's recent lecture on the subject delivered at the Department of Psychiatry, St. Michael's Hospital, University of Toronto. The views expressed in the Epilogue reflect the evolution of the author's thoughts on the subject, greatly assisted by the psychological autopsies he had done in one of his earlier published books on the lives of 11 well-known personalities from five different countries.

A book of this nature and magnitude could not have been written without the cooperation, assistance and encouragement of many individuals and organizations. At the risk of omitting many that deserve mention, the author would like to first acknowledge his gratitude to the Division of Social Science at York University (especially to Dr. Jane Haynes, then Chairperson of the division), which encouraged him to do research and also to offer a seminar on suicidology at a time when social taboos against suicide were much stronger than today. Thanks are also due to numerous grants from the Social Sciences and Humanities Research Council of Canada (including both small research grants and cultural exchange programmes with many different countries, enabling the author to conduct field research), the Faculty of Arts Research Grants Committee at York University; the Academy of Sciences of Hungary, ministries of health in Italy and the Netherlands, Society for the Promotion of Science in Japan, Centre National de la Recherche Scientifique (C.N.R.S) in France, Deutscher Akademischer Austaus Dienst der Bundesrepublik Deutschland, Institut d'Etude Demographique in Paris, Institute for Social Ecology at the University of Negev in Beer Sheva, Israel. The Bureau d'Accueil des

Professeurs Etrangers in Paris provided much appreciated and scarce office space and clerical help. Thanks are also extended to medical examiners' offices, crisis units at hospitals and research centres in Japan, United States, Canada, France, Spain, Portugal, Germany, Hungary, Italy, Belgium, the Netherlands, Denmark, Sweden, Finland, Greece, the former Yugoslavia, the ex-Soviet Union, People's Republic of China, Macao, and Israel.

At the individual level, the following persons deserve the author's special appreciation and gratitude for his cross-cultural research. In Japan, Dr. Yukio Saito, Executive Director of Tokyo Lifeline (known as INOCHI-NO-DENWA in Japanese), has opened many doors to the author over the years, enabling him to gather invaluable data on the telephone crisis lines in Japan. The late Professor Hiroshi Inamura, M.D., Department of Psychiatry at Hitotsubashi University, informed the author in no small measure on suicide behaviour in Japan through his numerous books and personal discussions. Also the late Professor Kan'ichiro Ishii, a pioneer in suicide prevention and intervention activities in Japan, had an indelible impact on the author through his research and personal friendship. Professor Hisashi Kurosawa, M.D., Nippon Medical College, was instrumental in helping the author appreciate the clinical dimension of psychiatry vis-a-vis suicide attempters in Tokyo. By any yardstick, he is one of the most distinguished suicidologists in Japan, whose work has enlightened some parts of the present volume. Professor Hisao Naka, a sociologist known in Japan for his major work on Emile Durkheim, invited the author to Japan for joint research on suicide, which further deepened the latter's understanding of Durkheim's contribution to suicidology. During the period of the said joint research with Professor Naka, the author's basic research on *seppuku* (Japan's ritual self-disembowelment, known in the West as "hara-kiri") was completed. Ms Yoko Koizumi, Executive Director, Ichijoji Research Centre, certainly deserves a special mention for her friendship and assistance in providing lodging and research facilities at her centre. It is Ms Koizumi who introduced the author to the world of *Naikan*, a time-honoured, Buddhist-based ethnotherapy in Japan.

In Europe, Dr. K. Szombathy of the Hungarian Academy of Sciences helped the author to better understand suicide in Hungary, a country that has demonstrated the highest suicide rate for decades, by making necessary arrangements to see specialists and making trips to every part of the then Communist country. Professor Francois Raveau, director of the Charles Centre for the Study of Social Maladaptation in Paris, warmly welcomed the author as a guest researcher during the author's long stay in Paris and France. Dr. Jean-Claude Chenais at the National Institute of Demographic Study in Paris provided a vast amount of information and valuable data on suicide across Europe covering over a century. Frau Barbara Radovic at the Deutscher Akademischer Austaus Dienst der Bundesrepublik Deutschland (in the Berlin headquarters) was most helpful in providing the author with housing and making arrangements to visit major research centres, hospitals and crisis centres throughout Germany. Dr. C. Kulessa, University Clinic, University of Heidelberg, offered not only temporary lodging for the author but opportunities for observation and discussion with many German scientists, researchers and clinicians. Ms Tal Perry, Executive Director of Jerusalem's ERAN (Emotional First Aid) is credited for enhancing and deepening the author's understanding of telephonic emergency services in Israel. It should also be mentioned that Tal Perry is certainly one of the most effective and empathetic telephone befrienders the author has ever encountered anywhere in the world. The author owes to her the cross-cultural appreciation of the effectiveness of the phone helpline.

In North America, Professor Mamoru Iga, formerly of Japan and later of the University of California at Northridge, has been one of the individuals who sparked the author's interest in comparative suicidology. His sharp and critical observations have taught the present author the true meaning of objective sociological study. Dr. Rosemary Barnes, formerly at Self-Harm Assessment Research and Education (S.H.A.R.E.) at Toronto Hospital, regularly exchanged and shared information with the author. Dr. Al Evans, one of the long-standing and eminent suicide researchers in Canada, St. Paul's College, University of Waterloo, was the very first colleague in this country to initiate professional dialogue on suicide with the author almost 20 years ago, and has stimulated the author's thinking ever since. He is one of the colleagues who read the original manuscript and made valuable suggestions. Mr. Gordon Winch, Emeritus Director of Distress Centre I in Toronto, taught the author about the importance of contributions lay volunteers can and do make in suicide prevention and intervention. In the field of telephonic emergency services, Gordon has stood as a model of unparalleled lay wisdom; he is certainly and primarily responsible for the founding and current prestige of the crisis line in Ontario. Dr. Isaac Sakinofsky, M.D., Clark Institute of Psychiatry, a dear friend and colleague in suicidology for years, is certainly one of the most distinguished suicidologists in Canada; he not only read the present author's manuscript but also graced the volume with his foreword.

Ms Miriam Freifeld, a doctoral student at York University, has been an extremely able and loyal friend and a junior colleague in suicidology; she has taught the author what it means to be a survivor victim. Ms T. Gomes deserves a mention as a dedicated and very resourceful research assistant who has gone beyond the call of duty in preparation of several chapters in the present volume. Ms Enza Mancuso, a graduate student in clinical psychology at the Ontario Institute for Studies in Education (O.I.S.E.), has also been a research assistant for this author for some years; she is responsible for assisting in the preparation of the first three chapters. She continued to assist the author even when her father was suffering from terminal cancer. Ms Heather Johnson collaborated with the author in the writing of a pilot study on the textbook analysis of suicide information for health-care professionals. Ms Francis McKenzie rendered clerical assistance with precision, persistence and a good sense of humour. The author also wishes to express his thanks to all crisis workers, researchers, clinicians and volunteers in more than 40 countries around the world who have cheerfully and graciously accepted the intrusion of the author, welcomed him into their midst and helped him deepen his understanding of their long and selfless work on crisis lines and crisis intervention centres. Special thanks in this regard go to all the volunteers at Scarborough Distress Centre, as some of the theoretical and practical implications mentioned in the last chapter are derived from the author's experience as a volunteer at the centre. In a sense, this book is dedicated to all these people whose work does make a difference in the question of life or death.

The teaching of suicidology and the writing of the present volume have been made enormously easy by the cheerful and resourceful assistance of my support staff over the years, including Alda Lone, Jackie McConnel (now Administrative Assistant in Department of Sociology), Jacqueline Selman and Allyson Young of the Division of Social Science, Faculty of Arts, York University. Certainly the author must thank all his students, past and present, both graduate and undergraduate, who have given necessary feedback on his teaching and research in the classroom, challenging and at times forcing him to revise his concepts. My special and warm thanks are extended to Ms Megumi Fusé (and Dr. Megumi Fusé in the not-too-distant future), a doctoral student in the field of biology who cheerfully and ably assisted her proud father in the latter's suicidology seminar on the role and function of neurotransmitters (e.g., serotonin) in human mood and behaviour. Last and most important, the author must express his deepest felt gratitude to Lois Prochaska-Fusé, the author's longest and most faithful unofficial and "unpaid" assistant-editor-proofreader-bibliographer-critic over the past 36 years, without whose loyal and resourceful help and support the present book would not have been possible. Though deeply indebted to all these organizations and individuals, it goes without saying that the author assumes full and entire responsibility for the content of the book.

Toronto 1997

Foreword

It is an honour, as someone who considers Professor Toyomasa Fusé to be both a colleague and a friend, to contribute a foreword to his new book on suicide. Toyomasa Fusé brings to this book a career of scholarship and research into suicide, and the advantage of being able to bridge the crucial cross-cultural gulf in understanding it from the viewpoints of some forty societies he has studied and/or experienced directly. Coming from an Oriental background, he then did research in Europe for several years, and in the most recent phase of his career he has taught social science at Toronto's York University where he pioneered a highly regarded seminar program in suicidology. Though skilled in several languages this is his first major foray into a publication in English, and hitherto manuscripts have been written in Japanese, published first in that country, and then translated into other languages. As a result his work is probably best known in the Orient and he is frequently invited there on lecture tours, which also function to keep him constantly abreast of developments in that part of the world.

There are today very many books about suicide, but there will be very few that will compare with this one in its author's expertise in the cultural dimensions of suicide, especially those that differentiate East from West. Professor Fusé's familiarity with cross-cultural nuances in suicidology is immediately apparent throughout this comprehensive volume, undoubtedly enriching his material in a manner beyond the reach of most North American suicidologists. In the very first section he deals with the etymology of suicide, tracing its lineage in European and Indo-European languages, then points out how there are more than thirty words that mean "suicide" in Japanese carried out in as many ways, so embedded has the phenomenon become in its history and its culture. Unlike the case in Western cultures none of these terms carry connotations of ethical or moral value judgment, making it more understandable to us why ritual suicide (*seppuku*) and *kamikaze* have become such well-known behavioural phenomena associated with the former Japan.

Professor Fusé next addresses the epidemology of suicide, not only the statistical data about its frequency and prevalence in particular societal groups but also the vital question about the validity of international suicide statistics and how they are collected and ascertained in the province of Ontario and around the world.

Chapter 3 is a meaty section which discusses theories of the causation of suicide, primarily from the sociological and psychological standpoints, but also covering the newly burgeoning biological areas. As a sociologist himself there is a proper acknowledgement of the seminal role played by the great nineteenth-century French sociologist, Emile Durkheim, whose landmark book, *Le Suicide*, laid the groundwork one hundred years ago for the sociological study of suicide. This section begins with interesting and little known biographical material and discusses the influences on his thinking and his break with the humanities and emergence into the field of science applied to social problems. Durkheim's theories are clearly presented and later attempts to replicate and/or test their validity are carefully dealt with. This section is illustrated by case examples of well known personalities (like Ernest Hemingway) who have taken their own lives. After this discussion Fusé proceeds to the work of Weber, Douglas, Baechsler and others, and then turns to the psychological theories of Freud, Menninger and (more recently) Shneidman, Farberow and Beck. A strength in this section is that after the theories of each group or individual have been explored there follows an account of how they have been empirically evaluated by others. Although not a biologist Fusé covers this field quite clearly, making this important area of endeavour meaningful to other non-biologists.

In Chapter 4 the author reviews the evidence that suicide is related to psychiatric illness, behavioural and cognitive theories of depression and also the biological studies. The subsection on culture is, predictably, of particular interest. The theme is taken up again in Chapter 5 where *seppuku* is explored in depth as a study of suicide in a cultural context; this is undoubtedly one of the highlights of the book for this reader and represents an authoritative reference on an important area for Western suicidologists. Chapter 6 discusses studies on suicide among physicians, a surprisingly large section of the book for such a special sub-population, but possibly reflecting the author's curiosity about the paradox implicit in the saying, *physician heal thyself.*

The final section of the book is about the prevention and treatment of self-destructive behaviour, and thus possibly the most useful to those for whom it is intended. Professor Fusé discusses the management of personal crises in detail, starting with the theory of crisis and how it developed with Lindemann and Caplan. Telephone crisis services are fully discussed, making special use of methodology from Ontario and from the pioneering Los Angeles Suicide Prevention Center. The various phases of secondary intervention (after suicidal behaviour) are dealt with, assessment of further risk, medical treatment and whether to recommend hospitalisation. As usual Fusé puts his familiar imprimatur on the section by a fascinating discussion of Japanese indigenous ethnotherapies, *morita* and *naikan*, deriving from Zen and Jodo Shinshu Buddhist teachings respectively. *Naikan*, in particular, has been credited in Japan with positive results in the treatment of suicide attempters. In light of our current interest in alternative therapies and the popularity of Tai Chi it would not be surprising if *Naikan-Ryoho* caught on in a similar fashion among readers of this book.

Isaac Sakinofsky, MB, ChB, MD, DPM(Lond), FRCP(C), FRCPsych(UK)
Professor of Psychiatry & Preventive Medicine & Biostatistics,
Clark Institute of Psychiatry, University of Toronto

CHAPTER 1

Suicidology—What it is, its fields of inquiry and its historical development

ETYMOLOGY OF "SUICIDE"

Simply defined, culture is a collective design for living. A bit more elaborately, it is a set of values, norms, artefacts, and symbols that provide a distinctive way of collective living and have been socially but not biologically transmitted to certain social groups. Language is certainly one of the most important and essential tools and means of expressing and transmitting a culture.

Language provides frameworks for creating and transmitting thoughts, knowledge, individual and collective wishes, aspirations, fears, joys and other feelings of humans. The mode of thinking, mores and other strongly held values as well as behavioural standards and cues (both prescriptions and proscriptions) of a culturally defined social group are usually reflected and contained in its language. Insofar as human language reflects the way of life, thinking and values of a cultural group as influenced by such artefacts as religion, law, customs and folkways, mode of socialization, collective history and tradition, the general attitudes and feelings about the act of suicide (either completed or attempted) are often shaped by and/or reflected in the very etymology of a given language.

Etymology refers to historical tracing of a linguistic form (such as its vocabulary) in its earliest recorded occurrence in the language where it is found. Hence, the etymology of "suicide" may provide us with some important clues to understanding the culturally related attitudes as well as some deeply felt religio-moral values and sentiments of a given social group about suicide.

In European languages, the word "suicide" is a compound noun and is derived from Latin—*sui* (of itself, him-/herself) and *cida* (to cut off, to kill).[1] It is "suicide" in English and French, *suicidio* in Italian and Spanish, and *selbstmord* in German. In an extensive investigation by the present author, in all Indo-European languages as well as some non-Indo-European languages like Hebrew and Arabic, the word "suicide" has always had the connotation of "self-killing" or "self-murder". "Suicide" made its debut in English back in 1642 in Sir Thomas Browne's *Religio Medici* (Section XLIV), and subsequently in the *Oxford English Dictionary*.[2] As its original connotation ("self-murder") suggests, the word and the implied meaning are definitely moral-evaluative and judgmental-condemnatory, reflecting the negative, religio-moral judgment and condemnation against such an intentional, self-harm behaviour as suicide.

In Japanese, by contrast, there are more than thirty words equivalent to the afore-mentioned "suicide".[3] Just a few examples in Japanese and the appropriate translations are given in Figure 1.

"*Ishi*," the first word in Figure 1, literally means "death by self-strangulation;" "*toshin*," the second on the list, refers to "death by jumping off from a high place;" "*nyusui*" indicates "death by self-drowning;" "*seppuku*" (also known as "*hara-kiri*") literally means "slitting one's abdomen;" "*shoshin*" means "self-immolation;" "*joshi*" refers to love suicide pact or "double suicide;" "*ikka-shinju*" means "suicide pact of the entire family;" "*boshi-shinju*" ("mother-child[ren] suicide"); "*fushi-shinju*," ("father-child[ren] suicide"); "*jibaku*," or "suicide by self-explosion," denoting the suicide by one's own explosives such as the kamikaze; "*jijin*," or "death by one's own sword," referring to the suicide of the samurai or by high-ranking military officers and soldiers as well as some civilians; "*ichimonji-bara*," meaning "slitting one's abdomen sideways just once;" and "*jumonji-bara*," meaning "slitting one's abdomen both horizontally and vertically as in cross," etc. It is important to notice in the aforementioned examples that these Japanese equivalents of "suicide" are characteristically devoid of any ethico-moral evaluation, judgment and/or condemnation. Rather, they are descriptive of the mode, means, number of people involved and type of

縊死 — *Ishi* (Suicide by strangulation)

投身 — *Toshin* (Suicide by jumping)

入水 — *Nyusui* (Suicide by drowning)

切腹 — *Seppuku* (Suicide by slitting the belly)

焼身 — *Shoshin* (Suicide by self-immolation)

情死 — *Joshi* (Suicide pact)

一家心中 — *Ikka-shinju* (Family suicide pact)

母子心中 — *Boshi-shinju* (Mother-child suicide)

父子心中 — *Fushi-shinju* (Father-child suicide)

自爆 — *Jibaku* (Suicide by self-explosion)

自刃 — *Jijin* (Suicide by sword)

一文字腹 — *Ichimonji-bara* (*Seppuku* by slitting belly sideways just once)

十文字腹 — *Jumonji-bara* (*Seppuku* by horizontal and vertical slitting of belly) human relationship of the deceased (e.g., lovers' suicide pact, family suicide).[4] Such etymology of the word "suicide" in Japanese is certainly reflective of the long-standing tradition in Japanese culture that has been tolerant of death in general and of suicide in particular.

Such etymological comparison cited above between European languages and Japanese reveals interesting differences in attitudes towards suicide. In Judaeo-Christian faiths, there has been a deeply felt belief that the ultimate human destiny involving life and death is in the hands of God the Creator: "God giveth and God taketh." Suicide as an intentional, self-inflicted death, therefore, has historically been denounced and condemned as one of the most serious sins and offences against God, resulting over the centuries in refusal of a religious burial.

In Japan's religio-moral tradition, by contrast, suicide has neither been a "mortal sin" in the religious sense nor a "crime" in legal terms. It is not difficult to understand that such historical tolerance of suicide in Japan has played a crucial role in the origin, development and institutionalization of such a time-honoured ritual suicide as *seppuku* as well as the widespread practices of the banzai charge (mass suicide by the Japanese military) and the kamikaze suicide attacks in the Pacific during World War II.

What Is Suicidology and What Does It Do?

Introduced for the first time in 1954 by an American clinical psychologist, Dr. Edwin Shneidman, the word "suicidology" is a compound word of Latin-derived "suicide" and Greek derivative of "*logia*;" as such, it means study of suicide. As one of the prominent suicidologists and the co-founder of the world-renowned Los Angeles Suicide Prevention Center, he is responsible for some seminal and pioneering work in the systematic study of suicide.

While working at the National Institute of Mental Health (NIMH) in Bethesda, Maryland, Shneidman published a quarterly entitled *The Bulletin of Suicidology* in 1964 and distributed it to medical schools, departments of public health, universities, crisis centres, suicide prevention centres, psychologists, physicians, etc. Gradually the word "suicidology" has taken root as denoting a field combining research and clinical praxis in relation to suicide behaviour. Shneidman was also instrumental in launching a new professional organization in 1968 devoted to suicide research on one hand and praxis (prevention, intervention and postvention) on the other. In its inaugural meeting, the organization adopted the name of American Association of Suicidology (AAS), which has become probably the best known professional association of people in the field, including both mental health specialists and trained lay persons.

Suicidology today refers to a systematic and scientific study of suicide, both attempted and completed, involving study and collation of suicide statistics in terms of socio-demographic variables (epidemiology), speculation and probing of presumed causes of such voluntary self-inflicted harm (theory), and adoption of prevention, intervention and postvention measures (praxis). Thus suicidology includes the three basic components of epidemiology, theory construction and praxis.

Epidemiology

Epidemiology is primarily a specialization in medicine, especially in its branch of epidemic control and public health that is concerned with the task of determining the origin, frequency and distribution of an infectious disease in relation to geographical and socio-demographic variables. Its ultimate aim is to control and prevent infectious diseases. As such, it has traditionally been involved with (a) clarifying disease characteristics in a given population or populations in general, (b) devising disease classification systems, (c) determining the pathogens and causes, and (d) working out effective prevention measures and public health programmes in affected areas as well as in the entire population. Epidemiology today, however, goes beyond the study of infectious diseases and deals with such problems as cancer, hypertension, heart disease, diabetes and accidents as well as the frequency and distribution of suicide, longevity and life expectancy and obesity.

With regards to suicide, the main concern of epidemiology is an inquiry into the increases and decreases of suicide rates in relation to geographical, demographic and sociological factors. Its main focus is on identifying certain sociological characteristics and attributes of suicide such as age, gender, occupation, residence, marital status, education, religion, race and ethnicity, means of suicide and/or motives. Identification of such socio-demographic traits is extremely useful in pin-pointing a target population and high-risk group(s). In terms of suicidology, its epidemiology has been primarily undertaken by demography, sociology, medicine, public health and central statistical offices and other governmental agencies. Probably the best known classical study of such suicide epidemiology is Emile Durkheim's *Suicide: A Study in Sociology* (1897). Practitioners involved in epidemiology of suicide include: demographers, sociologists, public health officials, statisticians in medical examiners' and coroners' offices, hospitals and police departments, etc. Both crude suicide rate (CSR) and age-specific suicide rate (ASR) are expressed in numbers of suicide in a given year per 100,000 inhabitants.

Theory

The second major area of suicidology is the inquiry into and speculation about possible reasons and causes for suicide. There are three major theoretical orientations and approaches in probing the causes of suicide: sociological, psychological and biochemical theories. Sociological orientations try to investigate and understand suicide behaviour in terms of social and group influences that may affect suicide; psychological theories, on the other hand, tend to look into both conscious and unconscious motivations, stress, depression and hopelessness, all at the individual level contributing to the final step of self-inflicted death; finally, biochemical speculations, which have gained much attention in the crest of mounting salience of biology and genetics in the latter part of the twentieth century, hope to look at suicide in terms of physiology, neurotransmitters and hereditary variables. Whichever approach(es) and orientation(s) appeal to the reader, the existence of many theoretical frameworks for understanding suicide suggests that there is no single, unifying theory of suicide to account for all types of suicide at this stage of the development of theory in suicidology. Until such time as the emergence of a general, unifying and cross-culturally valid and applicable theory of suicide is achieved, it is probably more prudent and fruitful to understand suicide in the context of all these theoretical orientations combined in a given culture (i.e., a synthesis of psychology, cultural orientations, sociology and biochemistry). Practitioners actively involved in theory building are: clinical psychologists, sociologists, psychiatrists, health-care professionals in emergency medicine (physicians and nurses), clinical social workers, psychotherapists, counsellors and scientists in life sciences (biochemistry, genetics, physiology, neuro-pharmacology, molecular biology).

Praxis (Prevention, Intervention, Postvention)

One of the special features of suicidology is the fact that it goes far beyond academic pursuit and scholarly research and includes activities and practices by professionals as well as trained lay persons in the fields of mental health, clinical medicine, psychology, nursing, sociology, police work, counselling and crisis intervention. As such, the domain of praxis in suicidology is generally divided into three areas of concern, research and practice: *prevention, intervention* and *postvention.*

Prevention activities include proper recognition and understanding of possible antecedent "clues" and "warning signs" for suicide ideation and suicidal act, which have thus far been identified by clinicians, mental health professionals, health-care workers, as well as by well-trained staff and volunteers at crisis intervention centres; they also involve public education and information dissemination, provision of facilities and necessary personnel for counselling, establishing and operation of telephone emergency services (e.g., distress centres, crisis centres, youth hot lines etc.). One of the unique attendant features of prevention activities has been the active involvement and contributions of trained lay volunteers who, since 1950s, have constituted the core and bulk of such prevention activities. The Samaritans in the United Kingdom, Telecare and Crisis Center in North America, INOCHI-NO-DENWA in Japan, Telefonseelsorge in Germany, SOS-Amitié in France, La Esperanza in Spain, ERAN in Israel, La Main Tendue in Switzerland and La Voce d'Amica in Italy are all cases in point. The extensive participation of lay persons at the frontlines of such suicide prevention activities may rightly be called the "Third Mental Health Revolution" and will be discussed in some length later in this book.

In addition to the aforementioned lay volunteers at telephonic emergency services, other people and organizations have usually been involved in crucial prevention activities. These include health-care professionals, mental health specialists, psychotherapists, teachers, counsellors and religious practitioners.

Intervention involves both prompt and appropriate medical and emotional first aid to those people who have gone beyond distress into self-perceived crisis such as panic, severe stress, depression, hopelessness, suicide ideation and initiation of suicidal act, all or some of which may call for immediate and appropriate intervention for the individual involved. By its very nature, it is usually professionals or highly trained lay persons that become involved in such intervention, including psychiatrists, emergency medicine health-care professionals (physicians, nurses, social workers, psychologists), police officers and some staff and/or trained volunteers at crisis intervention centres. The nature and type of crisis intervention will also be discussed in detail later. For suicide attempters, it has been customarily the health-care professionals in emergency medicine who render prompt and appropriate medical first aid. Subsequently mental health professionals including psychiatrists, clinical psychologists, psychiatric nurses, or at times some trained volunteers (e.g., at the Crisis Intervention Unit at East General Hospital in Toronto, to be discussed later), may take over. It is usually the practice that medical and physical intervention takes place first and then psychiatric intervention, followed by emotional and social support by professionals and trained volunteers, the details of which will be discussed later in this book.

The last part of praxis is called *postvention*, which includes both the follow-up care of suicide attempters after necessary primary care has been administered and support for surviving family members of suicide. For the former, it is ideally expected that the attempters would remain in close contact and consultation with health-care and mental health professionals after their release. But in reality such follow-up care has not always been pursued for many reasons such as refusal of the released client, privacy considerations, cutbacks in budget or lack of personnel. The story is different, however, in providing support and counselling for survivor-victims who have lost a family member to suicide. Typically in North America, where the program has been most flourishing, well-trained volunteers and "survivor-victim volunteers" (typically surviving relatives of a suicide) work closely together as a crisis intervention team and render prompt counselling and support to families that have just lost a member to suicide and may be in serious crisis. It is called the survivor support program. Shortly after the intervention has taken place in the form of counselling and support for the family, in their own home or elsewhere, the volunteer counsellors organize a self-help group for discussion and mutual support, thereby facilitating grieving, healing, recovery and eventual empowerment of survivor-victims. To be explained later in greater detail, there are numerous survivor support programmes all over the United States and Canada. This is a uniquely North American self-help group that provides the triple function of prevention, intervention and postvention: prevention, because it has been known for some time in suicidology that surviving family members of suicides run a much higher risk of self-harm than those who have not lost a family member to suicide, and the survivor support programme does contribute to reduction of such risk and prevention through its support services; intervention, because the survivor support programme, as a rule, sends a deputation team of two trained volunteers—as mentioned earlier, one is a non-victim volunteer and the other a survivor or victim who has in the past lost a family member to suicide—to offer crisis assessment and management at the very location of suicide (usually a home of the suicide), thereby providing immediate and prompt intervention to deal with the crisis and grief at the very location of the tragedy; and postvention, precisely because it offers surviving family members necessary support as well as programmes and opportunities for grieving, guilt and anger management, healing and self-growth that lead eventually and hopefully to self-empowerment.

If crisis intervention is primarily a preserve for health-care and mental-health professionals, prevention and postvention have become, in no small measure, the domain of trained lay volunteers. Thus, the main players in the field of suicidology have been both professionals and trained lay volunteers who at times work together (as in the case of the well-known and unique programme at the Crisis Intervention Unit of East General Hospital in Toronto). Such a double component of professional and trained lay workers constitutes one of the very unique features of suicidology, but could also be, as has been sometimes, the source of creative tension and problems. On the whole, however, it has been a remarkable feat that the field of suicidology has encompassed both trained professionals and trained lay volunteers and staff members, who not only stimulate but also complement the professionals.

In addition to the aforementioned fields, the following specializations are often included in the field of suicidology: medicine (especially emergency medicine), social science (anthropology, economics, sociology, psychology, political science and urban studies), public health (biostatistics, bioethics, public health programmes), family studies, gerontology, criminology (law enforcement science and forensic science), biochemistry (neurophysiology, neuropharmacology), biology (genetics, neurobiology, physiology, neuropsychiatry), psychoanalysis (both Freudian and Jungian), philosophy and ethics, religion and theology, mortuary science (funeral homes and their services), life-insurance system, mass communication studies and educational counselling.

The foregoing discussion now may be summarized in Figure 2 below.

Figure 2:	Field of Suicidology and Practitioners
Field and Subfield	**Practitioners**
(1) *Epidemiology*: gathering of data on distribution of suicide rates by socio-demographic variables (i.e., by region, age, sex, education, occupation, marital status, religion, etc.)	Sociologists, demographers, police, government ministries, hospitals, coroners' and medical examiners' offices
(2) *Theory*: assumed reasons and causes for self-inflicted harm in terms of : sociological factors psychological and psychiatric factors biochemical factors	Sociologists, psychologists, psychiatrists, phenomenologists, biochemists, physiologists, neuro-psychologists, etc.
(3) *Praxis*: activities in suicide prevention, intervention and postvention *prevention* (distress lines, counselling, education, etc.); increasing participation of lay persons; non-judgmental support *intervention* (active crisis management, physical and emotional first aid, non-judgmental support) *postvention* (follow-up care and counselling; survivor-victim support programmes, etc.)	Distress and crisis centre volunteers, counsellors, teachers, clergy, peer counselling and support, friends and other gate-keepers and support people Physicians, nurses, social workers, psychologists, etc. in emergency medicine; mental health professionals, trained lay volunteers, police, etc. Health-care and mental health professionals, survivor-victim support programme volunteers, etc.

Social Thought and Suicide: A Historical Review

People may wince at the slightest hint of suicide or may show an avid and extraordinary interest in the subject. Whatever the reaction may be, however, very few people are neutral or indifferent to the act and implications of self-inflicted death. It is not difficult to understand, then, that for centuries suicide has been a source of rich human drama in novels and theatre, East or West, North or South. A history of social thought on suicide is best understood in relation to the human quest for the meaning of life and death as well as ethico-moral and religious concepts as they developed and changed over the years. In this context, suicide has been debated and argued for and against by statesmen, philosophers, scholars and theologians as their legitimate domain of concern for centuries, especially and mainly in Western civilization.

The earliest known document on suicide is found in an Egyptian papyrus from the Middle Kingdom (2160 - 1788 B.C.), which is preserved at the Berlin Museum in a text entitled "The Dispute with His Soul of One Who Is Tired of Life." It seems to have been written by a man who was in despair and who had been rejected by society, presented in the form of a dialogue between a man and his soul about the pros and cons of burning himself to death (self-immolation). As such, it is a unique personal document concerning the worthiness of life and death.[5] One of the four poems in this document hints at the despair of the man for whom death is preferable to the misery of living:[6]

> To whom do I speak today? I am
> laden with wretchedness,
> without a faithful one.

During the Greco-Roman period, debates were exchanged about the acceptability of suicide. To Pythagoras (571 - 497 B.C.), life was considered as a training ground for humans, assigned by the gods. Pythagoras, known as a great mathematician of ancient Greece, conceived of a universe operated by certain mathematical rules and numbers, including certain fixed numbers of people. Hence, certain numbers must always be present and maintained in the universe, and suicide was considered to be an act to disrupt such numbers as ordained by the gods and so must be considered unacceptable.[7]

Socrates (470 - 399 B.C.), one of the best known philosophers in ancient Greece, was influenced by Pythagoreans and argued that humans are like domestic animals kept by the gods. Hence, suicide is an act that violates the gods' ownership of humans. Humans are here to serve gods, and suicide was likened to desertion from their post at the military camp and so was to be condemned. Socrates' concept that the soul was imprisoned in the body by the gods (known as the Orphic Doctrine), was best expressed in Plato's *Phaedo*:[8]

> It is not unreasonable that a man ought not to put an
> end to himself until God brings constraint upon him,
> as he does now upon me.

It is well known, however, that Socrates himself ended his own life with hemlock, from which the modern-day "Dying with Dignity" and other euthanasia groups often take their names, such as Hemlock Society in Los Angeles, which has become an advocacy group for euthanasia and right-to-die movements.

Even though Plato (427 - 347 B.C.) did make some allowance for suicide under certain conditions (e.g., patients with incurable illnesses), he was in principle against suicide. In his famous *Laws*, Plato states that those who commit suicide "from sloth or want of manliness" shall be buried in unmarked graves.[9] Such a concept, introduced by Plato, was later codified by the Roman Catholic Church as well as by most Western European nations for more than 1000 years. Neo-Platonists strongly emphasized the negative view of suicide, and its most prominent spokesperson, Plotinos (295 - 270 A.D.), insisted that so long as there is any prospect of progress in humankind, suicide should not be allowed.

Whereas the Pythagoreans opposed suicide on quasi-theological grounds, Aristotle (384 - 322 B.C.), perhaps Plato's best known disciple, advocated his opposition to suicide from non-theological and secular moral grounds as well as from the standpoint of a realistic assessment of the law in society. According to Aristotle, suicide is an act of inflicting self-injury on a person who is a citizen of a state; suicide, therefore, ought to be banned and punished by the state as an unjust and undesirable act. To Aristotle, moreover, suicide is a cowardly act, and a person of courage would not try to escape into suicide from poverty, problems and tribulations in love affairs or from physical pain and illness.[10]

If some of these prominent Greek philosophers, such as Pythagoreans, Platonists and Aristotelians, were against suicide, the

Romans were generally indifferent to the controversies of suicide and some even accepted suicide as an honourable alternative to a life of shame and misery. Such was the case with a group of Roman thinkers who came to be known as Stoics. One of the best known spokespersons of Stoics was the Roman poet Seneca (4 B.C.? - 65 A.D.?), who was a contemporary of the Emperor Nero. In general principle, Seneca was in agreement with the Roman law of the period that forbade suicide especially to soldiers and slaves because they were property of the state and hence were deprived of the right to die with their own hands. But it was a different story for free Romans. Seneca considered suicide as a possible alternative:[11]

> Do you like to live? Do you not like to live?
> It is in your power to return from whence you
> came.

Upon realizing that Nero, the Roman emperor of the period, wanted Seneca's death, he took his own life shortly after bidding farewell to his close friends. His last words were:[12]

> As one chooses his own boat,
> As one chooses his own dwelling,
> in facing death, I choose the best way
> of death for myself.

To Seneca, virtue does not lie in just existing physically but living well. Thus, a wise person lives out only his or her mandated period, not the livable period, as one wishes. The wise person's main concern is always with the *quality* not the *quantity* of life; to die early or late is not the issue, but to die well or to live out a miserable life is. To die well meant to Seneca an intentional escape from an unbearable, miserable and meaningless life. To him, it is not a virtue to be forced or condemned to live. Such a stand taken by Seneca certainly represented the spirit and essence of the Stoic school of philosophy in ancient Rome, which treasured, among other things, freedom of action and rational judgment.

Another famous Roman statesman, Cicero (106 B.C. – 43 B.C.) took a relativistic attitude: i.e., the appropriateness of suicide depends considerably on the individual character as well as specific circumstances. Hence, in the same circumstance, suicide may be quite appropriate for one individual while it may be wrong for another. He considered that a wise person might choose death even if he or she was completely happy; likewise, he conceded that if life became unbearable, a person might exit from such a life as one exits from a theatre or any other event. When one of his contemporaries, Cato (95 B.C. – 46 B.C.) lost a battle against Caesar and took his own life in Utica, Africa, Seneca praised Cato's suicide and composed a moving eulogy. Such thinking, which allowed the freedom of choice about one's life and death, was inherited by Epicurean philosophers as well. It could be said that, on the whole, Romans looked on suicide with neither fear nor revulsion but as a carefully considered and chosen validation of the way they had lived. Probably the best example was that of Cornellius Rufus, a Roman nobleman, who delayed his suicide throughout the reign of Domitian, saying that he did not wish to die under a tyrant. Then, no sooner than this powerful emperor died Rufus took his own life as a free Roman. The belief that "to live nobly also meant to die nobly and at the right moment" was in effect reinforced by Roman law. Suicide of a private citizen was not punishable if it was caused by "impatience of pain or sickness, or by another cause," or by "weariness of life.....lunacy or fear of dishonour."[13] Suicide was punishable only when it was utterly irrational; in other words, it was punished because it was irrational, not because it was a crime. Such an attitude was evident in one of the resolutions passed by the municipal council of Marseilles in Southern France during the period of the Roman Empire. The council resolution ruled that under the following conditions certain poison could be dispensed gratis to certain individuals: (1) pain and suffering from incurable diseases and/or extraordinary frailty due to advanced age; (2) escape from inerasable shame; and (3) in lieu of execution on the part of an individual sentenced to death.[14]

What about Judeo-Christian thought? It is interesting to note that there is neither a specific designation or word for suicide, nor an explicit proscription against such self-inflicted death anywhere in the Bible itself. To be exact, an examination of the Scriptures reveals that there are only seven instances of self-inflicted death reported: Saul and his armour bearer, to avoid defilement by the Philistines (First Samuel, 31.4); Abimelech, to avoid a more disgraceful death at the hand of a woman (Judges 9.54); Samson, as an act of vengeance against the Philistines (Judges 16.26); Ahitophel (Second Samuel 17.23); Zimri (First King 16.18) and Judas Iscariot (Matthew 27.5), each disgraced as a betrayer. In none of the cases is any moral judgment held against the act.[15]

According to Judaism, life is the highest gift given to man, and hence to cling to life is man's primary obligation:[16]

> Man has been given life by God, and he has to keep it. Negligence to keep life is a sin. Life should be sacrificed only for very worthy aims, and not be thrown away by neglecting the health.....the worst life is better than the best death.

One example of such "worthy-cause suicide" was certainly the mass suicide at Masada where almost 1000 Zealots at Masada (including soldiers as well as civilians, men and women, young and old), perished by committing suicide in 73 A.D. instead of surrendering to the Romans who surrounded the Masada fortress and cut off their food and water supply. As reported by a Jewish historian-general who surrendered to the Romans earlier, the story of Masada today stands as a symbol of Hebrew resistance against all kinds of enemies of freedom as well as a proud, justifiable and courageous death against shameful slavery. Recruits in the Israeli armed forces are taken to Masada and pledge an oath of defence against all enemies of Israel and its people.

In the heart of the Old Testament, however, death is meted out as punishment for man's rebellion against God's command, as revealed in the myth of the Garden of Eden. Thus, death is the "wages of sin" as mentioned in Genesis: as such, death has historically carried the connotations of "divine punishment," "undesirability," and "something negative." Such dark and negative aspects portray death as something to be conquered and overcome: thus, in the Old Testament, the Messiah (the Saviour yet to come in Judaism and Jesus of Nazareth for Christians) "will swallow up death in victory" (Isaiah 25.8). As Talmud was being systematized between 200 A.D. and 500 A.D., there emerged condemnatory tendencies against suicide. The developing Jewish tradition has affirmed the blessedness and sanctity of life as well as the injunction against destroying it as found in Genesis (Chapter 9). In the heart of Judaic beliefs, the ultimate human destiny of life and death is in the hands of God the Creator: thus, "God giveth and God taketh." In this spirit, therefore, the *Code of Jewish Law* condemns suicide in the strongest terms: none is a worse sinner than he who takes his own life. In the Jewish tradition, then, the taking of one's own life was permitted under certain conditions such as avoiding incest, denial of God (idolatry) and murder.[17] When and if suicide did occur, however, there was usually a negative judgment, and a religious burial could be and was often denied. Such strong sentiments and injunction against suicide seem to have become prevalent between 200 A.D. and 500 A.D. (Talmudic times). The following quote from the *Code of Jewish Law* demonstrates the aforementioned antipathy towards a self-destructive act:[18]

> There is none so wicked as the one who commits suicide. He who destroys one human life is considered as though he had destroyed a whole world. Therefore, one should not rend his garments or observe mourning for a suicide....He should not be ritually cleansed, dressed in shrouds and buried. The rule is, whatever is done in deference to the living should be done for him. If a man is found asphyxiated or hanged, if it is a possible murder he should not be considered a suicide. A minor who commits suicide is considered as one who took his life accidentally. If he is an adult and the act was prompted by madness or fear of torture, treat it as a natural death....

In other words, even a death by asphyxiation or hanging, which may cast some suspicion of possible murder in a seeming suicide, could be exempt from the classification of suicide. A minor's suicide should be considered an "accidental death" and ought to be so registered. Or, if the act of self-destruction was evidently prompted by insanity or mental derangement or by a legitimate fear of torture at the hands of the enemy, such a death could be considered a "death by natural causes."

Christianity parallels the Jewish tradition very closely as an offshoot of the latter. Yet, as mentioned earlier, *nowhere does the Bible censure or condemn suicide: it merely records it as fact.* It seems, therefore, that the early Church had difficulty in rationalizing its ban on suicide, since neither the Old nor New Testament explicitly prohibits it. In the early years of the Church, suicide was considered such a neutral subject that even the death of Jesus was regarded as a kind of suicide by Tertullian. Later, John Donne, the distinguished churchman and poet in Britain during the Renaissance, used Christ's death as an illustration to strengthen his first formal defence of suicide in his celebrated tome *Biathanatos*, saying "our blessed Saviour....chose that way for our redemptions to sacrifice his life, and profuse his blood."[19]

As a matter of fact, when Christianity was introduced into the Roman world suicide had been widely viewed as an acceptable alternative to a life of pain and suffering. For some Christians, suicide was perceived to be a way to achieve martyrdom, eternal glory in heaven and even sainthood. One of the best examples was Eusebius, Bishop of Caesarea (260-349 A.D.), who, in his *Ecclesiastical History*, cites the stories of Christians committing suicide as martyrs rather than be tortured. To Eusebius they are "the magnificent martyrs of Christ....regarding death as a prize snatched from the wickedness of evil men."[20] During the persecutions of Christians by the Emperor Diocletianus in the fourth century A.D., some ardent Christians trekked from afar just to choose martyrdom. In those days it was believed that martyrdom was a distinct honour and an effective means of achieving redemption for one's sins. The surviving family members of martyrs were often protected by the Church financially and socially. After the fifth century, however, the Church began to take an increasingly negative attitude towards suicide. The decline and eventual collapse of the Roman Empire, and the fear aroused by increasing ardour of martyrdom as well as ascending strength of neo-Platonists, may account for this change in the Church's attitude.

The turning point for the Church's stance towards suicide came with the powerful theological arguments of St. Augustine (354-430 A.D.). He argued that suicide is a "detestable and damnable wickedness," a mortal sin, for the following reasons: (1) suicide is a serious violation of one of the Ten Commandments, "Thou shalt not kill;" (2) the body is the temple of God; (3) each human body is the vehicle of an immortal soul, which will be judged not in this world but the next, and destroying it is a damnable wickedness; (4) life is the most precious gift of God, and man was made in His image, hence, to kill life is tantamount to killing Him, leading to deocide, calling for damnation; (5) Eusebius' example of the virgin who killed herself rather than be raped was in vain because it is the mind that sins and not the body; (6) committing suicide to atone for one's sins and crimes usurps the power and function of the Church and state; (7) suicide signifies a weakness and defect of one's character for, as soldiers of God, Christians must bear all pain and tribulations in life.[21]

It seems that Augustine's strong arguments against suicide were, at least partially, a response to the charges by Stoics and critics of

Christianity at the time who took more lenient attitudes towards suicide. As a slow change in the Church's stand began, a series of Church councils and synods passed resolutions with regards to suicide. Thus, at the Council of Orleans in 533, the Church denied burial to anyone who committed suicide while being accused of a crime. At the Council of Braga in 563, no funeral rites were allowed to *any* suicide, and this decision was written formally into the canon law. Canon law was to use two passages in the Old Testament to back up its injunctions against suicide: the first is in Exodus XX: 13: "Thou shalt not kill," and the second is taken from the Song of Moses in Deuteronomy (XXXII: 39):[22]

> I kill and I make alive;
> I wound and I heal
> and there is none that
> can deliver out of my hand.

Further, in 693 the Council of Toledo applied these laws to suicide attempters as well. Finally, at the Synod of Nimes in 1284, it was decreed that Christian burial was categorically denied to all suicides so that the burial had to take place outside the city walls in open fields. The only exception for this stringent rule at the time (and even today for the Roman Catholic Church) is allowed when a physician or credible witnesses can testify that the person who committed suicide was insane and/or unaware of his or her act.[23]

Another towering theologian in the Roman Catholic Church who expounded the opposition to suicide is Thomas Aquinas (1225-1274). He also supported the ban against suicide for several reasons. Firstly, God has given us life and only God can take it away; hence, taking one's own life is a challenge to God and is a mortal sin and crime. Secondly, suicide is a sin against justice because it means renunciation of one's responsibilities to one's community. Thirdly, it is a sin against charity, for instinctive charity each person bears towards oneself is the instinct of self-preservation, therefore, to go against such basic natural instinct is against nature.[24]

Thus far, concerns and caustic polemics on injunction against suicide as "self-murder" and "mortal sin" were essentially centred around ethico-moral perspectives of Judaeo-Christian thought. The central world view of the Middle Ages, in which the Roman Catholic Church completely dominated the thinking and behaviour in Christendom, is perhaps summarized in one dictum: "God is the measure of all things," as defined by the Roman Church authorities. Such fixed ideology, as represented by the Church, however, assured socio-political stability and the unity of *Weltanschauung*.

The period following the Middle Ages—roughly from the fifteenth century through the sixteenth—is called the Renaissance, in which the lost intellectual heritage of Greco-Roman civilization was rediscovered and its rebirth witnessed (hence the designation "renaissance," which means "rebirth" in French). It is the beginning of the rise of humanism in Europe and the efflorescence of a most creative intellectual and artistic energy and vitality in the Western world. Among many, the Renaissance signified a departure from the deo-centric view ("God is the measure of all things") to anthropo-centric view ("man is the measure of all things"), the assertion for the autonomy of knowledge, multiplicity of truth-claims and a belief that the human body must be looked upon as natural and good and not as a source of temptation and sin. Thus, the Renaissance witnessed some vanguard philosophers and thinkers who began to argue for accepting and affirming suicide under certain circumstances. One such heretical thinker, Sir Thomas More (1478-1535), argued in his *Utopia* that suicide should be accepted as a form of euthanasia for those afflicted with incurable diseases, thereby blazing the trail for later liberalization of the suicide taboo in the British Isles and the Continent. His thought was later echoed on the Continent by a French humanist thinker, Montaigne (1533-1592), who discussed the acceptability of suicide for unbearable pain and humiliation. His very modern way of thinking about euthanasia is revealed in his argument that the beginning of life (i.e., birth) is always determined by the will and choice of others, but death can be willed by an individual. To Montaigne, if there is no freedom of choice for death, living can be the submission to a miserable existence.[25]

During the Renaissance, there emerged perhaps the most powerful polemicist for suicide in the English language, John Donne (1572-1631). As one of the leading poets and churchmen of the period in England (as well as being a relative of Sir Thomas More), John Donne became Dean of St. Paul's Cathedral in London, drawing a huge congregation. What distinguished the Renaissance in terms of the attitude on suicide was its emphasis on individualism, insisting on the ambiguity of human moral judgment and arguing for transfer of the ethico-religious questions of life, death and ultimate responsibility from the decisions of the Church to the realm of individual choice. Thus, in his celebrated *Biathanatos*,

John Donne made a very erudite survey of suicide in non-Christian societies and in the ancient world, arguing that in all ages and places the world over people took their own lives. He made some pointed arguments on what he considered the inconsistencies of the Church ruling, pointing out that Lord Jesus Christ himself *chose death* (hence, willed death or suicide) for the redemption of mankind. Furthermore, he insisted that if the power and love of God the Almighty were really that potent, then He would certainly allow and forgive even the sin of suicide. The contemporary relevance of Donne's arguments on suicide lies in the very fact that he linked his constant feelings and propensity for suicide with his childhood spent among the oppressed Jesuits. Such implied hints and suggestions for a possible relationship between the emotional condition from childhood to later suicide ideation is certainly an amazing insight on the part of Donne.[26] Thus a new page was opened on European thought and attitude towards suicide.

The seventeenth century is usually known as the Age of Reason in which the power of reason reigned supreme and the belief prevailed that the mysteries of the physical universe could be understood by recourse to reason and through rational inquiry. It witnessed the efflorescence and denouement of modern physical science—especially mathematics and physics—and was pushed forward by such distinguished scientists as Galileo, Kepler, Copernicus and Newton. These men of science, together with the aforementioned Renaissance thinkers, also helped to further weaken the grip of the Church on the moral question of suicide through their powerful arguments for the importance of a rational approach to life.

The emergence and dominance of the Age of Reason laid the groundwork for demythologization and secularization. Thus Kepler established the presence of immutable physical laws that govern the planetary movements in the universe; Copernicus destroyed the prevailing geo-centric view of the universe ("the sun moves around the earth, and the earth is the centre of the universe"). The Age of Reason became an indispensable background for the Age of Enlightenment to follow.

The eighteenth century is called the Age of Enlightenment, which produced a host of powerful and influential social thinkers and philosophers in France, Britain and, to a lesser extent, other European countries. The spirit of the Age of Enlightenment was characterized by a number of dominant beliefs: belief in the power of reason to demystify and demythologize the *human world* just as physical sciences succeeded in demystifying the physical universe; belief in the infinite perfectibility of man; the attendant belief that progress is immanent in history; and the belief in liberalism as a tool of rationalizing every aspect of human activity including politics, economics, sociology, theology and ethics. The spirit and the thinking of the Enlightenment directly influenced the Bill of Rights and the Declaration of Independence for America as well as for the French Revolution, thereby leading further to a change in the area of legal sanction for those who committed or attempted suicide. Perhaps the best examples of social philosophers who became advocates for suicide were such French thinkers as d'Holbach, Montesquieu, Morpertuis and Voltaire. Montesquieu (1689-1755), for instance, insisted in his *Persian Letters* that suicide might be an acceptable solution for those who lost a purpose for living and/or those who faced an unbearable pain, incurable illness and unbearable humiliation in life.[27] It is interesting to note that all of these post-Renaissance social thinkers and writers argued for justification and acceptance of suicide, discussing it casually as though it were the most natural act in the world without really invoking the authority and the teaching of the Church but often citing Greco-Roman classics such as that of Seneca. The implications of such a frame of reference were enormous: challenge to the dogma of the Church and assertions of humanistic individualism and death as a rational choice.

Thus, the eighteenth century Enlightenment and the nineteenth century to follow further witnessed the weakening of the religious taboo against suicide. Beginning with the suicide of the poet Thomas Chatterton in 1770 at the age of 17, and extending through the short but intense lives of Keats, Shelley and Byron, a sort of idealism emerged that regarded life in this world as an imperfect antithesis to Eternity, as demonstrated in the quote below:[28]

> The purity and intensity of the poetic vision as it glimpsed Eternity caused life's energy to be spent quickly.... [The poets'] visions of Eternity consumed them and made life in an imperfect world, in an aging body, unbearable. For these Romantics, suicide became the natural consequence of living with that vision, to the point of being glorified as a perfection for a life turned to, and yet cut off from, the Eternal.

The French Revolution of 1789 was a monumental event not only for France but eventually for all of Europe, bringing about many changes in social institutions and thinking. For instance, it is well known that the mentally ill (who used to be called the "insane" or "deranged"), who had long been considered dangerous to others as well as to themselves and, therefore, had been chained and shackled in the dungeon, were released by the Paris Commune into the custody of a French physician, Dr. Pinel. Pinel proved the harmlessness and safe nature of these mentally ill patients in his custody. Probably the most important event for suicidology was the decriminalization of suicide by the Paris Commune, abolishing the ban and punishment of suicide and suicide attempt. It meant that the confiscation of property, refusal for burial, etc., for the surviving family as well as for attempters were no longer in practice. Such decriminalization of suicide, spear-headed by France at the time of the French Revolution, was followed by other European countries with the exception of Great Britain. Britain finally scrapped its stringent legal sanctions against suicide and suicide attempt in 1961. North America followed suit soon after, thereby acknowledging suicide as a "medical," but not a "religious" or "legal" problem.

Following the end of World War II, such liberal attitudes towards suicide gained slow but steady momentum, especially in Europe. Ascendancy of the euthanasia movement has certainly become one of the hottest ethical issues in modern society—variously called "euthanasia," "mercy killing," "dying with dignity," "physician-assisted suicide." Thus, in 1980, a book was published in Britain, entitled *Exit*, detailing the specific and least painful ways of suicide. It was followed in 1981 by a book in French, *Suicide: Mode d'Emploi* (Suicide: How to Do It). A wave of controversy followed the publication of *Final Exit* in 1992 by Derek Humphrey, then president of the Los Angeles Hemlock Society. His book shot up to the best seller list within a year after its publication. It makes a strong case for euthanasia in graphic detail on how to commit suicide. The controversy for physician-assisted suicide reached a crescendo with the much publicized suicide assistance rendered by a retired Michigan pathologist, Dr. Kevorkian, who devised a so-called "suicide machine" and has openly and defiantly assisted the suicide of selected individuals suffering from illnesses for which there are no known cures.

At the crest of increasing public saliency of euthanasia, the Netherlands became the first country in the world to not prosecute physicians who assist in the suicide of their patients under specific and well-supervised conditions. In 1995, a province in Australia became the world's first to legalize euthanasia under very liberal provisions; and in the United States, one state after another has begun to put the issue of euthanasia to referendum and election agenda.

In the case of Canada, the Québec Superior Court in the early 1990s upheld the appeal of "Nancy B.," who was completely paralyzed from the neck down, to be allowed to have her attending physician disconnect the life support system that had kept her alive in order to "let nature take its own course" and preserve Nancy's "quality of life." On the other side of the country, the British Columbia Supreme Court and later the Supreme Court of Canada in 1994 ruled against the repeated appeals of Sue Rodriguez, who was suffering with Lou Gehrig's disease, for physician-assisted suicide. Despite the rulings of both courts, Rodriguez went ahead with her physician-assisted suicide in the presence of a prominent and sympathetic M.P. (Svend Robinson). Her case created enough controversy and commotion in Canada as to compel the Canadian Parliament to debate the issue for a legislative action. Though the final decision in the Parliament was negative to euthanasia, the controversy is expected to continue in the years to come.

Such controversy and public concern have not been limited to the West only. Japan was also embroiled in the controversy: the nation's court indicted a physician at a prestigious university hospital who injected a lethal medication into a patient who had an incurable cancer. His participation in such active euthanasia was allegedly based upon repeated requests from the patient's family, but the court rejected such a defence. Despite the negative ruling by the court, the Ethics Committee of the Japan Medical Association recently recommended approval of euthanasia under strict and well-defined guidelines.

A BRIEF REVIEW OF RESEARCH ON SUICIDE

Since much of the debate on suicide had been dominated by ethico-religious arguments for centuries, more dispassionate and rational-scientific study and research on the subject began to emerge only after the Age of Enlightenment. The Age of Enlightenment was characterized by feverish intellectual activities of all sorts among encyclopaedists, social philosophers, political essayists and emergent advocates of new social sciences. The indisputable leaders in the Age of Enlightenment were definitely in France and Britain. In both countries the debate on suicide was increasingly divorced from theology and ethico-moral considerations and shifted to the domains of literature, history, philosophy and to sociology. It was Voltaire (1694-1778), one of the most prominent social philosophers of France, who wrote extensively on suicide in general and Cato's in particular. He also culled through the historical documents and newspaper articles of the period and collected specific reports on suicide, and then pointed out the seeming relationship between increasing urbanization and the rise in the numbers of suicide. His assumption was that urban dwellers who had been liberated from the monotonous physical labour of rural areas were now plagued by heretofore inconceivable amounts of leisure time, which led to an increase in depression with consequent increases in suicide rates.[29] Even if oversimplistic and inaccurate, Voltaire's approach to suicide was noteworthy in two respects: firstly, he based his arguments on empirical data rather than moralistic grounds; and secondly, there was an assumption of association between depression as a mood disorder and suicide. On the latter point, however, Voltaire was not the very first. Richard Burton, a Briton, already spoke of suicide in terms of depression in his *Anatomy of Melancholia* published in 1621.[30] George Cheyne, another Briton, published his treatise on what he considered the English malady of "nervous distemper" in 1733, arguing that the consumption of rich foods, physical inactivity and general conditions of large cities like London contributed to the increase in "nervous distemper" (e.g., depression, hypochondria, etc.) as well as the rise in suicide rates.[31]

A more dispassionate empirical and scientific study of suicide appeared in the nineteenth century with the appearance of the first suicide statistical tabulation by Falret in 1822. He presented some statistical tables on suicide for the region of Paris, with breakdowns in terms of gender, marital status, methods used, motives and classification between completed and attempted suicides. He foreshadowed contemporary suicidology of today by assuming the seeming association between mental illness and suicide, neuro-cerebral causation, as well as melancholia-related suicide being biochemically and genetically transmitted to descendants.[32]

Two other studies from the neuro-psychiatric orientation were introduced in the nineteenth century for the further advance of suicide research. In his *Des Maladies Mentales* of 1838, Esquirol discussed the issues related to the etiology of suicide. Implicit in his study was the assumption that any act or behaviour that goes against the human instinct of desiring life and avoiding death is, *ipso facto*, abnormal and hence related to psychiatric and mental aberration and impairment. A study by Brièrre de Boismont, *Du Suicide et la Folie Suicide* of 1856 was conducted in this vein as well. He collected 4595 cases of completed suicide and attempts (4330 suicides and 265 attempts) and examined 1327 suicide notes. It was a trail-blazing and pioneering work in the field of clinical study of suicide. Though many cases of suicide seemed to be related to insanity, de Boismont nevertheless did not assume the automatic link between mental illness and suicide. The relevance of his research to contemporary findings was rather surprising: his studies include the relationship between suicide and alcoholism, the unexpectedly high suicide rate among the elderly, the link between aggressive impulses in homicide and those in suicide which at times followed murder, and the increase in suicide rates in all age groups across the board as a result of pressures and ills of urban life, etc.[33]

By the nineteenth century, statistics as a science was fully introduced and gained much attention and acceptance. One of the best known figures in the new science of statistics was Adolphe Quételet (1796-1874), a Belgian astronomer and statistician. He was unique at the time in that he began to apply statistics extensively to various social problems and phenomena, leaving a great imprint on emergent social scientists who became enthusiastic about the potential use and implications of social statistics for both investigative and policy purposes. It could be argued that modern statistical epidemiology was established by Quételet and his nascent science.

Towards the latter part of the nineteenth century, inspired by a use of such statistical tools, two important sociological works appeared that dealt with the question of suicide in relation to societal factors: treatises by Thomas G. Masaryk and Emile Durkheim.

Thomas G. Masaryk (1850-1937), a Moravian scholar and later the first president of the Republic of Czechoslovakia after the Versailles Treaty of 1918, completed his doctoral thesis entitled *A Study of Suicide as a Social Phenomenon*, originally written in German in 1876 and later published in 1881 as *Suicide and the Meaning of Civilization*, outlining the assumed impact of sociological aspects of modern society on the individual. He examined the relationships between suicide and numerous variables—e.g., the possible impact of seasons, temperature and weather, correlation between suicide and social-economic-political environments, suicide inside the prison, gender, health condition, age, occupation, etc.[34] Such empirical work by Masaryk made an early contribution to the scientific study of suicide, but his work still was full of vague, quasi-moral and philosophical speculations on the subject of suicide. Masaryk's sociological work was followed in 1882 by Henry Morselli, who marshalled abundant statistics in Europe and demonstrated that suicide rates differed from one country to another, thus emphasizing possible social and cultural influences on suicide.[35] These works, though pioneering and insightful, were merely preparing the ground for the appearance of the *magnum opus* by a Frenchman who founded the discipline of sociology in France.

Emile Durkheim (1858-1917) published his monumental work *Suicide* in 1897, which is still being read today quite avidly by students of sociology and suicidology. It is interesting to note that the first systematic and most ingenious study of suicide came from a social scientist rather than from other fields and disciplines. In a section on theory, Durkheim's main theoretical points will be fully discussed in great detail, but a very short outline is in order.

By re-examining the suicide statistics of nineteenth-century Europe, Durkheim noticed the existence of "social facts" that were quite different from individual psychological conditions. Up to the time of Durkheim's work, it was quite common to seek the etiology of suicide in terms of emotional and psychiatric illnesses. True enough, Durkheim wryly observed, when one probes into the immediate and discernible motives of suicide, each suicide may manifest his or her own unique motives. If there are one hundred suicides, one would perhaps find one hundred different and individual reasons for suicide—e.g., jilted love, serious and chronic illness, financial failure, despair, etc. Yet, when one gathers a large number of suicides and classifies them in terms of their relationship to certain socially definable groups, discernible collective traits and characteristics in terms of group membership become apparent, the fact of which leads Durkheim to deny the legitimacy of the psychologistic approach to the study of suicide. When the socio-demographic data of all suicides are examined and the group rates of identifiable social groups are tabulated, one notices certain distinct group characteristics. Durkheim observed: (1) that national suicide rates, though there are some fluctuations from year to year, demonstrate a relative stability in rates, despite evident individual differences of the suicides; (2) that different national and group rates seem to indicate differences in the degree of individual integration into society; (3) that higher suicide rates are usually observed among the divorced, the widowed and bachelors than the married; (4) that Protestants register much higher rates than either Roman Catholics or Jews; (5) that men have higher rates than women; (6) that higher suicide rates have been observed among those who have a higher degree of individualism and who are socially isolated, such as writers, artists, intellectuals, etc; (7) that even in peacetime suicide is more frequently observed among certain groups of military personnel such as non-commissioned officers and commissioned officers than among enlisted men; (8) that, when faced with a serious collective crisis such as war or revolution, suicide rates usually decline dramatically.[36]

It was his contention that all these observed differences in group rates in suicide could be explained in terms of the individual's integration into social groups and society. Based upon such an assumption, he developed a typology of suicide: egoistic suicide in which the individual is least integrated into social groups and society; altruistic suicide, which is the opposite of the egoistic type, in which suicide occurs because of the over-integration into social groups on the part of the individual; and finally, anomic suicide in which social norms and regulatory mechanisms break down in a period of social change. That most of these aforementioned observations by Durkheim still hold true is an eloquent testimony to Durkheim's extraordinary genius and insight. Today Durkheim's monumental work is an indispensable part of the accumulated knowledge in suicidology, as will become evident throughout this book.

The main thrust of research on suicide in the twentieth century gradually shifted from France to Germany, Austria and then, after World War II, to Great Britain and the United States. Increasingly psychology and medicine, especially in its psychiatric speciality, became the main arenas of clinical study, research and treatment. Though a much more detailed discussion will appear later, a brief mention must be made of Freud's contribution to suicidology because most of the later psychological-psychiatric theories of suicide are offshoots of Freud's original insight or variations of it.

Freud (1856-1939) did not publish much on suicide but made some very seminal hypotheses on the possible etiology of suicide: the postulate of "object loss," and the subsequent melancholia, inner rage and aggressive impulses directed inwardly against the ego rather than externalized against someone else.

It is interesting to note that the very first symposium organized by the newly established International Psychoanalytic Society in 1910 in Vienna was about suicide among youths. Yet Freud was reportedly silent throughout the symposium, sitting in the back of the room. At the conclusion of the symposium in his concluding remarks Freud promised to produce a theoretical paper on suicide. He finally came up with one piece of work written on suicide, entitled "Mourning and Melancholia" in 1915, which was subsequently published in 1917. In this article, he hypothesized that killing oneself is either a symbolic act of killing an object with whom one has been closely identified, and/or internalizing and re-directing one's death-wish against oneself.[37] His theory of suicide as an "inverted aggression against one's own ego" became the background for later theorists such as Karl Menninger and others, as will be explained later in the chapter on theory. It cannot be denied, however, that suicide was a major interest of the original Psychoanalytic Society under the aegis of Sigmund Freud. It may also be mentioned parenthetically that eight out of the ten original members of the International Psychoanalytic Society—all physicians and psychiatrists— took their own lives!

The prolific aspect of suicidology research is attested by Dahlgren's survey, which revealed that from the turn of the twentieth century to the end of World War II almost 4000 research works on suicide had been reported.[38] Likewise, according to a computer search by the Calgary-based S.I.E.C. (Suicide Information and Education Centre), as of 1987 there had been more than 11,000 suicide research findings reported and these represent only the English-language ones.[39] When you include the works in French, German and other European languages as well as in Japanese, the estimate may easily be doubled. It should be mentioned that the bulk of research and investigations in suicidology around the world in recent decades has been carried out and reported by researchers in the field of psychiatric and clinical medicine overwhelmingly, followed by clinical psychology and to a much lesser extent sociology and social work. It is expected that such trends would continue in the foreseeable future. Some of these research findings and investigations will be introduced throughout the present volume.

The major breakthrough for the study of suicide in a systematic and scientific manner, unconstrained by the mere medical model, came when the young Shneidman happened to come across a pile of suicide notes. In 1949, while working at the Veterans Administration Hospital, he discovered several hundred suicide notes in the vault of the Los Angeles Medical Examiner's Office. Thereupon he devised an ingenious study of these notes in comparison to those simulated notes written by matched non-suicidal persons. The results were published in the famous small volume entitled *Clues to Suicide*. Without Shneidman's leadership and strong initiatives there would not have been modern suicidology as it is known today. He launched the famous Los Angeles Suicide Prevention Center in 1957-58 and assumed its first co-directorship with Norman Farberow, another clinical psychologist who left a deep imprint on the development of suicidology in the United States. Then, on March 20, 1968, in Chicago, Shneidman founded the American Association of Suicidology with the definite goals of developing suicidology and training suicidologists. In addition to holding an annual conference somewhere in the United States or Canada, the American Association of Suicidology (AAS) offers certification of individual crisis workers and crisis centres, publishes a well-respected quarterly journal, *Suicide and Life-Threatening Behavior*, for research papers and *Newslink* for suicide information and research abstracts, runs a national suicide information centre in Denver and operates a summer suicidology training institute in Aspen, Colorado. The latter Aspen Summer Suicide Institute offers continuing education for therapists, clinicians and any other qualified individuals for five days in July of each year. The Canadian version of the Suicide Information Center in Denver is the Calgary, Alberta-based Suicide Information and Education Centre (S.I.E.C.), which has since become a major mainstay of suicidology database, training, research and public education in Canada.

In review, the postwar years have seen dramatic developments in suicidology, as discussed in earlier pages, but the major trends seem to be headed towards three directions: continued socio-demographic study of epidemiology, psycho-social research centring on psychiatry, psychology and sociology, and increasingly eye-catching research findings in neurobiology and genetics. The future research efforts would certainly come from any one of these three main thrusts, and some of their important research work will be discussed in detail in the present volume.

Finally, it will be useful for the reader to be informed of the conclusion of a prominent archivist of suicidology in the U.S. David Lester, a clinical psychologist and former president of the International Association of Suicide Prevention (I.A.S.P.) who lists the following people as "major contributors" to the field of suicidology: Emile Durkheim for his contribution to sociological theory; Edwin Shneidman/Norman Farberow for developing suicidology and psychological theory of suicide; Aaron Beck for his study of hopelessness in suicidal individuals; and David Phillips for his study of "Werther effect."[40] To his list, however, the present author would also add the following researchers whose works will be either cited or discussed. Their contributions have added much in the accumulation of needed knowledge: Sainsbury and Barraclough, two outstanding medical scientists from Britain who wrote extensively on suicidology but especially in the area of suicide statistics and reliability of data; Jack Douglas and Jean Baeschler, an American and a French sociologist respectively, who introduced a new way of looking at suicide, different from the *ex-post-facto*, clinical perspectives.

Notes and References

1   *Webster's New Collegiate Dictionary* (Springfield, Mass.: G. & C. Merriam Company Publishers, 1990), p.286.

2   Alvarez, A., *The Savage God: A Study of Suicide* (Toronto: Penguin Books, 1990), p.68, reads: "Herein are they in extremes, that can allow a man to be his own assassin, and so highly extol the end and suicide of Cato."

3   Picken, Stuart D. B., *Suicide: Japan and the West* (Tokyo: The Saimaru Press, 1979). Picken is the first person to call attention to the linguistic richness of the Japanese language to the etymology of "suicide."

4   Fusé, Toyomasa, "Suicide and Crisis: Etymology and its Cultural Implications," *Focus on Listening* (Toronto: The Ontario Association of Distress Centres, 1993), Vol.2, No.2, Spring 1993, pp.1-2.

5   Valente, Mario, "History of Suicide," in Hatton, L. Corrine and Valente, Sharon M., (eds.), *Suicide: Assessment and Intervention*, Second Edition (Norwalk, Conn.: Appleton-Century-Crofts, 1989), pp.1-2.

6   Breasted, J., *Development of Religion and Thought in Ancient Egypt* (London: Hodder and Stroughton, 1912), pp. 188-198, cited by Hatton and Valente, *ibid.*, p.2.

7   The following discussions on the Greco-Roman attitudes towards suicide are from Ohara, Kenshiro, *Jisatsu-ron* (Treatise on Suicide) (Tokyo: Taiyo Shuppan, 1978), pp.159-164; also, Alvarez, A., *The Savage God, op. cit.,* pp.76-84.

8   Plato, *Phaedo* (Cambridge: Cambridge University Press, 1972), p.136, cited by Hatton and Valente, *op. cit.,* p.3.

9   Plato, *The Laws of Plato* (Manchester: The Manchester University Press, 1921), ix., p.873.

10 Fujii, Yoshio, *Aristotle* (Tokyo: Keiso Publishers, 1959); Aristotle, *The Nicomachean Ethics* (New York: Oxford University Press, 1980), V., p.11.

11 Seneca, L. A. *Letters from a Stoic* (New York: Penguin Classics), Letter 70, cited by Hatton and Valente, *op. cit.,* p.3.

12 Ohara, Kenshiro, *Jisatsu-ron, op. cit.*, p.161.

13 Alvarez, A. *op. cit.*, p.82.
14 Durkheim, Emile, *Suicide* (New York: The Free Press, 1980), p.330.
15 *A Handbook for Caregivers on Suicide Prevention* (Hamilton, Ontario: Council on Suicide Prevention and Hamilton Board of Education, 1987), p.2.1.
16 Ganzfried, Golden, *Code of Jewish Law* (New York: Hebrew Publishing Co., 1961), p.108; Jacobs, Louis, *Jewish Law* (New York: Behrman House, 1968), p.106.
17 See: Hatton and Valente, *op. cit.*; *A Handbook for Caregivers on Suicide Prevention*, (Chapter on "Cultural and Religious Approaches to Suicide"), *op. cit.*, pp.2.1-2.2; Alvarez, A., *op. cit.*, pp.63-69; Durkheim, E., *op. cit.*, pp.326-338.
18 Ganzfried, Golden, *op. cit.*, p.108.
19 Donne, John, *Biathanatos*, Part I, Distinction 3, Section 2 (New Facsimile Text Society, 1930), p.58.
20 Eusebius, *The Ecclesiastical History* (Cambridge, Mass.: Harvard University Press, 1957-59), 2 Vols., II, pp.288-293, cited by Hatton and Valente, *op. cit.*, p.3.
21 St. Augustine, *The City of God* (London: Everyman's Library, 1945), I, XV-XVII; Ohara, Kenshiro, *Jisatsu-ron, op. cit.*, pp.163-164; Alvarez, A., *op. cit.*, pp.86-89.
22 Hatton, L. and Valente, M., *op. cit.*, p.2.
23 Alvarez, A., *op. cit.*, p.89.
24 Aquinas, Thomas, *Summa Theologiae* (London: Blackfriars, 1975), Vol. 38, 2a 2ae, 64, 5.
25 Montaigne, *The Essays* (New York: Oxford University Press, 1946), Chapter 3, Book II.
26 Donne, John, *Biathanatos, op. cit.*, p.58; Alvarez, A., *op. cit.*, pp.173-192.
27 As he says: "when I am overwhelmed by pain, poverty and scorn, why does one want to prevent me from putting an end to my troubles, and to deprive me cruelly of a remedy which is in my hands....Life has been given to me as a gift. I can therefore return it when it is no longer." See, Montesquieu, *Persian Letters* (New York: Meridian Books, 1961), Letter 71.
28 "Suicide in Literature and Art," in *A Handbook for Caregivers on Suicide Prevention, op. cit.*, p.3.2.
29 Douglas, Jack D., *The Social Meanings of Suicide* (Princeton: Princeton University Press, 1967), pp.6-8.
30 Burton, Richard, *The Anatomy of Melancholy*, Vol.1 (London: Everyman's Library, 1932).
31 Cheyne, George, *A Treatise on English Malady* (London: G. Strahan, 1733).

[32]   Falret, J. P. *De L'hypochondrie et du Suicide* (Paris: Croullebois, 1822), pp.6, 95-96.

[33]   Brièrre de Boismont, *Du Suicide et de la Folie Suicide* (Paris: Baillière, 1856).

[34]   Masaryk, Thomas G., *Suicide and the Meaning of Civilization* (Chicago: The University of Chicago Press, 1970), originally published in German in 1881.

[35]   Morselli, Henry, *An Essay on Comparative Moral Statistics* (New York: Appleton, 1882). pp.1-35

[36]   Durkheim, Emile, *Suicide* (New York: The Free Press, 1960).

[37]   Freud, Sigmund, "Mourning and Melancholia," in James Strachey et al. (eds.), *Complete Psychological Works*, Vol.XIV (London: Hogarth Press, 1964), first German publication in 1917.

[38]   Dahlgren, Karl G., *On Suicide and Attempted Suicide* (Lund, Sweden: Hakan Ohlssons, 1945).

[39]   Fusé, Toyomasa, *Introduction to Suicidology in Cross-Cultural Perspective* (*Jisatsugaku Nyumon - Kurosu Karuchuraru teki Kosatsu*) (Tokyo: Seishin Shobo Publishers, 1990), p.11.

[40]   Lester, D., *Why People Kill Themselves: A 1990s Summary of Research Findings on Suicidal Behaviour* (Springfield, Illinois: Charles C. Thomas, 1992), p.438.

CHAPTER 2

Epidemiology of Suicide

W hat is epidemiology? Epidemiology may be defined as the "study of the distribution and determinants of diseases and injuries in human populations."[1] The fundamental task of epidemiology is threefold: to identify the demographic characteristics of a given illness or an injury; to measure and classify its frequency and distribution; and to establish appropriate policies in treatment, prevention and public health. Clues to the causes of a given disorder may be found by identifying variations in the frequency and distribution with which the condition affects different populations and then relating these variations to heterogeneity in their environments. Hence, in establishing specific treatment procedures as well as prevention and public health measures for a given disorder, identification of certain variables such as the physical location of the origin of the disorder, its frequency and distribution, as well as the age, background, residence, gender, medical history, amount of education, occupation, marital status, religion, ethnic and racial background of the afflicted population would be of importance. Perhaps the best example is the study of the 1849 cholera epidemic in London by John Snow. As he proceeded with his investigation, Snow began to observe that those districts and households most severely affected by the cholera outbreak were largely concentrated in specific reaches of the Thames River. He concluded that the cause of the cholera epidemic was the contaminated water from the Thames, thereby initiating the beginning of epidemiology in medicine. What is remarkable is that Snow identified the origin of the epidemic fully 25 years before the cholera micro-organism was discovered by Robert Koch and Louis Pasteur. In recent decades, the links between tobacco smoking and lung cancer, and between diet and heart disease, have been established beyond a reasonable doubt using similar epidemiological methods.

Of course, as clearly concluded by the chairperson of the National Task Force on Suicide in Canada, "suicide is an action, not an illness."[2] It is, however, certainly a self-inflicted "injury" consistent with the definition of epidemiology. Beginning with Sweden in 1749, data on suicide have been systematically collected by many countries and comparative studies of suicide epidemiology have provided cumulative knowledge and informed speculation about the etiology of suicide.[3]

Yet a word of caution is in order. Epidemiologists study collective social groups rather than individuals, and those findings related to a particular group may not be easily extrapolated to the individual. To do so would be committing what is known as an "ecological fallacy."[4]

At the macro level, suicide statistics constitute aggregates of all self-inflicted deaths of a given target population such as specific age groups, occupational groups, ethnic groups, and nations. One of the fascinating aspects of suicide epidemiology at the national level has been, as so astutely observed by Durkheim, that there have been remarkably consistent differences in rates between national, demographic and social groups as they have been recorded over a long period of time. Moreover, these differences persist despite political changes that in many countries have altered the suicidal death certification procedure, as will be discussed later.

SUICIDE KNOWLEDGE TEST

In his years of field research in many different countries in Europe, North America, the Middle East, Asia and Latin America, the present author has observed an extraordinary interest in the subject of suicide on the part of just about everyone, regardless of race, creed, nationality or colour. No one seems to be neutral or indifferent to the question of "suicide." Such ubiquitous and powerful interest in self-inflicted death across national and ethnic borders suggests the possibility (as hinted by Freud and others) that perhaps everyone may have entertained suicide ideation (thinking about suicide) at least once in their lifetime in one degree or another. It has also been the experience of the author in every country he has visited that such interest in suicide may not be matched with accurate knowledge of suicide epidemiology. It may be worthwhile to test the average reader's current knowledge of suicide epidemiology. Here is a set of questions designed to test such knowledge. The reader is encouraged to answer these twenty questions with a pencil and find out how accurate his or her current knowledge of suicide epidemiology is. The correct answers are provided at the end of the test. If the reader scores more than fifteen correct answers, he or she is considered "extremely knowledgeable;" scoring ten to fifteen correct answers may indicate "average" knowledge; and if the reader has less than ten correct answers, he or she may be considered "below average" in knowledge of suicide epidemiology around the world. It should be pointed out, however, that even if the reader's score is "below average" on this self-rating test, there is no need to be despondent about the result because the present volume has been written in such a way that all the questions contained in the following test will be explained and answered fully later on. It is hoped that by the time the reader finishes the present volume, he or she will have acquired enough information and knowledge that they will be able to answer adequately any such self-rating tests. Good luck and proceed!

(Read the following statements and decide whether the statement is TRUE or FALSE):

T F 1. Sweden has been known to have the world's highest suicide rate.
T F 2. In many countries of the world, suicide rates usually increase dramatically during periods of war and revolutions.
T F 3. In many countries of the world it is teens who commit suicide more than any other age group.
T F 4. At least in Europe and North America, women show higher rates of completed suicide than men.
T F 5. In attempted suicide men outnumber women.
T F 6. Married men are known to commit suicide much more than bachelors.
T F 7. Suicide rates are usually higher in developed countries than in developing countries.

T F 8. Suicide has been less common in traditional Roman Catholic countries.

T F 9. Japan, known for its hara-kiri and Kamikaze, usually shows the world's highest suicide rate.

T F 10. In the United States, immigrants have been known to commit suicide less than the native-born Americans.

T F 11. In most countries suicide increases during the winter months such as December, January and February and then decreases during spring.

T F 12. In many countries of the world, it is usually the elderly who have the highest suicide rate.

T F 13. In France, the Paris region has been known to have one of the highest suicide rates.

T F 14. In Canada suicide rates generally decrease as you move eastward from British Columbia to Newfoundland.

T F 15. Berlin has shown extraordinarily high rates for many decades.

T F 16. Tokyo has been known to have lower suicide rates than sparsely populated rural regions in Japan.

T F 17. Native populations in North America (i.e., Indians and Inuits) have been known to have lower suicide rates than whites.

T F 18. Physicians in Europe and North America have been known to have one of the highest rates.

T F 19. Orientals and blacks in North America have been known to have lower suicide rates than whites.

T F 20. Hungary has been the country with the highest rate of suicide for many decades.

(Correct answers: 1.F; 2.F; 3.F; 4.F; 5.F; 6.F; 7.T; 8.T; 9.F; 10.F; 11.F; 12.T; 13.F; 14.T; 15.T; 16.T; 17.F; 18.F; 19.T; 20.T.)

EPIDEMIOLOGY OF SUICIDE: WORLD TRENDS

In 1980s it was estimated by the World Health Organization that over 1000 people commit suicide every day in the world (or, an estimated total of over 365,000 suicides around the world every year) with several million attempts per annum.[5] When it is remembered that suicide is always under-reported rather than over-reported, and that in North America and most

European countries and Japan suicide has been ranked among the top ten causes of death, it certainly deserves serious concern in society as a public health problem. Moreover, while the mortality rate for some serious illnesses has declined, this has not often been the case with suicide. The magnitude of the problem is driven home powerfully when one is reminded that in most industrialized countries the number of people dying through suicide surpasses the number of people dying on the road through motor traffic accidents. According to a noted Dutch suicidologist, however, in all countries, without a single exception, the resources made available for preventive intervention in the case of suicide behaviour constitute only a very tiny fraction of what is available for the prevention of motor vehicle mortality.[6] Informed awareness, as well as an accurate grasp of the basic trends in suicide epidemiology, has become an important public health issue not only for policy-makers but also for students in medical fields and social sciences. A review of such epidemiological trends in suicide rates around the world enables suicidologists to observe discernible trends and patterns, some of which will be discussed in the ensuing pages. The question of whether or not the cross-regional and international comparison of such collective rates is feasible will be fully discussed in this section as well, but the persistent differences on the cross-national data seem to suggest that self-inflicted death varies in accordance with cross-national differences in traditions, customs, religious values and attitudes, environmental and climatic conditions and other factors influencing and regulating human behaviour. What is important is that, at least in Europe and North America, the statistical mean of suicide rates as well as the rank order of countries in suicide rate have remained rather constant. The following observations of trends and patterns of suicide for the period from 1955 to the 1990s have been based upon the analysis of data from fifty-seven countries on the basis of death certification for suicide, which was included in the World Health Organization mortality database.

(1) Despite the long-standing popular "myth," a careful perusal and examination of statistical data easily reveal that Sweden does not, and has not for years, led the world in suicide rates. The origin of such popular myth may go back to the days of the Eisenhower era in the United States where conservative Republicans vigorously opposed major social welfare programmes for citizens on the assumption that, by protecting the average citizen from the normal rigours of life, these programs render him incapable of facing and solving problems when such

problems inevitably emerge; moreover, such welfare programs eventually make citizens totally dependent on the state ("big brother" concept) and the resulting frustration leads to suicide.[7] But, of course, such a belief is totally belied by the fact that Norway has a similar welfare state system and a low suicide rate, while Denmark, another welfare state, has had a high rate of suicide for more than a century, long before the welfare state system was introduced.

(2) Historically, higher suicide rates have been always observed in Central Europe, Northern Europe and then in some West European nations. Hungary has had the highest rate for men (52.1 per 100,000—all ages), followed by Sri Lanka (49.6), Finland (37.2), then a number of other countries such as Austria (31.6 per 100,000), the former Soviet Union (now Russia, 30.0), the former East Germany (28.6), Denmark (27.5), Switzerland, France (25.2). Sri Lanka, a South Asian country, has registered persistently high rates of suicide, usually ranking right next to Hungary (with a rate of 49.6 per 100,000 for men and 19.0 for women in the late 1980s); it has had the highest certified suicide rate on a worldwide scale together with Hungary. In terms of suicide mortality in middle age (35-64 years of age), a substantial excess was evident in Hungarian males (96.7 per 100,000), followed by Finnish men (60.2 per 100,000).[8]

(3) As for the ethnography of suicide, the following generalizations could be made. The high suicide area has been historically European, especially Central-Northern and Western European; some countries in Europe, North America, Oceanic countries of European settlement (New Zealand, Australia) and Japan, together with some East Asian countries, fall into the intermediate-rate countries; and Southern Europe, most Asian countries, Latin America, the Middle East and Africa may be grouped as low-rate regions of the world.

(4) For Europe, countries in Southern Europe have the lowest rates, followed by the countries in the northwest (the United Kingdom and the Netherlands) with somewhat higher rates. The Nordic countries form a third group with again higher rates (except Norway), and a fourth group of countries with higher rates still are located in Central Europe, starting with Belgium and France in the west, via Switzerland, Austria and Hungary, ending in the east with Russia. Such a geographical suicide map or atlas has more or less been characteristic for the European region over the course of this century.

(5) In terms of the socio-cultural factors that may influence the national rates, it is interesting to note that exceedingly high suicide rates

of two European populations—those of Hungary and Finland—have a common ethnic background, although these same populations have been split for several centuries now and have considerably different socio-economic conditions.[9] In addition to being European (with the sole exception of Sri Lanka), higher suicide-rate countries are well developed socio-economically, either Protestant (state Lutheran church) in religious tradition or nominally Roman Catholic with a very high degree of secularism, and possess highly volatile population change and shifting political borders over the decades. Similarly, traditional and devout Roman Catholicism, warmer climates, lower economic development and large, consanguineous family system seem to characterize the lower rate countries in general.[10]

(6) The pattern for women has been quite similar to that for men, though absolute figures are considerably lower. The highest figures were in Sri Lanka (19.0 per 100,000), followed by Hungary (17.6) and several other European countries with rates between 9 per 100,000 to 15 (Denmark 14.98, Austria 10.62, Singapore 10.58, Belgium 10.36, Switzerland 10.18, the former East Germany 9.98, Japan 9.93, Finland 9.17 and France 9.14).[11] It may be noted that female rates are comparatively elevated in relation to male rates in East Asian countries such as Japan, Hong Kong and Singapore.[12]

(7) Japan, Singapore, Australia, New Zealand, Canada, U.S.A. and several other European countries have historically been characterized by intermediate suicide rates (between 15 and 24 per 100,000). Contrary to popular perception and belief, Japan has always been a middle-rank nation in suicide rates. Such popular misconceptions have undoubtedly been reinforced by Japan's time-honoured tradition of *seppuku* (ritual suicide by disembowelment, often called "*hara-kiri*" in the West), *kamikaze* in the last World War, legendary pressure-cooker lifestyle, "examination hell" that allegedly torments school kids to the brink of suicide, addiction to work resulting in "*karoshi*" (or death due to overwork), unbelievable urban population density (by North American standards), overcrowded living conditions and extremely well-controlled public behaviour. Yet Japan's suicide rate, though highest in Asia, has never been the highest in the world except in 1957; most of the time, Japan has belonged to the intermediate-rate countries.

With the commencement of the first suicide statistics in 1882, the rate of suicide in Japan in the Meiji-Taisho period (1868-1925) remained more or less steady, ranging between 16 to 20 per 100,000, accounting for about one percent of total deaths. During the turbulent Showa period

(1925-1989), however, there was much greater fluctuation in suicide rates from an all-time low of 12 in 1943 to an all-time high of 25.6 in 1957, the one year in which Japan became the country with the highest rate. From 1957, however, the rates began to decline to 14 to 17 in the period 1962-67, marking the lowest postwar rate of 14 in 1967. Since then it had begun to rise a bit through the 1970s but has more or less been stabilized, or even has dipped a little, to 17-20 per 100,000 in 1980s. From the late 1970s onwards, however, a steady decline of suicide among children was followed by a steady increase in the rate of middle-aged males in their 40s and 50s (36.7 per 100,000), a rate that is much higher in 1980s as compared to three decades earlier.[13] What alarmed Japanese health professionals in 1980s was the dramatic increase of suicide among Japanese men born in the late Taisho period and the first decade of the Showa period (called "Showa Hitoketa"). Some cohort analysis—an examination of the suicide rates of a given age group over different time intervals—conducted by Japanese sociologists and medical epidemiologists seems to confirm the increase in such age groups.[14]

(8) As for North America, the United States started from relatively high rates in the 1950s (15.1 per 100,000 for men, 4.2 for women) but showed a decline in the rates for men in middle age. In the U.S. in the past two decades, the percentage of suicide deaths by persons 15-25 years has increased, while the percentage of total suicide deaths by persons over 44 years of age has decreased. In the late 1980s, suicide mortality for both sexes was somewhat lower than in Canada, with the rates of 17.5 per 100,000 for men and 4.4 for women. The dramatic increase of suicide in the young age group between 1900 to 1990 is shown in Table 1.[15]

(9) In Canada, suicide mortality increased appreciably for males (from 11.7 to 19.7 per 100,000—all ages) between the late 1950s and the early 1980s and levelled off to 18.9 per 100,000 over the past 40 years or so. Rates for women were lower but more than doubled between 1955 to 1959 and declined thereafter to 5.2 per 100,000 in 1985-1989. The pattern in Canada was similar in middle age (35-64 years of age), although the upwards trends were proportionally smaller. Of particular concern in such countries as Canada, the United States, Australia and New Zealand is the steady increase of suicide rates for youths in the age group 19-25.[16]

(10) Overall certified mortality from suicide has been low for some time in the United Kingdom (8.8 per 100,000), Southern European countries (Italy with 8.25 per 100,000, Portugal 8.1, Spain 6.6, Greece 3.8), Latin

Table 1:	Percentage of Change between 1950 and 1988 for Suicide Rates by Age and Sex	
	Change (%)	
Age Group	Males	Females
15-24	237 %	65 %
25-34	87	27
35-44	7	-8
45-54	-32	-30
55-64	-43	-17
65-74	-34	-22
75-84	2	-20

Source: Tsuang, M.T., Simpson, J.C., & Fleming, J., "Epidemiology of Suicide," *International Review of Psychiatry*, 1992:4, p.120

America and reporting countries and areas in the Middle East, Africa and Asia (except Sri Lanka, Japan and Hong Kong). (Speculation as to why suicide rates had continually declined in England and Wales will be discussed later in this book when suicide prevention issues are presented). Suffice it now to mention that suicide rates have been persistently low in Latin American countries, which are, incidentally, all traditionally Roman Catholic, ranging from 4.2 per 100,000 for men and 0.7 for women in Mexico, to 13.1 for men and 3.3 for women in Uruguay and 15.5 for men, 1.9 for women in Puerto Rico. Such low rates have also been observed in Middle Eastern Islamic societies over the years.[17] As for Africa, epidemiological data suffer from the near-total lack of reported statistics except in Egypt and Mauritius. For Egypt, however, the reported mortality from suicide is extremely low (well below 1 per 100,000 in both sexes).[18] Some of the salient socio-cultural characteristics of these very low-rate countries are: warm, temperate climate; either traditional Roman Catholicism, which contrary to aforementioned nominal Catholicism with little meaning for daily life, seems to have stronger influence in the daily life of the majority of the populace, or Islamic faith with strong injunctions against suicide; much lower standard of living; prevalence of the traditional, extended family system with larger numbers of children.

(11) Throughout the world, suicide has always been more common in older age groups and in the male gender. In attempted suicide, however, such a rule is reversed—i.e., the female gender outranks the male by two to one, or even three to one ratio in favour of the female. These facts are almost universal axioms in suicidology. Even though the suicide rate for young adults has increased in both sexes in more countries than it has decreased, it has been a truism in suicidology for decades that in almost every country the elderly have shown the highest rates. A quick glance at an international comparison demonstrates extremely high rates in almost every industrialized country of the world in comparison to the national average, as shown in Figure 1.

With regards to such very high rates of suicide among the elderly, very interesting research findings came to light in Japan with regards to what kind of elderly are most likely to kill themselves. An investigation team from the Tokyo Metropolitan Medical Examiner's Office undertook in-depth interviews into the extremely high rates of elderly suicide in Japan in general and in Tokyo in particular. They came up with surprising findings. Contrary to their expectations, they found that those elderly people who lived with their married children and their grandchildren in a three-generation household had the highest rate of suicide, followed by those who lived with their unmarried children in a typical two-generation household. The lowest rate was observed among the old couples who lived by themselves separately from their married children and their grandchildren.[19] Implications are that, contrary to an idyllic and romanticized belief, the elderly in the "ideal" three-generation household may in reality encounter more stress, frustrations, disappointments and interpersonal frictions. Such findings, if cross-culturally tested and verified, would have important implications beyond the border of Japan for social and welfare policies in many countries in the future. This is certainly one of the urgent aspects of gerontology and suicidology that needs to be cross-culturally tested and verified.

In 1955, the elderly made up only 8% of the total population in Japan and in Western nations; by 2015, it is estimated that nearly 25% will be senior citizens in these countries. According to a study in Ontario, Canada, the elderly's rate of completing a suicide attempt, among males, is almost 20 times that of young people. Suicide attempts by those in their 20s end in death only one in 40 tries, but with those over 65 the rate is a grim one in two.[20] It is expected that as the share of the aged in

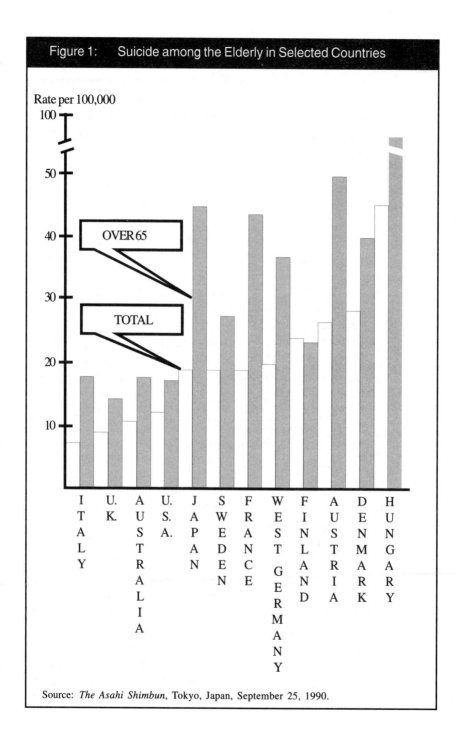

Figure 1: Suicide among the Elderly in Selected Countries

Rate per 100,000

Source: *The Asahi Shimbun*, Tokyo, Japan, September 25, 1990.

the national demographic structure increases, the future cohort analysis[21] would probably demonstrate a dramatic rise in suicide rates in highly industrialized countries of Europe, North America, Japan and elsewhere.

(12) All suicide rates of the countries that are reported in the WHO database could be grouped into three distinct patterns in terms of age: Pattern A, in which the rate for men increases steadily with age including Austria, Bulgaria, Chile, Cuba, the former Czechoslovakia, England and Wales, France, Germany, Hong Kong, Italy, Japan, Portugal, Spain; for women, Pattern A includes such countries as Austria, the former Czechoslovakia, Germany, Hungary, Italy and Singapore. Pattern B, on the other hand, shows a bimodal trend in which there are two demographic peaks—one peak in the young age group, 15-24, 25-34, or 35-44, and another sharp increase in the age group over 60. Such bimodal pattern for men has been observed in such countries as Belgium, Greece, Puerto Rico, Singapore, Uruguay, Venezuela and the U.S.A.; for women, such a trend was evident in Bulgaria, Hong Kong, Japan, Portugal and Spain. Finally, the third type, Pattern C, is characterized by a steady but gradual increase in rates in terms of age, but after 60 there is actually a slight decline and/or stabilization of the rate. Such a pattern was observed in rates for men in Canada, Norway, Poland; and for women in such countries as Australia, Canada, Denmark, the Netherlands, Poland, Sweden and the U.S.A.[22] These three patterns are presented in Figure 2.

(13) Durkheim's assertion that the common threat of war produces greater solidarity and cohesion in a community by maximizing collective efforts for survival is verified by the data for the two world wars of the twentieth century. In addition to such national solidarity, individual isolation, alienation and narcissism are usually minimized during wartime. Conversely, with the arrival of peace, suicide rates usually increase again.[23]

(14) Men complete suicide far more than women with a ratio of at least two to one or three to one, while women outnumber men in suicide attempts with a ratio of at least two to one. One of the main explanations for such gender difference is that men everywhere are likely to use more lethal means of self-destruction (e.g., use of firearms, hanging, jumping off high places, etc.), whereas women are more inclined to use non-violent means such as drug overdose. An exception to this basic rule in suicidology is made for some Islamic countries in the Middle East and some South Asian countries in which women's suicide rates sometimes approximate those of men.[24]

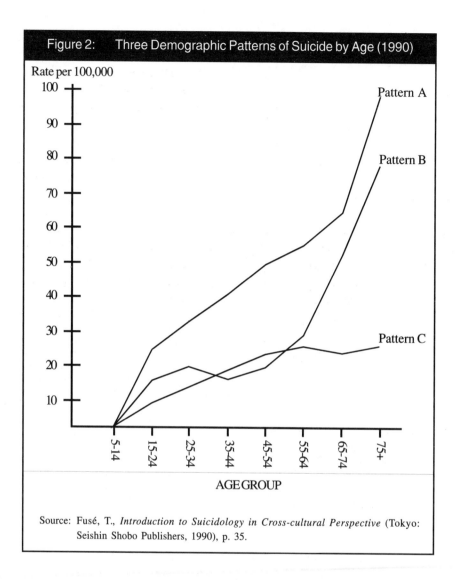

Figure 2:   Three Demographic Patterns of Suicide by Age (1990)

Rate per 100,000

Pattern A

Pattern B

Pattern C

AGE GROUP

Source: Fusé, T., *Introduction to Suicidology in Cross-cultural Perspective* (Tokyo: Seishin Shobo Publishers, 1990), p. 35.

The sex ratio in suicidology refers to the number of female suicides per 100 male suicides. In terms of the international comparison, European countries have persistently shown much lower ratios for women. A postwar international comparison of the sex ratio in selected countries and cities has confirmed such a generalization, as shown in Table 2.

As mentioned earlier, very high sex ratios in the Middle East and Southeast and East Asia seem to attest to the continuing stress and

Tabel 2:	Sex Ratio

By Country	Ratio of Female per 100 Males
Japan	77.4
United Kingdom	67.9
West Germany	51.2
Italy	43.4
Canada	40.0
Switzerland	38.7
France	36.2

Source: WHO *Statistical Report*, (Geneva: UNITED NATIONS, 1989), cited in Fusé, T., in *Introduction to Suicidology...*, *op. cit.*, p. 36.

tension women have to go through in most of the developing countries, where the burdens of life and family often affect females far more than in Euro-American societies.

(15) Historically, the rates of suicide for whites have been higher than for blacks, at least in North America, as shown in Table 3. It is interesting to note that such racial differences in rates between whites and blacks go way back to earlier periods: Morselli, in particular, observed that the suicide rate of blacks in New York City in 1870 was fourteen times lower than that of the whites! Differences have persisted since the turn of the century, as shown in Table 4.[25]

In 1989, the suicide rate for whites was 13.1 per 100,000, compared to 7.0 among non-whites.[26] In 1990, the suicide rate per 100,000 for white males in the United States was 22.0 and 5.3 for white females; for blacks the comparable figures were 12.0 per 100,000 for men, and 2.3 for women. When one compares the data for the rates by race for 1970, 1980 and 1990, one finds a steady increase for both white and black males but a decrease for both white females and black women (the decrease, however, is much more dramatic for white females).

It is interesting to note in this regard that the white suicide rates tend to increase with age, but the non-whites show very high rates in younger ages (15-24). Such pattern is also observed among native populations (i.e., North American Indians and Inuits), in which youths

Table 3:   Suicide Rates by Race (U.S.), per 100,000

	1970	1980	1990
White Male	18.0	19.9	22.0
Black Male	8.0	10.3	12.0
White Female	7.1	5.9	5.3
Black Female	2.6	2.2	2.3

Source: Bureau of the Census, U.S. Government, in *Newsweek*, April 18, 1994, p. 48.

Table 4:   Suicide Rates by Race (U.S.), per 100,000

	Whites		Blacks	
Year	Number	Rate	Number	Rate
1910	7 158	15.5	151	12.0
1920	8 529	10.8	261	3.6
1930	17 723	16.8	600	5.1
1940	18 284	15.5	623	4.6
1950	16 468	12.2	677	4.3
1960	18 121	11.4	920	4.5

Source: Chenais, J.C., *Histoire de la Violence* (Paris: Editions Robert Laffont, 1981), p. 181.

(15-24) demonstrate a very high peak accounting for almost 60% of all suicides in this age group, and then dramatically register declines in the older age group. This pattern among North American Natives and blacks has come to be known as "survivor phenomenon."[27]

(16) Durkheim suggested that married couples with children are at reduced risk for suicide, and that the risk decreases further with increased number of children. Table 5 shows that the suicide rates for widowed and divorced men are approximately four times those of married men; the rates run two to four times higher for widowed and divorced women than married women.[28]

Table 5:	Suicide Rates by Marital Status, for Males and Females in 1988 (U.S.)		
	Suicide Rate per 100,000		
Marital Status	Males	Females	
Single	29.44	6.42	
Married	18.94	4.68	
Divorced	72.61	16.47	
Widowed	92.13	8.85	

Source: Tsuang et al., "Epdemiology," *op. cit.,* p.121.

Very high rates for the divorced and the widowed suggest the possible impact of "object loss," which will be discussed later in the book.

(17) In terms of religious affiliation, Durkheim showed that rates are generally higher among Protestants than among Catholics and Jews. In one study in the United States, an inverse correlation was observed between the percentage of a state's Catholic population and its suicide rate—i.e., the higher the percentage of Catholics in a state's general population, the lower the rate of suicide.[29] In another study reporting suicide rates in New York City, the highest rates were found among Protestants (31.4 per 100,000); Jews had a medium rate (15.5) and Roman Catholics had the lowest rate of 10.9 per 100,000.[30]

(18) Information on the occupational backgrounds of suicides has been regrettably deficient and limited; neither has it been accurate because of the absence of a standardized classification system cross-culturally. It has been observed in some studies, however, that highly trained professionals such as physicians have shown very high suicide rates. Yet, as will be discussed later in this book, careful examinations of the data seem to disprove such an assumption. The physician suicide rate seems to be higher when it is compared to the entire general population, but when compared to a general population over 25 (the proper sample to be compared), physicians do not seem to kill themselves at a rate higher than the general population over 25.

The foregoing review of some world trends in completed suicides may suggest at least continued high rates in European countries, and probably increasing rates for North America and some non-Western countries, especially in East Asia, for a number of socio-economic considerations: a high and increasing divorce rate as a worldwide trend; a high unemployment rate, which may be interpreted as a measure of "anomie" (the state of normlessness and breakdown of regulatory values of human conduct), at least in European, North American and other highly developed countries in the Pacific Rim. In view of the increasing participation of females in occupations in these countries, the nearly universally rising incidence of female suicide rates may be observed. Finally, increasing trends in Europe, North America and Japan in the reduction of the population aged 15 and under, together with an increase in the percentage of the population aged 65 and over, may also increase the rates.

The following trends seem to be worthy of further and future research: persistently higher rates of suicide in European countries in terms of their relation to some cultural and social factors that may have contributed to the phenomenon over the centuries; the extraordinarily high rate registered by Sri Lanka, a South Asian country, which seems to be out of step with other countries in the region; a consistent and persistent decline in suicide rates observed by England and Wales over almost three decades; Hungary's excessively high rates over the centuries even by European standards; the much lower rate in Norway compared with other Scandinavian countries; the marked increase in rates for young adults especially in North America and some Oceanic countries such as New Zealand.

CERTIFICATION OF DEATH BY SUICIDE

In death certification both *cause* and *manner* of death are important criteria. Determining the *cause* of death—i.e., the actual, medico-physiological origin and process of death—usually requires certification by an attending physician who writes down what he or she believes to be the primary cause of death such as "death by malignant neoplasm" (cancer), myocardial infarction, pneumonia, etc., or any of the 137 causes of death in accordance with the International Classification of Death. The original classification was agreed upon in August of 1900 at an international conference in Paris, where 26 countries participated in the selection of causes of death for primary mortality tabulations. The basic classification of this scheme and the rules governing it are currently maintained by the World Health Organization in Geneva and are revised approximately every decade.

The *manner* of death, on the other hand, refers to medico-legal and forensic determination and judgment of *how* the death came about. For instance, in the case of a sudden unexpected death—e.g., accident, homicide, suicide—police and forensic authorities are always involved: i.e., police officers, coroners, medical examiners, pathologists, chemists and magistrates. Such sudden and unexpected death is also called "unnatural death," as opposed to "natural death" which is brought about by old age and/or by verified known diseases. In natural death, certification is a simple matter and poses little problem: the matter is simply settled by an attending physician writing out a death certificate. It is the unnatural death that presents problems. Suicide is classified, of course, as an unnatural death, requiring investigation and further examination by police, coroners, medical examiners and/or magistrates as the case may be. In the case of a suspected suicidal death, especially when there is no corroborating evidence such as a suicide note, the aforementioned medico-legal officials are required by law to determine, as much as possible, the identity of the deceased, time, place, cause and manner of death, using all available evidence and, when necessary, taking measures to collect further data and evidence. In the case of equivocal death (in which the cause and manner of death are undetermined), the coroner or the medical examiner is authorized to hold an inquest in order to obtain further clarification of the death.[31]

In the case of Canada, suicides demand special investigation in accordance with Coroner's Acts and Ordinances, but the word "suicide" is mentioned in only three of the Acts: those of Newfoundland (Summary Proceedings Act, 1979), Alberta (Fatality Inquiries Act, 1976) and British Columbia (Coroner's Act, 1975). These acts do not, however, specify the criteria to be used in determining the cause and manner of death; such decisions are left to the discretion of the investigating and certifying officials.[32] In addition to such ambiguity, absence of general nationwide standards for the qualifications of coroners is a major problem. At the moment, Ontario is the only province in Canada in which coroners are required by law to be physicians. In order to achieve even a minimal degree of consistency in death certification, the National Task Force on Suicide in Canada made a strong suggestion to develop a system of offering programmes of instruction to local coroners for guidance, in view of the diversity of backgrounds of coroners found in the various coroner systems in the country.[33]

At present, of the 37 countries reported in the World Health Organization, eight countries have a coroner's system, 20 have been practising a judiciary system of death certification by public prosecutor, district attorney and/or magistrate; in Japan, Scandinavian countries and others, medical examiners (medically trained professionals, usually physicians) and/or forensic specialists are in charge of the certification system.[34] In the United Kingdom, Scotland has always maintained a different system of death certification than England, Wales and Northern Ireland, and is listed separately in statistics. Whatever system may be followed, however, the following six points must be taken into account in determining death by suicide: (1) presence or absence of a suicide note; (2) statements and testimonies by surviving family members or next of kin, close friends, and witnesses; (3) police reports; (4) reports from hospitals or clinics; (5) coroner's or medical examiner's official reports; (6) autopsy report or the findings of the pathologist.[35]

A memorandum published by the Ontario Coroner's Office in 1993, entitled "Suicide – A Review for Ontario Coroners," mentions the following criteria for the determination of suicide: (1) pathological evidence (such as contact-type wound or powder residue on victim's hands that suggests the wound was made by the victim); (2) toxicological evidence (showing that the substance was available to the deceased and the lethal level was above the accidental or unintentional level of ingestion); (3) investigational evidence (such as police reports, diagrams, notes, photographs and physical and mental health records); (4) psychological evidence (demonstrating planning of suicide as shown by behaviour, communications, lifestyle, etc.); (5) statement of the deceased (either handwritten, typed, verbally or on cassette or video tape); and (6) statement by witnesses (either direct or by observation of the death, or indirectly by either explicit or implicit statements or observations of the deceased).

Since suicide is, by definition, intentional and self-inflicted death, equally central to the determination of death by suicide is the ascertainment of the intent to die—i.e., the deceased knew the method chosen to be lethal and/or that the action taken would usually result in death. There are usually three types of intent: (1) explicit intent (as demonstrated by writings or statements of the deceased in notes, diaries or by audio or videotape to the effect that the person is going to commit suicide); (2) implicit evidence of intent (which includes actions and statements by the deceased and observations by others that are not explicit but imply, perhaps retrospectively, that suicide was intended, e.g. such a statement as "life is not worth living" is a good example of an implicit statement from a suicidal individual); and (3) indirect evidence of intent (including depression, chronic alcohol or drug abuse, continuing great physical or psychic pain, chronic or terminal illness, farewell gestures such as making a will, recent loss of a significant other or loss of self-esteem and public standing, legal charges or incarceration, family history of suicide), but these risk factors should not be regarded as causal factors as they are also common in cases of natural or accidental death.

The following reproductions are examples of death certificates. Figures 3 and 4 are medical death certificates from France, which have been in use since 1866 and which require certification by the medico-legal (forensic) authority; they are then sent to the Central Statistical Office in Paris. Figure 5 is an example of death certification by the Ontario Coroner's Office. Figure 6 is a sample of the official police report for unnatural death (including suicide) for the Metropolitan Toronto Police Force, a copy of which is required to be kept in the file of the deceased together with a copy of the provincial Coroner's Report.

Finally it must be mentioned that controversy does exist where suspected death is associated with very young age, suspected insanity, impairment by drugs or alcohol, or an overdose in old age in the absence of a suicide note, etc. Statistics for young children's suicide pose problems because children under a certain age are considered too young to understand the irreversibility of death and/or the fatal consequences of their actions. Likewise, even though a previous or current diagnosis of mental illness does not rule out suicide, his or her actions can be ruled an accidental death in a court if the person is judged, on account of insanity, to have been incapable of forming intent and/or understanding the lethal consequences of the act. In U.S. insurance cases, suicide exemption is usually upheld by the courts where the words "sane or insane" are incorporated in the suicide exclusion clause of the policies.

Coroners completing death certificates and reports are likely to continue classifying as suicide any self-inflicted death initiated by the deliberate action of the deceased where suicide can reasonably be inferred from the circumstances surrounding the death. When parties disagree, the decision can then be taken before a judge or court.

Figure 3: Death Certificate (France)

CERTIFICAT MÉDICAL DE DÉCÈS

COMMUNE

N° DE L'ACTE

N° D'ORDRE DU DÉCÈS

(A remplir par la Mairie)

Document confidentiel

à détacher et à joindre au bulletin d'état civil
correspondant, au moment de l'envoi au Médecin
de la Santé Publique attaché à la Direction
départementale des Affaires Sanitaires et Sociales

Ne doit être ouvert que par le Médecin de la Santé Publique
attaché à la Direction départementale des Affaires Sanitaires et Sociales

---

Préfecture du Département

DU RHÔNE

Ne doit être ouvert que par
le Médecin de la Santé Publique
attaché à la Direction départementale
des Affaires sanitaires et sociales

Partie à détacher et à conserver dans les Mairies

CERTIFICAT DE DÉCÈS

Le Docteur _____, domicilié à _____

soussigné, certifie que la mort de M. _____

_____ [Nom et prénoms]

domicile _____

né.... le _____

survenue le _____, à _____ heure _____

à *(lieu du décès)* _____ est réelle et constante.

| N° d'ordre du décès à reproduire au verso | Décès ne posant pas de problème médico-légal | { Maladie contagieuse soumise aux prescriptions du décret n° 53-1087. |
| | | Maladie non contagieuse. |

Décès posant un problème médico-légal.
(Rayer les mentions inutiles).

A _____, le _____

Signature et cachet du médecin obligatoires :

La cause précise est indiquée dans la note confidentielle ci-annexée qui ne doit être ouverte que par le Médecin-Inspecteur de la Santé.

d _____

CERTIFICAT DE DÉCÈS

(Partie à détacher
et à conserver dans les Mairies)

_____ A remplir par le Médecin _____

COMMUNE :

NOM _____

Prénoms _____

Age _____

Domicile _____

Le Docteur en médecine soussigné, certifie
que la mort de la personne désignée ci-contre,
survenue
le _____ à _____ heure ,
est réelle et constante.
  La cause est indiquée dans le document
confidentiel ci-annexé qui ne doit être ouvert
que par le Médecin de la Santé Publique
attaché à la Direction départementale des
Affaires sanitaires et sociales.

A _____ le _____

Signature.

RÉSERVÉ A LA MAIRIE

Le numéro d'ordre du
décès sur le registre des
actes de l'état civil à ins-
crire ci-contre doit être
reproduit au verso.

N° D'ORDRE du décès

_____ A remplir et à clore par le Médecin _____

COMMUNE _____   DATE DU DÉCÈS _____

Renseignements confidentiels et anonymes sur la cause du décès

I. – Cause du décès

   a) *Cause immédiate de la mort* :

   (Nature de l'évolution terminale, de la complication éventuelle de la maladie, ou
   nature de la lésion fatale en cas d'accident ou d'autre mort violente) (1).

   qui est consécutive à :
   b) *Cause initiale*

   (Nature de la maladie causale ou de l'accident, du suicide, ou de l'homicide.)

II. – Renseignement complémentaire

   État morbide (ou physiologique, grossesse par exemple) ayant contribué à l'évolution fatale (mais non classable en I comme cause proprement dite du décès)(2).

   Une autopsie a-t-elle été pratiquée?   OUI   NON   (3)

   NOTE   Signature ou cachet du médecin.

   Ce document qui ne peut être communiqué
   ni en original, ni en copie, sera détruit par
   les soins du médecin chargé d'établir la statistique des causes de décès dès qu'il y aura puisé
   les renseignements indispensables pour cette
   statistique.

   (1) Mentionner ici le cas échéant le décès post-opératoire.
   (2) Mentionner ici le cas échéant l'état mental pathologique qui a pu être à l'origine du suicide.
   (3) Rayer la mention inutile.

_____ EXEMPLES _____

Décès par maladie	Décès par accident	Décès par suicide	Décès par homicide
I. a) Broncho-pneumonie	I. a) Fracture du crâne	I. a) Plaie du cœur par balle	I. a) Section de l'artère fémorale
b) Rougeole	b) Chute dans un escalier	b) Suicide par arme à feu	b) Homicide par coup de couteau
II. Rachitisme	II. Éthylisme chronique	II. État mélancolique	

Mod. 3103. - Berger-Levrault, Nancy (C).

Figure 5: Death Certificate—Ontario Coroner's Office (Canada)

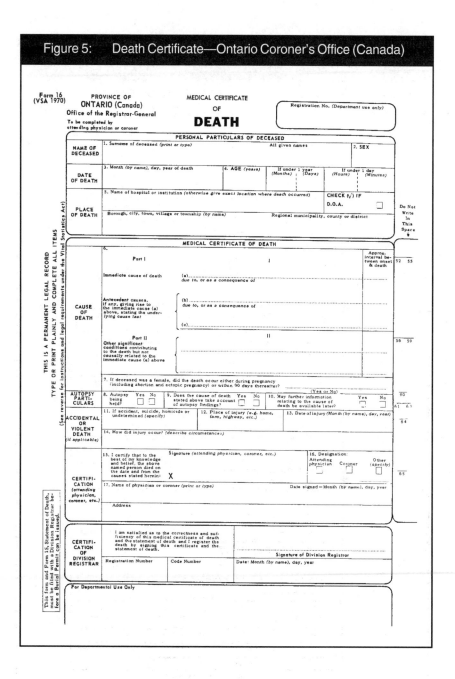

Figure 6: Police Report for Unnatural Death, Metropolitan Police Force (Toronto)

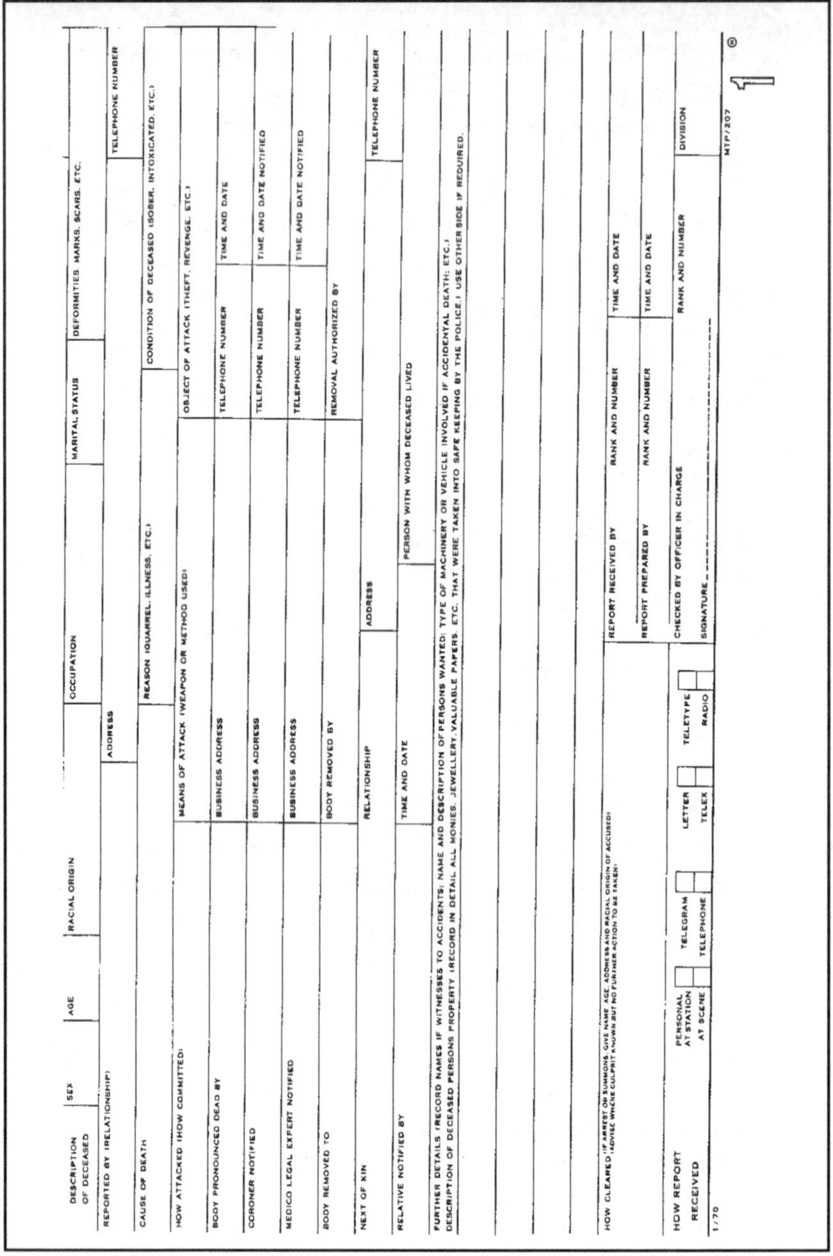

DESCRIPTION OF DECEASED	SEX	AGE	RACIAL ORIGIN	OCCUPATION	MARITAL STATUS	DEFORMITIES, MARKS, SCARS, ETC.
REPORTED BY (RELATIONSHIP)	ADDRESS	TELEPHONE NUMBER				
CAUSE OF DEATH	REASON (QUARREL, ILLNESS, ETC.)	CONDITION OF DECEASED (SOBER, INTOXICATED, ETC.)				
HOW ATTACKED (HOW COMMITTED)	MEANS OF ATTACK (WEAPON OR METHOD USED)	OBJECT OF ATTACK (THEFT, REVENGE, ETC.)				
BODY PRONOUNCED DEAD BY	BUSINESS ADDRESS	TELEPHONE NUMBER	TIME AND DATE			
CORONER NOTIFIED	BUSINESS ADDRESS	TELEPHONE NUMBER	TIME AND DATE NOTIFIED			
MEDICO LEGAL EXPERT NOTIFIED	BUSINESS ADDRESS	TELEPHONE NUMBER	TIME AND DATE NOTIFIED			
BODY REMOVED TO	BODY REMOVED BY	REMOVAL AUTHORIZED BY				
NEXT OF KIN	RELATIONSHIP	ADDRESS	TELEPHONE NUMBER			
RELATIVE NOTIFIED BY	TIME AND DATE	PERSON WITH WHOM DECEASED LIVED				

FURTHER DETAILS (RECORD NAMES IF WITNESSES TO ACCIDENTS; NAME AND DESCRIPTION OF PERSONS WANTED; TYPE OF MACHINERY OR VEHICLE INVOLVED IF ACCIDENTAL DEATH; ETC.)
DESCRIPTION OF DECEASED PERSONS PROPERTY (RECORD IN DETAIL ALL MONIES, JEWELLERY, VALUABLE PAPERS, ETC. THAT WERE TAKEN INTO SAFE KEEPING BY THE POLICE.) USE OTHER SIDE IF REQUIRED.

HOW CLEARED (IF ARREST OR SUMMONS, GIVE NAME, AGE, ADDRESS AND RACIAL ORIGIN OF ACCUSED) (ADVISE WHERE CULPRIT KNOWN BUT NO FURTHER ACTION TO BE TAKEN)	REPORT RECEIVED BY	RANK AND NUMBER	TIME AND DATE
	REPORT PREPARED BY	RANK AND NUMBER	TIME AND DATE
HOW REPORT RECEIVED: PERSONAL AT STATION / AT SCENE; TELEGRAM / TELEPHONE; LETTER / TELEX; TELETYPE / RADIO	CHECKED BY OFFICER IN CHARGE / SIGNATURE	RANK AND NUMBER	DIVISION

1/70 MTP/207

It goes without saying that in suicidology, as in all other related disciplines, accuracy and reliability of statistics and standards of criteria for certifying suicidal death are important for an epidemiological understanding of suicide behaviour and for cross-regional and cross-national comparisons. Suicide statistics—as collated aggregates of all intentional, self-inflicted deaths, which are then classified by certain socio-demographic variables such as age, gender, marital status, religious affiliation, educational level, rural-urban residence, occupation, etc.—are supposed to measure the distribution and frequency of suicide in a given population and delineate thereby the characteristics of targeted population groups. Such socio-demographic study through statistics, as was demonstrated so clearly in the work of Durkheim, may assist in the establishment of general associations between suicide and the characteristics of individuals who kill themselves. Suicide rates obtained from epidemiological studies of the general population provide public health officials and researchers with necessary information to establish and proceed with prevention programmes among high-risk groups and to set up prevention and intervention centres as well as effective programmes in those areas where the problems are most severe.[36]

Arguments Against Reliability of Statistics

The discussion of the question of doubting the reliability of suicide statistics could be reduced to the following points: the magnitude of under-reporting due to differences in certifying criteria used for suspected death by suicide, differing qualifications of certifying agents from one country to another (even from state to state, from province to province), and different attitudes of certifying officials.

As mentioned earlier, death by suicide is usually reported to the coroner's or medical examiner's office, and then sent to each country's central statistical office via village, town, county and municipal offices, state-provincial-prefectural offices, and on to the ministry of health and/ or national police agency. Finally, each country reports such data to the World Health Organization in Geneva. Any researcher in suicide epidemiology knows the frustration of encountering different figures of suicide even in the same country in the same year! Taking Japan as an example (and this is a country well known for accurate statistical information for years), suicide statistics for any given year are different for the White Paper of the National Police Agency and for the Ministry of Health! If this is the case within a given country, one can easily imagine the discrepancies one observes in cross-national comparisons.

It has been the experience of the present author in his first-hand field research in over 40 countries of the world that no country *ever* over-reports suicide. Under-reporting of suicide statistics was actually suspected even in the nineteenth century. Not only Esquirol but de Boisment and Morselli all expressed their serious doubts about the accuracy and reliability of official data and hinted at the widespread practice of under-reporting.[37] In the early twentieth century, another prominent French sociologist, Maurice Halwachs, pointed out that, despite the 1866 law which required the death certificate be written by a legally designated medical official, it had continued to be written casually by an attending police officer or any medical doctor in private practice, especially in small villages and remote towns.[38] In the United States, Louis Dublin estimated that at least 25% of all suicide deaths were unreported.[39] Such chorus of discomfort about official statistics was joined by other voices of distrust both in Europe and North America.[40]

L. T. Ruzika, an Australian demographer, in his special article in the *World Health Statistical Report*, concluded that, due to the unreliable nature of world suicide statistics, international comparison is not appropriate or possible.[41]

Jack Douglas, one of the best known suicide researchers in American sociology in the latter part of the twentieth century, joins Ruzika in his well-known work, *Social Meanings of Suicide*.[42] After reviewing the methods of collecting suicide statistics extensively from the nineteenth century to the present, Douglas expressed his profound distrust of official statistics. His scepticism is based on the suspicion that consistently low numbers of suicides may be due considerably to the nonreporting of cases as "suicide" because the coroners may not label a suicide death as such, unless a suicide note is found with the body. If the situation of death is ambiguous, the individual judgment and discretion of the certifying official become crucially important in determining the ultimate decision. In other words, the highly subjective view of the individual observer, such as the investigating police officer, coroner's investigator, coroner, medical examiner, as the case may be, will be an important factor in the verdict, especially in equivocal deaths. In dealing with such "undetermined death," there is a universal lack of standardized procedures and guidelines for verifying the equivocal case of death, such as those suspected of suicide.[43] It is well known that coroners, in their examination of unnatural deaths, consider it their primary responsibility to rule out homicide. If homicide is not confirmed, any further investigation to assess the possibility of suicide may be minimal. In other words, in socio-political terms, the determination of homicide often takes precedence over suicide.

Another contemporary researcher of suicide in France, Jean Baeschler—a French counterpart to Jack Douglas of the United States—fully echoes Douglas' misgivings about official suicide statistics. In his monumental work, *Les Suicides*,[44] which will be discussed later, he talks about the feasibility of using cross-national suicide rates for a comparative study but soon abandons such efforts because of his mounting distrust of the reliability of such statistics. Instead, both Douglas and Baeschler began to believe and argue that better understanding of suicide behaviour must be conducted at the individual, micro level of looking deeply into the inner subjective meanings suicide held for the deceased. They both insist that such micro-level study of individual cases in detail, almost social-psychological in nature, is much more fruitful in understanding such self-destructive behaviour.

One of the most important studies that casts strong suspicion on the reliability of suicide was conducted by Atkinson. He sent 40 cases of equivocal death suspected of suicide to English coroners and Danish medical examiners. The Danes consistently reported a significantly greater number of suicide (29%) out of these equivocal deaths than the English (19.25%), using the identical case material. In Denmark, the official diagnosis is given by a medically trained person (a physician), using a "balance of probabilities" as the criterion for determination of death. In England, by contrast, the verdict is given by the coroner, *in public* (in official gazette); the coroner requires proof of suicide intention "beyond a reasonable doubt" before he is permitted to return the verdict of suicide. These procedural criteria differences—i.e., the "balance of probabilities" approach vs. "beyond the reasonable doubt" approach—are significant in the light of the fact that Denmark has consistently reported a suicide rate higher than the international average, while England has always reported a rate lower than the international average.[45]

A study in Canada revealed that of 350 Ontario coroners, 33% (almost a third) of the coroners were reluctant to certify a death as suicide for such reasons as consideration of the emotional effect on the family, concerns for life insurance payment for the surviving family (if the insured's death came before the expiration of the exemption period, the insurance company is exempt from making the payment for the beneficiary), stigmatization of the deceased and possible legal consequences and/or religious and moral considerations. Moreover, as many as 38% of the coroners also admitted that, even in a case in which suicide was probable, they would either certify that death as "undetermined" or would simply fail to denote the manner of death.[46]

Another recent study by Phillips and Todd raises further questions about reliability. They examined the prevalence of the misclassification of suicide as "the other causes of death" through an analysis of computerized records of California death certificates from 1966 to 1990. Deaths from suicide, accidental barbiturate poisoning, single-car accidents, pedestrian accidents and ill-defined conditions are contrasted with a control group of deaths from multicar crashes and natural causes. While the control group did not exhibit the mortality peaks at symbolic ages characteristic of suicide, causes of death commonly suspected of containing misclassified suicides (e.g., barbiturate poisoning) and causes of death not hitherto suspected (e.g., pedestrian deaths) did display suicide characteristics or mortality peaks. Mortality peaks were found to correlate significantly with sex and race. Miscalculation was found in all time periods studied, large and small counties, and in each race and sex, raising some questions about the possibility of misclassifying suicide.[47]

Information on suicides in Alaska has been studied, using records obtained from the Alaska Bureau of Vital Statistics and the National Center for Health Statistics. To evaluate the accuracy of these statistics, both of these aforementioned records were searched for suicide deaths in Alaska in 1983-1984. Of 195 deaths meeting the case definition of suicide, only 141 (72%) appeared in Alaska Bureau of Vital Statistics records and 112 (57%) appeared in National Center for Health Statistics records. Native suicides were more likely to be under-recorded than non-native suicides, even after differences in recording district personnel were adjusted for. Errors resulted primarily from delayed determinations of the cause of death and failure to update the records.[48]

Also, informal discussions with staff members in a medical examiner's office about official reporting procedures suggest that investigative standards for assessing equivocal death among blacks may be minimal in comparison to the more uniform evaluations and documentation of questionable deaths for whites. Data pertaining to socio-economic characteristics, religious preference and the influence of interpersonal and intrapersonal factors thought to impact on the black victim's decision to attempt suicide are discussed on the basis of 55 non-white suicide case files. The findings suggest that the social worth criterion of the victims may influence the recording of suicide data.[49]

The reliability of official statistics in Third World countries regarding the reported low suicide rates was questioned in one study. Factors that possibly contribute to low suicide rates may be due to difficulty in discriminating suicide from other deaths. A case study as well as some interview data, obtained from 1960 to 1980 in sixteen Ecuadorean villages, are used to compute a suicide rate for the rural population, resulting in a rate similar to that of urbanized Latin American countries.[50] Though this particular study lacks methodological precision in itself, this is certainly one of the few studies that sheds light on the haphazard nature of data collection and death certification in developing countries. Even though Spain is not a developing country, a review of judicial proceedings revealed 775 cases of suicide in the Canary Islands between 1977 and 1983. This is twice the official number of 381, suggesting the lack of validity and reliability of official figures for suicide in Spain.[51]

Finally, the current practice in many countries of not reporting children's suicide under the age of ten can be another source of distorting the total picture of suicide through under-reporting. The present author learned, in the course of his field research trips to Israel in 1987 and 1994, that no suicide statistics are officially reported for children under 15; moreover, he was informed of the extreme reluctance of the medical examiner in Israel to determine death as "suicide," if and when vociferous objections are raised by a rabbi or religious community (the often repeated statement of a medical examiner was "I wouldn't touch it"). Since Israel consistently reports much lower suicide rates than the international average, such socio-cultural background factors behind suicide reporting must be fully taken into account when reviewing the rates from that country.[52] All of these foregoing studies support the conclusion of the WHO report that "...present official suicide statistics are only of limited value. Constructing epidemiological and socio-demographic theories about suicide, therefore, will remain hazardous."[53]

Arguments for Reliability of Statistics

It is interesting that the Working Group Report of the WHO Regional Office for Europe reached the opposite conclusion of the aforementioned earlier report by the WHO. The said Working Group expressed its collective view that the official statistics are reliable enough for comparative study and reference.[54]

The crucial question here is whether methods and criteria in identifying suicides vary so much among different populations that they may account for the differences in rates. In response to the criticisms raised by Douglas, Atkinson and others, the WHO Working Group made a careful examination of the reliability and usefulness of official statistics and came to the conclusion that differences in ascertaining procedures do not explain differences in suicide rates between populations. Such a conclusion is drawn from the following research findings and observations.

Scotland, unlike England and Wales, uses markedly different procedures for ascertaining death. Ross and Kreitman designed a study to show whether or not national differences are caused by different certifying procedures. They examined cases of men aged 25-44 and 65-84 years (the difference between the two areas was found the greatest for these two age groups). They found that certifying officials in Scotland, England and Wales agreed on the criteria used for reaching the verdict and concluded that the ascertainment process did not explain the difference in suicide rates.[55] In other words, the observed differences were real.

In a study by Sainsbury and Barraclough, the rank order of the suicide rates of immigrants to the United States from 11 different countries was compared with the reported rates of their countries of origin.[56] Immigrant suicide cases were all identified by the U.S. procedure, whereas suicides in their countries of origin were defined by the particular methods and procedures of each respective country. As shown in Table 6, the rank order of the two sets was nearly identical (r=0.90).

They concluded that *national suicide rates differed independently of the ways of defining and reporting a suicide.* Their study was repeated in Australia, and the same results and conclusion were drawn.[57]

Even though Holding and Barraclough found an estimated error of 22% in ascertaining cases of suicide, Sainsbury argued that there exists a net error of 16% in ascertaining deaths from cancer of the lung, but the

Table 6:   Suicide Rates for 1959 per 100,000 among Immigrants
           to the U.S. from 11 Countries

Country	A Suicide rate/100,000 of foreign- born in U.S.	B Suicide rate/100,000 of country of origin	Rank order of A	Rank order of B
Austria	32.5	24.8	2	2
Canada	17.5	7.4	9	8
Czechoslovakia	31.5	24.9	3	1
England and Wales	19.2	11.5	7	5
Germany, Fed. Rep. of	25.7	18.7	4	3
Ireland	9.8	2.5	10	10
Italy	18.2	6.2	8	9
Mexico	7.9	2.1	11	11
Norway	23.7	7.8	6	7
Poland	25.2	8.0	5	6
Sweden	34.2	18.1	1	4
U.S.	10.4			

$r = 0.90. \ p < 0.01$

Source: Sainsbury, P. and Barraclough, B.M., "Differences between Suicide Rates,"
          Nature, 1968: 220, p.1252.

conclusions drawn from official cancer statistics are never seriously questioned.[58] Persistent obsession and preoccupation with the accuracy of suicide statistics may actually reveal a deep-seated uneasiness about this form of self-inflicted death, which may surface in the form of pointed criticisms on the reliability of suicide data rather than other statistical information.[59]

A Canadian study demonstrated that, in contrast to other regions, suicide in Newfoundland and Labrador followed a stable pattern of low suicide rates, which were affected by the "new high-risk group" (such as young people) as witnessed in more urbanized areas in the rest of Canada. They confirmed that the suicide rate in Newfoundland and Labrador was less than half the national rate, even after allowing for under-reporting of suicides as well as the presence of the aforementioned "new high-risk group."[60]

In spite of persistent criticisms regarding their validity, official suicide statistics continue to be used in epidemiological studies that have substantial public health implications. On the question of which epidemiological findings might be affected by under-reporting of the suicide rate, one study estimates that the extent of potential under-reporting to be 17.5% for females and 12% for males.[61] It concludes that overall under-reporting is not sufficiently large that reasonable reformulations of the suicide rate substantially alter the findings, and that most epidemiological conclusions based on official rates are essentially correct.

A couple of other studies in Europe seem to affirm the reliability of suicide data. In a study of the suicide statistics of Greenland, with particular attention to and review of suicide among Inuits, the researcher concludes that the official statistics as published by the Danish Board of Health are generally reliable in Greenland.[62]

Also in a study in Belgium, various mortality indicators for suicide, undetermined deaths, accidental poisoning deaths and "estimated" suicide in 1968-1972 and 1978-1981 were compared. Results did not reveal important bias on national comparisons by under-reporting. But the biased distributions of undetermined deaths among the 43 geographical entities (districts) suggest that the assumptions about constancy of under-reporting are not always met and have to be checked if possible. But, the research concludes, the numerical weight of the under-reporting categories was not found heavy enough to bias the geographical pattern in Belgium.[63]

A 1991 Canadian study, for 1969 to 1982, estimated the suicide rate in Canada could be underreported an average 17.5% in females and 12% in males. Using a reformulating method that combines suicide deaths with selected undetermined and accidental deaths, this study concluded that national statistics are sufficiently accurate for most public health and epidemiological purposes. Epidemiological techniques such as reformulation do not produce new, accurate suicide rates but are simply attempts to measure and "even out" suspected unreliable statistics. If the number of suicide deaths is low because of under-reporting, a corresponding increase in accidental and undetermined deaths (misreporting) is expected.[64]

Question of Criteria for Ascertaining Death by Suicide

In certifying death by suicide, the determination of a death as "suicide" depends largely on the *inferred intention* of the deceased, which can only be established on a retrospective basis. If evidence of such intention is absent, death is quite likely considered "accidental," and the manner of death "undetermined." So-called "evidence" varies, however, and this variation may be influenced by the attitudes and values of certifying officials.

There are two distinct models of criteria for determining a death by suicide. One is based on the "balance of probabilities" approach in death certification, in which evidence is evaluated against the backdrop of physical autopsy results, psychological autopsy and toxicological examination reports, etc., and the most likely probability of the manner of death is decided. The aforementioned Danish medical examiners in the Atkinson study are a case in point. This approach may be also called the "medical-model criterion" because of the propensity of medical officers to follow this guideline.

The other criterion is the "beyond a reasonable doubt" approach, in which a death will not be certified as "suicide" unless it can be proven beyond a reasonable doubt. Such an approach is likely used by the legally trained personnel such as coroners and magistrates in England as shown in the preceding study by Atkinson. When a certifying official uses this latter model or approach, many probable suicides might go unreported. Since this is mainly related to a legal concept in criminal justice system, it may be called the "legal model."

Conclusion and Prospects for the Future

The preceding discussion hopefully presents a balanced evaluation of pros and cons for the reliability of suicide statistics. It is a well-known fact that suicide has been and will continue to be under-reported for a number of reasons enumerated in the foregoing pages, and that the rates are subject to many errors like other mortality figures in general. But the effective arguments presented in these pages also suggest that the errors in collective statistics are usually randomized, at least to an extent that allows researchers to compare rates between countries, within them and over time. Furthermore, these counter-arguments in support of the reliability of suicide statistics show that consistent differences in rates between national and social groups have been observed and recorded over very long periods (in some cases for more than a century), and that these differences have persisted despite considerable political and social changes that have altered the ascertainment procedures in these countries. On balance, then, the continued collation of official suicide data and study of the relative differences between official rates is not only heuristically useful but highly legitimate and fruitful for a comparative study in suicide epidemiology.

The question of the validity and reliability of suicide statistics may be evaluated on three levels: (1) the question of misidentifying or differentially identifying suicide deaths across jurisdictions or over time; (2) the degree of misidentifying suicide death, if any; and (3) if such misidentification does exist, the question of whether the degree of misidentifying is sufficient enough to threaten the validity of research based on suicide statistics. There is general agreement that suicides are likely under-reported for such reasons as the "beyond-a-reasonable-doubt" criterion used and for some socio-cultural reasons that may bias the reporting. There is not, however, much agreement as to the degree to which true suicides are undercounted. At least some of the inconsistencies in the findings of different investigators arise because of the variation in the suicide death certification system both internationally and intra-nationally. Much of this conflict is undoubtedly based on the lack of a genuine "gold standard" against which the verdicts of any given death certification process can be measured. In considering a central question of estimating the sensitivity of coroners and medical examiners in certifying suicide, the researcher of one study raises a question: "What proportion of true suicides are either equivocal or likely to go unsuspected by the coroner or medical examiner?" Another central question is one of "whether or not the degree and extent of under-reporting is such as to threaten the validity of research based on official statistics."[65] In this review of the controversy, the researcher concludes that, overall, it does not seem that very many true non-suicides are incorrectly certified as suicides.

What might be the necessary and useful steps for further improving the death certification system for suicide? The following points are expected to enhance the accuracy and reliability of suicide certification anywhere, if adopted: (1) an autopsy should be automatically ordered on all suspected suicides, including blood tests for as many drugs as possible; (2) the death certification ought to be based, if at all possible, on a "balance of probabilities" criterion, thereby decreasing the overuse of the "undetermined" category on the death certificate; (3) in the absence of a suicide note as well as in ambiguous situations, psychological autopsies should be mandatory; (4) uniform guidelines for certifying the death by suicide ought to be adopted, not only for all areas and regions in a given country but also ideally for the entire world under the aegis of a prestigious body such as the World Health Organization.

NOTES AND REFERENCES

[1] Mausner, J.D., and Bahn, A.K., *Epidemiology* (Philadelphia: W.B. Saunders Co., 1974), p.4.

[2] *Suicide in Canada: National Task Force Report* (Ottawa: Ministry of Health and Welfare, 1987), p.1.

[3] Murphy, H.B.M., "Suicide and Para-Suicide," in H.B.M. Murphy (ed.), *Comparative Psychiatry: The International and Intercultural Distribution of Mental Illness* (Berlin and New York: Springer - Verlag, 1982).

[4] Morgenstern, H., "Uses of Ecological Analysis," *American Journal of Public Health*, Vol. 72, 1982, p.1336-44.

[5] World Health Organization (WHO), *Prevention of Suicide* (Geneva: Public Health Papers, No.35), cited by *National Task Force Report, op. cit.*, p.3.

[6] Diekstra, R.F.W., "The Epidemiology of Suicide and Parasuicide," *Acta Psychiatrica Scandinavica*, 1993: Suppl. 371, p.9.

[7] Fusé, T., *Suicide and Culture* (Tokyo: Shinchosha, 1985), p.28.

[8] La Vecchia, C., Lucchini, F. and Levi, F., "Worldwide Trends in Suicide Mortality," *Acta Psychiatrica Scandinavica*, 1994: 90, 53-64. Hungary's increase towards reaching and maintaining the highest rate in the world began from an already high level more than four decades ago. The WHO Working Group quoted just as high rates of suicide in northern, industrialized and wealthier parts of the former Yugoslavia, as opposed to much lower rates in southern Yugoslavia such as Macedonia.

[9] Fusé, Toyomasa, "World Trends in Suicide—Its Regional Characteristics," *Clinical Psychiatry à la Carte (Kokoro-no Rinsho a ra Karuto)*, 1992: Vol.11, No.2, pp.15-17.

[10] Fusé, Toyomasa, *Introduction to Suicidology in Cross-Cultural Perspective, op. cit.*, pp.32-33, 79-88; La Vecchia et al., *op. cit.*, p.54.

[11] La Vecchia, C., et al., *op. cit.*

[12] Fukutomi, Kazuo, "Suicide among the Japanese: Its Statistical Characteristics," *Clinical Psychiatry à la Carte, op. cit.*, pp.18-20; Fusé, Toyomasa, "Suicide Behaviour of the Japanese and Implications for Modern Suicidology," in

Proceedings of the XXXIIth Congress of the International Institute of Sociology (Trieste, Italy: International Institute of Sociology, 1995), p.48; Kobayashi, S., "Increasing Suicide Rates among the Middle- Aged," *Indicator for Social Welfare,* 1988: Vol.34, No.4, p.203.

[13] Fusé, Toyomasa, "Trends and Patterns of Suicide in Japan: Some Observations in Suicidology," in Sekiné, T., Daly, D., (eds.), *Japan in Focus* (Ottawa: Cactus Press, 1994), Asia Pacific Research and Resource Centre, Carleton University, Ottawa, pp.244-245.

[14] Chenais, Jean-Claude, "La Violence Suicidaire" in Jean-Claude Chenais, *Histoire de la Violence* (Paris: Robert Laffont, 1982); Fusé, Toyomasa, *Suicide and Culture,* (Tokyo: Shinchosha Co., 1985), pp.47-49.

[15] Tsuang, Ming T., Simpson, John C. and Fleming, Jerome, A., "Epidemiology of Suicide," *International Review of Psychiatry,* 1992: 4, 117-129.

[16] *National Task Force Report on Suicide in Canada, op. cit.;* La Vecchia et al., *op. cit.*

[17] Fusé, T., *Introduction to Suicidology..., op. cit.,* pp.33-37.

[18] La Vecchia et al., *op. cit.* Mauritius, the only other country in Africa listed in the WHO database, actually belongs to the middle-rank group of nations as mentioned earlier, with appreciable upward trends over the last few decades, reaching 15.6 per 100,000 for men and 7.0 for women in the late 1980s.

[19] Ueno, M., Shoji, M., Nagasawa, S., et al., "Suicide among the Elderly Based on the Records of the Tokyo Metropolitan Medical Examiner's Office," *Medical Journal,* 1982: Vol.40, No.10, pp.1109-1119.

[20] *National Task Force Report on Suicide in Canada, op. cit.*

[21] "Cohort analysis" is a method of demographic analysis used in suicidology in which the rate of suicide, for instance, of a given age group is investigated and then followed up at different time intervals afterwards. The assumption is that any age group that manifests suicide propensity and vulnerability would maintain such tendency in later years as well. Solomon and Hellon showed that once a cohort of 15- to 19-year-olds had a high suicide rate, the group continued to exhibit an increased rate as that group aged. See: Solomon, M.I. and Hellon, C.P., "Suicide and Age in Alberta, Canada: 1951-1977, A Cohort Analysis," *Archives of General Psychiatry,* 1980: 37, 511-513.

[22] Lester, David, "The Distribution of Sex and Age among Completed Suicides: A Cross-National Study," *International Journal of Social Psychiatry,* 1982: 28, pp.256-260. This heuristic model was suggested by Inamura, H., *Suicidology* (Tokyo: Tokyo University Press, 1979) in which he originally labelled the Pattern A as "Hungarian," Pattern B as "Japanese," and Pattern C as "Scandinavian." But the Japanese trends changed in 1979 and have approximated the Hungarian model.

23 Durkheim, Emile, *op. cit.,* pp.217-240

24 Headley, L.A., (ed), *Suicide in Asia and the Near East* (Berkeley: The University of California Press, 1984).

25 Chenais, Jean-Claude, *Histoire de la Violence, op. cit.,* p.181.

26 Tsuang et al., *Epidemiology, op. cit.,* p.121.

27 Department of Indian and Northern Affairs, Government of Canada; Ottawa, 1973–1976 average, reported in *The Toronto Star,* September 25, 1982.

28 Tsuang, *op. cit.,* p.121.

29 Templer, D.I. and Veleber, D.M., "Suicide Rate and Religion within the United States," *Psychological Reports,* 1980: 47, pp.898.

30 Cross, C.K. and Hirschfeld, R.M.A., "Epidemiology of Disorders in Adulthood: Suicide," in Michels, R., Canenas, J., Brodie, H.K.H. (eds), *Psychiatry,* Vol.3 (Philadelphia: J.B. Lippincott, 1985), pp.1-15.

31 *Ontario Coroner's Act,* Provincial Government of Ontario.

32 *National Task Force Report on Suicide, op. cit.,* p.38.

33 *Ibid.*

34 Stengel, E. and Farberow, N.L., "Certification of Suicide around the World," *Proceedings of the International Conference on Suicide Prevention,* 1968, pp.8-15.

35 Fusé, T., *Introduction to Suicidology..., op. cit.,* pp.15-16.

36 Monk, M., "Epidemiology," in S. Perlin (ed), *A Handbook for the Study of Suicide* (New York: Oxford University Press, 1975).

37 Douglas, Jack D., "Social Meanings of Suicide," *International Encyclopaedia of Social Sciences* (New York: Collier and Macmillan Inc.,1968), pp.377-388.

38 Halwachs, Maurice, *Les Causes du Suicide* (Paris: Alcan, 1930).

39 Dublin, L.I., *Suicide: A Sociological and Statistical Study* (New York: Ronald, 1963).

40 Ovenstone, I.M.K., "A Psychiatric Approach to the Diagnosis of Suicide and Its Effect upon the Edinburgh Statistics," *British Journal of Psychiatry,* 1973: 125, pp.15-21; McCarthy, P.D. and Walsh, D., "Suicide in Dublin, Part 1: The Under-Reporting of Suicide and the Consequences for National Statistics," *British Journal of Psychiatry,* 1975: 126, pp.301-308; Liberakis, E.A. and Hoening, J., "Recording of Suicide in Newfoundland," *The Psychiatric Journal of the University of Ottawa,* 1978: 3 (4), pp.254-259; Brugha, T. and Walsh, D., "Suicide, Past and Present - The Temporal Constancy of Under-Reporting," *British Journal of Psychiatry,* 1977: 47 (2), pp.196-206; Atkinson, M., Kessel, N. and Dalgaard, J.B., "The Comparability of Suicide Rates," *British Journal of Psychiatry,* 1975:125, pp.247-256; Farberow, N.L., MacKinnon, D.R. and Nerlson F.L., "Suicide: Who's Counting?" *Public Health Reports,* 1977: 92 (3), pp.223-232; Nelson, L., Farberow, N.L.,

MacKinnon, R., "The Certification of Suicide in Eleven Midwestern States: An Inquiry into the Validity of Reported Suicide Rates," *Suicide and Life-Threatening Behavior,* 1978: 8, p.2; Walsh, N., "Implications of the Coroner's System for Official Suicide Statistics in Ireland," *Proceedings of the 10th International Congress of Suicide Prevention,* 1979: 2, pp.67-69; Syer-Solursh, D., "Attitudes of Coroners toward Suicide Certification Procedures," Educational Course for Coroners, Annual Seminar: Part I, Toronto (Toronto: Ontario Ministry of the Solicitor General, 1981), pp.78-86; Fusé, T., *Introduction to Suicidology...*, *op. cit.,* pp.24-31; Baeschler, Jean, *Suicides* (New York: The Free Press, 1975).

[41] Ruzika, L.T., "Suicide: 1950-1971," *World Health Statistics Report,* Vol.29, No.7, 1976, pp.396-413.

[42] Douglas, J.D., *Social Meanings of Suicide, op. cit.*

[43] The present author knows firsthand that in the coroner's office in many countries staff members, entrusted with investigating and verifying the suspected cases, often lack any qualification in chemistry, pathology or forensic science. In one case, in a highly developed country in the West, the official in charge of clarifying the so-called "undetermined death" was a high school graduate without any background or training in the aforementioned disciplines.

[44] Baeschler, Jean, *Suicides* (New York: The Free Press, 1975).

[45] Atkinson, M.W., Kessel, N., Dalgaard, J.B., "The Comparability of Suicide Rates," *British Journal of Psychiatry,* 1975: 125, pp.247-256.

[46] Syer-Solursh, D., and Wyndowe, J.P., "How Coroners' Attitudes toward Suicide Affect Certification Procedures," Educational Course for Coroners, Part I (Toronto: Ontario Ministry of the Solicitor General, 1981).

[47] Phillips, D. and Todd, R.E., "Adequacy of Official Suicide Statistics for Scientific Research and Public Policy," *Suicide and Life-Threatening Behavior,* 1993: 23: 4, pp.307~319.

[48] Hlady, W.G. and Middaugh,J.P., "The Underreporting of Suicides in State and National Records in Alaska, 1983-1984," *Suicide and Life-Threatening Behavior,* 1988:18: 3, Fall, pp.237-244.

[49] Peck, D.L., "Official Documentation of the Black Suicide Experience," *Omega:* 1983-84: 14: 1: pp.21-31.

[50] Tousignant, M. and Transito, C., "Suicide in Third World Countries: The Case of Rural Ecuador," *Omega:* 1991: 23:3, pp.191-198

[51] Ruzicka, L.T., "Suicide: 1950-1971," *World Health Statistics Report,* 1976: 29, 7, p.413.

[52] Fusé, Toyomasa, "Suicide in Israel," in "Epidemiology II," *Introduction to Suicidology...*, *op. cit.,* 1990, pp.69-75.

53 *WHO Chronicle,* 1975: 29, *op. cit.,* pp.188-193.

54 *Changing Patterns in Suicide Behaviour: Report on a WHO Working Group,* (Copenhagen: WHO Regional Office for Europe, 1982), EURO Reports and Studies, No.74.

55 Ross, O. and Kreitman, N., "A Further Investigation of Differences in the Suicide Rates of England and Wales and Scotland," *British Journal of Psychiatry,* 1975: 127, p.575.

56 Sainsbury, P. and Barraclough, B.M., "Differences between Suicide Rates," *Nature,* 1968: 220, p.1252.

57 Sainsbury, P., "Suicide: Opinion and Facts," *Proceedings of the Royal Society of Medicine,* 1973: 66, p.579.

58 Holding, T.A. and Barraclough, B.M., "Psychiatric Morbidity in a Sample of Accidents," *British Journal of Psychiatry,* 1977: 130, pp.244-52.

59 Sainsbury, P., "Validity and Reliability of Trends in Suicide Statistics," *World Health Statistics Quarterly,* 1983: 36, pp.339-48.

60 Malla, A. and Hoenig, J., "Suicide in Newfoundland and Labrador," *Canadian Journal of Psychiatry,* 1979: 24, pp.139-46; Malla, A. and Hoenig J., "Under-Reporting of Suicide," *Canadian Journal of Psychiatry,* 1983: 28, pp.291-367.

61 Speechley, M. and Stavraky, K.M., "Adequacy of Suicide Statistics for Use in Epidemiology and Public Health," *Canadian Journal of Public Health,* 1991: 82: 1, pp.38-42.

62 Thornslund, J. and Misfeldt, J., "On Suicide Statistics," *Arctic Medical Research,* 1989: 48: 3, 124-30.

63 Moens, G.F., "The Reliability of Reported Suicide Mortality Statistics: An Experience from Belgium," *International Journal of Epidemiology,* 1985: 14: 2, pp.272-275.

64 Speechley, M. and Stavraky, K.M., "Adequacy of Suicide Statistics for Use in Epidemiology and Public Health," *op. cit.*

65 Sainsbury, P., "Validity and Reliability of Trends in Suicide Statistics," *op. cit.,* p.345-346.

CHAPTER 3

Theories of Suicide

T. S. Kuhn, a historian of science, proposed three important stages in the development of scientific revolution: (1) an early developmental stage, in which there is competition between various theories, each building its own empirical base and methodology but without systematic accumulation of knowledge as in the case of mature branches of science like physics and chemistry; (2) a normal scientific stage in which one particular theoretical approach is accepted by most individuals in the field with some basic accumulation of knowledge achieved; (3) a scientific revolution, during which some facts or information are discovered not fitting into the accepted theory, thereby challenging the established theory and spurring the development, testing and accepting of a new theory.[1]

A glance at the field of suicidology somehow convinces an observer that, in terms of the above requirements set by Kuhn, it is still largely at the first, or at best moving towards the second stage of scientific development, in which three major branches of theories have been competing for saliency, dominance and hegemony, each with its own theoretical base making different assumptions, concepts and methodology with some accumulation of knowledge achieved. These three main orientations in theory in the field of suicidology are *sociological, psychological* and *biochemical*.

Sociological theories, pioneered by Emile Durkheim who founded the discipline of sociology on the strength of his work on suicide, try to understand suicide behaviour in the context of its relationship to social groups and socio-cultural factors in society. Psychological theories, on the other hand, probe deeply into the individual's inner psyche and emotional dimensions propelling the person to suicide. If the unit of inquiry for sociology is the human collective (groups, nations and social institutions), that of psychology is the individual. Biochemical theories explore the etiology of suicide in terms of physiology, biology, neurochemistry and genetics. That there have been three distinct theoretical orientations in suicidology is a good indication that the field still lacks a unified general theory. It is expected, therefore, that in the foreseeable future these three main branches of theoretical orientations will continue to develop along their own paths, building in the process their own empirical base and evaluating their concepts in accordance to their own basic assumptions and methodology.

The criteria for a good theory are usually based upon the following considerations: (1) comprehensiveness—i.e., the question of being able to explain *all* types of suicide; (2) simplicity—i.e., the question of being simple, consistent and coherent; and (3) verifiability—i.e., the question of being able to generate postulates and hypotheses that can then be operationally and empirically tested and verified.[2]

In the ensuing pages some of the important theories from these three main orientations will be discussed and then evaluated in terms of the supporting empirical data and findings.

SOCIOLOGICAL THEORIES

Emile Durkheim (1858-1915)

Biographical Background:

Emile Durkheim was born at Epinal (Vosges) in the eastern French province of Lorraine on April 15, 1858. His descent from a long line of distinguished rabbis influenced his early decision to study Hebrew, the Old Testament and Talmud. But his pursuit of these studies was short-lived due to his brief encounter with a Catholic instructress, who seems to have had quite an impact on him. Be that as it may, from his Judaic background and training, Durkheim gained a deep and permanent concern for universal law and the problem of ethics. Evidently he was a very serious young man without much humour and with somewhat heavy-handed traits redeemed by his overpowering dedication to sociology and by his vast learning.[3]

His first formal schooling started in his native city at the Collège d'Epinal. His outstanding performance led to a variety of honours and prizes. It was from here that he transferred to one of the great French high schools, the Lycée Louis-le-Grand and then prepared himself for the arduous, nationwide admissions examination to the renowned École Normale Superieure, the traditional training ground for the intellectual elite of France. After two unsuccessful attempts at the entrance examination, he was finally admitted in 1879. At the École Normale he developed a strong distaste and contempt for what he perceived to be the prevalent "dilettantism" at the school and for the strong emphasis placed on the humanities (such as reading of Greek verse and Latin prose) at the expense of "solid" and systematic learning.

Durkheim had two great mentors at the École Normale who had a great impact on his thinking and learning at the time: the great historian, Fustel de Coulanges, who assumed the directorship of the school in 1880, and Emile Boutroux, the equally eminent philosopher from whom much of present-day French philosophy stems. To Fustel, who preceded Durkheim in the advocacy of the comparative method and the conception of the importance of religion in social life, Durkheim dedicated his Latin thesis (on Montesquieu). To Boutroux, who impressed Durkheim most by his penetrating and objective way of reconstituting thinking systems, Durkheim dedicated his French thesis, which was entitled "Division of Labour."[4] It seems that Durkheim was not so influenced, as might be expected, by Auguste Compte, an eminent French social philosopher who coined the term "la sociologie" ("study of society"), because Durkheim objected to being identified as a "positivist" and rejected Compte's metaphysics and his conception of sociology.[5]

Durkheim graduated from the École Normale around 1882, and between 1882 and 1887 he began his teaching career in philosophy at a lycée. But he took time off from teaching from 1885 to 1886 in order to study and do research in Germany, culminating in the publication of two articles, one on German scientific methods in philosophy and the other on the overall importance of ethics. During his stay in Germany, he was reportedly most impressed by the rigour and scientific thoroughness of Wilhelm Wundt, the founder of Gestalt theory. He attentively witnessed Wundt's work in his famous physiological laboratory. In fact, Durkheim was most favourably impressed by many German intellectuals of the period,

> [as] he approved of their insistence on treating moral facts as empirical data *sui generis*. He agreed with their view that moral duty was social in nature and origin, and applauded their desire to have ethics take its place as an independent positive discipline alongside of the other social sciences.[6]

According to one biographer of Durkheim, this time in Germany confirmed Durkheim's conviction that the Kantian type of study of ethics was a thing of the past and that he should devote his intellectual energies to the scientific study of "moral life," which, to Durkheim, was society itself.[7]

In 1887, Durkheim was invited to join the faculty of the University of Bordeaux, which was offering a course in social science, the very first of its kind in all of France. In 1896, nine years after his appointment to Bordeaux, Durkheim was promoted to a full professorship, which he held for six years. In 1902, he was finally called to the Sorbonne, first as a chargé de cours (assistant professor) and later as Professor of the Science of Education in 1906. In 1913, by a special ministerial decree, his chair was changed to "Science of Education and Sociology," marking the first time that sociology was recognized as a legitimate, official chair in any French university. Durkheim continued to teach until 1916, when, experiencing severe sorrow over the death of his only son on the battlefield in World War I, he became seriously ill. On November 15th, 1917, at the age of 59, Durkheim passed away.

This talented sociologist is best remembered for the following major works: *De la Division du Travail Social, (Division of Labour in Society,* published in 1892); *Les Règles de la Méthode Sociologique (Rules of Sociological Method,* 1895); *Les Forms Elémentaires de la Vie Réligieuse (The Elementary Forms of Religious Life,* 1912); *Suicide: L'Étude Sociologique (A Sociological Study of Suicide,* 1897); *Éducation et Sociologie, (Education and Sociology,* 1922); *Sociologie et Philosophie (Sociology and Philosophy,* 1924). He is also known as the first editor of *L'Année Sociologique,* an influential French journal of sociology, which was first published in 1898 under Durkheim's aegis. It is probably no exaggeration to say that Durkheim's contribution to the new field of sociology was responsible for establishing the discipline as a recognized branch of social science in France, and later throughout the world. Certainly, "in France during his lifetime he was sociology."

Durkheim lived through a turbulent period in French history —the traumatic recovery from the aftermaths of the French Revolution, the tumultuous change wrought by the Industrial Revolution, the crushing defeat of the Franco-Prussian War of 1870 to 1871, the establishment of the Third Republic in 1875, which had some semblance of stability but contained within the ever-constant vulnerability to collapse and chaos. From the standpoint of the sociology of knowledge, Durkheim's intellectual concerns for social cohesion and solidarity must be understood in the context of a country that had been going through turbulent transformations and frequent fractious disruptions.

His Theory of Suicide

Throughout his career as a university professor he distinguished himself with outstanding research on social institutions such as the family, education, religion, economy, etc. One of his main preoccupations, however, was with establishing a new discipline, separate and different from all other existing fields. He began to advocate the creation of a new positivistic and empirical science (i.e., sociology), the central purpose of which was the study of "social facts" that are supra-individual in nature. Durkheim argued that cohesion in human relations, solidarity in family relationships, customs and mores in society, legal systems and traditions, religious, linguistic and educational systems, etc., ought to be legitimate and proper areas of inquiry for modern sociology. All of these objects of sociological inquiries were the products of collective social life which Durkheim called "social facts." As such, social facts are characterized by three distinct traits: (1) being external to the individual; (2) being measurable through such indicators as group rates (i.e., birth rates, suicide rates, divorce rates, crime rates, etc.); (3) and yet having a constraining influence on the individual.

Social facts exist often independently of the will of each constituent individual in society and cannot be explained adequately by individual-oriented approaches such as those of psychology. For example, if a particular individual could not obtain a job after much trying, it is still possible to render an individual analysis of his failure at getting a job, (e.g., perhaps his school transcripts were not good enough, or maybe he did not give a good impression at the job interview, his tardiness at work or certain idiosyncrasies in his life style, etc). All of these possible reasons are based upon his personal and individual attributes. But, if more than 20,000 persons of similar age with similar educational and work backgrounds were found unable to obtain jobs, the level of analysis must *ipso facto* switch from the aforementioned individual attributes (poor academic records, tardiness, bad interview results etc.), to social-structural analysis, i.e., the inability of the economic system to absorb qualified job seekers. Thus, during such massive economic dislocations as recession and depression, the central focus of analysis is no longer on the probing of individual quirks and attributes but rather the adequacy of the economy itself. Hence, according to Durkheim, a social fact such as the economic system must be explained by supra-individual facts such as the rate of unemployment and economic indices, etc. In other words, social facts must be explained by social facts; individualistic and psychologistic explanations of social facts, if attempted, are not only inadequate but often false.

In human social sciences one often has to deal with such intangible objects of inquiry as "social cohesion," "solidarity" and "social integration," that are not readily accessible to visual and/or tactile verification. Durkheim's response was that sociologists could indirectly measure such social reality, just as the human temperature, though real, could not be gauged directly but could be measured indirectly by the fluctuation of mercury in the thermometer. Likewise, the degree of "social cohesion" in a given society could also be measured indirectly by an assessment of divorce rates, crime rates, unemployment rates, suicide rates, etc. In line with such argument, therefore, his celebrated study on sucide was published.

In his study of suicide as a sociological inquiry, Durkheim noted that suicide rates in European countries in the nineteenth century had shown remarkable stability over the years, suggesting that such collective rates may be independent of individual whims and psychological states. Until this time it was the rule to seek answers for suicide almost exclusively in individualistic psychological factors. To be sure, if one examines 100 suicide notes, one is bound to find 100 different reasons and motives for suicide. Yet, if all social and demographic data are collected on these suicides, one notices certain discernible traits and characteristics that may remain constant over a period of time. Durkheim observed that: (1) suicide was consistently more common among the widowed, divorced and single than among the married (especially the married with many children); (2) suicide rates invariably decrease during wars and revolutions that involve the entire nation; (3) men are more prone to suicide than women; (4) suicide rates are consistently higher among Protestants than Roman Catholics and Jews; (5) suicide is observed more among writers, artists, highly skilled professionals and other intelligentsia, all of whom are characterized by a highly developed sense of individualism; (6) suicide rates are higher among military personnel than civilians, and within the military there is more suicide among the non-commissioned officers than enlisted men; (7) suicide rates are higher in times of sudden prosperity or sudden economic dislocations than in times of sustained economic stability or poverty.

At first glance, these observations seem to be disparate, unconnected phenomena and facts, but to Durkheim they represent certain distinct group properties and characteristics. Durkheim reasoned that since different groups have different suicide rates, there must be something about the social organization of the groups that deters or fails to deter people from suicide and that may even induce some of them to commit suicide. He maintained that individual reasons for suicide were many and varied, but they did not explain the fact that some groups are consistently more inclined to suicide than others. He suggested, therefore, that the degree to which the individual was integrated into group life determined whether or not he could be motivated to commit suicide. Hence, to Durkheim, suicide is an index of the degree of integration of the individual into society.

For Durkheim, suicide was primarily a social phenomenon, very much related to the particular social surroundings and conditions in which it occurred. As such, suicide was not considered by Durkheim as some sort of horrendous aberration of human behaviour, but rather as a social act quite in keeping with the particular societal conditions that prevailed at the time. He argued further that it was not so much an individual's particular proclivity towards suicide that caused him to commit the act. Instead, in most instances, the major inducement for an individual to take his or her own life was the peculiar societal circumstances involved. As he stated:[8]

> Each social group really has a collective inclination for the act, quite its own, and the source of all individual inclination, rather than their result.... These tendencies of the whole social body, by affecting individuals, cause them to commit suicide. The private experiences

usually thought to be the proximate causes of suicide have only the influence borrowed from the victim's moral predisposition, itself an echo of the moral state of society. To explain his detachment from life, the individual accuses his most immediately surrounding circumstances; life is sad to him because he is sad. Of course his sadness comes to him from without in one sense, however not from one or another incident of his career but rather from the group to which he belongs. This is why there is nothing which cannot serve as an occasion for suicide.

Indeed, societal pressures for Durkheim were by far the strongest influence upon an individual's actual behaviour. Thus, each society's particular suicide rate was primarily based upon the particular characteristics of that society at a particular period in its historical development.

In order to drive his points home, Durkheim embarked upon a clever polemic of debunking and eliminating the then-prevalent "causes" of suicide such as insanity and psychopathology, alcoholism, heredity, climate and seasonal impact, social contagion (imitation), etc., through manipulating a vast amount of suicide statistics from many European countries. The end result was that the only explanation left after such an elimination process was the social one. In order to thus proceed with his own theory, he provides the reader with a typology of suicide with three distinct types: *egoistic, altruistic* and *anomic* suicide.

Egoistic Suicide

When an individual is only weakly attached to society and least integrated into his social group, he loses the restraints which intense participation in the group imposes on him. In Durkheim's own words:[9]

In this case the bond attaching man to life relaxes because that attaching him to society is itself slack. The incidents of private life which seem the direct inspiration of suicide and are considered its determining causes are in reality only incidental causes. The individual yields to the slightest shock of circumstance because the state of society has made him a ready prey to suicide.

Under such circumstances, if he has any inclination to commit suicide, he is not deterred because of deeply felt commitments to others. Nor does he consider the consequences of his suicide for the group. To the extent that the individual is not bound to others, he is free of any claims they may have upon his life. The individual loses the emotional support which deep immersion in group life can provide, and he also forfeits the emotional attachments which made life worthwhile and less self-centred. He is thrown back upon his own resources; he gains no satisfaction from the achievements of the group. Success or failure is his alone.

Hence, wrongdoing is no longer defined solely by group standards but becomes a matter of personal judgment and responsibility. Under the burden of his individual responsibility, the individual is susceptible to the emotional disturbances which may lead to suicide, and he cannot fall back upon relations with others to help him over a personal crisis. Egoistic suicide is self-centred rather than group-centred; it is the type of suicide most likely to occur because the individual is uninvolved, isolated and detached.

In order to lend support to his notion of egoistic suicide, Durkheim stated the following three propositions: suicide varies inversely with the degree of integration of religious groups; suicide varies inversely with the degree of domestic integration (i.e., marriage and family); and suicide varies inversely with the degree of political integration. Durkheim reasoned that religion, marriage and family, and politics were the important social ties that held individuals together to society. He then proceeded to cite evidence illustrating that individuals who were less influenced by such integrating organizations in society were more likely to commit suicide than those who were more strongly under such influence. Durkheim determined that Protestants were more likely to commit suicide than Roman Catholics because Protestantism was indeed far less integrated than the Roman Catholic faith. As he says:[10]

> So if Protestantism concedes a greater freedom to individual thought than Catholicism, it is because it has fewer common beliefs and practices.... It socializes men only by attaching them completely to an identical body of doctrine and socializes them in proportion as this body of doctrine is extensive and firm. The more numerous the manners of action and thought of a religious character are, which are accordingly moved

from free inquiry, the more the idea of God presents itself in all details of existence, and makes individual wills converge to one identical goal. Inversely, the greater concessions a confessional group makes to individual judgment, the less it dominates lives, the less its cohesion and vitality. We thus reach the conclusion that the superiority of Protestantism with respect to suicide results from its being a less strongly integrated church than the Catholic Church.

Durkheim then cited evidence indicating that perhaps the Jews had an even lower rate of suicide than the Roman Catholics, if other variables could be controlled for. Jews were more likely to belong to occupational groups of a more professional nature, and such occupational groups invariably had higher rates of suicide in Europe at the time. However, if occupation was held constant, it might very well be that Jews have the lowest suicide rate of all. Durkheim argued for this assumption on the rationale that persecution and virtual isolation from the mainstream of society had perhaps tended to make Jews an even more closely knit religious group. In Durkheim's words:[11]

Their need of resisting a general hostility, the very impossibility of free communication with the rest of the population, has forced them to strict union among themselves. Consequently, each community became a small, compact, and coherent society with a strong feeling of self-consciousness and unity. Everyone thought and lived alike.... The Jewish church has thus been more strongly united than any other, from its dependence on itself because of being the object of intolerance.

To Durkheim, however, it was not the actual content of religious beliefs that persuaded believers against suicide. Rather, it was the structure of beliefs that was the most important factor. As he says:[12]

If religion protects man against the desire for self-destruction, it is not that it preaches the respect for his own person to him with arguments *sui generis*; but because it is a society. What constitutes this society is the existence of a certain number of beliefs and practices common to all the faithful, traditional and thus obligatory. The more numerous and strong these collective states of mind are, the stronger the integration of the religious community, and also the greater its preservative value. The details of dogmas and rites are secondary. The essential thing is that they be capable of supporting a sufficiently intense collective life.

Durkheim then studied the effect of marriage and family (in his terminology "domestic integration") on the likelihood of suicide. He came to the conclusion that after a long time of marriage, married people (both male and female) were less likely to commit suicide than the unmarried. The unmarried are both socially and emotionally isolated from others and they have fewer responsibilities as well as fewer attachments. The married, on the other hand, are restrained by both formal obligations and emotional ties, and they are less self-centred.

Durkheim looked at family life and concluded that it led to less likelihood of suicide for either sex. "It appears that marriage has indeed a preservative effect of its own against suicide...the fact remains that the family is the essential factor in the immunity of married persons, that is, the family as the whole group of parents and children."[13] He cited as evidence that widowed persons were less likely to commit suicide if they had had children in their marriage. Furthermore, argued Durkheim, the bigger the family unit, the more dense the interaction, and hence the chance of suicide was reduced even more.[14] In the larger family, the married have to care for others in the family, and they develop shared interests and values and find emotional support in their personal relations with members of the family.

Lastly, Durkheim looked at political integration as a factor involved in egoistic suicide. He discovered that wars, revolutions or major national disasters of any duration drastically reduced the suicide rate. As Durkheim observed, "great social disturbances and great popular wars rouse collective sentiments, stimulate partisan spirit and patriotism, political and national faith alike, and concentrating activity toward a single end, at least temporarily cause a stronger integration of society," and as a consequence "force men to close ranks and confront the common danger, [and] the individual thinks less of himself and more of the common cause."[15]

Altruistic Suicide

When the individual is tightly bound into a highly integrated group with a strong sense of solidarity, he accepts the values and norms of the group as his own. He does not distinguish between his interests and those of the group, nor is he likely to think of himself as a unique individual with a life separate and apart from the group. Under these circumstances, he will be more inclined to sacrifice his life for the group's goals and survival.

Durkheim also viewed altruistic suicide as a "primitive" form of suicide, which frequently occurred within primitive societies. Only in the military was one likely to encounter any instances of altruistic suicide in a modern society. According to Durkheim, altruistic suicide contrasts most strikingly with egoistic suicide and is related to "the crude morality which disregards everything relating solely to the individual."[16]

The collective suicide at Masada in 73 A.D., the kamikaze pilots during World War II and the mass suicide in Jonestown, Guyana in 1978 are cases in point. In highly integrated societies where there is a strong sense of social solidarity, self-destruction may be looked upon as self-affirmation and fulfilment; death as well as life has meaning and value.

In these examples, identification with the group can be so intense that group condemnation is tantamount to self-condemnation. Such suicide, stemming from an excessive degree of group integration, is committed for the sake of the group or according to group norms of "right" conduct. Closely related to this kind of suicide is a form of ritualistic suicide in such countries as Japan and India. In Japan it has been known as *seppuku* and has become a time-honoured ritualistic self-disembowelment among the samurai warrior class. In India it has been called "suttee" and performed by a woman upon the death of her husband. Durkheim called suttee fatalistic suicide as a subtype,[17] which often occurs as a result of too strong a social regulation.

In altruistic suicide, the individual takes his or her entire self-respect on approval of one particular group; when that is withdrawn, he or she has no other basis for self-esteem. Such suicide may be found where the individual is over-committed to one group and is socially isolated from other groups; they may be the military, the police, tightly-knit religious cults or other cohesive, self-contained groups.

Durkheim used his theory of altruistic suicide to explain why the suicide rate was higher for soldiers than for civilians, higher for non-commissioned officers than for enlisted men and higher for volunteers and those who re-enlisted than for conscripts. He suggested that suicide increases more dramatically the more the soldier identifies himself with the values and norms of military life. The officer is more deeply intergrated into the military organization than the ordinary soldier; the volunteer more committed to the military life than the ordinary conscript. The more the soldier is integrated into military life, the greater is his isolation from other groups in society, and the more he takes his self-respect from success in the army. Identification with the group can be so intense that group condemnation is tantamount to self-condemnation, often driving the individual to suicide.

Anomic Suicide

When a group is highly integrated and unified, it develops a set of norms to regulate behaviour and interpersonal relations. Norms include a clearly defined code of what is proper and improper for people of various ranks and classes. When it is felt that the individual should not presume beyond a certain station in life, the norms set strict limits on individual aspiration and achievement, but they provide people with a sense of security. Success may be limited, but it is genuine. Not only in matters of achievement but also in matters of moral behaviour, the individual knows what is expected of him. If he conforms to the standards set by the group, he is assured of its approval. The group provides the individual with a sense of security by establishing clear rules of right and wrong, and by limiting his aspirations to what he can achieve. When group norms are weakened, there is less restraint set upon the individual's aspirations and behaviour. At the same time, he loses the security which group control and regulation can provide. His aspirations soar beyond possible fulfilment; he is uncertain of what is right and wrong.

According to Durkheim, a society which lacks clear-cut norms to govern and regulate individuals' aspirations and moral conduct is characterized by "anomie," meaning "lack of rules" and "normlessness." Durkheim argued that anomic suicide was likely to occur when there was any sort of disturbance in what he termed the societal equilibrium, whether this change be for better or for worse. Thus, Durkheim stated that "whenever serious readjustments take place in the social order, whether or not due to sudden growth or to an unexpected catastrophe, men are more inclined to self-destruction."[18]

Durkheim found two pieces of evidence to support his theory that the lack of limiting norms might increase the suicide rate. He noted that the suicide rate was higher in countries that permitted divorce than in countries that did not permit it, and the rate was even higher where divorce was frequent. He suggested that where divorce was allowed one of the most important regulative principles in society was weakened and that the weakening of marriage norms was associated with a less firm application of other group norms. The other evidence he found was that of economic crisis. This is most evident in periods of recession and depression, but also occurs during periods of sharp business expansion and rapid social mobility. Durkheim interpreted this as a result of anomie. Although recession brings hardship, poverty by itself does not inspire suicide. As a matter of fact, in countries where poverty has been almost institutionalized over a long span of time, suicide rates tend to be much lower than in rich, affluent countries. Evidently economic shifts unsettle people's lives and make for greater uncertainty; consequently, people do not act on the basis of limited traditional aspirations and may find it difficult to accept frustrations.[19]

Anomic and egoistic suicide both spring from low social integration, but they are nevertheless independent. Although in the egoistic suicide the individual has severed the personal bonds which would deter him from suicide, he has not necessarily rejected the norms of the group. On the contrary, the egoistic suicide may be a highly moralistic person who feels a deep sense of personal responsibility for his behaviour. His morality, however, usually stems from his "principle" rather than from emotionally felt commitments or loyalties to other persons. Indeed, in such a case, one of the sources of his emotional disturbances may be that he is over-disciplined; he conforms in an overly rigid way. According to Durkheim, egoistic suicide is likely to occur among intellectuals and highly trained professionals, whose primary commitment is to ideas and values rather than to persons. In anomic suicide, on the other hand, the individual may be deeply involved in society, but group life fails to provide him with limiting norms and regulations. *The egoistic suicide may find life unbearable because of excessive self-discipline; the anomic suicide may find life unbearable because of inadequate self-discipline.*[20]

Durkheim assumed that anomic suicide was the more likely form of suicide to occur in contemporary society because the more traditional integrating institutions (i.e., religion, family, political unity, etc.) had lost most of their cohesiveness without replacing them with viable alternatives. It may be said, in an afterthought, that Durkheim's theory of anomie may have been a precursor of Erich Fromm's *Escape from Freedom*[21] in which Fromm argued that modern Western man's malaise and estrangement stems from his inability to replace the old primary bonds (such as religion, church and family, etc.) that used to provide security and anchorage.

Empirical Tests

Despite the fact that Durkheim's theory of suicide has long dominated the sociological study of suicide, cumulative theoretical advance within this tradition has been considerably stunted by a long hiatus in studies founded on it. Be that as it may, some competent studies have since empirically tested and verified his theory. Only some of them will be enumerated as examples in the following pages.

(1) One of the earlier sociological studies done in 1960s by a prominent suicidologist of sociological training has confirmed most of Durkheim's theoretical assumptions. In his extensive empirical study of suicide in Chicago, R. Maris was able to confirm the applicability of the sociological correlates of Durkheim's hypotheses on suicide.[22]

(2) Iga and Ohara, two Japanese suicidologists, tried to test out Durkheim's theory of anomie by interviewing both young male and female subjects who have made suicide attempts and survived, as well as young male and female subjects as a control who have never made an attempt. In this manner, Iga (sociologist) and Ohara (psychiatrist) hoped to illustrate the operationalizability of Durkheim's theory and then relate it back to individual cases. That is, they attempted to show that "the operational indices of Durkheim's types are obtainable and they might be applicable to both suicide rates and individual cases,"[23] and, in fact, their findings confirmed it.

(3) Pope and Danigelis analyzed the variables (i.e., marital status, religion, gender, age, etc.) from Durkheim's work as well as the French census data covering the period 1886-1931, together with the WHO data for thirteen countries between 1956 and 1962. While there were some exceptions, there was generally strong empirical support for the theory of Durkheim.[24]

(4) J.A. Blake re-examined Durkheim's theory of altruistic suicide in combat situations. Durkheim maintained that during military activities

heroic altruistic suicide or self-sacrifice would occur most often in groups exhibiting greater cohesiveness such as by members of the military elite. Relationships between cohesion and self-sacrifice as well as ranking and self-sacrifice are hypothesized for the combat situation and tested by using data concerning issuance of the Congressional Medal of Honor to World War II and Vietnam War recipients. Heroic self-sacrifice is identified by the act of throwing oneself on a hand grenade or in the line of hand grenade fire in order to save another person or to defeat enemy purposes. Supporting Durkheim's thesis, altruistic suicide during combat is found to be higher in more cohesive than in less cohesive groups.[25]

(5) Another approach was used by Biller. He theorized that if the national climate of mood could be made depressive by mass media coverage of a depressing event—e.g., the assassination of President Kennedy—then suicide would increase unless depression is not related to suicide during a time of great national focus. Such hypothesis was investigated by Biller through the use of a questionnaire requesting information concerning suicide rates for the period November 22 to 30, from 1956 to 1972. Data were collected from the Bureau of Statistics of 29 major cities nationwide. A total of 74 suicides (48 males and 26 females) was reported during the period of November 22-30 in 1962, the year of the Kennedy assassination. The finding that during a time of focused national crisis fewer suicides occur coincides with the findings of Durkheim.[26]

(6) Durkheim held that the degree of social integration (based on marriage and birth rates) and the degree of social regulation affect the suicide rate. To test this hypothesis, Lester analyzed the WHO data on suicide rates and marriage/divorce/birth rates for the period 1950-1985 for 21 nations in a multivariate time-series regression. Lester found that higher marriage rates were negatively associated, and higher divorce rates positively associated, with suicide rates, therby confirming Durkheim's hypothesis.[27]

(7) Pescosolido and Georgianna analyzed religion's effects on U.S. group suicide rates, with Roman Catholicism and evangelical Protestantism tending to lower rates, and institutional (mainstream) Protestantism tending to increase them, thereby confirming Durkheim's hypothesis on religion.[28] Conservative and cohesive religion such as Catholicism and evangelical Protestantism protect individuals from alienation and excessive individualism.

(8) Using cross-national comparative data from 52 nations and 15 independent variables, Conklin and Simpson concluded in their examination of Durkheim's theory of the family and suicide that family measures such as divorce are associated with higher suicide rates even after controlling for socio-economic differences among countries investigated.[29]

(9) Breault and Barkey conducted a comparative cross-national test of Durkheim's theory of egoistic suicide, using indicators of religious, family and political integration. They found the relationships between religious integration and suicide as well as between political integration to be non-linear, whereas the relationship between family integration and suicide is linear. Together, the indicators of religious, family and political integration explain about 76% of the variation in international rates of suicide.[30]

(10) Stack, a sociologist in the United States, examined Durkheim's theory of fatalistic suicide—i.e., the type of suicide that results from over-regulation. In order to operationalize over-regulation in political terms, a regression analysis utilizing 1970 U.N. data on 45 nations was conducted, with the results that indicators of totalitarianism—e.g., declarations of martial law and banning a political party—are significantly related to the rate of suicide, independent of the control variables. Thus he confirmed the relationship between governmental over-regulation in the form of martial law and the increase in suicide rates.[31]

(11) Wenz focused his research on a high suicide area (Census Tract A) in the city of Flint, Michigan. In fact, Census Tract A had had a suicide rate for two consecutive years (1971-73) ten times higher than that of the U.S. and three and one-half times greater than that of the remaining city of Flint. Furthermore, 65% of the suicides were either widowed or divorced. In the first phase of research, 250 suicides for the remaining city of Flint and 20 for Census Tract A were studied according to age, sex, marital status and race. Though the sample size was too small for Census Tract A, the result still served to offer some insight. During the second phase, social characteristics for both areas were compared with data obtained from a previously conducted social survey consisting of 85 subjects per group. Srole's Anomia Scale, Social Isolation-in-the-Present Scale, and Anticipation-of-Social-Isolation-in-the-Future Scale were used for the interviews. A further comparison was drawn on the basis of scores obtained from the same scales between a group of serious suicide attempters from Census Tract A and a general population sample

from the same area. It was found that the widowed were not only considered to be living in a state of "anomie" and social isolation but they also anticipated a future of social isolation. To a lesser degree, the divorced also shared in this predicament. Although different in the circumstances of age, both groups have suffered the loss of a loved object, and as such it can be concluded that the disintegration of personal relationships can lead one to an outlook of hopelessness in the future and a state of social isolation, or vice versa, such losses either through death or divorce can be associated with suicide. Finally, in the third phase of their research, they compared all three scales and their scores from the general population sample with those of the suicide attempt group. The findings indicated that the suicide attempters scored higher on all three scales than the general population. On the other hand, the pattern followed the same course as that of the general population, i.e., widowers scoring the highest, followed by the divorced, single and married.[32]

(12) Durkheim hypothesized that societies very high or very low in either social integration or social regulation would have high suicide rates. Lester tested such a theory of Durkheim's by investigating the relationship between measures of family integration and suicide rates from 1933 to 1985 in the U.S. and Finland. Finnish data were obtained from the Central Statistical Office and the U.S. data from the National Center for Health Statistics. Lester found that the Finnish data fit Durkheim's model quite well; as family integration increased, suicide rates decreased. Multiple regression analysis indicated that divorce rates were the best predictor of suicide rates.[33] Lester concluded his series of empirical studies for testing Durkheim's work by stating that some sociological findings, such as those of Durkheim's, hold up much better in cross-national replications than many other theories.

(13) Bille-Brahe in Denmark analyzed interviews with 89 suicide attempters, ages 20-69 years old, and calculated their level of social integration, using a Nordic model developed by himself, which was based upon Durkheim's work on the inverse correlation between suicide and social integration. Suicide attempters were interviewed as to their relationship with their close environment (family, friends, neighbours), their work environment and the community. Results show that those attempting suicide could be characterized as having inadequate contacts in the family, friends and neighbourhood. The level of social integration was significantly lower among the suicide attempters than in the

population generally, suggesting that Durkheim's theories are valid for explaining the incidence of suicide attempts as well.[34]

14) As mentioned in the main text, egoistic suicide often happens among individuals of ideas and power whose existence often depends on the consistency of ideas or on the presumed integrity of one's public image, etc. Figure 1 illustrates such a case. Figure 2, on the other hand, demonstrates the case of altruistic suicide in a society where individuals are extremely and inexorably integrated into a social group; in such a society, some individuals take their own life in order to defend the honour of a particular group to which they belong. Figure 3 is an illustration of a very high rate for Native Canadians who often symbolize socio-cultural uprootedness—i.e., anomie.

15) Even though Durkheim laboriously distinguished the aforementioned three types of suicide, he did not consider them as being mutually exclusive. Rather, he argued that egoistic, altruistic and anomic suicide could occur in various combinations, depending on the actual individual circumstances. For example, egoistic and anomic suicide often went together because an individual would find it increasingly difficult to remain integrated in a society which is increasingly losing its "moral equilibrium" ("anomie"), such as Hollywood. Figure 4 presents such an example in the suicide cases of celebrities and film stars.

Evaluation of Durkheim's Theory

There are a number of important positive contributions made by Durkheim in his highly original study that has since become a classic not only in sociology but in suicidology as well. The first of these is his astute and correct observation of the general stability of suicide rates over a long period of time, which seem to suggest some distinct group characteristics that persist. Precisely because of such regularity and stability, meaningful comparative study of suicide at the collective level is possible, as has already been discussed in the previous chapter. The credit for originally pointing out such relative stability of rates and making the first systematic comparative study must certainly go to Durkheim. Since social facts such as suicide are reproduced with relative uniformity and regularity, it must be admitted that they depend on forces *external to* and *independent of the individual* as has been insisted by Durkheim.

Another important contribution by Durkheim is the comparative study he commenced with such methodological precision and induction.

PUBLIC TRIBUTE: Mourners file past the entrance of Val de Grace Hospital in Paris yesterday to pay last respects to Pierre Beregovoy. The 67-year-old former premier committed suicide on Saturday.

Suicide leaves France asking 'why?'

PARIS (AP) — President Francois Mitterrand and hundreds of Parisians bearing roses paid respects yesterday to Pierre Beregovoy as the country debated who should share responsibility for the former premier's suicide.

Meanwhile, a French regional politician also took his life yesterday by jumping into a river near the town where Beregovoy died.

Police said Jean Roux, a 66-year-old Gaullist vice-president of a regional council, drowned in the Loire at La Charite, 24 kilometres (15 miles) from Beregovoy's hometown of Nevers.

They said he had been treated recently for depression.

Beregovoy's body lay in state at the Val de Grace hospital in Paris. Several prominent figures visited the closed flag-draped casket.

About 1,000 Parisians paid their respects after Mitterrand left. Many laid down single red roses, a symbol of the Socialist party that Beregovoy led to an electoral disaster in March.

Beregovoy was to be buried today in the central city of Nevers, where he had been mayor since 1983. It was here on Saturday that the 67-year-old politician shot himself in the head with his bodyguard's pistol.

The suicide has stunned France and left commentators groping to explain it. Blame has been directed at enemies, allies, media and investigators. Some have called for reform of the rough-and-tumble political system.

"The suicide of Pierre Beregovoy should cause many people to at the very least examine their consciences," former premier Laurent Fabius said in a letter to the newspaper Le Monde.

The conservative daily Le Figaro summed up national shock with a front-page editorial cartoon depicting Marianne, symbol of the French Republic, asking "Why?"

"He had been crucified," said Jacques Delors, president of the European Community's executive commission. "Not only because of the personal attacks, but because his policies were criticized, sometimes even by his friends."

Colleagues said Beregovoy had been distraught over the Socialist rout in the election as well as blame by some socialists for the lacklustre campaign.

He was also dismayed by reports in February that he received an interest-free loan in 1986 from a businessman later jailed for corruption.

Beregovoy insisted the loan was legal and entailed no favors. But his explanation that he repaid half the loan with old furniture and books prompted skepticism that he could not quickly shake.

Source: *The Toronto Star*, Tuesday, May 4, 1993.

Durkheim's *Suicide* was one of the earliest methodological masterpieces to fully utilize a vast amount of cross-national data. "Only comparison affords explanation. A scientific investigation can thus be achieved only if it deals with comparable facts and it is more likely to succeed [if] it has combined all those that can be successfully combined."[35] His comparative

JAL official kills self as atonement for jet crash

TOKYO. — A Japan Air Lines official who was negotiating compensation payments for families of the victims of the recent JAL jet crash died recently of knife wounds in an apparent suicide.

Hiroo Tominaga, a 59-year-old airline maintenance official, left a note saying, "I am atoning with my death."

Tominaga was found bleeding from neck and chest wounds in his home in Yokohama, south of Tokyo, in what police believed was a suicide. A 4-inch knife was discovered near his body.

A JAL spokeswoman said since Sept. 1 Tominaga had been assisting relatives of the victims of the Aug. 12 JAL crash that killed 520 people in the worst single-plane accident in aviation history. Four people survived.

Tominaga's duties included negotiating compensation payments with family members, the spokeswoman said.

"Mr. Tominaga was assisting the family members of the crash victims. It would be deeply sorrowful if the crash and his death were linked," said a statement issued by JAL.

Tominaga served as JAL's coordinator of maintenance at Tokyo's Haneda Airport. The JAL Boeing 747 that crashed took off from Haneda on a domestic flight.

The cause of the crash has not yet been determined, but investigators suspect it may be linked to improper repairs conducted on the plane's tail section by the Boeing Co. following an earlier accident.

Source: *Japan Times*, September, 1987.

study of suicide was certainly the first successful treatise in modern sociology to combine theoretical insight with masses of empirical data brought into focus in the form of verifiable hypotheses. Seemingly unrelated group statistics were brilliantly combined to lead to some very powerful and seminal insights on a topic that had never previously been

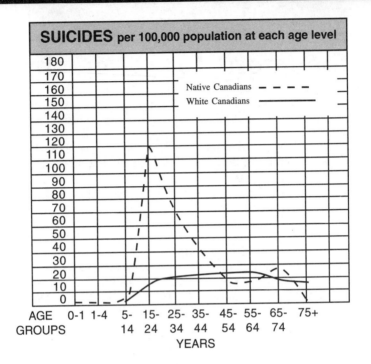

Figure 3:   Suicide among Native Canadians (Anomic Suicide)

SUICIDES per 100,000 population at each age level

Native Canadians – – – –
White Canadians ———

AGE   0-1 1-4   5-   15- 25- 35- 45- 55- 65- 75+
GROUPS   14   24   34   44   54   64   74
                              YEARS

Source: Department of Indian and Northern Affairs, Government of Canada, Ottawa, 1973-1976 average, as reported in *The Toronto Star*, September 25th, 1982.

elevated to the level of the social. His inductive method was indeed unparalleled in sociology and deserves a good review here.

After observing the remarkable stability in suicide rates among certain social groups, Durkheim then constructed a theory by extracting an abstraction of very high level from a mass of suicide data in certain European nations by resorting to the following reasoning process:

(1) Social cohesion provides psychic support to human social groups.

(2) Suicide rates are functions and indices of unrelieved anxieties, stresses and anomie to which persons are subjected.

1. Ernest Hemingway: This internationally acclaimed macho novelist was found dead in his house in Ketchum, Idaho, on July 2, 1961 with a double-barreled shotgun in his mouth, which blew his head off.

2. Gail Russell: A screen star of the 1940s, Russell was found dead at age 36 in her West Hollywood apartment, with an empty Vodka bottle and drugs by her side, in 1961.

3. Marilyn Monroe: A sex goddess of the 1950s, Monroe was found dead in her bed at age 36, on August 5, 1962, with sedatives and barbiturates by her side.

4. Alan Ladd: A handsome star of a Western, *Shane* (1954), Ladd killed himself at the age of 51 with an overdose of drugs shortly after a botched suicide attempt with a gun, on January 28, 1963.

5. Sylvia Plath: A highly gifted poet/novelist, Plath turned on the kitchen gas and put her head inside the oven on February 11, 1963.

6. Nick Adams: an action star of the 1960s, Adams took his own life with an overdose of drugs in the bedroom of his house in West Los Angeles on February 7, 1968.

7. Jimi Hendrix: At the age of 27, Henrix swallowed an overdose of drugs and suffocated on his own vomit in 1970.

8. Janis Joplin: Also at the age of 27, the popular rock singer was found dead in her apartment in Hollywood with an overdose of heroin on October 5, 1970.

9. Pier Angeli: An Italian-born beauty and a screen star of 1950s, she was married to Vic Damone. She committed suicide at the age of 39, following the tragic death of the then screen idol James Dean in 1971, with whom she had been rumoured to have been deeply in love.

10. George Sanders: Well-known for his golden voice and suave manner, the British-born star of the screen killed himself with drugs at the age of 65 in a Barcelona seaside hotel in 1972.

11. Gig Young: A debonair male star of the screen in 1940s and 1950s, Young shot his wife and then himself in his Manhattan apartment, October 19, 1978.

12. Sid Vicious: The well-known British punk rocker died of an overdose on February 2, 1979.

13. Jean Seberg: An Iowa-born beauty of the screen, who became famous for her screen debut in *St. Joan*, committed suicide in her car in Paris, Sepember 8, 1979, at the age of 41.

14. Freddie Prinze: A popular star of a T.V. sitcom "Chico and the Man," Prinze was found dead at the age of 21 at the pinnacle of his success. He killed himself with a 32 automatic, shooting himself through the temple, January, 1977.

15. Kurt Cobain: A popular rock star, committed suicide in 1994 after a long bout with depression.

16. Margaux Hemingway: The 41-year-old took her own life in her one-room Santa Monica apartment. A model and a fading film actress, she was a long-time victim of bulimia, epilepsy and alcoholism. Her apparent suicide occurred in July, 1996, just before the 35th anniversary of the day that her famous grandfather Ernest put a gun to his head. Her famous family has been plagued with suicide, including Ernest, his father, his brother and his sister.

(3)   Hence, suicide rates are an index of the degree of individual integration into social groups.

(4)   For example, Roman Catholics have much greater social cohesion than Protestants.

(5)   Therefore, lower suicide rates should be anticipated among Catholics than among Protestants.

In other words, Durkheim elevated the hitherto isolated empirical facts into an abstract relationship of a very high level, but *not* between religious affiliation and behaviour. Rather, he points out the relationship between social groups with certain conceptualized attributes (e.g., social cohesion in his study of suicide) and social behaviour such as suicide. Likewise, several seemingly disparate empirical uniformities witnessed in a mass of data (e.g., suicide rates between non-commissioned officers and enlisted men, differences between single and married men, differential suicide rates in time of war and peace, etc.) are now seen to be conceptually related to his theory of the degree of individual integration into society and social groups.[36]

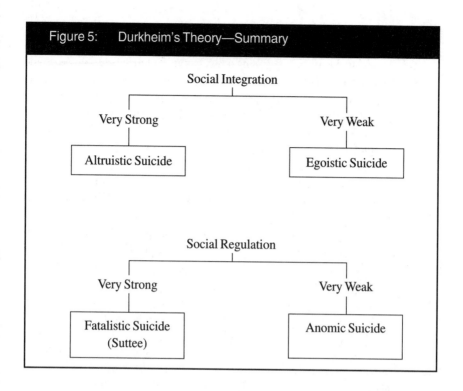

Figure 5:   Durkheim's Theory—Summary

Social Integration

Very Strong — Very Weak

Altruistic Suicide

Egoistic Suicide

Social Regulation

Very Strong — Very Weak

Fatalistic Suicide
(Suttee)

Anomic Suicide

Central to his theory of suicide have been the two major concepts—social integration and social regulation. The former is a social-psychological variable, whereas the latter a social-instititional one. Thus, when social integration is excessively high, probabilities for altruistic suicide increase; when it is extremely low, it is likely to lead to egoistic suicide. Likewise, when social regulation is extremely low, it is likely to result in anomic suicide; when it is excessively high, it will lead to fatalistic suicide. Such paradigm of Durkheim's theory can be now summarized in Figure 5 .

His brilliance notwithstanding, findings of modern suicidology have rectified some of Durkheim's rhetorics against some non-sociological correlates of suicide such as psychopathology, alcoholism, heredity, climate, seasonal impact, social contagion (imitation), etc., as mentioned earlier. As will be discussed later, the association between depression (and especially hopelessness) and suicide is hard to dispute today, suggesting a strong link between some types of emotional disorder and suicide. Likewise, a correlation between alcoholism and suicide is firmly established; climatewise, it is a direct challenge to Durkheim that the warm, temperate Mediterranean region has always been characterized by much lower suicide rates, suggesting a link between climate and suicide. Some extensive and highly competent studies by such prominent sociologists as David Phillips in the past two decades have clearly established the probability of "imitation" suicide shortly after publicity of celebrities' suicides. Furthermore, additional cautions and criticisms must be raised in spite of Durkheim's heuristically very useful theoretical system.

First, Durkheim cannot escape from the charge of extreme sociologism. In his scheme, individuals are reduced to mere victims of particular societal circumstances: society acts on the individual, but the individual seems to have no influence on society. Such an approach, i.e., extreme sociologism, is tantamount to the neglect of the importance of the role of the individual in the act of suicide. Throughout his work, Durkheim tried to extrapolate the group characteristics of suicide to explain individual occurrences of suicide. Certainly this is a type of ecological fallacy mentioned earlier in the previous chapter. Thus, temptation exists, for example, in the tradition of sociological research on suicide à la Durkheim, to relate the findings of certain suicide rates and characteristics of a particular goup to the etiology of individual suicide. One of the prominent suicidologists in North America with sociological training argues that Durkheim's generalizations concerning the causes of suicide operate on such a high level of abstraction that Durkheim was tempted to demonstrate how his explanations of the suicide rate are causally related to individual suicides.[37] Moreover, Durkheim's sociologism seems to be blind to the fact that, after all, suicide ultimately is the taking of a *single human life*. Any explanation of suicide which ignores this fact becomes totally callous and irrelevant to the pain and suffering of a suicidal individual.

Finally, another important methodological corrective must be mentioned as well. Durkheim did not take seriously the frequency and importance of altruistic suicide in contemporary society because he believed it was more common in primitive societies where collective solidarity is strong. Furthermore, his impressive suicide data did not include the statistics of civilians who willingly and voluntarily sacrificed their lives for a cause during wartime. One still hears about such sacrifice suicide for the sake of one's group: politically motivated terrorists and highly patriotic civilians are examples. For instance, the official suicide rate in Japan in 1943 was recorded as 12 per 100,000 of the civilian population, the lowest rate ever recorded in this century for Japan, appearing as if the statistical data confirmed Durkheim's theory that the suicide rate drops substantially during a war on account of the heightened degree of collective solidarity and cohesion. Such a rate, however, reflects only the civilian population deaths inside Japan proper, and is exclusive of the military and civilian populations overseas and on battlefields who committed suicide. Peacock, in one of her interesting studies, examined the mass suicides in Guadalcanal, Saipan, Iwo Jima and Okinawa by culling through the documents and archives of the World War II casualties. Though statistical data indeed showed that the suicide rate in Japan declined during the war in accordance with Durkheim's theory, Peacock argues that the suicide rate would demonstrate a dramatically higher rate if and when the incidences of altruistic military and civilian suicides in the Pacific were taken into account. In an age when one hears almost daily about the suicide bombings and acts of terrorism by highly motivated and patriotic civilians (as in the Middle East), one may be forced to re-evaluate suicide rates in a new light.[38]

Over the years, modern social science has found it necessary to critique Durkheim and will undoubtedly continue to do so in the future. Be that as it may, students of sociology can never be too grateful for the impetus and insight he gave them, the new horizons he showed them and the unexplored regions he charted for them.

"Social Action" Theory

In addition to Durkheim, modern sociology owes its origin and development to another great precursor of the discipline, Max Weber (1864-1920), a phenomenally creative German social scientist. Against the Durkheimian approach to society, which emphasized the objective observation of social facts and indirect measurement through measurable indices such as suicide rates, Weber insisted that the most fundamental purpose of sociology is the *understanding (verstehen)* of human *social* interaction as well as the *inner subjective meaning* of such social action.

Human behaviour cannot be understood merely in physiological terms and in a cultural vacuum but must be appreciated in the matrix of cultural symbols, common values, social roles, etc. In other words, socially and culturally defined meanings to human behaviour are the crucial points of inquiry. To give an example, if a person is walking down the street, a biologist would probably describe that action by saying that the person is walking down the street coordinating muscular movements, at five miles per hour, expending 200 calories of energy per hour and accelerating the heart beat at such and such pulse rate. As such, it is a description of physical action. But a sociologist would describe the action and situation differently: a sociologist would say that the person is going to church to pray, thereby giving a specific social (as opposed to biological) purpose and motivation for this physical movement. The sociologist may also give social and cultural meanings to the person's motility by saying that he or she is going to church to pray. This is an explanation of why he or she is going to church rather than somewhere else. If the former example simply refers to the physical action (i.e., a biological explanation), the latter is describing the socio-cultural behaviour and motivation (i.e., a social explanation) as a goal-oriented action. For sociology, then, all human behaviour must take into account such social and cultural meanings behind physical behaviour. As summarized by Max Weber himself, "action is social insofar as, (...it is a behaviour with) *the subjective meaning attached to it by the individual* (emphasis added)."[39] Weber called such an approach *Verstehende Soziologie* (understanding sociology). It is a type of social science which attempts the interpretive understanding of social action in order to arrive at a causal explanation of its course and effects. This is certainly a different approach from that of Durkheim, as is evident in the following quote by Weber:[40]

> A correct causal interpretation of typical action means that the process which is claimed to be typical is shown to be both adequately grasped *on the level of meaning* and at the same time the interpretation is to some degree causally adequate. If adequacy in respect to meaning is lacking, then no matter how high the degree of uniformity and how precisely its probability can be numerically determined, it is still an incomprehensible statistical probability (emphasis added)....

The fundamental element of sociological investigation in Weber is therefore "social action," and the single individual is the basic unit or the atom of society. Thus, Weber defined sociology both as the study of social action in its subjective meaning and as the study of typical social action—"the ideal type."

Such a Weberian approach received powerful support from a branch of phenomenological philosophy. Phenomenology rejects both the empirical assumptions of behaviourists and the biological explanations of human behaviour. Philosophically, phenomenology is characterized by a belief that human experience is the foundation of all knowledge, that all human beliefs and behaviours are based on the person's own perceptual experience of the world, that the ultimate source of reality, therefore, is subjective experience and meaning rather than empirical validation. As such, phenomenologists study the unique perceptions and inner meanings of each human being rather than trying to discover universal laws about human perceptions. In general, phenomenologists want to know first, how the individual views his or her world and second, how these unique perceptions and meanings influence the person's thinking, acting and feeling.[41]

Jack Douglas, an American sociologist, applied such insights from Weber and modern phenomenology to the study of suicide by rejecting standard statistical approaches pioneered by Durkheim. Douglas argues against the statistical suicide data on the well-accepted ground of unreliability due to under-reporting, as well as on the assumed nature of the so-called stability of group rates, which is at best questionable. To Douglas, it is much more productive to move the focus of research from the external fact of suicide (as revealed in suicide rates) to the inner meanings of the suicide act of the person who killed himself or herself. For such an approach and methodology, Douglas argues that the Weberian orientation of social action is far more fruitful, in which suicide motives constitute the core of inner meanings to the person who took his or her life.

To Douglas, the suicidal action is either the result of the factors external to the individual (typically a sociological approach), or the action is the result of something internal to the person (typically a psychologist's orientation), or it is the result of some interaction of these two approaches. Whether the specific meanings realized by the act of suicide will be attributed to the actor's self or to his or her situation will depend on the imputations of causality mode by the various persons in the situation: i.e., seeing the individual as the cause of his or her own actions (endogenous causation), or seeing the individual as having been induced (or driven) to commit suicide by circumstances such as divorce, spousal death, loss of job or family trouble (exogenous causation). Hence, according to Douglas, the only way one can go about studying the meanings of suicidal phenomena is by studying the specific meanings of real-world phenomena as the individuals involved construct them. As he states:[42]

In the Western world, death is thought and felt to be a permanent transformation of the substantial self from the realm of the time-bound, space-bound, worldly, everyday meanings to the realm of the timeless, infinite, otherworldly meanings. Death, then, is fundamentally meaningful in itself, and any actions performed within the realm of the complex of death meanings take on these meanings.

For Douglas, suicide is generally believed to follow an individual's summing up of his or her entire life, its worth, etc. Consequently, this summing-up process gives to suicidal actions the individual's statements about his or her whole self. Thus, individuals, at least in the Western world, can often make use of suicide actions to transform the meanings of themselves, of what they fundamentally are. In short, it is a statement about themselves, their social relationships and their social world. Suicidal action, therefore, is usually believed to mean something fundamental about the self committing it, or about the situation in which the person committed it, or about both of these. Hence, suicidal actions are socially meaningful actions, and individuals commit them in order to communicate something to themselves and others about themselves and others. Even an individual whose primary goal is death will not commit suicide unless he or she can do so in such a way as to communicate to himself or herself and to others just the right meanings. In other words, suicide is an act in which the individual makes a statement and transmits certain meanings. A study of suicide acts as socially meaningful—cognitively, affectively and normatively—opens up new directions and avenues of highly fruitful research.[43] This type of approach probably explains why there have always been religio-moral suicides in history: e.g., a string of religious martyrdom, *seppuku*, kamikazes, Masada, mass suicide in Jonestown, and most recently the Heaven's Gate mass suicide.

Jean Baeschler, a professor at the European Centre for Sociology and at the National Centre for Scientific Research (*Le Centre National de la Recherche Scientifique* or CNRS) in Paris, has fully incorporated the insights and orientations of both the social action theory of Weber and modern phenomenology into a paradigm as originally developed by Douglas. Baeschler, like Douglas before him, raised serious objections to the Durkheimian methodology to suicide. For, according to Durkheim, the meaning and cause of suicide are revealed not at the level of the individual case, as it appears to friends and relatives, but at the supra-individual, macro-social level. Baeschler is opposed to such an approach on the following grounds: (1) at the methodological level, the degree and extent of accuracy of statistics and the problems of under-reporting have not been answered adequately; (2) the small number of cases reported (only 20 to 30 per 100,000) make any validity of drawing conclusions from the correlations highly dubious and questionable; (3) in general terms, statistical correlations do not allow the construction of psychological or social suicide types. Baeschler was thus led to conclude that one must not begin the study of suicide with statistical correlations but with the analysis of individual cases. Baeschler argued that the uncertainty of the figures and the possible errors committed by looking for intelligibility with the help of concepts bear no relation to the spontaneous interpretations of the actor.

It is, therefore, necessary first to understand each suicide as it was understood by the one who killed himself or herself, or by those close to the individual, before looking for a so-called scientific explanation on a macro-sociological scale.[44] In other words, suicide, like any other human social action, has a particular meaning to a particular individual. Moreover, an individual or a group of individuals kills himself or herself or themselves in response to a situation. So, to Baeschler, suicide is often a positive act by which a subject tries to resolve an existential problem. Thus, one tries to push an investigation of suicide further by asking the decisive question of "why," to which one can give two series of radically different answers: those that begin by an adverbial phrase of "in-order-to..." and those that follow "because...." To Baeschler this distinction is fundamental to understanding human activities and behaviour in the framework of a phenomenological method introduced by a German philosopher, Alfred Schutz.

Alfred Schutz distinguished between the "*Um-zu-Motiv*" ("in-order-to motive") and the "*Weil-Motiv*" ("because motive"). The former designates the result that must be attained by a subject in such a way that the subject's project is realized. Hence, to Baeschler, if someone has just killed himself at the end of a period of mourning, it would not be right to say "he killed himself *because* he lost a dear one," but rather, "he killed himself in order to join the deceased in death." In other words, he killed himself *in order to* resolve the problem posed by the loss of this person who meant a great deal to him. As Baeschler says:[45]

> Our fundamental thesis is that every suicide is a
> solution to a problem. An act of suicide is always

undertaken in order to resolve a situation in a certain way. Consequently, the typical meanings that we are going to study are nothing more than the different *Um-zu-Motiv* of suicide, that in view of which a suicide is committed or attempted. The *Weil-Motiv* is entirely different. Whereas, in the preceding case, the question hinged on the end that gave meaning to an action, now it is concerned with the project itself: what is happening that such a subject understands that such an action will attain such a goal?...As regards suicide, investigation of the *because* would try to answer the following question: What is happening that such a subject has sought such a solution to such a problem by killing himself or trying to do so? Or, more briefly: Who is looking for what solution to what problem?

It follows that the *"Weil Motiv"* (because) is always retrospective—whereas the *"Um-zu-Motiv"* (in-order-to) is prospective—and can be distinguished only after the project is constituted. The most fundamental orientation in Baeschler's scheme is that the "in-order-to" (*Um-zu*) necessarily precedes the "because" (*Weil*) since the project effects a choice among several possibilities. Only after the choice has been made, is it possible to begin investigating the factors that led up to this choice.[46] To Baeschler, therefore, an individual is a being who pursues ends and must resolve problems that confront him or her in the pursuit of ends. Suicide can in fact be interpreted as the ultimate sign of human freedom because, in deciding for oneself the moment and modality of one's own death, one escapes the radical contingency of the human condition—one becomes the master of one's own life and death.

Since there is not just one act of suicide but many *suicides*, the problems confronted and the sought-for solutions are multiple. Thus, Baeschler constructs a typology of suicide, or the enumeration of typical meanings of the act whereby a person makes an attempt on his or her own life with the firm intention of dying. Baeschler gives a fourfold classification of suicide: escapist, aggressive, ablative and ludic, with eleven varieties—flight, grief and punishment belong to the first class; crime, vengeance, black-mail and appeal to the second; sacrifice and transfiguration to the third; and ordeal and game to the fourth.[47]

Empirical Test

Though challenging and highly provocative, the social action theory, originally expounded by Max Weber and followed by the seminal works of Douglas and Baeschler, faces one of the endemic problems of such theoretical orientation—i.e., a paucity of empirical research to lend support to its central arguments. Briefly discussed below are a few examples that are available to verify such theoretical orientation.

(1) How valid are Baeschler's theoretical assumptions and his typology? Three psychiatrists at the Groupe Hospitalier Cochin in Paris decided to test out Baeschler's typology and its usefulness in the clinical setting. They started out with his definition of suicide as "a voluntary, self-inflicted harm, which is neither normal nor pathological but merely a subjectively logical response to an existential problem."[48] Thus, to Baeschler, suicide is a purposive, and even a logical, act to an existential situation. In order to test this hypothesis, these three clinical psychiatrists studied the suicide attempts of French teenagers treated at the hospital. The sample consisted of 80 suicide attempters under the age of 20. Using Baeschler's typology, they obtained the following results: 10% of the sample fit into the "escape" category, 20% into the "mourning" class, 70% into "aggressive and black-mail" categories (including a small percentage of revenge and appeal). They found a correspondence between the "escape" attempts and the acting out of psychopaths, the "mourning" attempts and the acts of depressive subjects with a neurotic or pre-psychotic and even psychotic structures often preceded by a pre-suicidal syndrome. The aggressive attempts are likely to be found among the narcissistic or those who have a slight tendency towards character disorder, intolerant of frustration. They concluded that Baeschler's typology appears to be valid and useful in the clinical situation, as it cuts across the three populations of the teenagers.

(2) As discussed previously, Jack Douglas argues against attempts to interpret suicide rates in terms of social influences and social pressures and notes that the relative stability of suicide rates for national statistics is a result of the variability of the rates for their constituent towns and cities, which can produce a stable overall rate. Cresswell supports Douglas's contention by examining the suicide rates for county boroughs in England and Wales that show a considerable amount of yearly variation while their national rates over the years remain stable, as suggested by Douglas.[49]

(3) Brown examined the Sara Nar of south central Chad, a people among whom suicide is common. In this culture it is believed that suicide normally results either from bereavement or anger over accusations, insults or reminders of dead loved ones. Brown investigated the information on 11 suicides and seven attempted suicides in order to determine what situations actually lead to suicide in this culture and concluded that, of the various sociological and anthropological theories available and examined, the theory of Jean Baeschler best fits this culture. Baeschler's theory developed a typology of possible meanings for suicide, exploring specific social reasons for one meaning being dominant and prevalent in a particular society. In the Sara Nar case, the triangle relationship involving the husband-wife-and-third party appears to give the situation a specific meaning for suicide—that of disengagement from troublesome relationships.[50]

(4) After reviewing Baeschler's theory, Shneidman, the founder of modern suicidology, summarizes the central question of Baeschler's investigation as follows: "What kind of people seek what solutions to what problems by means of suicide?" Shneidman argues that the principal problems of human beings relate to the frustration of a variety of psychological needs. Thus, a full accounting of human needs might furnish a psychologically meaningful basis for a better understanding of suicidal events. Shneidman finds such an explanation in Henry Murray's theory of need system, which adequately classifies suicide acts, thereby lending support to the heuristic utility of Baeschler's typology.[51]

(5) Jean Baeschler undertakes an analysis of the mass suicide in Jonestown with data and materials published during the three months following the tragic event. Baeschler rejects the hypothesis of a religious sect responding to its own imminent destruction by the "forces of evil," and proceeds with a three-step interpretation of the event in accordance with the theoretical approaches he himself developed. First, Jones's biographical analysis reveals a life plan leading to inevitable failure, thus making suicide a probable way of sanctioning it. Second, the sect that Jones founded became his main psychological support system, so much so that he failed to see the distinction between himself and his creation and had to take it with him at the time of death. Finally, because the sect had selected members with a particular psychological make-up and biography, they also perceived the prospect of the sect's dissolution as an insupportable catastrophe.[52]

(6) *Seppuku* (ritual suicide by disembowelment, known in the West as *hara-kiri*) has been a popular theme in Japan's literature, theatre and folklore for centuries. It has been a time-honoured, traditional form of suicide among the samurai class in Japan. Fusé, in his investigation of the origin, development, types and reasons for this kind of ritual suicide (to be fully discussed later in this book), argues that a study of *seppuku* puts into question a discernible and dominant propensity in the West to understand suicide behaviour in terms of psychopathology. *Seppuku* in Japan has been nurtured in Japan's socio-cultural tradition as one of the socially and culturally prescribed and positively sanctioned role-behaviour in a highly formal and well-regulated society. Ultimately, the best way of understanding *seppuku* is to appreciate what social and cultural meanings *seppuku* held for Japanese samurai and military officers in war, lending support thereby to the appropriateness of the implications of social action theory such as those of Weber, Douglas and Baeschler.[53]

(7) Social action theory, especially the theory of Baeschler, has emphasized the importance of the "death meaning" to the suicide. Such premium placed on what death might have meant to the deceased certainly coincides with the methodology of "psychological autopsy" which examines, among many clues, what subjective meanings that death held for the deceased as revealed in the suicide note and lifestyles as well as in interviews with the surviving family members and friends. In his studies of eleven personalities (Ernest Hemingway, Marilyn Monroe, Judy Garland, Alan Ladd, Virginia Woolf, Jean Seberg, Jo Roman, Arthur Koestler, Yukio Mishima, General Maresuke Nogi, Dr. Josef Goebbles), Fusé found that, despite differences in nationality, religion and cultural backgrounds, the suicide behaviour of all these individuals could be understood in a common ground of what death meant to their existential suffering and problems. In other words, meanings of death somehow equalize and provide common grounds of their suicide beyond their apparent sociological differences, thereby lending strong support to the arguments and orientations provided by Weber, Douglas and Baeschler.[54]

Evaluation

Social action theory, originally expounded by Weber and then effectively deployed later by both Douglas and Baeschler, stressed the importance of subjective meanings that actors attach to their own behaviour and to the behaviour of others. The grasping of subjective meaning of an action is facilitated through empathy and a reliving of the experience to be analyzed. In terms of suicide research, then, such an approach enables the investigator to achieve a greater degree of appreciating and understanding the inner subjective meanings of the deceased. Social action theory, therefore, serves as a link between sociology and psychology—social psychology in the truest sense of the word. In such an approach, both sociology and psychology merge into one effective methodology to probe into what death has meant to the deceased and how such death-meaning may have propelled the individual to suicidal action.

Be that as it may, its strengths may easily slide into weakness. Modern psychoanalysis teaches us about the strong undercurrents of unconscious motivations that undergird much of our conscious behaviour. Social action theory may be tempted to ignore such powerful forces of unconscious motivations in human social action that may regulate and control much of overt human behaviour. It cannot explain away many suicides that have been committed as a result of clinical depression and other psychopathologies which may give distorted understanding and meanings to life and death. The distinction between the "normative" and "abberant" has often been blurred at best and ignored at worst in social action theory. Inability to take into account many sucides that have been propelled by mental and emotional illnesses has been one of the major weaknesses of this otherwise very insightful theory.

PSYCHOLOGICAL THEORIES

Sigmund Freud (1856-1939)

Psychoanalysis, developed and nurtured by Freud and his disciples, attained much popularity and acceptance, at least in its early history, especially in North America more than in Europe where it was born. Its theory reflects the founder's incredibly fertile mind and knowledge, delving into such diverse fields as literature, law, mythology, religion, philosophy, history, politics, physiology and neurology. Its influence and fame peaked in 1950s in North America; since then, however, it has declined little by little in the midst of competing theories and development of short-term therapies. Yet, most of the important psychological theories of suicide are heavily indebted to the original insights of Freud's theory, even though Freud himself wrote little about suicide. Hence, an examination of his seminal ideas is not only necessary but also fruitful in understanding the psychodynamics of suicide behaviour.

Sigmund Freud was born on May 6, 1856, in Moravia (now Pribor, in Czech Republic) in the then Austro-Hungarian Empire, into a middle-class Jewish family. At age nine, he entered high school (*Sperl Gymnasium*) and quickly became head of his class and graduated *summa cum laude*. At age 17, he moved on to the Faculty of Medicine at the University of Vienna, at the same time continuing his study of classic literature, linguistics, and philosophy. He graduated from the university with distinction, but due to financial reasons and his ethnic background many avenues of advancement were closed to him. So he went into private practice as a clinician in neurology. In 1882, he joined the staff of a psychiatric clinic as an "assistant physician." The director of the clinic, Dr. Theodore Meynert, was a brilliant anatomist of the brain and a psychiatrist, and he gave Freud the first hint of a hypothesis he later developed, the so-called "wish-fulfillment" hypothesis, which was to play an important part in his later major work, *The Interpretation of Dreams*. In that year Freud's relationship with Breuer, a Viennese physician and physiologist, developed. Breuer had treated a 21-year-old girl with complex psychosomatic symptoms after the death of her father. This young woman was to become famous in the annals of psychoanalysis as Anna O. Following her father's death, Anna's sight and speech were seriously disturbed, and she recoiled from food. She could change, with remarkable ease and facility, from relatively normal behaviour into the role of a recalcitrant child with alarming symptoms—a now familiar case of hysteria. Once, however, while she began to relate to Breuer the details of one severe episode, he was astonished to observe that the symptoms gradually disappeared. Breuer subsequently supplemented his procedure by inducing hypnosis, thereby obtaining for a time some startlingly successful results. Freud discussed the case over and over again with Breuer. The result of their joint work was the celebrated *Studies in Hysteria*.[55]

Then, in 1885, Freud obtained a fellowship to travel to Paris for his famous encounter with Jean Charcot, the most renowned professor in neuropsychiatry in Europe at the time. Freud tried to interest Charcot in the aforementioned "talking cure" in Vienna, but the professor showed no interest. During his study in Paris, Freud learned firsthand Charcot's effective use of hypnosis that induced such conditions as tremors, paralysis, anaesthesia and other symptoms of spontaneous hysteria.

Though Freud was not that much impressed by hypnosis as a clinical tool, he was nevertheless convinced that hysterical symptoms originated through the energy of the mental process which was being withheld from conscious influence and diverted into bodily symptoms (i.e., conversion). In other words, Charcot's demonstrations impressed upon Freud that the symptoms of hysteria could be removed by thought alone and that there thus must be a powerful psychogenic factor in their origin.[56]

The joint work of Freud and Breuer led to Freud's insistence that the basic origin of neurosis is due to repression of sexual conflicts. But such an idea was much too radical in Europe of that period, and Breuer himself was unable to accept it. Subsequently he parted company with Freud on that issue. But Freud persisted alone, and published his most original work, *The Interpretation of Dreams*, in 1900, followed by such works as *Psychopathology of Everyday Life* (1901) and *Three Essays on the Theory of Sexuality* (1905), in the latter of which he related his own sexual arousal by seeing his mother naked. His theory of infantile sexuality created a storm of aversion, controversy and eventually led to ostracism not only in Vienna but throughout Europe. Yet, among certain practitioners Freud's fame spread, and such figures as Jones from Britain, Jung from Switzerland, Ferenczi from Budapest, Brill from New York, Abraham from Berlin and Adler from Vienna flocked around Freud. After the rise of the Nazis, however, Freud fled to London and died in exile in 1939 at the age of 83. The compendium of his publications in English number 24 volumes, marking him as the most influential figure in medical psychology.

Freud's Theory of Suicide

Freud's theory of suicide is primarily based upon a very few writings by him, because, as mentioned earlier, he did not write much about the subject of suicide directly. Yet the implications derived from his original ideas have proven extremely accurate and relevant to both suicide ideation and behaviour. His theory, in short, may be quickly summarized in the three following postulates: a theory of *death instinct*, which according to Freud exists in every human psyche together with its twin, love instinct, and includes powerful human drives toward nothingness and self-extinction; a postulate of the *loss of love object*, which results from a traumatic sense of losing one's dearly loved person(s) or highly treasured things that are felt to be irreplaceable; and finally, *pathological melancholia*, which is generated by the above "object loss," and which eventually turns rage and aggression internally against the ego as a result of the ego's inability or inadequate way of grieving the loss.

Freud called the fundamental human life energy "id," which is further divided into eros (life instinct) and thanatos (death instinct). The former refers to an instinct which, at the collective level, strives towards the preservation of the human species and its perpetuation, and at the individual level works for sustaining and preserving one's life. Eros further has two components: *libido* and *ego*. Libido represents the energy which works towards the preservation of the human species through sexual union between the sexes, while in the spiritual and emotional dimension it tries to maximize individual bonding and connecting through friendships and/or sexual love. In a word, libido is the basic sexual sentiment observable in all biological organisms and is largely controlled by the pleasure principle and is expressed as sexual desire, self-centredness, narcissistic tendencies and the pursuit of pleasure. But the libido contains in itself some danger that is fundamentally "anti-social," hence in every society such demand for relentless pursuit of pleasure and its gratification is controlled and restrained for the sake of social harmony and peace. Due to its inherent potential for conflict with societal demands, therefore, libido is usually pushed back deep into the unconscious.

The other constituent of the life instinct (eros) is ego, which is primarily governed by the reality principle, taking into account the reality of social regulations and some constraints placed upon man's pursuit of pleasure. Ego tries to either obey social regulations or to gratify the needs in such ways as to be acceptable to society. In daily life, if the individual desires are very strong and satisfying them would violate social regulations, some defence mechanisms such as repression or sublimation would be employed by the individual. Repression refers to the process and mechanism of pushing such thoughts and desires into the inner recess of the unconscious in order to avoid inevitable negative sanctions of others and society. Sublimation simply means to express and rechannel one's desires into socially acceptable forms such as scholarly pursuits, sports, music, poetry, etc. According to Freud, sublimation would be necessary because if man were permitted to pursue his pleasure as his biological impulses dictate, society would turn into an inferno. Hence, repression and sublimation would be necessary ingredients for the creation and continuity of human civilization, according to Freud.[57]

As mentioned earlier, however, there exists another instinctual force in man side by side with eros—*thanatos* or death instinct. Thanatos as such refers to that inner striving in every organism that propels itself towards the inorganic state or extinction. It often works against eros by trying to destroy friendships, bonding and love relationships that have been formed by eros. It represents the destructive side of man and is governed by aggression and the nirvana principle. One of the extreme forms of such death instinct is, of course, homicide and suicide. Whether it will be homicide or suicide depends on the direction of aggression: when it is externally expressed against another person, it is homicide, and when it is internally directed against the self, it is suicide.[58]

The duality of eros and thanatos is expressed usually in ambivalence—the co-existence of opposing tendencies that are yet closely linked and related. Love and hate is often cited as a *prima facie* example of such ambivalence. Another example would be the case of sadism and masochism. According to Freud, in this latter example, sadism is a fusion of love and aggression (eros and thanatos), whereas masochism symbolizes a union of love and aggression being now directed internally against the self.[59] This hypothesis of Freud's was published in his article, "Mourning and Melancholia," and gradually developed into his theory of death instinct.

In April, 1910, the first meeting of the International Psychoanalytic Society was held in the form of a special symposium on suicide among students. It was reported that Freud had remained silent throughout the symposium, but at the conclusion of the said symposium he reportedly stated that suicide would not be understood completely unless complex processes and relationships between mourning and melancholia due to object loss had been fully clarified. He tried to do so in this now famous article originally presented in 1915.

According to Freud, an individual's libido, largely represented by sexual energy and directed by the ego, identifies with and invests its energy in a person or any symbolic representation of deep attachment. The objects of embodiments of symbolic representation of deep attachment are usually one's parents, spouses, intimate friends, one's occupation, health and self-respect. When the relationship with the person or symbolic representation is lost or threatened, either through death, divorce, separation, illness, rejection or disappointment, it was called "object loss" by Freud. In "Mourning and Melancholia," written five years after the symposium on suicide, Freud developed his theory of suicide as displaced hostility directed internally against the self. The analysis of melancholia showed Freud that "...the ego can kill itself only if, owing to the return of the object cathexis, it can treat itself the hostility which relates to an object and which represents the ego's original reaction to objects in the external world...."[60] He argued that in mourning and melancholia the ego tries to restore to life whatever has been lost by identifying with it and then incorporating or introjecting the lost object in itself. In "normal" mourning, the painful process of coming slowly to terms with the fact that the loved object really no longer exists in the outside world is gradually compensated for by establishing the lost objects within the ego as something loved, loving and strengthening. By contrast, in "pathological" melancholia, guilt and hostility are now inverted against the self. The suffering individual believes, for instance, that the lost love object has been murdered by him; it serves as an internal prosecutor and punishing agent, seeking revenge and expiation. In other words, he is both the guilty party who has committed murder and the innocent victim of the object loss, in which he may take his own life partly to atone for his fantasied guilt for the death of someone he loves and partly because he feels the dead person lives on inside him. Thus, according to Freud, the process of mourning is completed when whatever has been lost, for whatever reason, is restored to life within the ego of the mourner.[61] But when the loss occurs at a particularly vulnerable age, the slow process of introjection becomes not only more difficult but also more hazardous. In this remarkable insight, one can observe the well-known phenomenon in suicidology that a child or young person with an experience of object loss at an early period in life runs a greater risk of suicide later on. For every child who loses a parent or someone loved equally passionately and helplessly must cope as best as he or she can with a confusion of guilt and anger and an outraged sense of abandonment. As he or she does not understand this in his or her innocence, the natural grief is made doubly painful.

The presence of and conflict between opposing forces in the human psyche, i.e., eros and thanatos, became Freud's major theme in the latter half of his career. The theme was developed gradually from his study of mourning and melancholia. Freud's ingenuity perceived that the pain of melancholia could itself be a source of pleasure.[62] Freud was then beginning to realize that masochism is not secondary to sadism, as he had earlier thought, but was instead a primary impulse as strong as eros.

It is well known that his most original work, *The Interpretation of Dreams*, is based upon the assumptions that all dreams are wish-fulfilling. But in his own clinical work, Freud began to notice "repetition compulsion" in some of his patients: the patients' dreams and fantasies seemed to be compelling them to suffer again and again in all their anguish and without any of the usual dream distortion and displacement. In other words, he began to realize that in certain types of neurosis, a force is at work to powerfully oppose any pleasure principle. No wishes were fulfilled, no gratifications, however perverse, were achieved. Instead, the purpose to the repetition compulsion was to attempt to obtain this overwhelming *un*pleasure principle, i.e., death instinct (thanatos). In other words, by obsessively repeating the trauma, the sufferer was trying to gain control over it. From all these various strands, Freud gradually wove his theory of the death instinct, a non-erotic primary aggression present from the very beginning of life and working continually to unbind connections, to destroy, to return to an inorganic state of nothingness.[63] In his development of a theory of suicide, Freud concluded that the death instinct took over in melancholia and triumphed over the love instinct, even leading to suicide:[64]

> [In melancholia] we find that the excessively strong super-ego which has obtained a hold upon consciousness rages against the ego with merciless violence, as if it had taken possession of the whole of the sadism available in the person concerned. Following our view of sadism, we should say that the destructive component had entrenched itself in the super-ego and turned against the ego. What is now holding sway in the super-ego is...a pure culture of the death instinct, and in fact it often enough succeeds in driving the ego into death....

The foregoing discussion is now summarized in Figure 6 and Figure 7.

Empirical Tests

As revealed in his clinical study of cases in medical psychology, Freud's brilliance and ingenuity was certainly unparalleled in portraying and describing the mysterious interiors of the human psyche. Yet the

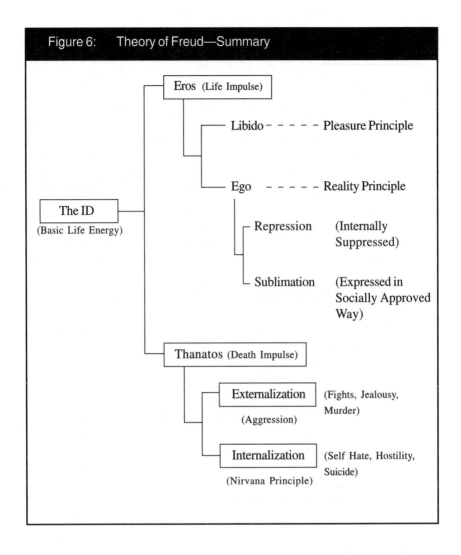

Figure 6:　　Theory of Freud—Summary

central thesis of Freudian theoretical system—that the world of human consciousness is merely the tip of an iceberg and that the real motivating force in human desires and behaviour lies deeply hidden in the unconscious—was not accepted by orthodox psychology for years. Partly because the field of psychoanalysis had only been open to those with a medical degree, at least in North America, and partly because it had lacked an acceptable methodology and empirical verification, it had long been met with hostility and suspicion by academic psychologists.

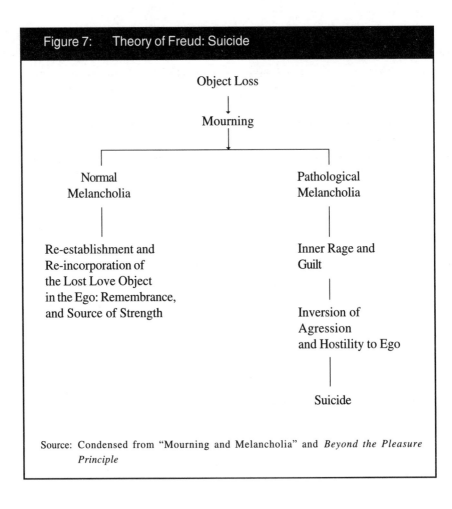

Figure 7:   Theory of Freud: Suicide

Object Loss

↓

Mourning

↓

Normal
Melancholia

Re-establishment and
Re-incorporation of
the Lost Love Object
in the Ego: Remembrance,
and Source of Strength

Pathological
Melancholia

Inner Rage and
Guilt

Inversion of
Agression
and Hostility to Ego

Suicide

Source: Condensed from "Mourning and Melancholia" and *Beyond the Pleasure Principle*

Since 1960s, however, the door of psychoanalysis has been opened to psychologists and others without a medical degree in North America. Since then the field has entered the stage of experimentation and empirical testing. Since World War II, clinical psychology, which has begun to show much interest in motivation and personality theories, has also started to turn its attention to psychoanalysis as well and has blossomed into present-day ego psychology. Under such changed circumstances, Freud's psychoanalysis itself and its tributary theories have begun to be examined carefully under the rigorous lens and instruments of orthodox academic psychology. Thus Kline, for instance, who surveyed almost

700 research articles and experiments, has argued that Freudian theory can no longer be ignored by academic psychologists.[65] Another work by Fisher and Greenberg has also demonstrated that much of Freud's analytical theory has been empirically verified on the basis of numerous works testing his assumptions and ideas.[66]

Central to his theory of suicide is the hypothesis about "object loss," as has been already discussed. Today this assumption seems to have been considerably supported by much empirical work and constitutes the core of the theory of Survivor Support Programme. In object loss, the relationship with the person or symbolic representation is lost or threatened either through death, separation, divorce, illness, disappointment or rejection. Since the self must detach itself from the object which is still in the mind, a period of intense psychic pain follows after which the libido is redirected onto another object. The correlation between suicide and depression is so great and persistent that there have been at least several hundred research articles on the subject in the period 1985-1995 alone. But the very precursor of depression, according to Freud, is object loss, which is expressed in divorce, separation, quarrels with a loved one, death of a significant other, loss of health or wealth or termination of a relationship.

One of the important indicators of such object loss is certainly divorce or widowhood: at the group level, when a great many people in a given population experience divorce, it is certainly expected that a suicide rate in that given population may rise. On the individual level, on the other hand, such object loss gives rise to increased risks of suicide for a particular individual. In the following pages, then, the impact of such object loss as defined in the death of a spouse, divorce and/or separation from spouse, and childhood absence of one or both parents through death, divorce or separation, will be discussed with some examples, both at the collective level (in the examination of suicide rates) and at the individual level in terms of the impact of such a loss for individuals. It is interesting to note that Freud's concept of object loss such as divorce and widowhood certainly interfaces with the sociological theory of divorce as anomie by Durkheim.

(1) All suicides in Montreal (Quebec, Canada) between ages 10 and 20 years were chosen for 1978-1982, and 17 individuals were identified who left suicide notes. The content analysis of the notes lends support to a Freudian psychoanalytic perspective that views suicide as the result

of object loss, an ambivalent attachment to a love object, internalization and direction of aggression against the self.[67]

(2) As mentioned earlier, divorce is an important object loss. Trovato conducted a longitudinal analysis of the association between divorce and suicide mortality in Canada using time series data from 1950-1982. Investigating the aggregate information with respect to suicide, divorce, unemployment and female labour force participation, results revealed that the higher the divorce rate, the higher the national suicide rate, even after the effects of unemployment and female labour force participation are taken into account simultaneously. The findings generally confirm both the Durkheimian and Freudian proposition: that at the national level of analysis, divorce is directly related to suicide mortality because it represents a significant breakdown in the social integration of the marital institution (i.e., anomie); at the same time, Trovato's study lends strong support to Freud's theory of object loss in divorce as having a significant relationship to suicide.[68]

(3) In an attempt to test whether the relationship between suicide and divorce was spurious, genuine or attributable to a third factor, Stack examined the association between suicide and divorce in relation to the following variables such as long-distance migration, race (white or non-white), age and family income. Through regression analysis, the relationship between suicide and divorce was tested while all other variables were controlled. Then, in the final phase of the research, quantitative effects of divorce on suicide were examined. Stack found that the higher the divorce rate, the higher the suicide rate ($p<0.01$), and that the higher the interstate migration index, the higher the divorce rate ($p<0.01$). As for this latter relationship, one can either postulate that the aftermath of divorce influences interstate migration or that interstate migration is an added culprit in weakening family and primary group ties. Stack concluded that the higher the divorce rate, the higher the suicide rate as well; and moreover, for every 1% increase in the divorce rate, there is a 0.54% increase in the suicide rate.[69] Thus, divorce as an index of object loss has a direct impact on suicide.

(4) Data on suicide and divorce in Denmark between 1951 and 1981 were examined in terms of regression analysis by the same researcher. Results were found to replicate the U.S. pattern. The divorce index is more closely associated with changes in the suicide rate than the unemployment rate. That is to say, 1% increase in divorce is associated with a 0.32% increase in suicide. Divorce trends also predict the incidence

of youth suicide. Such findings confirm the generalization that links significant loss such as divorce to suicide in contemporary societies.[70]

(5) Motohashi investigated suicide rates in Japan for two periods, 1953-1972 and 1973-1986, using 12 socio-economic indicators. Multiple regression analysis showed that the indicators affecting suicide rates were not identical in the two periods examined. For the period 1953-1972 (a period of Japan's very rapid and robust economic expansion and development), the suicide rates were closely related to the unemployment rate and the labour force; but for the period between 1973 and 1986 (a period of economic maturity as revealed in the growth of tertiary industry), divorce rates and the proportion in the service industry were most influential. Such a trend in the ascending importance of divorce is a further support to the preceding study of an increasing association between suicide rates and a rapid change in marital relations such as divorce.[71]

(6) In contrast to the U.S., Norway has a relatively high degree of cultural homogeneity, a national character thought to act as a buffer against suicide and a relatively low divorce rate. In addition to these factors and other features of Norwegian society that can affect the negative effects of an upswing in divorce, a study was undertaken to determine if research on the impact of divorce on suicide based on a single nation (the U.S. for instance) may be replicated for other nations. Analysis demonstrates a definite relationship between divorce and suicide: a 1% increase in divorce is associated with a 0.46% increase in suicide, despite Norway's institutional and cultural protection against taking one's own life. Moreover, the researcher found that the effects of divorce on suicide are independent of the trends of religiosity.[72]

(7) Loss of a spouse through death is commonly associated with the elderly population for obvious reasons. MacMahon and Pugh wanted to find out whether or not bereavement was of etiological importance for the suicide rate of the widowed. If bereavement was a determining factor, the suicides should cluster around the date of the spouse's death. In testing this hypothesis, they compared 246 widowhood suicides and 255 widowhood deaths due to miscellaneous causes other than suicide (control group) in Massachusetts. Both groups were matched according to five-year age groups, sex, race, date of death and duration of widowhood. The researchers found that an excess number of suicides clustered around the date of their respective spouse's death. Although the frequency of suicides lessened with the length of

widowhood, it only levelled off during the fourth year after bereavement. It was also found that 48 suicides in the first four years of widowhood were attributable to bereavement alone. Due to the significance of four years, the interval of four years or more was assigned an arbitrary risk of 1.0. Relative risk of suicide during widowhood was found to be as follows: under one year of widowhood (2.5), one year of widowhood (1.6), 2 years of widowhood (1.5), and 3 years (1.4). The following miscellaneous observations were also made: the rate of suicide was higher for males than females, suicides in the cases of older subjects clustered around the death of their spouse in shorter intervals and a higher rate of suicide was found among subjects who were 70 or over. In fact, in 71% of the suicide cases, the subjects were over 60, while only 7% were less than 50 years of age, showing that the loss of a spouse is an important factor for increasing the risk of suicide among the elderly.[73]

(8) Paykel, Prusoff and Myers examined retrospectively the events six months prior to the suicide attempt. All subjects for the suicide attempt group were randomly selected through the general hospital emergency service files in New Haven, Connecticut. Two control groups were also randomly selected—a group of psychiatrically diagnosed depressives and a general population sample. The depressive group was selected from a community mental health centre, while the general population sample was obtained from a previously conducted survey. Both groups were matched on age, sex, race and social class with all subjects in the suicide attempt group. Each group consisted of 53 subjects—a total of 159 subjects ranging in age from 18 to 65. Subjects were interviewed by trained researchers and followed a given questionnaire consisting of 32 events. While the general population was interviewed at home, others were interviewed in the hospital while well onto recovery. In terms of the total number of events reported, the suicide attempt group differed from the depressives and general population. In the preceding six months, the attempters had four times as many events occur compared to the general population and one and one-half times more events than the depressives. In terms of object loss or threat thereof, the suicide atempters reported significantly more serious arguments with a spouse (i.e., the threat of object loss). This threat of object loss was further evident where the suicide attempters reported more serious illnesses within the immediate family. Although the attempters and the depressed overlapped, they differed in that the suicide attempters reported more events with

threatening implications—more undesirable events of significant loss such as separation and/or divorce, more "exit" in their immediate social field and work (retirement), more events at major intermediate levels of upset and more uncontrollable events. Although previous studies indicated a relationship between divorce, death of a spouse and suicide, the frequency with which these losses were sustained by the suicide attempt group in Paykel et al.'s study did not reach levels of significance. In fact, those significant events were related to object loss insofar as they were threats of such loss. Hence, there exists the possibility that it is through a series of object losses or the threat of such losses that an adult may be induced to commit suicide or attempt suicide.[74]

(9) Dorpat, Jackson and Ripley examined the family history of subjects who either committed suicide or attempted suicide. The main independent variable was "broken home" defined as the absence of one or both parents for more than a period of four years prior to the subject's eighteenth birthday. All subjects were residents of King County in Washington. Two groups were set up: an attempted suicide group of 111, and the completed suicide group of 88. In both groups, those having had broken homes were identified and examined as to their age at the time of the loss and the types of losses. They found that 64% of the suicide attempters and 50% of the completed suicide group had experienced a broken home before the age of 18. Furthermore, the loss of a parent through death was particularly high (45%) among the completed suicides, while losses due to divorce were noted during the adolescent stage (12-17 years of age) with a particularly high proportion occurring in the group of completed suicides. Moreover, the majority of attempted suicide subjects had experienced a serious quarrel with a loved one prior to the attempt, while the completed suicide group appeared to have suffered the death of a loved one prior to the suicide.[75]

(10) Birtchell examined the relationship between attempted suicide, depression and parental death before the age of 19. He selected all subjects from a psychiatric hospital population at Crichton Royal Hospital, Sussex, England. Two groups were set up: one group of 104 suicide attempters, and the other, a group of 110 subjects who had neither contemplated or threatened suicide (control). Both groups were matched on age (19-59) and sex. Initial analyses of the suicide attempters showed that the male/female ratio was 1:1.7. In comparing the attempters and the controls (no previous threat or inclination to suicide), it was noted that the attempters differed significantly ($p < 0.05$). A larger proportion of

attempters were severely depressed. In re-grouping the two groups according to parental loss prior to age 19 and depression scores, an excess amount was found among the group of suicide attempters (66.7%).[76]

(11) In examining suicide ideation associated with parental loss and suicidal behaviour, the Canadian researchers Adam and his associates focused their research on the relationship between early parental loss (before the age of 16) to suicide ideation and suicide attempts among a group of university students. Over a period of four years, subjects were randomly selected from the university mental health clinic records on the basis of age range (17-27) and the availability of family history. Subjects were then categorized into three groups: a group of 40 who experienced the death of one or both parents prior to the age of 16, a group of 35 who experienced parental loss through separation or divorce before 16, and another group of 61 subjects from intact homes, all matched on sex, age and religion. Taped interviews were obtained and analyzed. Particular insights were obtained on family stability, suicidal ideation and parental loss. A significant difference was noted among the early parental loss group and the control group: of the subjects who had lost a parent through death, 47% were found to have suicide ideation, while of those subjects who lost a parent through divorce or separation, 34% were found to have suicide ideation. The parent-death group with suicide ideation had a pattern of family stability prior to the loss after which it became either unstable or chaotic. On combining these two groups, the following pattern was observed: a period of instability prior to the loss, a period of instability and chaos following the loss and an even greater degree of family instability in the long term. Researchers concluded that there did exist an association between an early object loss (through parental death, divorce or separation) and later suicide. This association is one whereby the seed of death or wish to die may have been implanted. This seed is further maintained if the loss is followed by a series of disruptive events adding a sense of instability to one's social environment.[77]

(12) The research of Humphrey et al. focused on the lives of suicide victims and the disruptive social events in their lives. The purpose was to isolate a consistent pattern of problematic events under the assumptions that the greater the incidence of disrupted social relations the higher the risk of suicide. Subjects consisted of completed suicides from 1968 to 1970 in New Hampshire, for whom psychological autopsies could be compiled. In total, 160 subjects and psychological autopsies were compiled and analyzed according to disruptive life events. Twenty

events were isolated, which were sequentially ordered according to their frequency of occurrence and the statistical procedure of scalability was used to measure the accuracy of the ordering. Events which occurred infrequently were excluded. Table 1 summarizes the findings below. The table illustrates the sequential ordering of events deciphered from the psychological autopsies of 160 suicide victims. The percentage corresponding to the event indicates the proportion of time that the event has preceded all other events being analyzed. For example, "parental abandonment" occurred 86% of the time before all other events, common to both the male and female sample. It is clear that object loss, such as parental abandonment (86%), death of a parent (79%), placement in a foster home (78%), has a dramatic impact on the suicide process.[78]

(13) In his extensive and longitudinal study of student suicide at the University of Kyoto, Iga in Japan found a strong association between suicide ideation and suicide itself and early parental loss among these students. His study is important because it gives empirical verification of Freudian postulates from non-Western samples.[79]

(14) Internalizing depression onto the self and consequently to suicide has been consistently verified by empirical research done at the Mental Health Clinic of New York University.[80] In the field of clinical psychiatry, Freud's thesis that guilt feelings and subsequent depression are usually generated when aggression against others is directed internally against the self has been substantiated. It is widely accepted by clinical psychiatrists that depression as a form and type of emotional disturbance and mental illness is closely associated with suicide and suicidal feelings. It has been pointed out by mental health professionals the world over that a history of depression is often seen among suicide attempters and that among in-patients in mental hospitals depressive illness occupies a disproportionately higher percentage among suicide attempters. (There will be far more detailed discussions on this problem later in this book.)

(15) On the evidence of 50 attempted suicides, two New York psychiatrists made an interesting discovery: in 95% of all their cases there had been "the death or loss under dramatic and often tragic circumstances of individuals closely related to the patient, generally parents, siblings, and mates."[81] In 75% of their cases, the deaths had taken place before the patient had completed adolescence. Such findings seem to lend support to Freud's point on the impact of early loss on suicide in later adult life.

Table 1:	The Suicide Process	

		Mean Percentages
	Parental Abandonment	86%
	Death of a Parent	79%
	Foster Home	78%
(M)	Childhood Institutionalization	72%
	Loss of Student Role	64%
(M)	Sibling Death	59%
(M)	Alcoholism	55%
(M)	Ill Health	48%
(M)	Death of a Close Relative	46%
(M)	Arrest	45%
(M)	Incarceration	41%
	Suicide Attempt	40%
	Sexual Incompatibility	36%
	Divorce	36%
	Psychiatric Hospitalization	31%
	Loss of Occupational Role	31%
(M)	Violent Assault	28%
	Abandonment of Spouse	27%
(F)	Death of a Child	26%
	Suicide Threat	24%

M – Peculiar to Males
F – Peculiar to Females

Note: The scalability measure for the noted table indicated a moderate to strong level of accuracy.

Source: Humphrey, J., French L., "The Process of Suicide: The Sequence of Disruptive Events in the Lives of the Suicide Victims," *Diseases of the Nervous System*, 1981: 35, p.28.

Evaluation

All the findings cited thus far seem to give credence to Freud's original insight into the link between object loss and suicide. A preliminary investigation by the present author suggests that a particular type of object loss—divorce especially—seems to be one of the most closely associated variables to suicide.

One other extremely important variable is the issue of the linkage between depression and suicide. This problem will be dealt with in another chapter in greater detail, but suffice it to mention here briefly that Freud's hypothesis of aggression internally directed against the ego and thereby contributing to suicide has been consistently verified by empirical and clinical research. It has long been pointed out by many mental health professionals that emotional illness such as clinical depression is closely related to suicide and suicidal feelings. It has been observed cross-culturally today that a history of affective disorders such as depression is often seen among suicide attempters and that among in-patients in psychiatric hospitals depressive illness occupies a higher percentage among attempters.[82]

Yet caution must be taken because, according to the National Task Force in Canada, only 4% of suicide completers in their study had a history of psychotic depression.[83] Rather, neurosis—anxiety states and reactive depression—the much more common mental disorder, was shown to be present in suicide completers at twice the rate of suicide attempters and at four times the rate of individuals who died natural deaths. Though suicide completers were more depressed in the two months prior to death than individuals who died natural deaths, they were less depressed than suicide attempters.[84]

Finally, Freud's theory of thanatos (or death impulse) assumes that it exists together with eros (or love impulse) in every human. Its universal presence somehow presupposes normativeness—if everyone has it, it is a part of the universal human condition, and as such not necessarily an aberrant or abnormal phenomenon or trait. Curiously enough, then, Freud's theory talks about "pathological" mourning as a precursor to inner rage, depression and inversion of aggression onto the self but without really defining or clarifying it.

The presence of death impulse, which is certainly related to self-destruction, according to Freud, is an ever-present human impulse and as normative as its counterpart love impulse. The deciding factor for suicidality, in the theory of death impulse, then, is whether or not the death impulse tips the balance and becomes paramount in the individual's psyche. The question of how such an imbalance occurs is certainly one of the ambiguities in Freud's otherwise remarkable theory.

Theory of Karl Menninger

Karl Menninger elaborated on the death impulse, which was originally developed by Freud. According to Menninger, suicide may be better understood as a highly complex form of death involving three distinct psychic elements: the wish to kill, the wish to be killed and the wish to die. The suicidal person first entertains murderous desires which may be directed either upon himself, herself or upon other persons. In suicide, the person must direct these impulses directly upon his or her own person in the violent act of *self-murder*. And he or she must truly wish to die with all the force of his or her unconscious psychic drives. Only then can the suicide act be consummated. The first of such aggressive impulses is the "wish to kill." It refers to the primordial destructive impulse in humans as expressed in hate and hostility. Usually, however, such hate and hostility is directed against those in intimate relations with the ego such as parents, siblings, lovers, wives, husbands and very intimate friends. This is certainly in line with the theory of ambivalence. Hence, its outright expression is culturally and interpersonally discouraged in most societies; consequently, it is more often than not directed internally against the ego itself.

The second impulse, "the wish to be killed," represents the very outcome of the repression of the first impulse. When aggression and hostility are directed against the self, they are usually accompanied by a strong sense of guilt and self-blame. A desire to be killed represents an attempt on the part of the ego to eliminate the tension of guilt and self-remorse by wishing to be killed so that the very source of such guilt may be eliminated. Psychoanalytically speaking, however, this second impulse is simply a transformation of the first wish.

The third impulse, "the wish to die," represents a wish for a chronic, slow process as opposed to the acute nature of the first two impulses. As such, the wish to die is usually expressed in such forms as despair, exhaustion and prolonged discouragement. It usually crystallizes after a long period of conflict, depression and suffering. During this period, some people begin to develop suicide ideation and rationalization of self-destructive behaviour such as suicide. It is usually related to the type of suicide caused by long-standing, chronic illness and suffering.

According to Karl Menninger, the suicide attempter may entertain violent and murderous intentions upon himself or herself, but at the same time he may not wish to surrender his or her life completely, nor whatever satisfaction he or she might find in this world. The one wish is active, the other is a passive resignation. The two are often not reconciled. In such cases, the person really does not want to die. The individual may thus look forward to the thought of dying without fully realizing its implications. In other words, he or she may derive unconscious pleasure from the prospect of forgetting one's anxieties in the permanent sleep of death; he or she may unconsciously hope to gain the love of certain persons after having committed suicide; or the person may think that he or she is placating his or her superego by punishing oneself through suicide. For these and other reasons, the individual may entertain the fantasy of suicide and may even make a suicide attempt. The person may be unconsciously attempting to have a cake and eat it, too. One may desire the satisfaction that will allegedly come from punishing one's conscience through the dramatic gesture of suicide, but at the same time one does not wish to give up completely the joy of life either.[85]

Empirical Test

There are a couple of important studies that examined the validity of Menninger's thesis; one is an American study by the noted suicidologist, Edwin Shneidman, in Los Angeles, and the other by a well-known Japanese psychiatrist who pioneered suicide research in that country.

Shneidman analyzed 619 suicide notes culled from the Los Angeles County Medical Examiner's Office according to the typology developed by Menninger. He found the following tendencies among men as revealed in their suicide notes. In general, as men grow older, they will manifest fewer tendencies towards the wish to kill or the wish to be killed. With an increase in age, the wish to die will dominate. Among youths, however, 31% expressed the aggressive wish to kill, as opposed to 23% among the middle-aged and 11% among the elderly. As for the wish to be killed, 27% of the young people, but 16% of the middle-aged and 10% of the elderly showed such tendencies. With regards to the third impulse, the wish to die, the breakdown was that 23% of youths, 35% of the middle-aged, but 57% of the elderly expressed such tendencies. As for the suicide notes among women, basically similar trends were observed. The wish to kill and the wish to be killed decreased as age increased. The reverse trend was observed in the wish to die: as age increased, the wish to die tendencies increased.[86]

Ohara, a Japanese suicidologist, examined suicide notes at the Medical Examiner's Office in Tokyo and essentially confirmed the

Shneidman study in Los Angeles. The tendency to express aggression and hostility was most prominent among the suicide notes of youths and young adults, but as age increased, less aggressive trends were observed. The only salient difference found between the Japanese sample and the American counterparts was the target of such aggression: the Americans tended to direct such hostility to their spouses and intimate friends, but the Japanese expressed their aggression less towards their immediate family members and spouses than towards others in workplace and secondary relations.[87]

Evaluation

It is evident that the theoretical base and predecessor of Menninger's orientation is Freudian theory. It is essentially an extension of Freud's ideas about death impulse, aggression, ambivalence and inversion of aggression onto the self. As such, it is not a very original idea or a concept but a useful tool for providing categories for types of dominant death wish. Hopefully there will be more empirical testing of Menninger's typology in the future.

Other Psychological Theories: E. Shneidman, N. Farberow and A. Beck

(1) Edwin Shneidman, a founder of modern suicidology and a clinical psychologist, proposes and illustrates a theoretical formulation in relation to the psychological components of suicide behaviour. According to Shneidman, the following four elements are identified as necessary and probable for the suicidal state: heightened inimicality (increased danger of harm to oneself as well as to others—i.e., lethality); exacerbation of perturbation (heightened emotional upset and psychic pain); increased constriction of intellectual focus (serious cognitive disturbance as revealed in inability to concentrate and think straight, together with collapsed or diminished coping skill); and the idea of cessation (desire to escape from the present pain even at the risk of life). Shneidman proposes that when all of these four factors are above a danger threshold, the suicidal state exists.[88]

Moreover, on the basis of his clinical experience and research, Shneidman attempts to re-evaluate conventional notions of death and suicide and creates a psychologically oriented classification of death phenomena by developing four categories in relation to the role of the individual in his or her own demise: *intentioned, subintentioned, unintended* and *contraintended*. The intentioned categories include death seekers who intentionally kill themselves, whereby rescue would be impossible or unlikely; death initiators who may disconnect their life-support system because of their terminal illness or unbearable pain; death darers who will take a chance even though the probability of their survival is quite low (such as Russian Roulette); death ignorers who do not play an active role in facilitating their deaths but who nevertheless contribute to their deaths by being careless, forgetful, inattentive, etc. (such as the abandoned elderly and troubled teens). The subintentioned include death chancers, hasteners, capitulators and experimenters. Categories for the unintentioned cessation include death welcomers, acceptors, postponers, disdainers and fearers. Contraintentional cases are death feigners and threateners.[89]

(2) Norman Farberow, a long-standing colleague of E. Shneidman and a co-director of the world famous Los Angeles Suicide Prevention Center, is credited for developing some seminal theoretical insights of suicide behaviour combining both psychological concepts and clinical experience. Farberow categorizes suicidal motivations into both interpersonal and intrapersonal factors. Even though both factors are often involved in almost all cases of suicide, one or the other aspect will often predominate.

Interpersonal factors in suicide motivations may be attempts on the part of the suicidal person to bring about an action on the part of another person or persons or to effect a change in attitudes or feelings within another person or persons, or both. The suicidal act can thus be seen as an instrumental and manipulative behaviour to induce change in the attitudes and behaviours of the other person or persons—a means to influence, persuade, force, manipulate, stimulate, change, dominate or reinstate feelings or behaviour in someone else. The other person is usually someone very close to the suicidal person such as spouse, lover or member of the family—a so-called "significant other." An example may be someone, typically in the younger and/or middle-aged groups, reacting to a loved one or to divorce or separation. Suicide behaviour is used to express anger or feelings of rejection and to force a change in the rebuffing person or to arouse guilt feelings in the other party.[90]

Intrapersonal motivations for suicide most often involve older persons and occur in situations in which ties with others have dissipated, expressing the pressures and stresses from within and fulfilling important needs in the suicidal individual. As Farberow states:[91]

The typical person is a male aged 60 or over who has recently suffered the death of a loved one, whose physical condition has deteriorated so that there is illness or pain, or whose children are married and so live their own separate lives. There are intense feelings of loneliness, feelings of not being needed any longer, of no longer being able to work effectively, perhaps because of physical condition, or feeling that life has been lived and holds no more. The mood is often depressed, withdrawn and physically and emotionally exhausted.

Farberow also hypothesizes, on the basis of his famous study of suicide notes together with Shneidman, that suicide behaviour acquires a clearer perspective when one looks at the suicide act as a communication process, which may be verbal or non-verbal, written or simply behavioural. In most instances, the suicidal activity occurs at the end of a long train of events that have finally led the person to the conclusion that life is no longer worth living. Accompanied by many communications along this course, the suicidal act itself often becomes a communication in itself (which may have many meanings and much significance as already revealed in the previous discussion on the theories of Douglas and Baeschler). According to Farberow, in most interpersonal situations the communication is directed to a specific person or persons; the communication may be overt or indirect. Often it is a "cry for help," a pleading to be rescued, a means for expression of hostility and hate, a final fixing of blame, a way to assume blame, absolve others and expiate one's own guilt. Most persons considering suicide will identify themselves by communicating this tendency either behaviourally or verbally long before any specific act occurs.

Farberow identifies some salient traits of the suicidal person characterized by the following: ambivalence—co-existence of the wish to die and the wish to live; feelings of hopelessness and helplessness; feelings of either physical or psychological exhaustion, or both; unrelieved anxiety or tension, depression, anger and/or guilt; cognitive confusion of feeling too disorganized to restore order; mood swings, for example, from agitation to apathy or withdrawal; tunnel vision and inability to see alternatives; loss of interest in activities, which used to interest him or her; and physical distress such as insomnia, anorexia and other psychosomatic symptoms.[92]

Farberow, moreover, was instrumental in working out a list of criteria from his experience in the Suicide Prevention Center in Los Angeles for evaluating the suicidal person in terms of the relatively immediate potentiality of lethal acting out, including: suicidal plan; absence of social resources and support; prior history of suicide attempt; onset of suicidal behaviour (the actual suicidal behaviour may be more immediately serious but also more amenable to intervention); the presence of masked depression as in the guise of physical complaints for which no organic cause can be found; loss of a loved one because of death, separation, quarrel or divorce; and the breakdown or collapse of communication.[93]

It was Farberow who emphasized the importance of work for suicide prevention. For the middle-aged group who experienced premature dissolution of relationships, work becomes the principal source of self-worth and self-esteem. The non-personal aspects of the work itself, rather than the people involved with whom interaction on the job occurs, becomes very important. So long as one is able to function in one's job and to lose oneself in its details, there is sufficient defence against suicidal impulses. For the very severely and chronically depressed person, work may provide a cover for the feeling of emptiness and void from which he or she is continually trying to escape. The routine or work keeps one busy and prevents one from thinking about oneself. Not to work provides the person with time during which the individual is free to think about himself or herself and to feel useless and empty. Once the work is lost, perhaps through some personal difficulty, physical crisis or enforced retirement, a crucial defence seems to be breached and suicidal impulses may burst through.[94]

Farberow's theory, developed in the bosom of modern clinical psychology and nurtured and reinforced by his clinical and practical experiences at such places as the Veteran's Administration Hospital and the Los Angeles Suicide Prevention Center, has made an important contribution in the field of suicidology.

(3) Aaron Beck is another important figure in suicidology today. Depression has always seemed to be associated with suicidal behaviour. Depression is a type of dysphoria that affects vast numbers of people at one time or another in their life, at least in North America and Europe and probably in many other parts of the world as well. It is often assumed that depression as an antecedent is an important determinant of suicide. Although research shows that only a small percentage of suicide victims have been free of such a psychiatric disorder as depression, it must also

be remembered that a substantial percentage of individuals with depression do not commit suicide. If depression alone is not enough to account for suicide, then what does? Aaron Beck, director of the Mood Disorder Clinic at the University of Pennsylvania, has been arguing that hopelessness, a core characteristic of depression, serves as the possible link between depression and suicide. According to Beck, both suicide ideation and intent is related to hopelessness rather than depression. Depression is a despair and pessimism about the perception of one's present condition; hopelessness, on the other hand, is an emotional and cognitive state characterized by a negative perception and expectations of one's future. As such, hopelessness is accompanied by despair, pessimism and feelings of helplessness to change the future, as well as a sense of impending dread due to an unchangeable and meaningless existence.[95] The French word "*desespoir*" says it well: loss of hope.

To Beck, hopelessness as negative expectations for the future is the critical factor in the suicide: it is the critical link between depression and suicide intent. The suicidal person views the future as negative, anticipates more suffering, more hardship, more frustration without any hope of improvement. Such a person considers himself or herself incompetent and worthless, alone, unwanted and unloved and suffers from ever-increasing self-reproaches, regret and guilt. The suicidal person's thoughts (i.e., cognitive interpretation of the situation) are arbitrary, full of factual errors and distortion. He or she views the situation as hopeless and regards suicide as the only possible solution to their perceived, unsolvable problem (situation). Desperate to escape from such unbearable pain and suffering, death is often thought of as being preferable to life.

Beck devised a 20-item, true-false test and showed that suicide intent in attempters correlated more highly with hopelessness than with depression.[96]

It is not difficult to understand that those who are experiencing feelings of hopelessness and helplessness consider ending their lives as they see no possibility or prospect of an end in sight to their present unbearable pain. Suicide prevention specialists generally lend their support to Beck's assertion by saying that such unbearable psychic pain and the resultant hopelessness are the most common stimuli in suicide. Thus, Beck's theory of hopelessness has gained enormous support in the past two decades.

Evaluation

(1) In a study by Wetzell et al., the researchers found that the correlation between hopelessness and suicide intent was r=0.75 (p<0.05), whereas that between depression and suicide intent was merely r=0.36 (p<0.05). Moreover, when the effect of hopelessness was removed statistically, there was no relationship between suicide intent and depression. These researchers argue, therefore, that the observed correlation between depression and suicide intent is due solely to the frequent combination of hopelessness and depression.[97]

(2) In one bi-cultural study by Heisel and Fusé of depression, hopelessness and suicide ideation among psychiatrists, nursing students, suicidology students and students in a humanities-class (control) between Canada and Japan, the preliminary findings indicate that hopelessness was indeed associated with suicide ideation much more than depression per se.[98]

(3) In another study, using 217 individuals in an intensive outpatient programme targeting suicidal behaviour among young adults, Dixon and his research team found that hopelessness had a significant direct effect in predicting suicide ideation, as well as a significant indirect effect for problem-solving appraisal in predicting suicide ideation.[99]

(4) Lester operationalized each of 15 known theories of suicide with 10 statements, and these 150 statements were then rated as present or absent in the lives of 30 famous suicides for whom a biography was available. It was found that the theory of A. Beck was most applicable in the analysis of these deceased individuals.[100]

(5) Finally, a prospective study of 1958 outpatients found that hopelessness, as measured by the Beck Hopelessness Scale, was significantly related to eventual suicide. Those who scored high on the scale were 11 times more likely to commit suicide than the rest of the outpatients. Hence, this research team is led to conclude that the Beck's Hopelessness Scale may be used as a sensitive indicator of suicide potential.[101]

Because of the limitation of space, not all empirical studies done for evaluating the theory of Beck have been presented in this section, but a preliminary computer indexing indicates a vast amount of research, most of which seems to verify the relevance, applicability and predictive value of Beck's theory. It seems, therefore, that Beck's theory, by any measure, is certainly one of the most fruitful and predictive instruments of suicidality in the field of suicidology in the past 25 years.

BIOCHEMICAL THEORIES

Biochemistry and Suicide

Biologically oriented theories stress the importance of genetic, biochemical and physiological causes, focussing on genetic factors, chemical imbalances, role of neurotransmitters, damage to the central nervous system caused by infections and nutritional disorders and other factors. Even though most biologically oriented scientists seem to assume that biological factors and environmental stresses jointly cause aberrant behaviour, biologically oriented hypotheses for certain human behaviour including suicide have gained enormous support and interest in recent years.

In 1975, Marie Asberg, a researcher at the Karolinska Institute in Stockholm, Sweden, and her research team made a new discovery. While studying depression, she and her co-researchers found that 40% of a group of depressed patients who had lower than normal levels of 5-HIAA (5-hydroxyindoleacetic acid) had attempted suicide. Among depressed patients with normal levels of 5-HIAA, the suicide attempt rate was just 15%. Moreover, the attempts by those in the group with less 5-HIAA were serious and violent—attempts by firearms, jumping from buildings— in comparison to the other group of patients who had mostly resorted to drug overdose. Asberg also found that among patients who had been hospitalized for suicide attempts, those with low levels of 5-HIAA were ten times more likely to have died from suicide after one year than were those with higher levels of 5-HIAA. In other words, Asberg and others identified a deficiency of a special chemical—serotonin—in the brains of some people who are prone to take their own lives in the face of difficulties.[102]

Since 1980, other researchers in Europe and the U.S. further confirmed the link between suicide and the serotonin level. In 1985, Herman Van Praag at Albert Einstein College of Medicine in New York City reported that low levels of serotonin seem to be a biochemical danger signal for those depressed people who are prone to suicide.[103] A new hope was raised, therefore, that a drug could eventually be developed to correct the biochemical deficiency and imbalance and thereby prevent at least some future suicides. It has been observed that in almost all societies men are more prone to complete suicide than women. It is conceivable, therefore, that such "impulsive violence" as homicide and suicide may be largely due to serotonin deficiency in men. It is generally assumed that serotonin, one of dozens of amino-acid-based neuro-transmitters that control some activity of brain cells, is instrumental in regulating certain brain activities, including emotion, along with other brain chemicals.

A word of explanation is in order for the role of neurotransmitters. The brain is essentially like an electrical system. The nerves (like electric "wires") communicate their electrical signals to each other by way of chemical messengers. If the nerves become depleted of these chemical messengers, the wiring in the brain develops faulty connections, resulting in mental and emotional static. It is almost like music that goes haywire with a loose wire in the tuner of a radio. The emotional static may be likened to depression. The manic states, in which the person is overwhelmed by an uncontrollable, emotional high, seem to indicate an excessive level of activity of these chemical messengers, leading to hyperactive nerve function. As shown in Figure 8, an electrical impulse travels along Nerve 1 until it reaches the terminal region. Here, tiny packets containing chemical messengers rupture and the chemical messengers spill into the synaptic region. The synapse is the fluid-filled junction between Nerve 1 and Nerve 2 in Figure 8. The chemical messengers then migrate across the fluid-filled synapse and become attached to the membrane of Nerve 2, triggering an electrical impulse in Nerve 2. The chemical messengers are then destroyed and the waste products are excreted from the brain and ultimately go out of the body in urine. Nerve 1 must constantly manufacture fresh chemical messengers to replace those that are lost. A deficiency of messengers is thought to lead to depression. (Antidepressants compensate for the assumed deficiency by raising the levels of chemical messengers or by increasing the potency of the chemical messengers in the synaptic region).[104]

Coming back to Asberg, she and her research team coined the term "serotonin depression" after reviewing the interesting results from their study on the relationship between the concentrations of cerebrospinal fluid (CSF) called 5-HIAA (5-hydroxyindoleacetic acid) and primary depressive disorders (including both endogenous and exogenous depression). They found that the distribution of 5-HIAA concentrations in 68 depressed patients was bimodal: significantly more of the depressed patients in the "low" CSF 5-HIAA group had attempted suicide in comparison with those in the "high" CSF 5-HIAA group. Similarly, in other studies of personality-disordered individuals conducted in 1979 and 1982, patients with a history of suicidal behaviour were found to

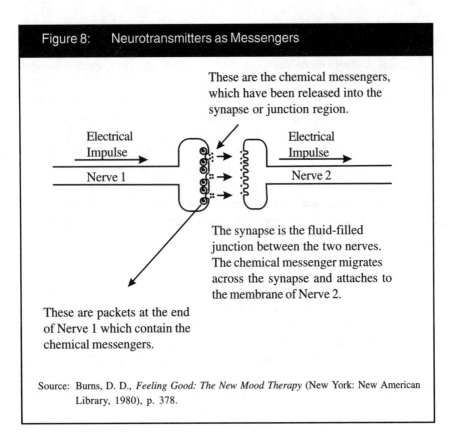

Figure 8:   Neurotransmitters as Messengers

These are the chemical messengers, which have been released into the synapse or junction region.

Electrical Impulse
Nerve 1

Electrical Impulse
Nerve 2

The synapse is the fluid-filled junction between the two nerves. The chemical messenger migrates across the synapse and attaches to the membrane of Nerve 2.

These are packets at the end of Nerve 1 which contain the chemical messengers.

Source: Burns, D. D., *Feeling Good: The New Mood Therapy* (New York: New American Library, 1980), p. 378.

have significantly lower CSF 5-HIAA levels than patients without such a history.[105] Thus, a group of neuro-biological scientists suggest, on the basis of the serotonin deficiency as determined by measuring levels of one of its main metabolites (e.g., 5-HIAA) in the brain during autopsies or from spinal fluid drawn from the living, that low CSF 5-HIAA levels may have some significant correlation with suicidal behaviour. Moreover, these test results also suggest that such low levels of serotonin may be an indicator of suicidal tendency as violence towards oneself. Furthermore, more impressive is the finding that even in the non-depressed subjects suicide attempts were strongly associated with low CSF 5-HIAA concentrations.[106] Another study compared a group of suicidal schizophrenic patients with a matched group of non-suicidal schizophrenics and found that, despite the psychiatric diagnosis, the suicidal group had significantly lower CSF 5-HIAA concentrations, thereby concluding that "low CSF HIAA may be a generalized marker of aggressive behaviour against the self and others."[107]

Current prevailing understanding is that serotonin deficiency occurs in people more prone to impulsive violence and that, when they also become depressed, they are then more likely to commit suicide than others. In short, serotonin deficiency and depression, in combination, increase the risk of suicide more than either factor alone. Since the trailblazing work of Asberg, an increasing volume of biochemical and neuro-pharmacological research findings have been accumulated, lending support to the presumed biochemical base of suicidality.

Genetics and Suicide

Another major scientific phenomenon in the field of biological sciences in the latter half of the twentieth century has been the impressive development of modern genetics and its application. It is no accident, therefore, that some research has been shedding light on the genetic implications of suicidality.

The founder of modern genetics, Gregor Mendel (1822-1884), discovered the following in his studies of garden peas: inherited characteristics (such as colour and shape, for instance) are produced by genes; genes occur in pairs on chromosomes which are carried in every cell; genes are passed along from one generation to another; members of a pair differ in their effects; one gene of a pair dominates the other; during egg or sperm formation, members of each pair of chromosomes recombine independently; and one member of the offspring's chromosome pair comes from each parent. Though his land-mark study was not appreciated in his lifetime, it was discovered and recognized for its worth years after Mendel's death.

The three main methods of assessing the contributions of genetics to mental illness and other inheritable diseases are family risk studies, twin studies and adoption studies. In the family risk studies, the incidence of abnormality among members of the biological family of mentally disturbed persons are compared with the incidence of mental illness or abnormality in the general population. If the family data show a clear association between the degree of biological kinship and the incidence of mental illness among relatives of a mentally ill person, they are suggestive evidence for the role of genetics in the production of the mental illness and other aberrant behaviour such as suicide.

One of the best known family risk studies for suicide is the "Amish Study," in which a group of researchers reported on the suicide data obtained from the study of affective disorders among the Old Order Amish Community of Lancaster County in southeast Pennsylvania. Almost 75% of the 26 suicide victims over the last 100 years in the said Amish group were found to cluster in four family pedigrees, each of which committed a heavy loading for affective disorders and suicide. Interestingly, however, the converse was not true, as there were other family pedigrees with heavy loading for affective disorders but without suicide. Thus, Houseman et al. suggest in their study that they indicate an increased suicidal risk for people with a diagnosis of major affective disorder and a strong family history of suicide. As they concluded, "the clustering of suicides in Amish pedigrees follows the distribution of affective illness in the kinship and suggests the role of [genetic] inheritance."[108] They even identified the gene responsible for it to lie within a narrow portion of the chromosome designated as Number 11. Members of the family who inherited the gene had an 85% chance of suffering bipolar depression or related conditions such as suicide propensity during their lifetimes. If the Amish gene can be isolated and its role in the etiology of depression and suicide completely clarified, it will give a very important clue into how mental illness and suicide propensity can be genetically induced and subsequently controlled and prevented.

One other well-known study of the family risk factor and suicide is that of Alec Roy. He found that a family history of suicide significantly increased the risk of a suicide attempt in a wide variety of diagnostic groups. For instance, almost half (48.6%) of the 243 patients with a family history of suicide had attempted suicide themselves. Furthermore, more than half (56.4%) of all the patients with a family history of suicide had a primary diagnosis of an affective disorder; and more than a third (34.6%) had a recurrent unipolar or bipolar affective disorder. Hence, a positive family history for violent suicide should be considered a strong prediction of active suicide-attempting behaviour in major depressive illness.[109]

A second source of evidence of the role of genetics is the twin study, in which concordance rates are calculated for identical twins (monozygotic twins, or MZ in abbreviation, and 100% shared genes). Concordance measures the probability if one identical or fraternal twin is abnormal in some particular way that the other twin will also be afflicted with a similar abnormal behaviour.

Some strong evidence of such genetic links has been found in the twin pair studies of the etiology of schizophrenia. It has been found in one study, for instance, that in slightly over 86% of all identical twin pairs in which one twin shows symptoms of schizophrenia, the other member of the pair also shows them, i.e., the two are concordant for the schizophrenic trait; in the remaining 14%, the twins are discordant, i.e., one lacks the trait.[110] Schizophrenia clearly develops much more easily in some genotypes than in others, indicating a strong hereditary predisposition to the development of the trait.

In his review of 149 sets of twins in which one twin was known to have committed suicide, Roy found that there were nine sets of twins where both twins had committed suicide. All of these nine twin pairs were monozygotic twins, and there was not one set of dizygotic twins (i.e., fraternal twins) concordant for suicide ($p<0.0001$).[111]

The adoption study is the third source of evidence of the effect of genetic influence. This method involves data collected from children who have been released at an early age by their biological parents for adoption into an unrelated family. Roy reviewed a study in Denmark, which has screened a register on the 5483 adoptions in greater Copenhagen for the period 1924-1947. An examination of causes of death revealed that 57 of these adoptees eventually committed suicide. Probing of the causes of death revealed that 12 of the 269 biological relatives of these 57 suicides among the adopted had committed suicide themselves, compared with only 2 of the 269 biological relatives of the 57 adopted controls. None of the adopted relatives of either the suicide or control group had committed suicide. In a related study, it was also found that significantly more of the biological relatives of the adoptees with affective disorder than their controls had committed suicide. Particularly, those adoptee suicide victims with the diagnosis of "affect reaction" had significantly more biological relatives who had committed suicide. This diagnosis described an individual in a situational crisis, often an impulsive suicide attempt, generating a suggestion that a genetic factor in suicide may be an inability to control impulsive behaviour which has its effect independently of, or additively to, psychiatric disorder, which may be genetically transmitted.[112]

Empirical Tests

The assumption that there is a substantial association between the degree of genetic relation between individuals and the likelihood that biological relatives will develop similar psychiatric disorders and traits has received powerful support from an increasing amount of biochemical and neuropharmacological studies in recent years. Limited space and the highly specialized and technical nature of these studies preclude a full presentation of them without running a serious and real risk of doing gross injustice to them. Just a sample of these studies, however, will suffice for this section.

(1) In the past two decades since the introduction of the 5-HIAA postulate, some important cross-national studies have confirmed the Asberg hypothesis. Van Praag's study of Dutch depressed patients found that there was an increase in suicidal behaviour in patients with low levels of 5-HIAA. The same results were obtained in studies conducted in the U.S., Britain, India, Finland, Hungary, Spain and Japan.[113]

(2) Alec Roy reviewed several studies on the subject, showing that lower serotonin levels had been found not only in those who had committed suicide but also among several impulsive or violent groups. A study in Finland of 36 murderers, for example, found that those who had killed on impulse, as opposed to those who had carefully planned their crimes, had lower levels of serotonin. The Finnish researchers also found lower than normal levels among a group of convicted arsonists, suggesting the possible links between serotonin deficiency and impulsive violence such as homicide, arson and suicide.[114]

(3) In his review of multiple causes for suicide, Holden identified various factors associated with suicide and suicide risk. He suggested that suicide is seldom the abnormal act of a normal individual, but it is often associated with serious psychiatric disorder, typically, depression. Individual psychological factors appear to play a role in suicide risk, but vulnerability to suicide may ultimately be rooted in biology and biochemistry. As support to this contention, he presents epidemiological evidence that suicide runs in families as well as recent studies on a serotonin deficiency in suicides.[115]

(4) In 1981, the investigators reported additional powerful evidence for a genetic relationship to susceptibility for manic-depressive or depressive disorder. Their previous study permitted the measurement of genetic blood "markers" located on the surface of the white blood cells of subjects with a history of depressive (or manic-depressive) disorder as well as their close family members (siblings, children, parents who did not have a history of these depressive disorders). In the later study, 20 of 120 families studied in Toronto and Rochester had at least two close

family members with a history of such depressive disorder. Each member of these 20 families was subjected to an identical clinical diagnostic interview and samples of blood were flown to the genetic laboratory at the University of Rochester for analysis within 36 hours of drawing the blood. The laboratory staff in Rochester were unaware of the clinical diagnoses of both the patients and their normal relatives so as to prevent bias in the laboratory measurement. As the depressive disorder, including manic depression, is the most common major psychiatric disorder, it was important to replicate the earlier finding on a much larger cohort than in the earlier study. The replication study used a total of 751 subjects from 116 families, including the 20 families reported in the 1981 study, 86 newly identified Ontario families and 10 previously assessed Newfoundland families. The analysis reconfirmed the original results leading to the conclusion that a certain chromosome (in this case Chromosome 5) constitutes one of the elements in the multifactorial etiology of depression and manic depression, further bolstering the ongoing discussion of the role of genes in the etiology of illness.[116]

(5) Mann argues that biochemical markers such as low cerebrospinal fluid (CSF) levels of the serotonin metabolite 5-HIAA and related indices of serotonergic function appear to correlate with violent and suicidal behaviour. These and other biochemical changes may have predictive value in determining suicide risk and could contribute to a more complete mode of suicidal behaviour analysis that combines genetic, biological, psychological and sociological factors.[117]

(6) Kushner offers a fascinating explanation why white male Austrians, Germans and Danes historically have had relatively higher incidences of suicide and depression than Irish and Italians, based on evidence regarding synthesis of the neurotransmitter, serotonin. Serotonin's chemical precursor, the "essential" amino acid, tryptophan must be supplied by diet. Once tryptophan enters blood plasma it must compete with other amino acids in order to cross the "blood-brain barrier" for brain uptake. When some carbohydrates, such as potatoes, are consumed, insulin is secreted, lowering the levels of other amino acids in the blood and allowing more tryptophan into the brain to be synthesized as serotonin. Competing amino acids are far more abundant than tryptophan in dietary protein. A meal low in protein but high in carbohydrates causes a maximum elevation of brain serotonin levels. Consequently, those West European groups such as Germans, Austrians and Danes who seem to have ethnic-specific diets higher in protein than

do the Irish and the Italians may have lower concentrations of serotonin and thus a greater susceptibility to depression and suicidal behaviour.[118]

(7) Creniter and his research team attempted to verify a link between the 5-HIAA level in the cerebrospinal fluid (CSF) and violent suicide attempts by comparing the 5-HIAA levels in subjects who attempted suicide violently and a control group. Five subjects (aged 18-50 years) who had attempted suicide and 12 controls were compared. The rate of 5-HIAA was significantly lower among suicide subjects. The researchers concluded that the 5-HIAA level may indeed be a biological indicator of severe suicide attempts and may, in particular, predict the risk of recurrence.[119]

(8) A team of researchers at the Karolinska Hospital studied suicide risk after attempted suicide, as predicted by CSF monoamine metabolite concentrations in 92 psychiatric mood disorder inpatients (aged 19-68 years) admitted shortly after attempting suicide. The potential of the serotonin metabolite 5-HIAA in the CSF to predict suicide risk within the first year after attempted suicide was studied by means of survival analysis. Eleven subjects (12%) committed suicide within one year after attempted suicide. Eight of these eleven suicides (or 73%) belonged to the below-the-median CSF 5-HIAA subgroup. Their research suggests that low CSF 5-HIAA predicts short-range suicide risk after attempted suicide in mood disorder psychiatric inpatients.[120]

(9) It is sometimes assumed that all antidepressants have a beneficial effect in reducing suicidal ideation or tendencies, but there is evidence to suggest a positive effect with some while others may even provoke suicide attempts. Possible provocation of suicide attempts may be involved to explain the high rate of attempts reported in a study with maprotiline compared with a placebo and the higher rate of deaths from overdose seen with some tricyclic antidepressants. Serotonin reuptake inhibitors (SRIs) have been rather consistently reported to have an advantage in reducing suicidal ideation and have been shown to have a protective effect against the emergence of suicidal thoughts.[121]

(10) Roy reviewed data which suggest genetic and biological risk factors for suicide. Studies from clinical populations, twin studies, the Amish study, data from the Iowa-500 study and the Danish-American adoption studies all indicate that there may be a genetic factor predisposing to suicide. Neurochemical data CSF, urine and postmortem studies suggest that diminished central serotonin and dopamine may be implicated in suicide behaviour.[122]

Evaluation

In view of the fact that many elderly have been known to have seen their general practitioners shortly before their suicide, the role of physical illnesses cannot be overemphasized. Moreover, taking into consideration the above fact, it is urgently desirable that front-line health-care professionals such as family physicians and nurse practitioners be trained well enough to detect the signs of deteriorating health and pain especially among their elderly patients. These "gate-keepers," so to speak, ought to be able to discern danger signals of increasingly painful chronic illnesses and/or ailments that are considered difficult or impossible to cure.

As for biochemical theories, there has been an impressive amount of neuropharmacological evidence since the early research work by Asberg and her team that lends strong support to the hypothesis of a link between low levels of cerebrospinal fluid (CSF) as measured by its metabolites such as 5-HIAA and suicide. As for a genetic connection, Alec Roy, one of the well-known suicidologists at the National Institute of Mental Health in the United States, has confirmed that almost half (48.6%) of suicide attempters had a history of some blood relative committing suicide. This is in addition to very high correlations between suicide attempt and psychiatric disorders among mental patients with a history of suicide attempts. In his review of the Amish study, Roy demonstrated a strong suggestion of genetic link in this religious sect that is characterized by a relatively pure genetic pool and a similar lifestyle (in other words, social factors such as differential lifestyle were controlled). As mentioned earlier, a strong genetic link was suggested in the study of suicide among monozygotic twin pairs in Denmark. Similar findings were also reported in Japan,[123] adding further support to the previously reported European and American twin studies on genetic link.

The foregoing discussion, though very promising both in the etiology and treatment possibilities of suicidals in the future, poses some problems for critics. Several of these criticisms and cautions are presented below.

(1) Most biochemical theories assume that a defect in metabolic process within the central nervous system produces mood changes and a propensity to mental illness and suicide. Moreover, even though some biochemical theories are based on the genetic inheritance of the metabolic imbalance, such biochemical defects need *not* be caused by genetic processes; biochemical abnormalities can be produced by environmental

stress, infection or trauma to the central nervous system as well as genetic factors. Besides, some genetically predisposed individuals, such as the identical twin of a schizophrenic person, do not *always* develop the disorder. Therefore, genetic factors cannot be totally responsible for the development of schizophrenia, much less suicide propensity.

(2) One of the most potent criticisms is that the heterogeneity of the suicidal population and the overlap of suicide and depressive illness make it difficult to find significant and replicable correlations between suicide and the various neurochemical, pharmacological, electroencephalographic and genetic factors that have been investigated as possibly contributing to suicide. One researcher actually insists that "incorporation of these scattered findings into a theoretically meaningful and clinically useful model does not appear to be a realistic possibility at the present time."[124]

Even the study of the serotonin level as measured by low 5-HIAA is under criticism. Hankoff argues that although findings in these biochemical areas offer some promise:[125]

> ...proven...biochemical characteristics which distinguish those individuals having the primary affective disorders from the general populations are confounding factors. Thus, those suicidal individuals drawn from the pool of depressed patients are apt to reflect the same biological findings as the rest of the group. In terms of research methodology, any findings specific to the suicidal group must be demonstrated to be distinct from those of the associated depressive condition.

(3) Research at the Mood Disorder Clinic at the University of Pennsylvania strongly suggests that pure "test-tube treatment" with antidepressant drugs alone is not the total answer because the researchers there obtained the best results with a combination of drug treatment and cognitive self-help therapy.[126] The latest confirmation of this comes from a prominent researcher and authority on depression who co-authored a number of definitive works on clinical depression and who confesses her own long-standing suffering with bipolar affective disorder. While admitting the powerful effects of such drugs as lithium, she argues forcefully for the indispensability of psychotherapy in conjunction with a drug therapy that alters the metabolic aspect of biochemistry.[127]

(4) In view of the fact that nerve endings responsible for sleep, appetite, memory, learning and sexuality, which characterize a typical depressive episode, are located in totally different regions of the brain, how is it possible that a single neurotransmitter (such as serotonin) could trigger the disruptions of the abovementioned multiple functions all at once?

(5) Other suicide researchers object to focussing exclusively on biochemical indicators by pointing out that emotional and psychological factors seem to play at least an equally strong or even stronger role than brain chemicals in the act of suicide. Edwin Shneidman, Dean of American Suicidology, has argued that reducing suicide to a biological basis ignores the psychological pain which drives it. According to Shneidman, there can be no pill that salves the human malaise that leads to suicide.[128]

(6) It may be too premature to assume that a single pathological gene is sufficient to produce behaviour such as suicide. The single-gene defect model may be supported in some disorders, but in others (including psychosis and suicide propensity) a diathesis-stress (which assumes the interplay of two factors for causation) model may be more useful and appropriate. According to this model, there is an inherited predisposition to develop psychiatric disorder and aberrant behaviour, and the predisposition may involve biochemical disorders or personality characteristics such as a high anxiety level. The diathesis-stress theory assumes that even though several genes produce defects or weaknesses in the victim's physiology, environmental stress is seen as a major contributor to the development of abnormal behaviour, allowing for both hereditary and environmental effects on behaviour. No matter which theory is more appealing, many investigators assume that defective genes or environmental stress or both cause chemical disorders in patients, and that these biochemical abnormalities, in turn, produce abnormal behaviour.[129]

(7) In the foregoing discussion, the question arises as to the nature of the temporal priority of the variables involved in the etiology of suicide. There are two possible hypotheses: Does suicide follow the emotional (either depressive or aggressive) consequences of a biochemical aberration as reflected in lowered 5-HIAA concentrations? or, Do our emotions, which are products of cognitions according to the cognitive theory, cause reduced 5-HIAA concentrations?

Much of the biochemical research cited thus far lends support to the first hypothesis—low levels of 5-HIAA are causally linked to negative cognition which leads to negative emotions and then to suicide. Yet, there is also some support for the second hypothesis. As cogently demonstrated by Beck and others, emotions are often products of cognitive processes— the emotional response is elicited by a complex cognitive appraisal of the significance of events for one's well-being. This is the central point and focus of cognitive theory pioneered by Aaron Beck: cognition may and does influence the nature and content of emotions.[130] In some studies it was found that most of the individuals perceived themselves as no longer in control of self or situation and entered a pronounced state of giving up, helplessness and hopelessness. Also impressive is the demonstration of such positive emotions as optimism and laughter contributing to a substantial increase in white blood cells, which are necessary for healing and prevention of illnesses.[131]

(8) Further evidence of psychological conditions influencing the physiological consequences is research by James Pennebaker. He indicated that if one does not confide their perceptions of hopelessness and other negative emotions, the chances of adverse physiological results are dramatically enhanced. According to Pennebaker, survivors of a family that lost a member to suicide have a statistically much higher rate of vulnerability to serious illnesses due to grief and bereavement. In comparison to family members who kept the grief to themselves (control), those who did confide their grief (to a diary, best friend, religious practitioner, therapist, etc.) experienced less vulnerability to serious illnesses.[132] It seems, therefore, that the specific trauma induced by hopelessness in addition to the specific responses of non-confiding could lead to decreases in serotonin turnover, a predetermined vulnerability in physiological responding which may lead to suicide. Confiding serves several important functions as the individual receives social comparison of information suggesting that others have also had similar feelings and problems. Also, the confiding process helps to organize structure and find meaning in one's experiences. Coping aids, such as legal aid, counselling, financial assistance, could also come about as a result of confiding. Hence, it stands to reason that psychotherapy, which facilitates confiding, would be highly effective in reducing the negative and physiological consequences of perceived hopelessness, as revealed in the reduced vulnerability to serious illnesses. This is probably one of the important and powerful arguments for the *raison d'être* of telephone emergency services. Psychotherapy and other means to confiding directly reduce stress by allowing the cognitive reorganization process to occur and nullify the need to inhibit: by so doing, cognition contributes to more positive emotions and reduces vulnerability to serious illnesses.

(9) Another well-known study further reinforces the importance of psychotherapy beyond neuropharmacology. In a longitudinal study, Aaron Beck and his colleagues studied 44 depressed patients who were treated with either imipramine hydrochloride, a facilitator of serotonergic synapses, or with cognitive therapy over a 12-week period. Although both groups experienced reduced levels of depression, the cognitive therapy group showed greater improvement of symptoms and a higher treatment-completion rate. One year later, self-rated depressive symptomatology was significantly lower for those who had completed cognitive therapy than for those who had been in the clinical pharmacotherapy treatment only. While most patients were generally asymptomatic after a year, patients who received cognitive therapy, with or without pharmacotherapy, were doing significantly better on various measures of social functioning.[133]

(10) Some problems exist in biochemical research in general. First, some of the so-called "clinical research" in the medical setting have very small samples. It is understood in behavioural sciences that for a sample to be considered valid it must have more than 39 subjects in each group.[134] Second, conclusions drawn from the research do not differentiate the possible influence of the differences between endogenous or reactive (exogenous) depression (at the present stage of neuropsychiatry it is not possible to differentiate the two effectively). Third, in the field of research on suicide attempt researchers usually do not differentiate between attempted suicide with a genuine intent and attempted suicide for other ambivalent or manipulative reasons. Fourth, although most of the studies do give statistical significance between paricular variables, this does not indicate a cause-and-effect relationship between them. The best they can tell us is that we can probably expect to see the same results occur over and over under the same circumstances.

CONCLUSION: TOWARDS A UNIFIED THEORY

At the present stage of development in suicidology the reasonable conclusion is that there is no general unified theory available that can explain all types of suicide for all motives and in all cultures. In the foregoing discussion, three major models in suicide theory have been presented: sociological-epidemiological, psychological-psychiatric and biochemical-genetic.

Durkheim's sociological analysis of suicide focused its attention on collective rates of social groups, relative regularity and stability of such rates over time, supra-individual characteristics of suicide and suicide tendencies linked to membership in certain social groups. As such, it has become an indispensable basis of the modern epidemiology of suicide research. Its epidemiological utility and applicability notwithstanding, Durkheim's approach to suicide cannot appreciate and assess the depth and degree of individual psychic pain and hopelessness that often precede and accompany the suicide act. In short, its heuristic value in collective data analysis cannot be transferred to the understanding of individual motives for suicide or empathize with the pain of the individual involved. Moreover, strong trends in suicide research and prevention in recent decades are primarily and largely informed by psychiatric and psychological orientations that stress the importance of individual psychic mechanism, personality structure and emotional disturbance and hopelessness. Increasingly, sociological orientations are given a secondary role in the etiology of suicide except in the area of the *ex post facto* gathering of suicide rates.

Yet, one of the major developments out of Durkheim's theory has been the increasing use and importance of "cohort analysis," which has become a standard demographic-sociological analysis of suicide data in modern suicidology. Originally, "cohort" meant a small military unit in the ancient Roman Empire, but it has now become an analytical concept in demography meaning "the same-age group." It is based upon a Durkheimian notion that the suicide rate differs by temporal, spatial, geographical, cultural, gender and age factors. In the process of analysis it raises important questions such as "why are certain individuals suicide-prone who belong to a certain age-specific group?" It makes possible a linkage between macro-analysis and micro-analysis as well as a transfer from minute statistical analysis to qualitative, structural analysis. In other words, it can become a methodology in suicide research that delineates certain characteristics of a similar birth-age group that shares suicide propensity at the temporal and spatial level. In their stages of development, people experience a developmental transition from a primary group (the family) to a secondary group (social groups); in the socialization process, people come under the influence of the culture, politics, moral values, economy and technology of the period. Patterns of thinking and ways of life certainly differ among people due to their particular periods in history and geographical factors; in fact, such differences are referred to often as "generation gap." Cohort analysis is certainly useful to delineate certain central tendencies in suicide rates among certain age-cohorts. Besides, cohort analysis makes possible certain predictions in sucide rates and is capable of clarifying certain risk groups and makes possible prevention policies for decision-makers.

It goes without saying, moreover, that Durkheim's theory provides an enormously useful tool: through gathering group rates, researchers are able to delineate the characteristics of different groups and to pin-point the risk groups and target specific social policies (e.g., towards the elderly, young adults in their 20s in Canada). Thus the Durkheimian theory provides the basic framework for suicide epidemiology, for identifying high-risk individuals in a given group, for recognizing certain group characteristics that are highly correlated to certain socio-demographic variables (marital status, age, gender, rural-urban differential, methods used, religion, occupation), and assisting social policy-makers in the formation and adoption of appropriate measures for the prevention, intervention and postvention of suicide.

Weber's social action theory, on the other hand, was instrumental in providing a background for the importance of "subjective, inner meanings" of the suicide act to the particular individual involved. It encourages the other party (observer) to step closer into the subjective thinking of the person who killed himself or herself. It has opened the door for a social-psychological approach to suicide, as evidenced by the theories of Douglas and Baeschler. These two social scientists emphasized the importance of understanding the possible inner meanings attached to the act of suicide. As such, their theoretical orientation is much closer to that of psychologists. Moreover, their theory will likely acquire much more saliency and public visibility in the years to come in terms of the right to die and/or dying with dignity movement, which considers the primacy of what death as well as "quality of life" mean to a particular individual. Finally, the theoretical orientations of Weber, Douglas and Baeschler provide a link between sociology and psychology.

As opposed to Durkheim's approach, the psychological theories of suicide focus on the individual as the unit of analysis: personality structure, inner feelings and psyche, often hidden deep in the inner recess of the unconscious; stages of psychological development and certain specific impediments in the psychological growth; dramatic trauma experiences such as object loss, depression and hopelessness; interpersonal difficulties; and stress of all sorts. Its merits have been the understanding of certain, suicide-prone personalities, the impact of "object loss" and its relation to suicide behaviour, and the role of dysphoria in the etiology of suicide. The major contribution of such psychological theories and orientations have been their derivatives: the generation of empathy to feel and mitigate the psychic pain that often accompanies suicide ideation, and, subsequently, an offer of a therapeutic process to the person in crisis that may succeed in averting the crisis and in healing the psychic wound. Without the psychological theories, it is impossible to understand and appreciate modern suicide prevention activities. In this regard, the contributions of Freud, Menninger, Shneidman, Farberow and Beck must be fully appreciated. A unique feature of these psychological theories is that their theories were developed in conjunction with or after clinical dealings and experiences with real suffering by real individuals. On the surface, such individualistically oriented psychological theories seem to differ considerably from the more impersonal, collectively oriented sociological theories. Yet, as has been already shown, Freud's theory of object loss can be effectively gauged in terms of the suicide rates of individuals who either experienced separation or divorce themselves or come from broken families. Herein lies the important linkage between psychology and sociology: divorce or widowhood as object loss can be understood both at the collective (suicide rates of the divorced and/or widowed) and at the individual level.

The theories of Farberow and Shneidman reflect their direct involvement with individuals in distress and crisis. The painful psychological process of personal crisis leading to suicide has been effectively conceptualized by these pioneers of modern suicidology. Today, all major telephone crisis lines and suicide prevention centres around the world have incorporated the theories of Farberow and Shneidman.

Aaron Beck, founder of modern cognitive therapy, has been credited with developing the theory of hopelessness as the link between depression and suicide intent, which has been verified by one study after another. It is probably no exaggeration to say that his theory of hopelessness as "negative cognition" (negative expectations) has been one of the best indicators of eventual suicide behaviour.

From the standpoint of a more exact science, biochemical theory seems to be very promising. It could entail medical and pharmacological intervention of suicide ideation, propensity and behaviour in the future. Yet, as has already been mentioned, it is still fraught with certain methodological difficulties and uncertainties.

At the very outset of this chapter, the three criteria of comprehensiveness, simplicity and empirical verifiability were presented for exploring whether the various theories are relevant to a similar set of facts, and also for examining the stage of development for each theory. In reviewing all the theories introduced in this chapter, every one of them has met all of these criteria: they are fairly simple, comprehensive and operationizable for empirical verification. The present author, however, would like to add one more criterion: cross-cultural validity. In view of the fact that Euro-Americans represent a fraction of world humanity, it is questionable to assert universal validity of theories that have been found applicable only to Euro-Americans.

In conclusion, it seems to be appropriate to say that, rather than trying to choose the best from among the various theories, it may be better to ask whether the existing theories produce insights into different types of suicide behaviour. Specifically, it may be that instead of being comprehensive, alternative theories of suicide behaviour are mutually complementary. Each may deal with an important but not overlapping set of suicide behaviours. Moreover, no "immature" theories should be rejected simply because they are less well developed or less well tested than more comprehensive, older theories. New theories may turn out to account for important phenomena as they mature. In this spirit, then, a synthetic model of suicide behaviour will be presented, fusing most of the relevant insight from psychological, sociological and biochemical theories. Such a synthetic model would take into account a predisposing personality structure, which is characterized by a propensity to think in a rigid, "either/or" way in which issues and people are usually bifurcated into "good" and "bad," "all" or "nothing," and no grey zones are perceived or accepted. When such a rigid personality experiences serious object loss such as the loss of parent(s), lover, spouse, friend, child, job, health, self-respect, social standing, wealth, etc., he or she undergoes acute psychic pain. Individuals under such psychological conditions are said to be in crisis: they cannot solve the problem facing them because of drastically reduced or collapsed coping mechanisms. Such individuals, then, are likely to experience a deep sense of despair and hopelessness. All of these factors mentioned combine and lead to suicide ideation and to the suicide act itself. Such psychological processes and factors would certainly be bolstered and augmented by the presence of certain environmental-sociological factors such as the family backgound in which object loss was experienced, separation and/or divorce, social isolation, retirement, unemployment, bankruptcy, absence of support group and crisis intervention resources to restore coping skills. And finally, both psychological and sociological factors may combine with certain biological factors such as physical illness, biochemical imbalances affecting psychic well-being, substance abuse and chronic pain, propelling the individual to the ultimate act of self-destruction. In terms of the foregoing discussion, it is heuristically appropriate to consider such a synthetic, unified theoretical approach to such a complex behaviour as suicide. Such a unified theoretical model is presented in Figure 9.[135]

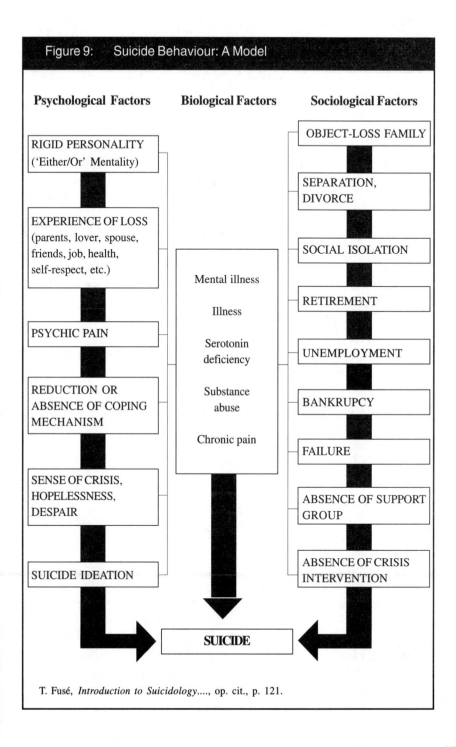

Figure 9:   Suicide Behaviour: A Model

Psychological Factors **Biological Factors** **Sociological Factors**

RIGID PERSONALITY
('Either/Or' Mentality)

OBJECT-LOSS FAMILY

SEPARATION,
DIVORCE

EXPERIENCE OF LOSS
(parents, lover, spouse,
friends, job, health,
self-respect, etc.)

SOCIAL ISOLATION

Mental illness

RETIREMENT

Illness

PSYCHIC PAIN

Serotonin
deficiency

UNEMPLOYMENT

REDUCTION OR
ABSENCE OF COPING
MECHANISM

Substance
abuse

BANKRUPCY

Chronic pain

FAILURE

SENSE OF CRISIS,
HOPELESSNESS,
DESPAIR

ABSENCE OF SUPPORT
GROUP

SUICIDE IDEATION

ABSENCE OF CRISIS
INTERVENTION

SUICIDE

T. Fusé, *Introduction to Suicidology....*, op. cit., p. 121.

NOTES AND REFERENCES

1   Kuhn, T.S., *The Structure of Scientific Revolution* (Chicago: The University of Chicago Press, 1962).

2   Hall, C.S. and Lindzey, G., *Theories of Personality* (New York: John Wiley and Sons, 1980), pp.9-15.

3   Simpson, George, *Emile Durkheim* (New York: Thomas Y. Crowell, 1963), p.1.

4   LaCapra, Dominick, *Emile Durkheim: Sociologist and Philosopher* (Ithaca, N.Y.: Cornell University Press, 1972), pp.30-31.

5   Alpert, Harry, *Emile Durkheim and His Sociology*, (New York: Russel and Russel, 1939), p.25.

6   Coser, Lewis, A., *Masters of Sociological Thoughts* (New York: Harcourt Brace Jovanovich, 1981) pp.129-174.

7   Alpert, H., *op.cit.,* p.41.

8   Durkheim, E., *Suicide,* (New York: The Free Press, 1966), pp.299-300.

9   *Ibid.,* pp.214-215.

10   *Ibid.,* p.159.

11   *Ibid.,* p.160.

12   *Ibid.,* p.170.

13   *Ibid.,* p.198.

14   *Ibid.,* p.201.

15   *Ibid.,* p.208.

16   *Ibid.,* p.227.

17   *Ibid., op. cit.,* pp.217-228.

18   *Ibid.,* p.246.

19   *Ibid.,* pp.241-276.

20   *Ibid.,* p.258.

21   Fromm, Erich, *Escape From Freedom* (New York: Holt, Rinehart and Winston,1950).

22   Maris, R., *Suicide in Chicago: An Examination of Durkheim's Theory of Suicide*, Ph.D. Thesis, (Urbana, Ill.: University of Illinois, 1965), p.215.

23 Iga, M. and Ohara, K., "Suicide Attempts of Japanese Youth and Durkheim's Concept of Anomie: An Interpretation," *Human Organization*, 1968: Vol. 26, Nos 1-2 (Spring and Summer), p.67.

24 Danigelis, N. and Pope, W., "Durkheim's Theory of Suicide as Applied to the Family: An Empirical Test," *Social Forces*, 1979: 57, 4, June, pp.1081-1106.

25 Blake, J.A., "Death by Hand Grenade: Altruistic Suicide in Combat," *Suicide and Life-Threatening Behavior*, 1978: 8, 1, Spring, pp.46-59.

26 Biller, O.A., "Suicide Related to the Assassination of President John F. Kennedy," *Suicide and Life-Threatening Behavior*, 1977: 7, 1, Spring, pp.40-44.

27 Lester, D., "Domestic Integration and Suicide in 21 Nations, 1950-1985," *International Journal of Comparative Sociology*, 1994: 35, 1-2, Jan.-April, pp.131-137.

28 Pescosolido, B.A., and Georgianna, S., "Durkheim, Suicide, and Religion: Toward a Network Theory of Suicide," *American Sociological Review*, 1989: 54, 1, Feb., pp.33-48.

29 Conklin, G.H. and Simpson, M.E., "The Family, Socio-Economic Development and Suicide: A 52 Nation Comparative Study," *Journal of Comparative Family Studies*, 1987: 18, 1, Spring, pp.89-112.

30 Breault, K.D. and Barkey, K., "A Comparative Analysis of Durkheim's Theory of Egoistic Suicide," *Sociological Quarterly*, 1982: 23, 3, Summer, pp.321-331.

31 Stack, S., "Durkheim's Theory of Fatalistic Suicide: A Cross-National Approach," *Journal of Social Psychiatry*, 1979: 107, 2, April, pp. 161-168.

32 Wenz, F.V., "Social Areas and Durkheim's Theory of Suicide," *Psychological Reports*, 1976: 38, 3, Part 2, June, pp.1313-1314.

33 Lester, D., "The Relationship between Family Integration and Suicide and Homicide in Finland and the U.S.A.," *Psychiatrica Fennica*, 1992: Vol.23, pp.23-27.

34 Bille-Brahe, U., "Attempted Suicide in Denmark: II. Social Integration," *Social Psychiatry*, 1985: Vol.20, 4, October, pp.163-170.

35 Durkheim, E., *op. cit.*, p.41.

36 Merton, R.K., *Social Theory and Social Structure*, (New York: The Free Press, 1978), pp.96-99.

37 Maris, R., 1965, *op. cit.*

38 Peacock, D., "Altruistic Suicide in Contemporary Society: The Case of Japan during World War II," *Proceedings of the World Congress of Asian and North African Studies,* (Hamburg: University of Hamburg, 1990).

39 Weber, Max, *Basic Concepts in Sociology*, (New York: The Citadel Press, 1964) p. 29. (Italics by the author)

40   *Ibid.*, p.99. (Italics mine)

41   Weber, M. in Parsons, T., *The Structure of Social Action, op. cit.*, p.642.

42   Douglas, J.D., *The Social Meanings of Suicide* (Princeton, N.J.: Princeton University Press, 1968), p.285.

43   *Ibid.*, pp.285-286; 377-543.

44   Baeschler, J., *Suicides* (New York: Basic Books, 1979), pp.xii-xiii.

45   *Ibid.*, pp.53-54.

46   Schütz, Alfred, *The Phenomenology of the Social World* (Evanston, Illinois: Northwestern University Press, 1967), pp.86-96; Baeschler, J., *ibid.*, xiv, pp.52-54.

47   *Ibid.*, pp.59-206.

48   Peigne, F., Elis, B., Bavouzet, J., "One or Several Types of Suicide?" *Service de Psychiatrie Clinique du Groupe Hospitalier Cochin, Université Paris V.,* presented at the International Congress on Suicide, Ottawa, Canada, May 1979, p.85.

49   Cresswell, P., "Suicide: The Stable Rates Argument", *op. cit.*, pp. 151-161.

50   Brown, E.P., "The Ultimate Withdrawal: Suicide among the Sara Nar," *Archives Europeennes de Sociologie*, 1981: 22,2, pp.199-228.

51   Shneidman, E.S., "A Possible Classification of Suicidal Acts Based on Murray's Need Systems," *Suicide and Life-Threatening Behavior*, 1980: 10:3, Fall, pp.175-181.

52   Baeschler J., "A Strategic Theory," *Suicide and Life-Threatening Behavior,* 1980: 10,2.

53   Fusé, T., see Chapter 5 on *seppuku.*

54   Fusé, T., *Profiles of Death: Biographical Autopsies of Eleven Personalities* (Tokyo: Seishin Shobo Publishers, 1991).

55   Freud, S., "An Autobiographical Study," in Gray, Peter (ed), *The Freud Reader* (New York: W.W. Norton and Co., Inc., 1989),pp.3-41.

56   Hall, C.S. and Lindzay, G., *op. cit.*, pp.36-70; Jones, E., *The Life and Work of Sigmund Freud,* (New York: Basic Books), Vol.I, 1953, Vol.II, 1955, Vol.III, 1957; Nelson, B., (ed), *Freud and the 20th Century* (New York: The World Publishing Company, Meridian Books, 1968); Amacher, P., "Freud's Neurological Education and Its Influence on Psychoanalytic Theory," *Psychological Issues*, Vol.4, (No.4), 1965, pp.1-93.

57   Freud, S., *Civilization and Its Discontents* (London: Hogarth Press, 1961), (the first German edition, 1930).

58   *Ibid.*

59   Freud, S., "Mourning and Melancholia," in James Strachey et al., (eds), *Complete Psychological Works*, Vol.XIV (London: Hogarth Press, 1964), (the first German edition, 1917).

[60] Freud, S., *ibid., op. cit.*, p.247.

[61] *Ibid.*, p.253.

[62] Freud, S., *Beyond the Pleasure Principle* (London: Hogarth Press, 1964).

[63] Freud, S., *Civilization and Its Discontents, op. cit.*

[64] Freud, S., "Mourning.....," *op. cit.*, p.252.

[65] Kline, P., *Fact and Fancy in Freudian Theory* (London: Methuen, 1972). Also see: Klein, G.S., *Psychoanalytic Theory: An Exploration of Essentials* (New York: International Universities Press, 1976).

[66] Fisher, S. and Greenberg, R.P., *The Scientific Credibility of Freud's Theories and Therapy* (New York: Basic Books, 1977).

[67] Posener, J.A., LaHaye, A. and Cheifetz, P.N., "Suicide Notes in Adolescence," *Canadian Journal of Psychiatry*, 1989: 34, 3, April, pp.171-176.

[68] Trovato, F., "A Longitudinal Analysis of Divorce and Suicide in Canada," *Journal of Marriage and the Family*, 1987: 49, 1, Feb., pp.193-203.

[69] Stack, S., "Relation of Marital Separation and Divorce to Suicide," *Suicide and Life-Threatening Behavior*, 1978: 8, 4, Winter, pp.217-224.

[70] Stack, S., "The Effect of Divorce on Suicide in Denmark, 1951-1980," *Sociological Quarterly*, 1990: 31, 3, Fall, pp.359-370.

[71] Motohashi, Y., "Effects of Socio-economic Factors of Secular Trends in Suicide in Japan, 1953-1986," *Journal of Biosocial Science*, 1991: 23, 2, April, pp.221-227.

[72] Stack S., "The Impact of Divorce on Suicide in Norway, 1951-1980," *Journal of Marriage and the Family,* 1989: 51, 1, Feb., pp.229-238.

[73] MacMahon, B. and Pugh, T., "Suicide in the Widowed," *American Journal of Epidemiology,* Vol.81, 1965, pp.23-31. Due to the significance of four years, the interval of four years or more was assigned an arbitrary risk of 1.0. Relative risk of suicide for sexes during widowhood was found to be as follows: Under one year of widowhood (2.5), one year of widowhood (1.6), two years of widowhood (1.5), and three years (1.4).

[74] Paykel, E., Prusoff, B. and Myers, I., "Suicide Attempts and Recent Life Events," *Archives of General Psychiatry*, Vol.32, 1975, pp.327-333.

[75] Dorpat, T., Jackson, J. and Ripley, H., "Broken Homes and Attempted and Completed Suicide," *Archives of General Psychiatry*, Vol.12, 1965, pp.213-216.

[76] Birtchell, J., "The Relationship between Attempted Suicide, Depression and Parent Death," *British Journal of Psychiatry,* Vol.116, 1970, pp.307-313.

[77] Adam, K., Lohrenz, J., Harper, D. and Streiner, D., "Early Parental Loss and Suicide Ideation in University Students," *Canadian Journal of Psychiatry*, Vol.42, 1980, pp.275-281.

78 Humphrey, J., French, L., "The Process of Suicide: The Sequence of Disruptive Events in the Lives of Suicide Victims," *Diseases of the Nervous System*, Vol.35, 1974, pp.275-287.

79 Iga, M. and Ohara, K., "Suicide of Japanese Youth," *Suicide and Life-Threatening Behavior,* Vol.11, 1981, pp.17-30.

80 Silverman, L.H., "Psychoanalytic Theory: 'The Reports of My Death Are Greatly Exaggerated,'" *American Psychologist,* 1976: pp.621-637.

81 Moss, Leonard, M. and Donald M. Hamilton, "Psychotherapy of the Suicidal Patient," in Edwin S. Shneidman and Norman L. Farberow (eds), *Clues to Suicide* (New York: Madenhead, 1963), pp.99-110.

82 Ennis, John, "Suicide and Mental Illness: A Review," Director, Self-Harm Assessment, Research and Education (S.H.A.R.E.), Department of Psychiatry, Toronto General Hospital, a special lecture given at a suicidology seminar, Division of Social Science, York University, Toronto, Canada, February 3, 1988; Kato, Masa-aki, "Neurosis, Mental Illness and Suicide," in Ohara, K., (ed), *Jisatsugaku—Jisatsu no Shinrigaku: Seishin Igaku* (Suicidology—the Psychology and Psychiatry of Suicide), (Tokyo: Shibundo, 1965), Vol.2, pp.147-156. For an extensive and one of the best treatises on the development and substance of Freud's theory of death instinct in its relationship to suicide, see: Okonogi, Keigo, "On Theory of Death Instinct," (*Shi no Honno Ron*) in Ohara, K. (ed), *Jisatsugaku: Jisatsuno Seishin Byori* (Suicidology: Mental Pathology of Suicide), (Tokyo: Shibundo, 1964), Vol.1, pp.53-73.

83 *National Task Force Report on Suicide in Canada, op. cit.,*p.24.

84 *Ibid.,* p.27.

85 Menninger, Karl, A., *Man Against Himself* (New York: Harcourt, Brace and Wold, 1938).

86 Shneidman, E.S. and Farberow, N.L., *Clues to Suicide* (New York: McGraw Hill, 1957).

87 Ohara, K., "Suicide Notes," in Ohara, K. (ed), *Suicidology: Mental Pathology of Suicide, op. cit.,* pp.175-197.

88 Shneidman, E., "A Psychological Theory of Suicide," *Suicide and Life-Threatening Behavior*, 1981: 11, 4, pp.221-231.

89 Shneidman, E., *Death of a Man*, as cited in Grollman, E.A. (Boston: Beacon Press, 1988).

90 Farberow, Norman L., "Suicide," in *Encyclopaedia of Social Sciences* (New York: Routledge, Chapman, Holt, 1972) p.392.

91 *Ibid.,* p.393.

92 Shneidman, E. and Farberow, N.L., "summary," in Shneidman, E. and Farberow, N.L., (eds), *The Cry for Help* (New York: McGraw-Hill, 1960), pp.290-321.

93 Farberow, N.L. and Litman, R., "Emergency Evaluation of Self-Destructive Potentiality," in Farberow, N.L., Shneidman, E., (eds), *The Cry for Help, op. cit.,* pp.48-59.

94 *Ibid.*

95 Beck, A.T., Weissman, A., Lester, D. and Trexler, L., "The Measurement of Pessimism: The Hopelessness Scale," *Journal of Consulting and Clinical Psychology,* 1974: 42,6, pp.861-865.

96 Leenaars, A., "Psychological Perspectives on Suicide," in Lester, D. (ed), *Current Concepts of Suicide* (Philadelphia: Charles Press, 1990), pp.159-167.

97 Wetzell, R.D., Margulies, T., Davic, R. and Karani, E., "Hopelessness, Depression and Suicide Intent," *Journal of Clinical Psychiatry,* 1980: 41, 5, May, pp.159-160.

98 Heisel, M. and Fusé, T., "Depression, Hopelessness and Suicide Ideation: A Bicultural Study," forthcoming, York University, Toronto, 1998.

99 Dixon, W.A., Heppner, P.P. and Rudd, M.D., "Problem-solving Appraisal, Hopelessness and Suicide Ideation: Evidence for a Mediational Model," *Journal of Counseling Psychology,* 1994: 41, 1, Jan., pp.91-98.

100 Lester, D., "A Comparison of 15 Theories of Suicide," *Suicide and Life-Threatening Behavior,* 1994: 24, 1, Spring, pp.80-88.

101 Beck, A.T., Brown, G., Berchick, R.J., Stewart, B.L. and Steer, R., "Relationship Between Hopelessness and Ultimate Suicide: A Replication with Psychiatric Outpatients," *American Journal of Psychiatry,* 1990: 147, pp.190-195.

102 Asberg, Marie, Traskman, L. and Thoren, P., "5-HIAA in the Cerebral Fluid: A Biochemical Suicide Predictor?" *Archives of General Psychiatry,* 1976: Vol.33, pp.1193-1197.

103 Van Praag, H., *Violence and Suicidality* (New York: Brunner and Mazel, 1990).

104 Burns, D.D., *Feeling Good: The New Mood Therapy* (New York: New American Library, 1981), pp.377-378.

105 Ricci, L., "Monoamines: Biochemical Markers of Suicide?" *Journal of Clinical Psychology,* 1990: 46, p.109.

106 Orland, L., Wiberg, A., Asberg, M., Traskman, L., Sjostrand, L., Thoren, P., "Platelet MAO Activity and Monoamine Metabolites in Cerebrospinal Fluid in Depressed and Suicidal Patients and in Healthy Controls," *Psychiatry Research,* 1981: 4, pp.21-22.

107 Ninan, P., Van Kammen, D., Scheinin, M., Linnoila, M., Bunny, W., Goodwin, F., "CSF 5-HIAA Levels in Suicidal Schizophrenic Patients," *American Journal of Psychiatry,* 1984: 141, 4, pp.566-569.

108 Houseman, D.E., Egelland, J.A., Gerhard, P.S., Pauls, D.L., Sussex, J.N., Kidd, K.K., Allen, C.R. and Hostetter, A.M., "Amish Study: Bipolar Affective

Disorder Linked to DNA Markers on Chromosome 11 Manic-Depression," *Nature,* 1987: 325, Feb. 27, p.783.

[109] Roy, A., (ed), *Suicide* (Baltimore: William and Wilkins, 1986), p.54-58.

[110] Kallmann, F.J., "The Genetic Theory of Schizophrenia," *American Journal of Psychiatry,* 1946: 103, pp.309-322; Kallman, F.J. and Roth, B., "Genetic Aspects of Preadolescent Schizophrenia," *American Journal of Psychiatry,* 1956: 112, pp.599-606.

[111] Roy, A., "Genetics of Suicide," *Proceedings of the 20th Annual Conference of the International Association of Suicide Prevention and the American Association of Suicidology,* San Francisco, May 25-30, 1987, pp.155-156.

[112] *Ibid.*

[113] Roy, A., (ed), *Suicide, op. cit.,* pp.54-58.

[114] Roy, A., "Serotonin Levels and Impulsive Violence," presentation at the Academy of Sciences, October 7, 1985, Albany, New York.

[115] Holden, C., "A New Discipline Probes Suicides's Multiple Causes," *Science,* 1992: 256, 5065, June, pp.1761-1762.

[116] Stancer, Harvey, *A Study to Determine Genetic Vulnerability to Depressive Illness: Strategies for Prevention* (Toronto: Clarke Institute of Psychiatry, 1983-1986); *Canada's Mental Health,* Vol.36, No.4, December 1988, p.22.

[117] Mann, J.J., "Psychobiologic Predictors of Suicide," *Journal of Clinical Psychiatry,* 1987: 48, Supplement, pp.39-43.

[118] Kushner, H.I., "Biochemistry, Suicide, and History: Possibilities and Problems," *Journal of Interdisciplinary History,* 1985: 16, 1, Summer, pp.69-85.

[119] Creniter, D., et al., "Serotonin and Suicide: A Preliminary Study Concerning a Sample of Violent Suicidal Patients," *Progress in Neuro-Psychopharmacology and Biological Psychiatry,* 1994: 18, 5, September, pp.871-878.

[120] Nordstrom, P., et al., "CSF 5-HIAA Predicts Suicide Risk After Attempted Suicide," *Suicide and Life-Threatening Behavior,* 1994: 24, 1, Spring, pp.1-9.

[121] Montgomery, S.A., "Suicide Prevention and Serotonergic Drugs," *International Clinical Psychopharmacology,* 1993: 8, Supplement 2, November, pp.83-85.

[122] Roy, A., "Genetic and Biologic Risk Factors for Suicide in Depressive Disorders," Special Issue, *Psychiatric Quarterly,* 1993: 64, 4, Winter, pp.345-358.

[123] Tsutsumi, S., "A Study on the Genetic Relationship in the Suicide among Mental Patients," *Journal of Psychiatry,* 1969: (Tokyo), Vol.5, No.895.

[124] Struve, F.A., "Clinical Electroencephalography," in Hankoff, E.D. and Einsidler,

B., (eds), *Suicide: Theory and Clinical Aspects* (Littleton, Mass.: P.S.Q. Publishing Co., 1979), cited by Welfare Canada, *Suicide in Canada, op. cit.,* p.25.

[125] Hankoff, L.D., "Physiochemical Correlates," cited by *Suicide in Canada, op. cit.,* p.25.

[126] Burns, D., *Feeling Good: The New Mood Therapy, op. cit.,* pp.394-398.

[127] Jamison, K.R., *The Unquiet Mind,* (New York: Alfred Knopf, 1995).

[128] Leenar, A., (ed)., *Suicidology, op. cit.,* p.4.

[129] Lazarus, R., "Thoughts on the Relations between Emotion and Cognition," *American Psychologist,* 1982: 37, 9, pp.1019-1024.

[130] Burns, D., *Feeling Good..., op. cit.*

[131] Cousins, N., *Anatomy of an Illness as Perceived by the Patient* (New York: W.W. Norton, 1986); Pelletier, K., *Holistic Medicine: From Stress to Optimum Health* (New York: Delacorte Press, 1979), p.32.

[132] Pennebaker, J. and O'Heeron, C., "Confiding in Others and Illness Rate among Spouses of Suicide and Accidental Death Victims," *Journal of Abnormal Psychology,* 1984: 93, 4, pp.473-476; Pennebaker, J., "Traumatic Experience and Psychosomatic Disease," *Canadian Psychology,* 1985: 26, 2, pp.82-95, cited in Fusé, T., *Personal Crisis and Ethnotherapy* (Tokyo: Chuo-Koronsha Co., 1992), pp.50-73.

[133] Rush, A.J., Beck, A.J., Kovacs, A.T. and Hollon, S., "Comparative Efficacy of Cognitive Therapy and Pharmacotherapy in the Treatment of Depressed Outpatients," *Cognitive Therapy and Research,* 1977, 1, 1, March, pp.17-38.

[134] Agnew, N., Pyke, S.W., *The Science Game: An Introduction to Research in the Social Sciences* (New Jersey: Prentice-Hall, 1987).

[135] Fusé, T., *Introduction to Suicidology in Comparative Perspective, op. cit.,* p.121.

CHAPTER 4

Continuities in Suicidology Research— Suicide and Mental Illness

There has been strong evidence to suggest a close link between suicide and some forms of diagnosable mental disorder at the time of death. A survey of such a link between suicide and depression, for instance, produced a staggering number of works (over 850), most of which were published just for the period of 1990-1995 in the English language alone, confirming the relationship.[1]

An extensive survey by an American suicidologist examined suicide completers, attempters and people who died from natural causes and found: a higher incidence of psychiatric disorders was observed among suicide completers and attempters than the control group of those who died from natural causes; more than a 50% incidence of mental illnesses among suicide completers; for both completers and attempters (40% and 50% respectively), psychiatric hospitalization was found to be common, as compared to the control group of natural deaths (3%); neurosis (anxiety states and reactive depression) was observed among the completers at twice the rate of attempters, and at four times the rate of those who died from natural causes; both suicide completers and attempters showed more manifestations of hopelessness, dissatisfaction, isolation from others and the desire to die; suicide completers demonstrated a greater degree of depression in the two months prior to death than the control group; among the general psychiatric patient population, depressives had the highest suicide rate.[2]

There seems to be some range of variance in the incidence of mental disorder among suicide completers, ranging from 20% to 94% among the nations of the world.[3] As for North America, the comparable figure ranges from 50% to 90%,[4] reflecting the conclusion of the Working Group for Suicide Research organized by the World Health Organization that "the majority of suicide victims have an unequivocal mental illness...."[5]

It seems appropriate to state, therefore, that a general agreement exists among mental health professionals for a very close link between suicide and pre-existing psychiatric disorder, except for sociologists who have traditionally taken normative, non-psychiatric approaches to suicide.

One of the most prominent research findings in this regard is a British study, which utilized psychological autopsies based on interviews with relatives and physicians of suicide victims.[6] It revealed the following: 93% of their sample had been diagnosed for a major mental illness; 48% of the suicides paid a visit to a doctor within one week of death, usually with psychiatric complaints; 82% of them had been on medication for some form of affective disorder; 70% of these suicide victims showed depression; and 66% of the alcoholics were judged to have been clinically depressed, suggesting a close association between depression and alcohol addiction as well as the high-risk nature of such a group.

In a review study, which examined all the studies done from 1980 to 1990 on the question of a relationship between mental illness and suicide, it was concluded that suicide behaviour is more common among individuals with such psychiatric illnesses as affective disorders, schizophrenia, substance abuse, borderline personality disorder and eating disorders.[7] A very extensive Ontario health study in 1995 concurs with the above findings: those with mental illness, mood disorders, anxiety disorders, substance abuse, anti-social personality or eating disorders show an elevated risk of suicidality, and such risk is tripled among those diagnosed with pre-existing mental disorders in accordance with the *Diagnostic Statistical Manual*, third revision (*DSM-III-R*).[8] In this study, 1000 psychiatric outpatients were screened for past suicide attempts as well as for present suicide ideation and were diagnosed by the aforementioned *DSM-III-R*. It was found that subjects with major depression and borderline personality disorder were most likely to have current thoughts of death, wishes to be dead, thoughts of suicide and actual plans for suicide.

Yet in another study it was found that 68% of subjects with borderline personality disorder had made one or more attempts; 34% of subjects with major depression and 33% of those with borderline personality disorder had actual plans to kill themselves; suicidal thoughts were significantly more likely in subjects with major depression plus borderline personality disorder than in subjects with major depression alone; and suicide plans were significantly more likely among those outpatients with anxiety disorder and borderline personality disorder than anxiety alone. Clearly comorbidity among such psychiatric factors seems to increase suicidality.[9]

Another study in New Zealand, called the "Canterbury Suicide Project," examined a series of issues relating to the antecedents, correlates and risk factors for suicidal behaviour as an ongoing case control study of suicide. The study compared three groups: a consecutive series of 200 deaths in the Canterbury region which were deemed suicides, a consecutive series of 300 individuals who made suicide attempts for which hospitalization was required, and a control group of 1000 randomly selected adults over age 18. Preliminary findings suggest a high level of psychiatric illness in the sample of completed suicides and attempters.[10]

Still another study examined the relationship between specific mental disorders and their comorbidity with suicide among young men. For this study 75 subjects in the age group 18 to 35, whose deaths were adjudicated as completed suicides, were compared with 75 living subjects, matched for age, gender, marital status, living area and neighbourhood and occupation. Using *DSM III-R* as a diagnostic tool, researchers found that 88% of subjects who committed suicide and 37.3% of the comparison (control) group had at least one *DSM III-R* Axis I disorder, and 57.3% suicide subjects and 25.3% of the control group had at least one Axis II disorder (for a brief explanation of *DSM* Axes, see p.199-200). The most frequently diagnosed disorders were major depression, substance abuse (both alcohol and drug) and borderline personality disorder. Of the subjects who completed suicide, 28% had at least two of these disorders, while the rate was zero percent among the comparison control subjects.[11]

In Israel the effect of mental illness on suicide completion risk was assessed using the data from 1307 single and multiple suicide attempters. The subjects were followed up retrospectively from their first attempt in the period 1972 to 1983. It was found that about 18% of suicide attempt repeaters completed suicide, and that mental illness was one of the most important factors that affected suicide completion. Moreover, in terms of the suicide probabilities risk, it was found that two-thirds of the attempts due to mental illness were in the high suicide risk.[12]

Further support for such close association between suicidality and mental disorders is also obtained in a study conducted in Finland, where researchers found that of 229 suicide completers, 59% had evidence of depressive disorders and 43% had alcohol dependence.[13] A study in Copenhagen also suggests that personality disorder and affective psychosis are among some of the major predictors of later suicide.[14]

Likewise, an examination of the records of 300 Navajo, Pueblo and Apache youths age five to 29 who killed themselves over a 31-year period revealed that males accounted for 90% of all suicides; the highest rates occurred in the ages 20-29; firearms and hanging were the predominant methods used; and the significant factors most commonly observed were alcoholism/intoxication and depression/mental illness.[15]

Another study of trends in the epidemiology of parasuicide in Europe, conducted for the World Health Organization Euro-Multicentre, concluded that even though the overall parasuicide rates among Europeans aged 15 years or older varied among different European countries, 70% of the sample studied were diagnosed with a known diagnosable mental illness—usually affective psychoses, personality disorders and adjustment and relational disorders.[16]

Such strong association was reflected in research conducted in Toronto as well. Thus, according to a report by Self-Harm Assessment, Research and Education (SHARE) at Toronto Hospital, completed suicide was most prevalent among the depressive patients (30-70%), followed by alcohol addiction (15-25%) and schizophrenia (2-10%). For para-suicides, chronic schizophrenia was found to be most closely associated with suicide attempt, and almost 56% of attempts were found to have received previous psychiatric services.[17]

Another researcher reported that among patients hospitalized at the Clarke Institute of Psychiatry in Toronto for psychiatric disorders, almost half (49%) were known to have planned a suicide attempt.[18]

The influence of psychiatric illness versus social and behavioural risk factors on suicide in young males was investigated in a longitudinal study of 50,467 Swedish men, ranging in ages from 18 to 20, who were drafted for military training in the period 1969-1970 and were followed through to 1983. It was found that among the 247 suicides that occurred during the follow-up, a psychiatric diagnosis during in-patient care was the strongest predictor of suicide.[19]

In Japan, some clinical researchers have also reported a close relationship between psychiatric disorders and suicide. An earlier study by a prominent suicidologist in Japan reported the high incidence of endogenous depression and neurosis among 1457 in-patients in psychiatric hospitals in Japan. When the incidence of suicide attempt among such psychiatric in-patients was compared to the normal population, it was shown to have been far more frequent than that of the control group.[20] According to this researcher, among such psychiatric patients, suicide attempts were made within one year of hospitalization. Inamura, another suicidologist in Japan, reported that among the schizophrenic in-patients the suicide rate was found to be 365.7 per 100,000.[21] The Department of Emergency Medicine at Nippon Medical College Hospital reports that such disorders as neurosis, depression, alcohol addiction and schizophrenia are closely associated with suicide attempt.[22] It was also reported that among in-patients in psychiatric hospitals in Japan suicide attempt was observed previously in the very early stage of hospitalization, but in recent years it has been observed much more frequently among the long-term in-patients.

The foregoing discussion suggests a strong association between some diagnosable psychiatric disorders and suicide, for which there seems to be no lack of evidence. Retrospective studies cited thus far, together with the biographical autopsies conducted on certain well-known individuals by the present author,[23] have indicated that the vast majority of suicide victims suffered from some form of diagnosable emotional and mental disorder at the time of their deaths. Thus, the assumption that psychiatric disorder is a major determinant of suicide behaviour has gained considerable support over the years not only among mental health professionals but also among the public at large. Today it seems almost beyond debate that the incidence of suicide has been higher among individuals identified by their contact with some type of psychiatric service. This is particularly true, it seems, among the hospitalized population: studies of in-patients as well as discharged patients have reported incidence rates ranging from 18-100 per 100,000 to 50-500 per 100,000. These are certainly much higher than the rate found in the general population.[24]

As discussed in the first chapter of this book, the dominant approach to suicide in Europe and North America since the nineteenth century has been one of the "medico-psychiatric model," or the so-called "disease model:" it is a medical and psychiatric orientation that regards suicide as the manifestation of inherent and underlying psychiatric-pathological disorders. Just about all major studies in the tradition of the "medico-

	mentally ill	affectives	N. of study
Table 1: Prevalence of Psychiatric Diagnoses and Depression in Retrospective Studies of Suicide			
Robins et al. (1959)	94%	45%	134
Dorpat and Ripley (1960)	100%	30%	114
Seager and Flood (1965)	85%	?	325
Barraclough et al. (1974)	96%	70%	100
Chynoweth et al. (1980)	76%	55%	135
Rich et al. (1986)	92% <30	35%	133
Rich et al. (1986)	91% >30	52%	150
Rich et al. (1986)	91% all	44%	283

Source: Sakinofsky, I., and Webster, G., "Risk Factors for Suicidality in the Community: The OHS Study," Clarke Institute of Psychiatry, Toronto, Ontario 1995.

psychiatric model" would lend strong support to the assumption of such relationship and association between a pre-existing psychiatric disorder and suicide. Table 1 summarizes some of the major studies which examined the relationship between suicides and mental illness as well as affective disorders.[25]

Such overwhelming evidence notwithstanding, it is necessary to remember that "mental disorder is not a sufficient cause of suicide, given the large number of mentally ill individuals who do not commit suicide."[26] It seems appropriate to reproduce a conclusion of a team of experts in Canada on this assumed association:[27]

> It is generally accepted that pre-existing mental disorders and alcoholism are important determinants of suicide. However, this does not imply sole causation.

Although research shows that only a small proportion of suicide victims have been free of psychiatric disorder, reports also point to a large percentage of individuals with mental disorders who do not commit suicide. Mental disorder should be considered as only one factor, albeit a significant one, with many other influences such as social, psychodynamic, developmental and constitutional factors acting in an interactive fashion.

Dr. Inamura, one of Japan's prominent psychiatrists, also echoed the above sentiment. He asserted for many years that as accuracy and precision of data in suicidology improved, the tendency to equate suicide too hastily with psychiatric illness would be weakened. According to him, "such an equation is still in the realm of prejudice and bias, often obscuring the interpretation of data."[28]

It is interesting to note that psychiatric researchers in Europe and North America are more likely to report higher percentages of mental illness in the etiology of suicide than their Japanese counterparts. A director of the psychiatric branch of the Osaka Prefectural Public Health Institute accepts the relationship between mental illness and suicide, especially depressive illnesses. Yet he cautions against the easy equation of mental illness and suicide, arguing that whether or not a depressed person will commit suicide depends upon many other non-psychiatric factors.[29] He argues that suicidal patients with schizophrenia do not get well easily even with several years of treatment; yet in his many years of clinical experience he had known only two cases of suicide among schizophrenic patients. He concludes that the percentage of the mentally ill who are suicidal is at best around 30%, and that in his personal opinion as a clinician "the vast majority of suicides are unrelated to known mental illness."[30] Another suicidologist in Japan, who had also served as a psychological counsellor at University of Kyoto, made a survey of clinical reports on student suicide by psychiatrists and other mental health professionals and then concluded that, on the basis of his 27 years of experience as a crisis counsellor at the said university, the percentage of association between mental illness and suicide must be, at best, less than 10-20% of all student suicides at his university. In his clinical experience, those students who showed any sign of mental disorder comprised less than 17% of all suicides.[31] He stated that he had not encountered a single case of delusion, auditory hallucination or other tell-tale symptoms of genuine mental disorder; moreover, his experience with these suicidal students suggested the far greater relevance of what he considered "non-psychiatric" symptoms such as a sense of maladjustment, decline in intellectual performance, stagnation in studies or a sense of despair for one's self. He attributes all these manifestations as expressions of a desire to "escape from the predicament," which is also observed among the normal population and is by itself not a symptom of psychiatric disorders. He even recalled many instances of students who committed suicide who, just before the act, came to bid farewell to him, calm and well collected without any sign of emotional perturbation, saying "thank you very much for all your help in the past." This well-known suicidologist in Japan, Ishii (who also was one of the founders of the Kyoto telephone crisis intervention line), warned against an easy equation of mental illness with suicide on the basis of his 27 years of experience as a suicidologist in counselling students, some of whom committed suicide.[32]

Japanese examples notwithstanding, very few people commit suicide when they are in a happy mood and in good mental health, at least in Euro-American societies. That suicide seems to be connected with pre-existing and diagnosable disorders seems to need little explanation. What is needed, however, is a deeper and clearer understanding of the nature and type of psychiatric illnesses in general and affective disorders in particular because of the latter's widely assumed affinity to suicide ideation, attempts and completion.

There are a few fundamental issues that remain unanswered. If psychiatric disorders are indeed causally related to suicide, why is it that not all the psychiatrically ill commit suicide? What are the specific criteria used for diagnosing psychiatric illnesses? Are they observable cross-culturally? Since depressive illnesses seem to be very closely associated with suicide ideation and acts, it is necessary to have a basic understanding of the nature and type of this particular emotional disturbance that affects so many individuals in modern society. The following pages contain a brief background of the diagnostic history of depression, some problems that may still exist in the diagnostic process inherent in the discipline of psychiatry and, finally, some cross-cultural research findings that may shed light on the thorny issue of whether or not the phenomenon of depression as has been known in Euro-American societies is similar to the core experiences of people in non-Western countries.

WHAT IS DEPRESSION?

Suicide is not likely to occur if an individual is content and sees value in his or her own life. The act of suicide seems to be most often committed by people in depressive states. Schizophrenic and paranoid disorders primarily reflect cognitive disturbances (i.e., disturbances of thought and perception sufficiently strong to cause a loss of contact with reality such as delusional beliefs and bizarre hallucinations), which are called psychosis. Most, but not all instances of mood disorders fall short of this level of disturbance. All mood disorders (also called affective disorders) represent a range of persistent affect of sufficient intensity as to be clearly maladaptive for sufficient periods of time. When a person experiences a mood change detrimental to the person's emotional well-being, it is called emotional disturbance. In this regard it is probably appropriate to define what is meant by "mental disorder." According to the American Psychiatric Association's *Diagnostic and Statistical Manual IV* (*DSM-IV*), the most authoritative guidebook for mental illness diagnosis, a mental disorder is a syndrome or pattern of behaviours, thoughts and feelings that are associated with *present distress* (a painful symptom); or *disability* (impairment in one or more important areas of functioning); or *significantly increased risk* of death, pain, disability or an important loss of freedom. To qualify as a mental disorder the behaviours, thoughts and feelings must be more than an "expectable" response to a traumatic event such as the death of a loved one.[33]

What is depression, then? It is an emotional state usually characterized by sadness, pessimism, unsatisfied and generally negative self-image, lethargy and reduced life activity. It is not necessarily an illness but is often associated with mental and physical disorders. It may be a fleeting or a permanent experience, mild or severe, acute or chronic. It is unpleasant and discouraging. In its less serious form it is self-limiting, does not last long, follows no regular course and has no particular or specific outcome.[34] In its severe form it can be devastating and debilitating to the person's physical condition and emotional state.

Depression can be any of the following three things: a transitory mood ("blues") which is experienced by everybody at some time in life and may be considered "normal depression;" a symptom which is associated with a variety of psychiatric disorders, from milder anxiety disorders to severe and at times even debilitating diseases such as schizophrenia; or a mood disorder in itself. In other words, it can be considered a passing mood, a symptom of something else, or an emotional illness itself. For the discussion in this chapter, however, it is meant to be more than just feeling sad or "blue;" rather, it is a state of dysphoria which, in contrast to the ups and downs of everyday life, can and does distort life at home and work by interfering with the daily function of living. As such, depression can and does affect any person, young or old, man or woman, white or black, at any time in the course of the person's life.

In terms of its etiology, depression may be considered endogenous or exogenous. Endogenous depression does not necessarily arise from a negative life experience but may be associated with a biochemical imbalance in the brain or a change in the body chemistry as related to brain damage, tumour, heredity or menopause. Or, it may be considered an exogenous or reactive depression which is assumed to be caused by precipitating factors external to the individual. The very wording "reactive" suggests the nature of this type of depression. Such a dichotomy has been questioned by some clinicians and scientists because such bifurcation may actually obscure the understanding, as has been the case in the dichotomy of psychosis and neurosis. Rather, it may be more heuristically useful to differentiate types of depression by different patterns of behaviour or by the degree of severity instead of judging by the presence or absence of precipitating environmental events. For example, in terms of the pattern of behaviour and affect, it may be argued that the endogenous depressives are more likely than the exogenous depressives to manifest deep depression, motor retardation, loss of interest in life, lack of reaction to the environment, insomnia and other attendant physical symptoms. Or, in terms of the degree of severity of suffering, depression can be classified on a continuum from the most severe to the least severe; it then can be judged, for example, that endogenous depression is more severe than exogenous.[35] Thus, using this criterion of severity, depression can be arranged on a continuum from passing (or normal depression) to mild/moderate to severe depression. The moderate and severe degree of suffering may be unipolar depression (major depression) or bipolar depression. In the case of unipolar depression, which is much more frequent, the person has one or more major depressive episodes and the absence of any manic episodes.

Persistent depressed mood is accompanied by such somatic and cognitive dysfunctions as poor appetite, insomnia, psychomotor retardation, decreased sex drive, fatigue, feelings of guilt and worthlessness, inability to concentrate and thoughts of death or suicide.

In bipolar depression, the person experiences major depressive episodes, as mentioned in relation to unipolar depression, but in addition has one or more manic episodes.[36] (Mania is characterized by intense and unrealistic feelings of excitement and euphoria, and in the bipolar disorder mania often accompanies and alternates with deep depressive mood). It is considered that major mood disorders such as unipolar and bipolar depression are primary and physiological in origin, whereas reactive and neurotic depression is secondary and psychological.

It is rather difficult, as mentioned earlier, to determine what is endogenous or exogenous depression because they often overlap and there is no objective and effective test at the moment to differentiate one from the other. Likewise, it is equally difficult to determine what is "normal" or "pathological" in terms of depression: only the degree of intensity relative to the precipitating events and the degree of interference with routine functioning of daily life determines whether a depression is pathological or not.

What is the prevalence of depression? When it comes to "normal" or passing and transient types of "blues" just about everyone experiences them. As for the more severe types of depression, it is estimated that 8 to 10% of North Americans—about 25 million Americans and almost 2.5 million Canadians—may experience a more severe type of depressive episode; and 1 to 2% of North Americans will likely suffer from bipolar disorder. Depression occurs often in puberty, but the majority of cases occur between the ages of 25 and 65, even though it is known that such mood disorders affect young children as well. For instance, one study found a depression rate of 5.2% among some 3000 third to fifth graders.[37] There is no lack of clinical evidence for the occurence of even major depression among children.

Since major mood disorders such as bipolar mood disorder (i.e., manic-depression) and unipolar depression (i.e., major depression) seem to be primarily associated with biochemical imbalance, the suffering individual is not likely to respond to psychological counselling—the person is likely to benefit from antidepressant medication. Conversely, such antidepressant drugs have been found to be of little use in the treatment of milder depressions.[38] Aaron Beck and his research team found, on the other hand, that even for severe types of depression the best results have been obtained through the combined use of antidepressants and a type of psychotherapy known as cognitive therapy.[39]

Theories of Depression

There have been a few theories to explain the etiology of suicide from the vantage point of each discipline from which the theory is derived. Likewise, psychologically based theories of depression try to explain it in terms of childhood experience and training, an experience of dysphoria as a result of an "object loss," distorted cognitive perception and beliefs, and/or in terms of learned helplessness or lack of reinforcements. Sociological and social-psychological orientations try to explain depression in terms of social values, events and stages in the life cycle that have great bearing on one's emotional state and behaviour. Biological theories assume that a chemical imbalance or genetic factors cause depression.

The Psychodynamic Orientation

The psychodynamic approach, founded and developed by Freud, emphasizes the mechanics of subterranean, unconscious feelings and reactions in the psyche to the actual loss or a feared or fantasized loss of a significant person or an object, usually earlier in life. The earliest serious attempt at a psychoanalytic theory of grief and depression was published by Freud in 1917 in a paper entitled "Mourning and Melancholia," in which Freud and his student Karl Abraham suggested that a consequence of oral fixation at an oral-dependent stage makes a person dependent on others for self-evaluation; such a dependent personality with oral fixation, when faced with the later loss of a loved one or an object, would generate serious depression. After a person experiences "object loss," pervasive feelings of sadness, anger and dejection accompany and assail the suffering person, and the lost person or any object of great significance is mourned and unconsciously introjected (or incorporated) into the mourning individual as a means of "undoing" the loss. Because of the ambivalence of the feelings of love and hate towards the lost person, the mourner introjects some of the anger and rage onto himself or herself, generating resentment and guilt for feeling such anger and rage. Thus, in the course of mourning, the mourner eventually recalls memories of the one who is lost and separates the mourner from that lost person. Freud considered this to be the normal process of grief. Melancholy, as Freud called it, was essentially grief gone haywire, because the grieving becomes excessive and prolonged, and often unrelated to the environment. In "Mourning and Melancholia" Freud described both normal mourning and depression as responses to the loss of someone or something loved and cherished. Thus, internally directed resentment and anger, and subsequent and consequent guilt following a loss become the basis of depression.[40] As such, depression is a concomitant of object loss and grief that went out of control. Normal grief reactions generally move towards a resolution of profound and pervasive sadness following bereavement, when the mourner readjusts to the loss and begins to rebuild a new life after a year or two. In many cultures and religions, whether Western (i.e., Christian) or Eastern (e.g., Buddhist), a social designation of one year's "mourning period" somehow speaks eloquently about the wisdom of pre-modern age.

If grief is other-centred in the sense that it is an emotional reaction to the loss of someone other than the self, depression is primarily self-centred with such attendant feelings of self-hate, self-blame and self-pity.[41]

Socio-Psychological Orientation

Sociologists, cultural anthropologists and social psychologists emphasize the importance of socio-cultural values pervasive in society. Thus, in highly developed industrial societies, a great premium is usually placed on the extrinsic merits of high productivity and income which greatly enhance one's standing and prestige in society. Retirement as an unavoidable life event symbolizes for many individuals a forced withdrawal and exclusion from the productive process of society. Hence, in all industrialized societies, retirement often brings about dysphoria and depression. In Chapter 2, a dramatic increase in suicide rates among the population over 65 years of age was discussed as evidence for the importance of such a life event as retirement, which may influence one's self-worth and sense of usefulness to society. The fact that the highest rate of suicide is observable among the elderly in almost every nation also dramatizes the saliency of such devastating events as retirement, declining health, death of a spouse and/or close friends, decreasing social status and importance in society, reduced income, increasing vulnerability to serious illnesses and ascending threats to emotional health. All of these life events contribute to a profound sense of loss, which in turn may lead to depression, despair and social isolation as these men and women face a loss of meaning in their lives when they begin to realize that the inevitable and irreversible process of aging is encroaching, that their life's ambitions are not going to be totally met and that they will soon be replaced by younger persons.

One of the best known theorists in this orientation is Daniel Levinson.[42] Following in the footsteps of Erikson, Daniel Levinson made a study of life crises in relation to stages of life for men. He observed that in their middle years of life grown men were often found to be groping like adolescents in the midst of fading passions, dashed dreams and intimations of mortality as their physical prowess declines. His study of the life stages of middle-aged American men is one of the most ambitious accounts of the adult life cycle since the classic work of Erik Erikson, leading to the coinage of the terminology and concepts of "male menopause" and "mid-life crisis," which increase the propensity to confusion, depression and despair.

According to Levinson, every man passes through a sequence of stable and transitional periods in life, each usually lasting four to eight years, during which a man builds, modifies and rebuilds the basic structure of his life. Of the men in Levinson's study, about 60% experienced moderate to severe crises in their 30s: the most dissatisfied got divorced, jettisoned their favoured career plans or faced the demoralizing realization that they would never climb very high in their own or society's eyes and often became depressed.

When men cross the meridian age of 40, they enter Mid-Life Transition; by this time, a majority face up to the disillusioning fact that they will never realize their dreams, and even some of those who have find that it did not bring the magical sense of completeness they had expected. Whatever the catalytic event—or even without one—every man faces a mid-life crisis in his 40s that forces him to appraise his past and to prepare for a seemingly uncertain future. The typical North American male is saddled with heavy responsibilities both at home and at work. He finds himself in a dead-end job without much hope of further advancement but with added responsibility. At home he is confronted with recalcitrant teenage children in a spirit of rebellion and with aging and increasingly dependent and often disabled parents. Moreover, in addition to making external changes in his life, the middle-aged male must also rebuild "the internal aspect" of his life structure. For many men in their mid-life, depression is a much too common phenomenon.

The phenomenon of female menopause is a much better known and talked about life event of both biological and psychological consequences. The emotional hazards of menopause constitute a minefield: some women appear to wend their way through relatively unscathed, while others are devastated by unpredictable mood swings. Anxiety may be internalized as a sensation of growing panic or depression. It may aggravate memory lapses and reinforce a feeling of incompetence. If one feels slightly out of control, making decisions becomes more and more difficult. The variations are many but the result, for countless women, is a debilitating loss of self-confidence and depression. No woman, traditional or highly liberated, will be free from the devastations of menopausal crisis, including depression, as the following quote testifies:[43]

> As a modern liberated woman, the major myth I had to overcome was the one which maintained that menopause was only a problem for neurotic women. I was taught that, if a woman was physically active, busy, enjoying life, career-oriented and fulfilled, she would not experience any special discomfort during menopause. I am healthy, very busy and active, and was amazed to discover that certain menopausal symptoms did indeed occur. Night sweats, joint pains, dreadful nervous instability, terrible feelings of anxiety and depression, impending disaster....

In addition to these crucial events in the life cycle of individuals, other adverse sociological and environmental factors seem to precipitate severe mood disorders as well. Beck provided a broad classification of the most frequently encountered precipitating social-psychological circumstances for the onset of serious mood disorders such as depression: i.e., social situations that tend to lower self-esteem; thwarting of important goals, or emergence of an insoluble dilemma; single stressor of overwhelming magnitude; several stressors occurring in a series or at once; and physical disease or abnormality that activates ideas of deterioration or death.[44] Beck's points have been strongly supported by Paykel who has made a comprehensive review of the literature on life events that occurred before the onset of the episodes of affective disorders such as depression. Life events that involved the loss of important people in one's life (object loss) were found to be closely associated with the emergence of depressive states. When such serious losses are combined with the minimal or virtual absence of social support resources, the onset of depression is very likely, especially among the elderly.[45]

Behavioural-Learning Theories

Learning theory as a part of the behavioural theory in psychology assumes that depression is related to lack of reinforcement: responses which used to be rewarded in the past are no longer reinforced because of the important losses such as the loss of a relationship, the loss of a job, the death of a spouse and so forth. When the reinforcements are withdrawn, the person becomes passive and withdrawn and as a result is often labelled depressed. For example, following a painful divorce one may find few other people rewarding or interesting and simply withdraw from social interaction and relationships, thereby further contributing to social isolation and depression.

The support for such an assumption in behavioural-learning theory came from studies which found that when very depressed persons were placed in highly rewarding situations their affective state improved.[46] Depression, in this theory, is considered a dysfunction in self-reinforcement systems, which produces feelings of worthlessness and inadequacy. Thus, depression follows the loss of positive reinforcers in the life of a person.

In the theory of "learned helplessness," Seligman proposes that anxiety and depression develop into feelings of helplessness—feelings that are learned. According to this approach, a person suffers from anxiety when faced with a very stressful problem or situation, which develops into depression when that person comes to believe the problem is uncontrollable, cannot be changed or solved. When such a perception becomes paramount and overwhelming, the person feels helpless and comes to believe that all efforts to cope with the problem are useless.

People learn to be helpless as a result of certain situations they encountered in the past. According to this theoretical orientation, depression is a form of learned helplessness stemming from the inability to escape from negative stimuli; withdrawal and helplessness follow the stressful event and the depressed person receives sympathy and special attention from friends, relatives and colleagues who do not now expect too much from the depressed.[47] Learned helplessness, in short, is analogous to depression in that it is the behavioural equivalent of the subjective experience of depression.

Seligman's theory of learned helplessness assumes that although anxiety is the initial response to a stressful situation it is later replaced by depression if the person comes to believe that it is beyond his or her control. His theory emerged as a result of a series of experiments in which animals developed manifestations of learned helplessness after they were exposed to 15 daily sessions of inescapable shock. Soon after receiving the repeated shocks they stopped running around in a distressed manner; instead, they seemed to give up and passively accepted the painful stimulation, just lying in a corner and whining (helplessness). They appeared to lose the ability and motivation to learn to respond in an effective way to painful stimulation. On the basis of such experiments, Seligman and his associates conducted experiments with humans that yielded results very similar to those of the animal experiments. People who were subjected to inescapable noise, inescapable shock or who were confronted with unsolvable problems later failed to escape noise and shock and solve simple problems.[48]

Seligman's theory has helped to partly explain depression among women. The higher frequencies and levels of depression among women may be due, according to this theory, to a lack of personal and political power and to social roles that do not encourage them to feel competent.[49] Likewise, Viktor Frankl's existential therapy (also called logotherapy, after the Greek word *logos*, translatable as meaning) is useful in this regard. Frankl, an Austrian psychiatrist who had spent three years in Nazi concentration camps, concluded that in order to survive in the midst of terrible suffering and tribulations in life one must somehow find meaning in suffering and relate it to a deeper spiritual life. Such spiritual understanding gives the individual freedom to transcend circumstances, enables the person to overcome helplessness and makes one responsible for one's own life. To Frankl, psychopathology such as depression ensues when a person has no purpose in living and feels utterly helpless. Hence depression is essentially a learned helplessness. Thus, his proposed logotherapy is a way of reversing such learned helplessness by helping people to accept responsibility for their lives and find some meaning even in face of trying circumstances, suffering and tribulations.[50] The theory of learned helplessness may assist in meeting the need of the depressed to achieve a sense of competence and of control over events in their lives as well as responding to the deep need to command their own destinies.

Cognitive Theory

Cognitive theories are derived from the assumption that cognitive processes are important determinants of emotional behaviour and that the same experience may affect two people differently. In other words, according to this theory, depression is primarily a disorder of thinking rather than of mood and is made up of a cognitive triad of *negative thoughts*, the *situation* and the *future*. As discussed in Chapter 3, the most influential and best known proponent of this important psychological theory of depression is ironically not a psychologist but a psychiatrist, Aaron Beck. Beck proposed that individuals become depressed because they have developed distorted cognitive beliefs and see ordinary events as somehow reflecting on their own competence. Depressives are not necessarily illogical, but they tend to draw unnecessarily illogical conclusions inconsonant with reality when it comes to evaluating themselves and their situations, thereby generating unwarranted pessimism, negative expectations and hopelessness. Illogical thinking (cognition), therefore, distorts reality and produces emotional reactions that are negative, unrealistic and false.

Beck noticed that depressed patients reacted to the events with a sense of self-blame, catastrophe, self-devaluation and the like. This sense of catastrophe would be interpreted by a normal person as simply irritating or inconvenient. The depressed seem to only perceive impending personal failings, misfortunes and overwhelming difficulties without much hope of improvement. Thus, their illogical way of thinking makes depressives expect to fail most of the time, to feel worthless and responsible for all their misfortunes. In contrast to Freud, Beck argues that one's emotional reactions are the result of the way one interprets the events and the world. Many studies lend strong support to the assumptions of cognitive theorists that cognition is invariably distorted among depressives and that the cognitive distortion of depressives is not the effect of an emotional disturbance but may in fact be a cause of the depressed mood.

Beck's theory of hopelessness has been found to be one of the best predictors of suicidal danger; it can and does alert the caregiver to the realization that depression does exist and may indeed lead to suicide ideation and act. Hopelessness is indeed an accurate indicator of suicidal state and is often expressed in such statements as "nothing feels good to me anymore and never will," "things will never work out," or "I can't imagine that things will ever be different," and so forth. Hopelessness is a logical link to depression.[51]

Research has shown that a psychotherapy based upon Beck's cognitive theory (called cognitive therapy) is more successful in alleviating unipolar depression than the administration of an antidepressant drug such as tricyclic imipramine (Tofranil), even though previous research findings had shown imipramine to be superior to insight-oriented psychotherapy in the treatment of depression. It is all the more impressive, therefore, that Beck's cognitive therapy was better than a standard course of pharmacotherapy.[52] One of the studies conducted by the chief proponent of the theory of learned helplessness, Seligman, found that unipolar depressives who were treated at Beck's centre for cognitive therapy at the University of Pennsylvania showed a reduction in learned helplessness, conceding to the potential superiority of the cognitive theory over his own.[53]

Biological Theories

In recent years biological theories of depression have gained much attention. Biogenic theories of depression are based upon the observation that severe manic and depressive disorders, once they occur, tend to run their course or are interrupted by drugs or other intervention.

As mentioned earlier, major affective disorders can be either unipolar depression or bipolar manic-depressive episodes. In unipolar depression the person is depressed for long intervals, whereas in bipolar disorder the individual experiences elation followed by an interval of depression in a recurring pattern. It is possible that manic states do not occur alone but as one phase of bipolar depression. Biological theories assume that biogenic and genetic factors play an important role in the etiology of depression.

Biochemical theories assume that biogenic amines that transmit neural impulses, such as catecholamines (including dopamine and norepinephrine) and indolamines (serotonin), are the main agents for the etiology of depressive illness. The depletion or a low level of serotonin or norepinephrine seems to be related to depressive episodes. A number of studies cited in Chapter 3 render strong support to such a hypothesis, especially the research findings of Marie Asberg.

As for the genetic transmission theory, it has also been supported by a number of family risk studies, twin studies and adoption studies as also discussed in Chapter 3. The family risk study assumes that biological relatives share a greater proportion of their genes than biologically unrelated people do and that the closer the relationship, the greater the number of shared genes. If a disorder is genetically determined, the individuals who are closest in heredity to the diagnosed person (called the "proband" or "index case") should be at the greater risk of showing signs of the disorder. The researcher compares the prevalence of a disorder in relatives of affected individuals with its prevalence in the general population. Available data reveal that the more genes two individuals share the greater the risk of the disorder for one when the other has a disorder, which supports the assumption that a predisposition to certain disorders (physical or mental) can be transmitted genetically. But it must be remembered that in the family risk studies the genetic relationship is not the sole factor in etiology, in view of the possible influence of environmental factors such as the common experiences a parent's behaviour may have on a developing child.[54]

Twin studies try to control the problem of possible environmental factors influencing the outcome by finding an individual who has an identical twin with a certain known disease or disorder. Ever since the early work by Kallmann, many studies were repeated to ascertain the presumed genetic transmission of a predisposition to certain psychiatric disorders such as schizophrenia and depression.

Monozygotic (MZ) twins are produced from the same fertilized egg and therefore have identical heredity; dizygotic (DZ) twins, by contrast, are produced from two separate eggs fertilized simultaneously, thereby having the same genetic relationship as any other brothers and sisters. The twin studies method estimates the probability that both twins will develop a certain disorder given one twin who is already afflicted with the disorder: such probability is called "concordance rate," which is usually reported separately for identical (monozygotic, or MZ) twins and fraternal (dizygotic, or DZ) twins. Thus, Kallmann found the concordance rate for mood disorders and schizophrenia to be much higher for identical than for fraternal twins; for instance, Kallmann revealed that his study of 27 pairs of identical twins received a concordance rate of 93%, and 55 pairs of fraternal twins showed the concordance of 24%.[55] Rosanoff measured 23 pairs of identical twins and 67 pairs of fraternal twins and found that the concordance rate for mood disorder was 70% for identical and 16% for fraternal twins.[56] A series of other studies supports the assumptions of genetic transmission of some psychiatric disorders such as schizophrenia and depressive illness. Expectancy rates for affective disorders among relatives is shown in Table 2,[57] and a summary of major European family and twin studies of the genetics of schizophrenia is shown in Table 3.[58]

Table 2: Expectancy Rates for Affective Disorders Among Relatives

Kinship	Number of Studies	Median Expectancy Rates	Percentage Range
MZ Twins	6	70	50-93
DZ Twins	6	20	0-38
Parents	10	8	3-23
Siblings	9	9	3-23
Children	6	11	6-24
Uncles and Aunts	2	3	1-4
Grandchildren	2	3	2-3

Adapted from Rosenthal, D., *Genetic Theory and Abnormal Behavior*, (New York: McGraw-Hill, 1970), p.285.

As convincing as the evidence may be from the twin studies, there are some basic problems. Because identical twins are virtually always of the same gender and share very similar physical characteristics and appearances, including level of attractiveness, they are likely to have more similar environmental reactions to themselves than are fraternal twins. Hence, the observed high concordance in psychopathological outcome could as much reflect environmental as genetic commonalities. Recognition of such basic problems in the twin studies method led to the third method of possible genetic transmission—adoptee studies. This method evaluates the psychiatric background of those people who were adopted out of their biological families at an early age and then compares their disorders with those of their biological and adoptive family members. If a predisposition to develop a given disorder is inheritable, it should

Table 3: Family and Twin Studies of the Genetics of Schizophrenia (European Countries)	
Relation to Proband	Percentage Schizophrenic
Spouse	1.00
Grandchildren	2.84
Nieces/nephews	2.65
Children	9.35
Siblings	7.30
DZ twins	12.08
MZ Twins	44.30

Adapted from Gottesman, McGuffin and Farmer, "Clinical Genetics as Clues to the 'Real' Genetics of Schizophrenia," *Schizophrenia Bulletin*, 1987: 13, pp.23-47.

show up more often among biological as opposed to adoptive relatives of the affected adoptees.

Working with Danish samples of 71 mood-disordered subjects and 71 matched normal control adoptees, Wender at al. assessed independently the psychiatric status of the close biological and adoptive relatives of these individuals. For major mood disorder, i.e., major depression and bipolar disorder, unipolar depression was eight times more likely to occur among the biological relatives of the depressed subjects as compared with control cases; suicide was 15 times more likely among biological relatives.[59]

This body of evidence indicates that genetic factors play an extremely important role in the development of such disorders as depression and schizophrenia.

As impressive as these studies are, however, these biological theories of depression do not promise a perfect causal correlation. Cautions are necessary, therefore, in evaluating biochemical theories. Neither the levels of such crucial neurotransmitters as norepinephrine nor serotonin could be measured directly within the brains of the depressed. Hence, the metabolites of these neurotransmitters and the by-products of the breakdown of serotonin and norepinephrine are found in urine, blood serum and the cerebrospinal fluid but are not direct reflections of brain levels of either norepinephrine or serotonin.

The same caution must be taken in terms of the genetic transmission of such disorders as depression and schizophrenia. In none of the studies quoted thus far was there a perfect causal relationship, hinting that some other factors than biological or genetic factors must be at play in the etiology of depression.

Depression and Culture

Depression, thus far discussed, seems to be expressed in the following symptoms: 1) a sense of sadness, emptiness and anxiety; 2) irritability over trifle matters and quick anger; 3) a sense of hopelessness and profound pessimism; 4) noticeable decrease in cognitive ability such as concentration, memory and decision-making; 5) sleep disorders such as insomnia, oversleeping, fitful sleep, frequent waking up and the inability to go back to sleep; 6) eating disorders such as excessive eating or drastic loss of appetite; 7) loss of interest in activities and people; 8) loss of interest in sex; 9) withdrawal from friends and family and increasing isolation; 10) experience of physical pain and/or disorder for which no organic cause can be found; 11) increasing indifference to personal hygiene and appearance. These known characteristics of depression may be grouped into three major dimensions: affective dimension (numbers 1, 2 and 3 of the above), cognitive dimension (number 4 of the above), and somatic or physical dimension (numbers 5 through 11 of the above). It is significant that physical or somatic and behavioural characteristics are most numerous in the aforementioned symptomatology of depression, the fact of which may have some important implications—i.e., that somatization may be a core symptom of melancholia rather than psychologization or cognitive aspects.

One of the important questions that has to be raised in this section is: Is the experience of depression as known in Euro-American societies universal even in the non-Western world, or does it vary in its nature and content from culture to culture? The following survey of a number of cross-cultural studies supports the assumption that some real variations do exist in the experience and type of depression among people in different cultures.

(1) Some extensive reviews of cross-cultural aspects of psychiatry (or transcultural psychiatry) suggest the importance of devising appropriate and culturally sensitive strategies for studying culture as well as psychiatric disorders. Overall, these reviews suggest that feelings of guilt, self-punishment and self-devaluation are predominant in Western cultures, whereas somatic symptoms (physical complaints) of depression appear to be more prevalent in non-Western regions such as Africa, Asia and Latin America.[60]

(2) It was reported in earlier studies that even in those non-industrialized countries where depressive disorders are relatively common they seem less closely associated with feelings of guilt and self-recrimination than in Western countries. In one of such studies conducted among several groups of Australian Aborigines, researchers found not only an absence of guilt and self-recrimination in depressive reactions but also no incidence of attempted or completed suicide, indicating that the absence of suicide may be explained as a consequence of strong fears of death and also because of the tendency to act out behaviourally and externalize hostile impulses.[61]

(3) In order to examine whether or not different types of somatization may be a core symptom of melancholia, researchers in Germany studied 51 Turkish patients and 51 education-matched German patients with melancholic depression. They found that Turkish patients had higher frequencies of somatic preoccupation and hypochondriasis (i.e., abnormal concern with physical symptoms). Their tentative conclusion from this study is that somatization may be a neurobiological core symptom of melancholia or it may be a culture-bound symptom in the sense of being excessively concerned with physical symptoms—a tendency fostered and nurtured by certain cultures.[62]

(4) In a study of the prevalence of psychiatric disorders in Japan in comparison to the United States and Europe, a researcher found the Japanese to be particularly prone to somatization in reference to depression, the fact of which may account for the differences in rates, raising questions of cultural explanations and methodological problems in cross-cultural psychiatric epidemiology. It suggests that the diagnostic instrument such as *Diagnostic Statistical Manual* (*DSM*) widely in use

in North America may reveal some implicit assumptions of the parochial culture of psychiatry as an ethnoscience.[63]

(5) In Benin, West Africa, 92 adult patients with major depression were rated using Comprehensive Psychopathological Rating Scale. The study revealed a lower frequency of suicidal thoughts and guilt feelings and a higher frequency of somatic complaints.[64]

(6) Some researchers point out the linguistic problems involved in identifying depression. For instance, in a study that interviewed patient samples in nine countries—Denmark, England, the former Soviet Union, Czechoslovakia, Colombia, India, Nigeria and Taiwan—it was reported that in Nigeria and Taiwan, countries where the language is not Indo-European, their languages have not differentiated bodily and psychological experiences to the extent that Indo-European languages have. Chinese and Africans, therefore, have more difficulty differentiating emotional states than do Indo-Europeans. This fact may explain that they tend to express depression in somatic rather than psychological terms.[65]

(7) In an interesting research on the word association studies on depression, investigations were conducted to find out if cross-cultural variations exist in the subjective experience of depression among 150 Japanese nationals who were born and raised in Japan, 158 Japanese-Americans who are racially Japanese but were born in the U.S. and raised as Americans, and 146 Caucasian-American college students. Researchers examined word association for the equivalent words of "depression" for the Japanese-Americans and Caucasian-Americans, and for the Japanese word "yu-utsu" (Japanese equivalent of depression or "feeling down"). Results indicate that Japanese nationals in Japan associated the word "yu-utsu" to more external referent terms such as "rain" and "cloud" as well as somatic referent terms such as "headache" and "fatigue," whereas, by contrast, both Japanese- and Caucasian-Americans associated predominantly internal mood-state referent terms such as "sad" and "lonely" to the word "depression." These observed differences are attributed to differential degrees of individuation mediated by each culture and reflected in the subjective experience of depression. Thus, it is assumed that Japanese self-structure was essentially "unindividuated" while American self-culture was considered to be more "individuated," accounting for the latter's tendency to use more internal referents for their mood-state.[66]

(8) In a study by an American psychiatrist during his sabbatical year in China, it was found that in China rates of depression are low but tend

to be expressed as somatic symptoms. In examining out-patients at Hunan Medical College Clinic, Kleinman found that there is no Chinese word which is the equivalent of "depression" in English; instead, the Chinese clinicians still use a diagnostic category of neurasthenia, which went out of use in North America in the 1950s, and which designates somatic symptoms much more than psychological ones.[67]

(9) The Student Suicide Ideation Measure (SSIM) was developed to examine the association between suicide ideation and various predictive variables such as depression and hopelessness. Using such a scale, Heisel and Fusé compared five samples in Canada and Japan: 123 Canadian undergraduate students enrolled in an introductory psychology course, 59 Canadian undergraduates enrolled in a course on suicidology, 70 Japanese physician-students enrolled in a post graduate programme in psychiatry, 88 Japanese undergraduates enrolled in a social science course, and 62 Japanese nursing students in a school of nursing. The results indicated that the Canadian samples generally experienced suicide ideation as an affective construct that was most strongly predicted by feelings of hopelessness and sub-clinical depression in support of Beck et al. (1985) and Weishaar and Beck (1992). Conversely, the Japanese samples generally experienced suicide ideation as a behavioural construct, with suicide ideation most strongly predicted by previous suicidal behaviour, negative coping skills that included both intentional and unintentional self-harm behaviour, and use of drugs and alcohol when sad. In short, psychological variables of depression and hopelessness are correlated with suicide ideation for the Canadian samples, but for the Japanese counterparts behavioural variables are much more correlated with suicide ideation than depression or hopelessness.[68]

(10) A comparative study was made about the self-report of depressive symptoms as measured by the Self-Rating Depression Scale (SDS) with students in Korea, the Philippines, Taiwan and the United States. The mean score of the 966 college students varied significantly across nationality boundaries for depressive symptoms. Furthermore, there were marked differences between countries in symptomatic manifestations. In the United States and Taiwan, depression was reported primarily in the form of psychological symptoms, but in Korea and the Philippines the most frequent symptoms were somatic.[69]

(11) Under the aegis of WHO, a collaborative study of depression was conducted in 1991 in Ankara, Athens, Bangalore, Berlin, Groeningen,

Mainz, Manchester, Nagasaki, Paris, Rio de Janeiro, Santiago, Seattle, Shanghai and Verona, by using a number of measuring instruments such as Composite International Diagnostic Interview (CIDI) and International Classification of Disease-10 (ICD-10). It was found that in terms of current depression such cities as Ankara, Groeningen, Mainz, Manchester and Santiago showed a much higher prevalence of depression than other cities. In other words, most of the cities in European countries and cities under strong Western influences seem to manifest a higher prevalence of depression. As for Japan, it was pointed out by the Nagasaki team that whereas in all other cities in the world the gender difference was 19.2% for men and 28.1% for women, indicating higher frequency of affliction with depression among females, in Japan the comparable percentage was almost identical with 8.9% for men and 8.4% for women. Moreover, the average estimated prevalence of depression for all cities in other parts of the world was 24.9%, but that of Nagasaki was 8.6%, suggesting a much lower prevalence in Nagasaki.[70] Similar results were obtained in another study in Japan that compared the prevalence of depression among outpatients at a university hospital general medicine clinic to that of the United States.[71]

(12) In an earlier study, Murphy et al. investigated the depression syndrome in 30 countries and confirmed the presence of such "classic" symptoms as "feeling down," "diurnal variation," "sleep disturbance," "loss of interest in the environment around him or her" in 21 countries, but such symptoms were less frequent in nine non-Western countries. Rather, in these non-Western countries, such somatic symptoms as fatigue and exhaustion, decline in appetite and sexual desires, and loss of weight (i.e., somatization) were more pronounced.[72]

(13) In a comparative study of depression conducted under the auspices of WHO, 473 outpatients were interviewed in Canada, India, Japan, Iran and Switzerland, using the WHO-designed SADD (Standardized Assessment of Depressive Disorders). It was found that there were indeed some cross-cultural differences: in terms of guilt feelings, 68% of the Swiss expressed such feelings as opposed to 32% of the Iranians; as for suicide ideation, 70% of Canadians experienced it as opposed to only 40% of the Japanese outpatients; as for somatic symptoms, 57% of the Iranians but only 27% of the Canadians expressed such complaints. Overall, the severity of depression was highest in Montreal, Canada and Basel, Switzerland.[73]

(14) A careful review of similar studies demonstrates that some differences are indeed observed in psychological symptoms between Western and non-Western countries. There is little difference in somatic symptoms between countries, suggesting that physical symptoms are much more basic aspects of "depression" than psychological conditions.[74] Such findings were further reinforced by a study of outpatients in Indonesia and Germany, which found that depressed Indonesian outpatients were more likely to express their dysphoria in somatic complaints, whereas German patients tended to express their depression in terms of the decline in their morale and productivity on the job, high degree of self-blame and suicide ideation.[75]

(15) Binitie studied a consecutive sample of patients attending a nervous disease clinic in a Nigerian city for a period of 18 months, comparing them with outpatients attending a London psychiatric clinic. He examined these patients, all of whom received a diagnosis of affective disorder utilizing the Present-State-Examination (P.S.E.)—a structured, systematic, psychiatric interview. Binitie found that both groups reported depressed mood, but feelings of guilt, anxiety and active contemplation of suicide were more characteristic of Londoners, whereas somatization and motor retardation were much more characteristic of Nigerians.[76]

(16) According to the Second Gujarat Suicide Inquiry Commission in India, it was revealed that the causes of suicide and attempted suicide in India are usually not related to psychiatric illnesses. The report insists that non-psychiatric factors are more significant in causing suicide than psychiatric disorders, at least in India. Such causes as worries over serious illness and quarrels with parents-in-law or spouses show up as important causes. The report asserts that the linear relationship that exists between depressive illness and suicide in Western countries is not characteristic of India. "Fewer depressives commit suicide in India than elsewhere. The ideas of guilt and sin possess a low suicide potential in the Indian culture...mental etiology was found in only 944 of the 4537 suicides studied by the Gujarat Commission....Chronic illnesses contribute heavily to the suicide toll."[77] Another study of attempted suicides in India found that of the 35 cases studied in the period beginning in April, 1977 the absence of depression was striking.[78]

(17) To be discussed in greater detail in the next chapter, *seppuku* is a time-honoured ritual suicide among the warrior class in Japan. One of the compelling factors in this form of ritual suicide is *inseki* or assuming responsibility for a particular behaviour or event, which continues as a

powerful motive for suicide even in today's Japan. One of the hallmarks of such ritual self-disembowelment has been the absence of antecedent depression. Fusé argues that *seppuku* has been nurtured in Japan's socio-cultural values and traditions as one of the socially and culturally prescribed and positively sanctioned role-behaviours. As such, *seppuku* has been unrelated to depression and hence is a necessary corrective to the Euro-American propensity to understand suicidal behaviour primarily in terms of psychopathology.[79]

Depression and Culture: Postscript

Even though the aforementioned studies pointed out some important differences in the experience of depression among different cultures, expecially between Western and non-Western cultures, it must be remembered that basic similarities outweigh the differences: the experience of depression in all cultures seems to include "feeling sad," "reduced cognitive ability" (such as concentration and memory), "sleep disorder" and "loss of interest in activities and people around the individual." For example, one researcher conducted a study of somatized distress among normal populations in seven different cultures by administering the MMPI (Minnesota Multiphasic Personality Inventory). In general, researchers who conduct general populations surveys, rather than hospital-based ones, seem to be more impressed with similarities than differences as well as with the stability of affective dimensions across cultures. On the other hand, those who work with clinical populations are more impressed by differences and variations.[80] In other words, according to some of these surveys, depression as an affect seems more alike than dissimilar across cultures, whereas depression as an illness—that which is recognized and handled by a societal health regulatory system—may vary greatly across cultures.[81]

This point was further buttressed by Beiser who has been pursuing studies of psychiatric disorders such as depression in different cultures for some time. Based upon the results of his findings in 1985 and 1994, he and his research associates insist that depressive disorders occur in many cultures in more or less invariant forms. They examined depression from comparable studies in Senegal, among Southeast Asian refugees in Canada and midtown Manhattan residents. They found that in all three samples the affect of depression is expressed in psychological terms, suggesting that neither the Senegalese nor the Southeast Asian refugees seem to lack a vocabulary for such expression and, therefore, that the expression is not an unfamiliar one. Their study in 1994 found that comparison samples of 319 resident Canadians and 1348 Southeast Asian refugees (58% males) showed similarities in the manifestation of three depressive categories: major depression, depression with panic and subclinical depression. Their conclusion is that depression seems to occur very much the same way beyond cultural differences.[82] It may be that a major difference between "normals" and psychiatrically depressed patients is that while depressive affect and somatization occur independently of each other among the normal population they may co-occur among the psychiatrically depressed patients.

Further support to their contention was rendered by another recent cross-cultural study of depression in India. An Indian research team examined 91 subjects (ranging in age from 15 to 78 years) diagnosed with depressive disorder using the Standardized Assessment of Depressive Disorders (SADD) developed by the World Health Organization. The ten most frequently mentioned symptoms were "sadness," "anxiety," "joylessness," "lack of energy," "hopelessness," "loss of interest," "disruption of social functioning," "irritability," "loss of ability to concentrate" and "lack of appetite." Results were compared with other available data on the SADD and the absence of culture-specific symptoms was noted.[83]

All of these studies, though limited and small in sample size, legitimately caution against too easy an argument for culture-specific aspects of depression. Granted that such caution be taken into consideration, there are nevertheless many research findings, cited in these pages and elsewhere, that suggest the probability of culture-specific tendencies towards somatization or psychologization: depressive individuals in the West are likely to express their dysphoria predominantly in psychological terms, whereas depression seems to be experienced in somatic symptoms in non-Western cultures. How does one account for such observed differences? There are some explanations for such cultural differences in the experience of depression.

One explanation, particularly strong in Euro-American societies and among their mental health professionals, is that psychologization is the main and genuine experience of depression and that somatic symptoms, therefore, are merely the indications of "masked depression." It is known that depressives often make repeated visits to family physicians for a wide range of physical complaints. It is assumed that 10 to 60% of outpatients who visit general practitioners seem to suffer from this "veiled" form of depression.[84] Thus, according to Lesse, the patient's "cry for help" may be expressed in such "masked" forms as hypochondriasis, psychosomatic disorders, impulse disorders, substance abuse, anxiety, indiscriminate promiscuity, truancy and phobias. The patient often hangs on to the extremely uncomfortable and distressing symptoms that cover up the depression. Depression, therefore, does not always receive proper and necessary treatment due to an excessively strong defence mechanism in the form of effective camouflage. At times, therefore, many health-care and mental health professionals fail to detect and recognize it in its disguised form. Such an argument for masked depression is reinforced by the fact that many completed suicides follow recent visits to physicians and therapists who apparently miss completely such signs of the "cry for help" because of the masking of the symptoms.[85]

The aforementioned cultural differences—i.e., the tendency to psychologize depression in the West and the prevalence of somatization in non-Western countries—raise a fundamental question: Why is it that people in Western countries are much more inclined to express depression primarily in psychological terms such as negative self-image, self-hate, guilt, etc., while non-Westerners are likely to express their distress in somatic terms?

One of the distinct hallmarks of Western civilization has been the development of individualism. Individualism treasures and cultivates a person's unique individual history, well-being and happiness together with the individual's personal feelings, emotions, sensitivity and interpersonal communication. Hence, in a society that values the individual, greater premiums are placed on the expression and portrayal of the interior world of the individual human being. By contrast, a society that treasures the collective tradition, values, survival and continuity of the group of which the individual is a part puts more emphasis on respecting the collective heritage. Such a traditional and collectivity-oriented society places less emphasis on the interior world of a particular individual and treasures and cultivates visible aspects of the plurality of individuals which sustains the solidarity, survival and continuity of the group. Physical conditions—somatic conditions—are an indispensable part of survival of group life, far more important than individual history or personal feeling. Thus, the emergence of individualism in the West seems to have created the corollary of paying much greater attention to individual feelings and the interior world of the individual. It was Max Weber (1864-1920), a founder of modern sociology in Europe, who maintained that one of the processes of modernization in Western civilization was the interiorization and intensification of the individual's unique experience and feelings. Such preoccupation with the inner world gave a powerful impetus to "psychologization" and to scientific pursuit of psychology as a discipline.[86] Societies characterized by a strong collective orientation, therefore, would not require as much preoccupation with the individual's interior world; rather, they would pay more attention to the description of physical conditions that are more visible, common and necessary for the preservation, prosperity and continuity of the particular group of which the individual is merely a part.

Kleinman points out that somatization is not uncommon, however, even among working-class British people who openly vocalize their physical discomfort in physiological complaints, a practice carefully avoided by the middle, upper-middle and upper classes. Even in the Victorian age, somatization was common and acceptable among the working class in Britain, but it came to be frowned upon and suppressed among the middle classes.[87] According to this theory, as somatization came to be suppressed it was gradually replaced with psychologization, which was much more acceptable to upper middle classes. Thus, instead of saying that "so-and-so is ill with such and such disease" in graphic detail, people may describe the condition in semi-psychological words like "so-and-so is indisposed."

It also seems that Christian ethics have had an effect on the nature and content of depression in the West. It seems that there are some fundamental differences in the nature of ethical commands between the Ten Commandments in Judaism and Jesus' teachings in Christianity. Moses' Decalogue is primarily behavioural, whereas Christian ethics are both behavioural and attitudinal. For instance, the Mosaic commands of "thou shalt not commit adultery" or "thou shalt not kill" are behavioural proscriptions. By contrast, Christian ethics goes beyond such behavioural proscriptions to inner psychological control and censorship: "he who looks at a woman with lust after her has committed adultery already in his heart" and "he who hates his brother has committed murder in his heart." The moral injunctions of the Decalogue were meant to regulate overt and external behaviour, but Jesus' teachings are extended to the censorship and judgment of a hidden, inner world of thoughts, desires and feelings. It means, therefore, the Christian individual stands in constant judgment before the Almighty God not only in terms of behaviour, which is visible, but also in terms of thoughts, desires and feelings, which are hidden and invisible. Christian faith, in contrast to Judaism, judges both the individual's behaviour and thoughts and feelings. Such religious orientation is likely to contribute to the generation of self-censorship, self-blame and guilt, whether or not one's conduct and/or thinking is hidden from the public knowledge. In this regard, it is no accident that modern totalitarianism, which is bent on regulating and subjecting every aspect of human behaviour and thinking to total control and censorship, appeared in highly advanced Western countries with a Christian background.[88]

Mental Illness and Problems of Assessment

The relationship between mental illness in general and depression and suicide in particular has been discussed here at some length. One of the important points that emerged in the discussion of depression is the variation of mental and emotional disorders in terms of culture. If the phenomenology of mental and emotional illness is dependent on the culture in which it finds itself, what ought to be the reasonably reliable criteria for determining the nature and type of mental illness? Better still, does there exist a reliable set of criteria to decide whether or not a particular mental and emotional disorder constitutes abnormality or illness? Is it possible at this stage in the field of mental health to definitively decide what is mentally and emotionally normal or abnormal? The straightforward and intellectually honest answer would be in the qualified negative at this time.

At present, in tune with the increasing medicalization of suicide prevention and intervention, both in behaviour and ideation, there has been a widespread tendency among both mental health professionals and lay people to regard suicidal behaviour and ideation as the result of irrational or abnormal mental states induced by mental illness. Of course, there has been considerable evidence to suggest a possible link between certain mental and emotional disorders and suicidal behaviour. But it is also an undeniable fact that not all mentally ill people commit suicide. The problem, therefore, rests in regarding all suicides as irrational and drawing a conclusion on the direct causal link between mental and emotional illness and suicide. One serious limitation of such a "disease model," which incidentally constitutes the very basis of the Western medical model, is illustrated by the fact that according to the National Task Force on Suicide in Canada, only 4% of the suicide completers had a history of psychotic depression.[89]

What then are some of the criteria used for determining mental illness? One criterion is statistical infrequency, measuring specific characteristics such as personality traits and ways of behaving and the distribution of these characteristics in the general population. According to the statistical infrequency criterion, an assertion of abnormality simply suggests that a particular individual deviates from the average in a particular trait or behavioural pattern. One of the problems of such an approach, however, is that it gives no guidance in determining what infrequent behaviour psychopathologists should study. Another criterion for diagnosis is the degree and extent of distress and anguish caused by the individual's behaviour. One of the problems of such a criterion is subjectivity; subjectively felt distress and emotional suffering are not synonymous with the objective measure of the severity of the problem. As "beauty may be in the eye of the beholder," distress and crisis are in the experience and feelings of the individual involved in a particular situation. Another criterion is the degree of disability and debilitation such as a phobia. And finally, some may consider that abnormal behaviour is whatever violates social norms and threatens or makes anxious those observing it—sociopathy. But there are some problems in such conformity to community mores and standards. In a society that imposes strict racial segregation rules backed up by a long-standing tradition of beliefs in racial superiority that justifies segregation (apartheid in the former South Africa or many southern states in the U.S. in pre-1954 racial practices), a decent individual who is disturbed by the injustices of such segregation may rebel against such practices, as had been the case among many civil rights protesters in the U.S., and may then be judged "abnormal." Some people indeed may argue that before such a person is judged normal or abnormal the sanity of the community or society must be examined and judged. In summary, the criteria may include statistical rarity, subjective experience of distress or violations of accepted norms. It is important to remember that the crucial implication of the paradigms for determining abnormality is that they determine how and where investigators look for answers. Thus, the investigators will interpret data differently according to their point of view with limited perceptions of the world and reality.

Under the present medical model, therapists must pay strict attention to assessment, diagnosis and classification standards in practice, even though at this moment there is no single definitional criterion for absolutely certain diagnosis. Despite such ambiguity in determining abnormality, there are some useful aspects in assessment even with the current tools and methodology: scientific merit in differentiating the causes of mental disorders, practicality and utility in dealing with different types of mental patients, and the desire for constant improvement. Moreover, the assessment provides an important step in understanding the causes of mental illness. Finally, as imperfect as it is, competent assessment has been used in courts of law to determine whether or not a particular individual is legally insane.

The history of diagnosis in medicine goes way back to before the Christian era, when diagnosis was often based upon astrology. Humankind has come a long way since then. The first "scientific" psychological assessment was undertaken by Sir Francis Galton in 1882 when he set up a laboratory in London to measure human abilities statistically using large samples of people so that he could establish statistical norms for the general population.

Modern psychiatric classification of mental illness was established by Emil Kraepelin (1855-1926), professor of psychiatry at the University of Munich from 1903 to 1921. He is generally considered to be the father of modern psychiatry, and his imposing statue still graces the entrance of the Max Plack Institute for Psychiatry in Munich today. As a physician he developed a comprehensive system of classification of mental illness on the basis of literally thousands of patients who were grouped into four assumed causes for all abnormal behaviours: metabolic dysfunction, endocrine dysfunction, brain disease and hereditary abnormalities.[90] Even though he did not include possible psychological, sociological and environmental factors (as the modern *DSM* does), his classificatory system was so comprehensive that it has since become the basis of all diagnostic tools and measurement instruments around the world, including the International Classification of Disease-10 and the *Diagnostic and Statistical Manual of Mental Disorders* of the American Psychiatric Association.

Each DSM category contains a specific description of abnormal behaviour with listings of both the essential and associated features of the disorder. Essential features are necessary for the diagnosis, and associated features are often present. As its name suggests, *DSM* is based upon the known demographic frequency distribution and characteristics of each disorder such as the age of onset, prevalence, family patterns, sex ratio and predisposing factors. *DSM* as a diagnostic guide allows the clinician to construct a profile of the patient across five dimensions or "axes," which are expected to offer extensive information about the patient. Thus, Axis I describes specific clinical syndromes, Axis II gives a list of personality disorders, with the inclusion of physical disorders in Axis III, necessary information about the current level of environmental stress in Axis IV, and the highest level of a patient's adaptive functioning during the past year in Axis V.

DSM-III, which was coordinated with ICD-9, was published in 1980. *DSM-III* introduced a number of important methodological innovations, including explicit diagnostic criteria, a multi-axial system and a descriptive approach that attempted to be neutral with respect to theories of etiology. Improving on consistency and clarity, the revised version of *DSM-III* was published as *DSM-III-R* in 1987. *DSM* represented a major advance in the diagnosis of mental disorders and greatly facilitated empirical research.

DSM-IV has benefited from the substantial increase in the research on diagnosis that was generated in part by *DSM-III* and *DSM-III-R*. The Task Force on DSM-IV and its working groups undertook comprehensive and sytematic reviews of the published literature, reanalyses of already-collected data sets and extensive issue-focused field trials. The last task compared *DSM-III*, *DSM-III-R*, ICD-10, and proposed *DSM-IV* criteria sets in five to ten different sites per field trial with approximately 100 subjects at each site. The 12 field trials included more than 70 sites and evaluated more than 6000 subjects. An attempt was made to strike an optimal balance in *DSM-IV* with respect to historical tradition (*DSM-III* and *DSM-III-R*) and compatibility with ICD-10. *DSM-IV* classification is organized on a dimensional model rather than the categorical model used in *DSM-III-R*. As such, the dimensional model classifies clinical presentations based on quantification of attributes rather than the assignment of categories and works best in describing phenomena that are distributed continuously and do not have clear boundaries.

Despite a constant improvement in diagnostic tools and skills, some questions of ambiguity still remain. The accuracy of any psychiatric diagnostic tool depends upon validity (i.e., a device that assesses what it is meant to measure) and reliability (i.e., repeated consistency as measured, for instance, by interjudge reliability). There has been a study that testifies to the merits and constantly improving reliability of the *DSM-III*, allowing professionals to produce interjudge reliability coefficients several times higher than those obtained by using *DSM-II* criteria.[91]

Such improvement in reliability notwithstanding, endemic and systemic problems of ambiguity and imprecision recur. It may be that the very problem lies in the fact that the modern classification system of diagnosis in mental illness originated in the medical model. For medicine itself is not an exact science but, at best, an art. This point was driven home by a recent study that compared the practice of medicine in Britain, France, Germany and the United States. It showed that at both macro and micro levels differences in national character, cultural values and professional responses to patients' problems are important determinants of medical care. The sanitation and living standards are just about the same in all these countries, and the citizens of these four countries are expected to live to the same respectable old age. Yet their physicians treat them in vastly different ways. The way physicians deal with patients and their ailments is largely determined by attitudes acquired from their cultural and national-historical heritage. Thus, American doctors, for instance, perform six times as many cardiac bypass operations per capita as English physicians do; an English patient would receive more anti-anginal drugs than an operation. Low blood pressure is rewarded with reduced life insurance rates in the United States, while in Germany it is treated as an ailment; an American suffering from prostate cancer would undergo major surgery, while a Frenchman would receive less invasive radiation therapy; in the United States a simple sinus condition often warrants a prescription for antibiotics, while Germans would not receive an antibiotic unless they were sick enough to be hospitalized; hysterectomies, performed infrequently in France, are the second most common major operation in the United States. Most disturbing of all, diagnosis may not always be uniform either.[92]

Similar problems confront psychiatric disorders as well. Before the mid-1960s, it was common knowledge in professional circles that basing diagnoses on the "clinical judgment" of psychiatrists was unreliable. The American schizophrenic might well have found his disease called manic-depressive disease or even neurosis if he sought a second opinion in Britain; in France he likely would have been diagnosed as having delusional psychosis. The Frenchman suffering from spasmophilia or the German from vasovegetative dystonia would be considered merely neurotic in Britain or perhaps a victim of panic disorder in the United States if he were considered sick at all.[93] One World Health Organization study found that doctors from different countries diagnosed different causes of death even when they were shown identical information from the same death certificates.[94] A psychiatric assessment and diagnosis can result in some patients being incarcerated. Yet when psychiatrists from six countries tried to agree on who was dangerous, the overall level of agreement was under 50% for three-quarters of the cases considered, and the psychiatrists did not agree any more among themselves than did non-psychiatrists.[95] Probably the best known experiment on the question of reliability of psychiatric assessment was that of Rosenhan.

Rosenhan asked his eight highly trained assistants with no previous history of mental illness to pose as "patients" and apply for admission to separate mental hospitals in different states in the United States. Using an alias, each assistant was instructed to provide an accurate personal history, with one important piece of false information—"hearing voices" when no one was there. This is a classic sign of schizophrenia, and all but one of the eight "pseudopatients" was diagnosed as schizophrenia and were subsequently admitted to the mental hospital. Upon their admission to the hospital, Rosenhan's assistants stopped mentioning about hearing voices and tried to act normally. They began to take notes about events inside the mental ward; and the staff of each hospital further diagnosed their "note-taking behaviour" as "disturbed." The irony was that the long-standing patients on the wards somehow believed that these "pseudopatients" did not belong there. It took these assistants from seven to 52 days to be discharged, with an average hospitalization of 19 days. From this experiment, Rosenhan argued that the diagnostic accuracy of the mental hospital was very low.[96]

Despite the claims of remarkable improvements in interjudge reliability, the subjective nature of assessment and diagnosis prevents the practice from achieving complete accuracy and reliability. Another study, for instance, compared Caucasian-American and Chinese-American therapists with regards to their conceptions of normality, empathic ability and their reactions to videotaped interviews of Caucasian and Chinese clients. Results indicated that even though both Caucasian- and Chinese-American therapist groups basically agreed in their perception of "normality," there were some differences observed. For instance, white therapists were more accurate in predicting self-descriptive responses of white clients than of Chinese clients. Besides, there were significant differences between ratings of the same clients given by white and Chinese-American therapists. Moreover, Chinese-American therapists judged the Caucasian clients to be more severely disturbed than did the white therapists. Such differences suggest a reflection of the therapists' perception of normality and empathic ability as seen by these two ethnically different groups of therapists. Moreover, this study reveals the very subjective nature of clinical judgment, which may be swayed by ethnicity, cultural values and perception as well as the mode of socialization of these ethnically different therapists.[97]

CONCLUSION

A review of some reputable studies cited in this chapter seems to give strong and compelling evidence of a correlation between some forms of pre-existing and diagnosable mental illness and suicide. One of the problems that stands out, however, is the wide range of such a relationship, with WHO estimates ranging between 20 to 94% worldwide, and between 50 to 90% in North America, and for Japan at most 33%. Even the highly respected report of the National Task Force on Suicide in Canada,for which the Canadian researchers received an award from the American Association of Suicidology, gives a conflicting figure: while generally admitting very high correlation, it also mentions that among suicide completers only 4% showed psychotic depression.

Another problem seems to be a persistent manifestation of cross-cultural variations in the type and content of mental illness, such as depressive disorders across cultures, the fact of which makes it impossible at this stage to draw any confident conclusion about the assumed relationship between mental illness and suicide. What has plagued the field of inquiry has been the acknowledged nature of diagnosis and assessment: by its very nature, psychiatric assessment has some distance to go before achieving any measure of accuracy and reliability. Such assessment *ipso facto* tends to be subjective and arbitrary and may lack the universal validity beyond cultural variations. Finally, the cross-cultural studies cited in this chapter raised the serious question of culture-bound aspects of psychiatric disorders such as depression.

What implications can one draw from the foregoing discussion? Some examples cited in the present chapter somehow reflect the caution of a medical anthropologist:[98]

> ...to be adequate, [psychiatric] phenomenology must begin not with professional categories but with universal [read cross-cultural] lay experience. When more than three-fourths of the world's population live

in non-Western cultures, and greater than 90 percent are unfamiliar with psychoanalytic and other clinical constructs, symptom phenomenologies to be valid must begin with core meanings and experiences that may seem alien to educated, middle-class Americans and Europeans but that have been normative for most of human history, including our own.

Notes and References

1   Gomes, T., unpublished report, Department of Social Work, York University, 1995.

2   Maris, R., *Pathways to Suicide: A Survey of Self-Destructive Behaviours* (Baltimore: Johns Hopkins University Press, 1981).

3   World Health Organization, *Changing Pattern in Suicide Behaviour* (Copenhagen: EURO Report and Study #74, 1982), p.2.

4   Adam, K., "Suicide and Attempted Suicide," *Medicine North America*, 1983: April, pp.3200-3207.

5   WHO, *op. cit.,* p.20.

6   Barraclough, B., Bunch, J., Nelson, B. and Sainsbury, P., "A Hundred Cases of Suicides: Clinical Aspects," *British Journal of Psychiatry*, 1974: 125, pp.355-373.

7   Lester, D., *Why People Kill Themselves: A 1990 Summary of Research Findings on Suicidal Behaviour* (Springfield, Illinois: Charles C. Thomas, 1992), pp.269-331.

8   Sakinofsky, I., Webster, G., "Risk Factors for Suicidality in the Community: The Ontario Health Survey," an internal paper, Clarke Institute of Psychiatry, Suicide Studies Programme, Toronto, Ontario, 1995.

9   Zisook, S., Goff, A., Shuchter, S., "Reported Suicidal Behaviour and Current Suicidal Ideation in a Psychiatric Outpatient Clinic," *Annals of Clinical Psychiatry*, 1994: March, Vol.6, 1, pp.27-31.

10 Beautrai, A., Joyce, P., Mulder, R.T., "The Canterbury Suicide Project: Aims, Overview and Progress," *Community Mental Health in New Zealand*, 1994: June, 8, 2, pp.32-39.

11 Lesage, A., Boyer, R., Grunberg, F., Vanier, C. et al., "Suicide and Mental Disorder: A Case-Control Study of Young Men," *American Journal of Psychiatry*, 1994: July, 151, 7, pp.1063-1068.

12 Sheiban, B., "Mental Illness and Suicide in Israel," *Medicine and Law*, 1993: 12-3-5, pp.445-465.

13 Henriksson, M., Aro, H., Marttunen, M., Heikkinen, M. et al., "Mental Disorders and Comorbidity in Suicide," *American Journal of Psychiatry*, 1993: June, 150: 6, pp.935-940.

14 Nordentoft, M. and Rubin, P., "Mental Illness and Social Integration among Suicide Attempters in Copenhagen: Comparison with the General Population and a Four-Year Follow-up Study of 100 Patients," *Acta Psychiatrica Scandinavica*, 1993: October, 88, 4, pp.278-285.

15 May, P., Van-Winkle, N., "Indian Adolescent Suicide: The Epidemiologic Picture in New Mexico," *American Indian and Alaska Native Mental Health Research*, 1994: 4, pp.5-34.

16 Schmidke, A., Bille-Brahe, U., Kerkhof, A., deLeo, D. et al., "The WHO/Euro Multicentre Project on Parasuicide: State of the Art," *Giornale Italiano de Suicidologia*, 1993: Oct., 3, 2, pp.83-95.

17 Barnes, R., "Suicide and Attempted Suicide," special presentation, Suicidology Seminar, York University, Toronto, March 7, 1989.

18 Roy, Alec, "Suicide in Chronic Schizophrenic Patients," *Canadian Journal of Psychiatry*, 1986: 31, pp.737-740.

19 Allebeck, P. and Allgulander, C., "Suicide among Young Men: Psychiatric Illness, Deviant Behaviour and Substance Abuse," *Acta Psychiatrica Scandinavica*, 1990: June, 81, 6, pp.565-570.

20 Ohara, K., *Nihonjin no Jisatsu* (Suicide of the Japanese), (Tokyo: Seishin Shobo Publishers, 1965), pp.147-156.

21 Inamura, H., *Jisatsugake* (Suicidology), (Tokyo: University of Tokyo Press, 1979).

22 Iwasaki, Y. and Kurosawa, H., "Consultation Liaison Psychiatry in a Critical Care Medical Centre," a special presentation, Crisis Intervention Unit, Department of Psychiatry, East General Hospital, Toronto, Ont., August 2, 1989.

23 Fusé, T., *Profiles of Death: Biographical Autopsies of Eleven Personalities* (Tokyo: Seishin Shobo Publishers, 1991).

24 *Suicide in Canada, National Task Force Report: An Update* (Ottawa: Ministry of Health and Welfare, 1994), p.27.

25 Sakinofsky, I. and Webster, G., "Risk Factors for Suicidology in the Community," *The O.H.S. Study*, (Toronto: Ontario, Clark Institute of Psychiatry, 1995).

26 *Suicide in Canada*, National Task Force, *op. cit.*, p.3.

27 *Ibid.*, p. 30.

28 Inamura, H., *Suicidology, op. cit.*, p.62.

29 Fujii, H., "Suicide as Observed by a Clinical Psychiatrist; Psychopathology of Suicide," Symposium of Japan Association of Insurance Medicine, *Insurance*, 1987: 2375, pp. 13-14.

30   *Ibid.*, p.14.

31   Ishii, K., "On the 'Myth' of Prevention Policies of Student Suicide," *Phoenix-Health*, 1984: 8, p.100.

32   *Ibid.*

33   *Diagnostic and Statistical Manual of Mental Disorders*, Fourth Revision, (Washington, D.C.: American Psychiatric Association, 1995), p.xxii.

34   Fusé, T., *Personal Crisis and Ethnotherapy* (Tokyo: Chuo Koronsha, Ltd., 1992), pp.74-81.

35   Endler, N., *Holiday of Darkness* (Toronto: Wally and Thompson, 1989), p.100.

36   *Diagnostic and Statistical Manual, op. cit.*

37   Lefkowitz, M.M. and Tesiny, E.P., "Depression in Children: Prevalence and Correlates," *Journal of Constitutional Clinical Psychology*, 1985: 53, pp.647-56.

38   Stewart, J.W., McGrath, P.J., Liebowitz, M.R., Harrison, W. and Quitkin, F., "Treatment Outcome Validations of DSM-III Depressive Subtypes: Clinical Usefulness in Outpatients with Mild to Moderate Depression," *Archives of General Psychiatry*, 1985: 42, pp.1148-1153.

39   Burns, D., *Feeling Good: The New Mood Therapy* (New York: Penguin Books, 1990).

40   Freud, S., "Mourning and Melancholia," originally published in 1917, in Strachy, J. (ed), *Complete and Psychological Works of Sigmund Freud* (London: Hogarth, 1957), Vol.14, p.246.

41   Abrahms, J.L., "Depression vs. Normal Grief Following the Death of a Significant Other," in Emery, G., Hollon, S. and Bedrosi, R., (eds), *New Directions in Cognitive Theory* (New York: Guilford Press, 1981).

42   Levinson, D., *The Seasons of a Man's Life* (New York: Knopf, 1978).

43   Boston Women's Health Collective, *Our Bodies, Ourselves* (New York: Simon and Schuster, 1976), p.330, quoted in "A Friend Indeed: for Women in the Prime of Life" (Montreal: A Friend Indeed Publications, 1988), Volume II, p.1.

44   Beck, A., *Depression: Causes and Treatment* (Philadelphia: University of Pennsylvania Press, 1967), cited in Carson, R.C., Butcher, J.N., Coleman, J.C., *Abnormal Psychology and Modern Life*, (Glenview, Ill.: Scott, Foresman and Co., 1988), p.298.

45   Paykel, E.S., "Life Events and Early Retirement," in Paykel, E.S., (ed), *Handbook of Affective Disorders*, (New York: Guilford Press, 1982).

46   Lewinsohn, P.M., "A Behavioural Approach to Depression," in Friedman, R.J. and Katz, M.M. (eds), *The Psychology of Depression: Contemporary Theory and Research* (New York: Holstead Press, 1974).

47   Endler, N., *Holiday of Darkness, op. cit.*, p.101.

48   Klein, D. and Seligman, M., "Reversal of Performance Deficits and Perceptual Deficits in Learned Helplessness and Depression," *Journal of Abnormal Psychology*, 1976: 85, pp.11-26.

49   Radloff, L., "Sex Differences in Depression: The Effects of Occupation and Marital Status," *Sex Roles*, 1975: 1, pp.249-265.

50   Frankl, V., *Man's Search for Meaning* (New York: Washington Square, 1963).

51   Beck, A., *Cognitive Therapy and Emotional Disorders* (New York: International Universities Press, 1976).

52   Simon, A.D., Murphy, G.E., Levine, J.L. and Wetzel, R.D., "Sustained Improvement One Year after Cognitive and/or Pharmacotherapy of Depression," *Archives of General Psychiatry*, 1985: 43, pp.43-48; Teasedale, J.D., Fennell, M.J.V., Hibbert, G.A. and Amies, P.L., "Cognitive Therapy for Major Depressive Disorder in Primary Care," *British Journal of Psychiatry*, 1984: 44, pp.400-406

53   Seligman et al., "Explanatory Style Change during Cognitive Therapy for Unipolar Depression," *Journal of Abnormal Psychology*, 1988: 97, pp.13-18.

54   Tsuang, M.T. and Vandermay, R., *Genes and the Mind* (Oxford: Oxford University Press, 1980); Gottesman, I.I., McGuffin, P. and Farmer, A.E., "Clinical Genetics as Clues to the 'Real' Genetics of Schizophrenia," *Schizophrenia Bulletin*, 1987: 13, pp.23-47.

55   Kallmann, F.J., *Heredity in Health and Mental Disorder* (New Norton, 1953); Kallmann, F.J., "The Genetic Theory of Schizophrenia," *American Journal of Psychiatry*, 1947: 103, pp.309-322.

56   Perris, C., "The Recent Perspectives in the Genetics of Affective Disorders," in Mendlewicz, J. and Shopsin, B., (eds), *Genetic Aspects of Affective Illness* (New York: S.P. Medical and Scientific, 1979); Mendlewicz, J., "Genetic Research in Depressive Disorders," in Bechham, E.E. and Leber, W.R., (eds), *Handbook of Depression: Treatment, Assessment and Research* (Homewood Ill.: Dorsey Press, 1985), pp.795-815.

57   Rosenthal, D., *Genetic Theory and Abnormal Behaviour* (New York: McGraw-Hill, 1970), p.285.

58   Gottesman, I.I., McGuffin, P. and Farmer, A.E., "Clinical Genetics.....", *op. cit.*, cited by Davison, G.C., and Neale, J.M., *Abnormal Psychology* (New York: John Wiley and Sons, 1990), Fifth Edition, p.387.

59   Wender, P.H. et al., "Psychiatric Disorders in the Biological and Adoptive Families of Adopted Individuals with Affective Disorders," *Archives of General Psychiatry*, 1986: 43, pp.923-929.

60   Marsella, A.J., "Depressive Experience and Disorder across Cultures," in H.C. Triandis and Draguns, J. (eds), *Handbook of Cross-Cultural Psychology*

(Vol.6), (Boston: Allyn and Bacon, 1980); Fusé, T., *Introduction to Suicidology in Cross-Cultural Perspective, op. cit.,* pp.173-195; Sougey, E.V., "Transcultural Aspects in Depression," *Brazilian Journal of Psychiatry,* 1992: May, 41, 4, pp.177-183.

[61] Kidson, M. and Jones, I., "Psychiatric Disorders among Aborigines of the Western Australian Desert," *Archives of General Psychiatry,* 1968: 19, pp.177-183.

[62] Ebert, D. and Martus, P., "Somatization as a Core Symptom of Melancholia Type Depression," *Journal of Affective Disorders,* 1994: 32, December, 4, pp.253-256.

[63] Kirmayer, L.J., "Culture and Psychiatric Epidemiology in Japanese Primary Care," *General Hospital Psychiatry,* 1993: July, 15, 4, pp.219-223.

[64] Bertschy, G., Viel, J.F., Ahui, R.G., "Depression in Benin: An Assessment Using Comprehensive Psychopathological Rating Scale and Principal Component Analysis," *Journal of Affective Disorders,* 1992: July, 25, 3, pp.173-180.

[65] For Nigeria, see: Leighton, A., Lambo, T., Hughes, C., Leighton, D., Murphy, J., Macklin, D., *Psychiatric Disorders among the Yoruba,* (Ithaca, N.Y.: Cornell University Press, 1963); for China, Tseng, W. and Hsu, J., "Chinese Culture, Personality Formation and Mental Illness," *International Journal of Social Psychiatry,* 1969: 16, pp.5-14, and Kleinman, A., *Social Origins of Distress and Disease: Depression, Neurasthenia and Pain in Modern China* (New Haven: Yale University Press, 1986).

[66] Tanaka-Matsumi, J., Marsella, A., "Cross-cultural Variations in the Phenomenological Experience of Depression: I. Word Association Studies," *Journal of Cross Cultural Psychology,* 1976: December, 7, 4, pp.379-396.

[67] Kleinman, A., *Social Origins of Distress and Disease: Depression, Neurasthenia and Pain in Modern China,* (New Haven: Yale University, 1985).

[68] Heisel, M. and Fusé, T., "A Cross-cultural Examination of College Student Suicide Ideation," unpublished paper, Department of Psychology, York University, 1996.

[69] Crittenden, K.S., Fujita, S.S., Bae, H., Lamug, C.B. et al., "A Cross-Cultural Study of Self-Report Depressive Symptoms Among College Students," *Journal of Cross-Cultural Psychology,* 1992: June, 23, 2, pp.163-178.

[70] Nakane, Y., Tsukahara, M., Michitsuji, S., "Characteristics of Depression in Japan: An Epidemiological Viewpoint," *Journal of Clinical Psychiatry,* 1994: 23, 1, pp.5-12.

[71] Sato, T. and Takeichi, M., "Lifetime Prevalence of Specific Psychiatric Disorders in a General Medicine Clinic," *General Hospital Psychiatry,* 1993: 15, pp.224-233.

72 Murphy, H., Wittkower, E. and Chance, N., "Cross-Cultural Inquiry into Symptomatology of Depression," *Transcultural Psychiatric Review*, 1964: 1, pp.5-21.

73 Satorius, N., Jablensky, A., Gulbinat, W. and Ernberg, G., "WHO Collaborative Study: Assessment of Depressive Disorder," *Psychological Medicine*, 1980: 10, pp.743-749; World Health Organization, *Depressive Disorders in Different Cultures* (Geneva: World Health Organization, 1983).

74 Takahashi, S. and Someya, T., "Some Specific Factors in Diagnosis of Depressive Disorders in Japan," *Clinical Psychiatry*, 1994: 23, 1, p.30.

75 Pfeiffer, W., "The Symptomatology of Depression Viewed Transculturally," *Transcultural Psychiatric Review*, 1968: 5, pp.121-123.

76 Binitie, A., "A Fact of Analytical Study of Depression Across Cultures—African and European,"*British Journal of Psychiatry*, 1975: 127, pp.559-563.

77 Headley, L.A., (ed), *Suicide in Asia and the Near East*, (Berkeley: University of California Press, 1984), pp.230-231.

78 *Ibid.*, p.234.

79 Fusé, T., *Suicide and Culture,* (Tokyo: Shinchosha Co., 1985).

80 Butcher, J.N. and Pancheri, P., *A Handbook of Cross-National MMPI Research* (Minneapolis: University of Minnesota Press, 1976).

81 Beiser, M.R., Benfari, C., Collomb, H. and Rand, J., "Measuring Psychoneurotic Behaviours in Cross-Cultural Surveys," *Journal of Nervous and Mental Disorders*, 1976: 163, pp.10-23.

82 Beiser, M.F., Cargo, M., Woodbury, M.A., "A Comparison of Psychiatric Disorder in Different Cultures: Depressive Typologies in Southeast Asian Refugees and Resident Canadians," *International Journal of Methods in Psychiatric Research*, 1994: October, 4, 3, pp.157-172.

83 Gupta, R., Singh, P., Verma, S., Garq, D., "Standardized Assessment of Depressive Disorders: A Replicated Study from Northern India," *Acta Psychiatrica Scandinavica*, 1991: October, 84, 4, pp.310-312.

84 Lesse, S., (ed), *Masked Depression* (New York: Jason Aronson, 1974).

85 *Crisis Intervention Manual* (Toronto: Crisis Intervention Unit, Department of Psychiatry, Toronto East General Hospital, 1990).

86 Weber, Max, *Economy and Society* (Berkeley: University of California Press, 1978), Vol.12.

87 Kleinman, A., "Neurasthenia and Depression: A Study of Somatization and Culture," *Medicine and Psychiatry*, 1982: 6, 2, pp.117-189.

88 Fusé, T., *Emotional Crisis and Ethnotherapy* (Tokyo: Chuo-Koronsha, 1992), pp.94-98.

[89] *National Task Force Report on Suicide in Canada, op. cit.,* p.24.

[90] Kraeplin, E., *Clinical Psychiatry* (New York: Macmillan, 1937), 6th edition, originally published in German in 1899.

[91] Spitzer, R.L. and Fleiss, J.S., "A Reanalysis of the Reliability of Psychiatric Diagnosis," *British Journal of Psychiatry*, 1974: 125, pp.341-347.

[92] Payner, L., *Medicine and Culture* (New York: Penguin Books, 1989).

[93] *Ibid.*, p. 25.

[94] WHO, "The Accuracy and Comparability of Death Statistics," *WHO Chronicle 21* (Geneva: World Health Organization, 1967).

[95] Harding, T.W. and Adserballe, H., "Assessments of Dangerousness: Observations in Six Countries: A Summary of Results from a WHO Coordinated Study," *International Journal of Law and Psychiatry*, 1983: 6, pp.391-98.

[96] Rosenhan, D.L., "On Being Sane in Insane Places," *Science*, 1973: 179, pp.250-258; Rosenhan, D.L., "The Contextual Nature of Psychiatric Diagnosis," *Journal of Abnormal Psychology*, 1975: 84, pp.442-452.

[97] Li-Repac, D., "Cultural Influences on Clinical Perception: A Comparison between Caucasian and Chinese-American Therapists," *Journal of Cross-Cultural Psychology*, 1980: September, 11, 3, pp.327-342.

[98] Kleinman, A., *Culture and Depression, op. cit.*, p.22.

CHAPTER 5

Continuities in Suicidology Research—
Seppuku as a Study in Suicide and Culture

INTRODUCTION

It is interesting to note that three well-known Japanese words pertain to martial activities: *judo, kamikaze* and *seppuku* (or *hara-kiri*). Furthermore, it is even more interesting to observe that the latter two refer specifically to *suicide*: *kamikaze* for *group* suicide and *seppuku* for an *individual* act of taking one's own life (with a few exceptions, as will be explained later).

The *kamikaze* style of self-destruction with explosives in one's own aircraft (which was devised by Lieutenant General Takijiro Ohnishi as a desperate attempt to slow down American advances toward Japan in the latter part of World War II) disappeared and "self-destructed" in postwar Japan.[1] Today the word "*kamikaze*," which originally meant "Divine Wind" in Japanese, refers to all sorts of suicidal attacks on a perceived enemy, fully bent on self-destruction but taking along the lives and *matériel* of the enemy. The only residue of this word in modern Japan is reserved almost exclusively for the world-renowned taxi drivers of Tokyo who seem to chill the spine of every foreigner visiting Japan for the first time. *Seppuku* likewise has ceased to be practised commonly by the Japanese in a ceremonial manner; yet, the method of self-harm by slitting one's belly still remains as one of the means of suicide even in contemporary Japan.[2]

Seppuku, ritual suicide by disembowelment in Japan, known in the West as *hara-kiri*, has been a popular theme in Japan's literature and theatre for years. It has been a time-honoured traditional form of suicide among the feudal samurai class as well as for many military officers in the twentieth century. There has been a propensity in the West to understand suicide behaviour in terms of psychological and psychiatric constructs and theories. One such tendency is, as has been discussed, a prevalent attitude and assumption associating any suicide behaviour with depression and other psychiatric disorders. As one prominent researcher in the field of culture and depression warns us, an adequate phenomenology of depression across cultures must begin not with professional and clinical categories but with universal and cross-cultural applicability. When more than 75% of the world population live in non-Western cultures, diagnostic classifications, in order to be cross-culturally valid, must begin with core meanings and experiences that may seem strange to educated, middle-class Euro-Americans but which have been normative for a large segment of humanity for centuries.[3] A study of *seppuku* casts some serious doubt on the validity and appropriateness of such psychopathological orientations as applied to non-Western cultures such as Japan.

Seppuku has been nurtured in Japan's socio-cultural tradition as one of the socially and culturally prescribed and positively sanctioned role-behaviours in hierarchical organizations, tightly-knit human groups and classes. *Seppuku* may have become extremely rare in contemporary Japan, but the type of suicide related to one's role-performance still continues today very much akin to the spirit and rationale of *seppuku*. Hence a study of *seppuku* helps in understanding better the unique cultural tradition and "aesthetics of death" in an otherwise highly technological and robust industrial society such as Japan. Ultimately, *seppuku* is one of the keys to appreciate the deep relationship between suicide and culture in Japan.

It is still remembered well that during World War II countless numbers of Japanese military officers and soldiers, and even some civilians, committed *seppuku* in Pacific islands in order to avoid the humiliation of capture by the advancing Americans as well as to offer an apology to His Imperial Majesty for having lost the battle. Moreover, immediately after the end of World War II in 1945, the serene outer ground of the Imperial Palace in Tokyo was dyed with the blood of many Japanese men and some women, both military and civilian, who ceremonially disembowelled themselves in tens and hundreds as an apology to the Emperor for having lost the war to the enemy. Then in 1970, the gory incident of Mishima's *seppuku* right after his failed coup attempt at the Self-Defense Forces Headquarters in Tokyo shocked the world, reviving the spectre of an old, Imperial Japan in a seemingly affluent and "Westernized" economic giant. The telecasting of the extremely popular *Shogun*, a ten-hour epic drama of seventeenth century Japan, captured an all-time high viewer rating. Some of the most enigmatic and fascinating aspects of the film were the episode of *seppuku* and the philosophy of death espoused by the Japanese in it. The powerful motives for committing *seppuku*—"saving one's honour," "making apologies" and "assuming one's moral (as opposed to legal) responsibility for one's own mistakes or one's superior or one's group"— still constitute some of the major reasons for suicide in contemporary Japan.

Origin of *Seppuku*

The first incident of *seppuku* was recorded in an episode in *Harima Fudoki* (*The Chronicle of Geography of Harima*) in 716 A.D. in which a young goddess allegedly committed suicide by disembowelment, reportedly out of jealousy and rage following a marital dispute with her god-husband. And according to legend, it is said there have been no fish with intestines in the near-by lake since then as the goddess disembowelled herself and threw the intestines into the lake in a fit of rage.[4] The second *seppuku*, a real historical incident, took place in 988 A.D., as recorded in *A Story of Ancient Matters, Volume II* (*Zoku-kojidan*) written in 1219. According to this account, Yasusuke Fujiwara, a well-heeled scion of a distinguished aristocratic family, turned to a life of robbery and murder. It was said that he was embittered by not having been recruited into the coveted court bureaucracy in Kyoto and subsequently chose the "profession" of robbery. One day, when he was at the house of a friend, he was surrounded by the police; realizing that there was no way out for an escape, he disembowelled himself and took out his intestines and threw them out, but he did not die immediately. He was taken to jail, where he died the following day.[5]

During the reign of the Emperor Kammu (737-805), the capital was moved from Nara to Kyoto and Japan enjoyed one of the great periods of cultural attainment and effervescence, elegance and refinement, largely due to the court nobility in Kyoto. They demonstrated their talent and competence in administration, statecraft and cultural pursuits, creating a distinct aristocratic culture. The rule of the aristocracy during this period was based on special claims of noble descent and the embellishment of culture from China. In contrast to such court nobility in Kyoto, Japan's military aristocracy emerged during the early part of the tenth century in response to the increasing decline of the police and military systems. The functions of local administration, land management and policing were combined as some minor local officials and members of influential provincial families took up arms. By the eleventh century, the samurai had begun to emerge as a separate and functional group, and by the twelfth century they were the dominant social-political-military group.

Following the ascendancy of the samurai, incidents of *seppuku* multiplied rapidly among the samurai as a way of showing their valour and honour, especially to escape the indignity of being captured alive by the enemy. It was observed more frequently among the Genji-clan samurai in the eastern region. One of the most famous *seppuku* incidents was the story of Tametomo Minamoto in the *Tale of Hogen*, one of the medieval military chronicles in Japan. Tametomo was exiled to Izu Island following defeat in an uprising known in Japanese history as the Hogen Incident in 1159. Soon thereafter, the Imperial Court sent more than 300 troops to capture and punish him. A fabled archer, he was reported to have sunk at least one ship with his arrows. He and his few retainers, however, were no match against the 300 men who came to arrest him. He thus retreated into his private room, stood against a pillar and began to disembowel himself, threw the intestines at the advancing enemy and expired at the age of 28. This is the first recorded case of *tachibara*, or "*seppuku* committed in a standing position." Prior to Tametomo's *seppuku*, his infant brother was captured and beheaded by the rival Heike Clan in 1156. Upon hearing the news, one of the retainers of the infant lord, Heita Naiki, rushed to the scene and committed *seppuku* with his infant lord's corpse in his hand. This is probably the first recorded incident of *oibara*, or a type of *seppuku* committed following the death of one's lord.[6]

Though the government was centred around the Emperor and the court nobility during the Nara and Heian periods, the reins of power now fell into the hands of the samurai with the advent of the Kamakura shogunate period (1192-1333). Upon eliminating the Heike Clan, Yoritomo Minamoto of the Genji Clan established the military shogunate at

Kamakura, marking the beginning of the 675-year-long military and feudal age in Japan, molding and nurturing the distinctly military values and ethos. One of the tragic sagas of this period was the *seppuku* of Yoritomo's younger brother, Yoshitsune. Despite his indisputable power, Yoritomo was becoming increasingly jealous and suspicious of his younger brother's alleged ambitions and threat as the latter had become an immensely popular folk hero of the period. Consumed with jealousy and mounting hatred, Yoritomo chased his brother away from the capital, drove him into hiding, sent troops to hunt him down and finally cornered him. Realizing this was the end, Yoshitsune committed *seppuku* with a sense of mortified chagrin, which came to be known as *munenbara*.[7]

The Hojo Clan came to power after the death of Yoritomo's second successor, further strengthening government by the samurai. During this period, there were attempts made by the Mongols to invade Japan. Incidents of *seppuku* reached one of their highest peaks during the battle with the invading Mongols. Many samurai committed *seppuku* in order to show their valour in face of the enemy, preserve their honour, escape from the indignity of being captured by the enemy and to assume responsibility for local defeats and tactical mistakes. From the Kamakura period on, the values and lifestyles of the samurai were firmly established in the military class, and *seppuku* took firm roots as a distinct military lifestyle of the samurai class. Deeply influenced by the philosophy of Zen and the Pure Land sect,[8] the samurai began to develop the samurai code of ethics, conduct and aesthetics, which together came to be known as *bushido* (the way of the warrior). *Seppuku* came to be considered a concrete expression in action of the spirit of *bushido*.

The reign of the Hojo Clan was characterized by a series of civil wars and dynastic plots involving the succession to the throne. In one of the fabled civil wars during this dual dynasty period (southern and northern dynasties), Kototoshi Sakurayama committed *seppuku* with 23 men after killing his wife and son first. Involved in this incident are two of the uniquely Japanese types of suicide: family suicide and group suicide. Also recorded is another group suicide in which Nakatoki Hojo committed self-disembowelment with 432 men under his command. Another collective *seppuku* was committed in 1328 by Masashige Kusunoki and his 72 surviving men following a decisive defeat. Later on, in 1347, his son, Masatsura Kusunoki, also committed *seppuku* with his men after a defeat. Upon witnessing the collective suicide of Masatsura and his men, a scout sent as a messenger committed *seppuku* himself out of sympathy for these comrades. This type of *seppuku*, committed for sympathy, came to be known as *gifuku*.

Another type of *seppuku*, a forced *seppuku* as a penalty for a serious crime committed by a samurai, was recorded for the first time in 1439. Mochiuji Ashikaga and his uncle were ordered to commit *seppuku* for their alleged conspiracy against the shogunate. Such penal *seppuku* became common later during the Tokugawa period. It was called *tsumebara*, or forced *seppuku*.[9]

Finally, Iyeyasu Tokugawa succeeded in unifying the country by establishing the strongest and longest lasting shogunate in Edo (or present-day Tokyo) in 1603. The Tokugawa period (1603-1868) ushered in an unprecedented period of national unity, uninterrupted peace and prosperity. The successive Tokugawa shoguns maintained a tight control over the entire nation. Before the Tokugawa period, *seppuku* was mainly a form of suicide among the samurai in the battlefield to demonstrate their courage in face of the enemy. But during the period of unprecedented peace lasting more than 250 years, even the conduct of the samurai and their *bushido* underwent some fundamental changes. Thus, *seppuku* began to be practiced in the context of certain political and administrative needs. During the Tokugawa period, the detailed ceremonial forms and rituals of *seppuku* were officially worked out in detail. Institutionalization, ritualization and standardization were completed. And now, *seppuku* also became a type of penalty for the samurai, who, as the privileged military class, had to be spared the indignity of ordinary punishment such as beheading, which was meted out for common criminals. Because the samurai were seldom put to death by court, they were given the privilege of committing *seppuku* for their serious offences rather than being executed like commoners. Ordered or forced *seppuku* came to be called "*ishi*" or "conferred death" under the criminal code.[10]

Prolonged peace in the Tokugawa era witnessed a type of *seppuku* called *junshi*—*seppuku* committed in order "to follow one's lord to the grave." In peacetime the samurai were deprived of occasions to show their military valour and loyalty to their lords so they felt the acute need of showing their sense of loyalty especially at the time of the death of their lords. Afraid that they might lose many capable men because of such practice, the Tokugawa shogunate strictly prohibited *junshi* among the samurai. But when Hidetada, successor to Iyeyasu, died, one of his high-ranking retainers committed *seppuku* (*oibara*); likewise, when the third shogun Iyemitsu passed away his death was followed by Kaganokami Hotta, the highest-ranking elder statesman. In other provinces it was reported that as many as 20 samurai followed their lords to the grave, and every province took secret pride in the number of such *junshi* as a visible badge of loyalty among its retainers.[11]

Probably the most famous incident of *seppuku* was that of the celebrated 47 ronin, exemplifying in the popular imagination the time-honoured Japanese values of valour, perseverance and selfless loyalty. The incident that led to this story took place in Edo in 1701, when Lord Asano, the feudal daimyo of Banshu Province and Akaho Castle, drew his sword and injured Lord Kira, the protocol officer at the shogunate Chiyoda Castle, on March 14, the Fourteenth Year of the Genroku period (1701). That was the day when the imperial court in Kyoto sent a special imperial envoy to the shogunate in Edo. The shogun was to receive the envoy and hand over his reply to the imperial court's earlier letter. Drawing one's sword inside the castle was strictly forbidden, was considered the most serious felony offence and was punishable by death. Subsequent inquiries revealed that Lord Asano was repeatedly humiliated and deliberately misinformed by Lord Kira about the protocol involving the reception of the imperial envoy, primarily because Asano did not send gifts as a bribe to Kira as had been expected. As a consequence of such a serious crime inside the castle, Lord Asano was ordered to commit *seppuku* by the shogunate, his feudal estate confiscated, his men dismissed and his family line discontinued. Such severe punishment was generally considered one-sided especially because nothing was done against Lord Kira who provoked Asano in the first place. Thereupon, 47 of his retainers pledged revenge for their Lord Asano. Thus, on December 14, 1702 (or the year Genroku 15), in the middle of the night, they finally took revenge for their lord by capturing and beheading their arch enemy. The incident was a sensation in Japan, arousing a massive popular sympathy from all strata of Japanese society for the courage, endurance and unswerving loyalty of these 47 ronin. After fierce and painful debates, the shogunate decided to uphold the existing criminal law and ordered these men to commit *seppuku* as a legal punishment for their crime of personal vendetta, which had officially been forbidden. Thus, on February 4, 1703, all the ronin, from a boy of 17 to the men in their late 60s, committed *seppuku* in a serene and dignified manner. The story of these loyal 47 samurai has been told and retold in Japan, providing a rich source of material for the theatre, movies and television dramas.[12]

Less dramatic but equally heart-rending is the story of fifty-three samurai who committed *seppuku* as a sign of legal-moral responsibility for a bungled job. In 1753-1754, Satsuma Province in southern Japan was ordered by the shogunate to undertake a flood control project. Satsuma had to underwrite 90% of the costs of the project as well as provide the necessary manpower, even though it was initially a shogunate project. The project was started in the Mino Plain covering the Kiso, Nagara and Seki rivers. When the project was not completed by the scheduled date, some Satsuma samurai committed *seppuku*—a type of *seppuku* called *inseki* or "*seppuku* for assuming responsibility." When the project was finally finished with much delay and an over-spent budget, more men committed *seppuku* as an official apology for and silent protest against the shogunate for imposing such an unreasonable project in the first place on their province. In all, 51 Satsuma samurai, one Mino samurai and one Tokugawa supervisor, a total of 53, died by self-disembowelment.

In terms of group *seppuku*, the story of the *Byakkotai* (White Tiger Squad) is almost as famous as that of the 47 ronin in the hearts and minds of the Japanese. On the eve of the Meiji restoration in the nineteenth century, some daimyo in the northern domains banded together and fought against the combined forces of Satsuma and Choshu (the two major daimyo domains that pushed the imperial Restoration by attacking the Tokugawa forces). Yet one by one these northern domains fell before the powerful combined forces of the Satsuma-Choshu domains with the Aizu-Wakamatsu Castle the only remaining symbol of resistance. Suffering from total fatigue and manpower attrition, the feudal domain of Aizu was forced to recruit teenagers aged 16 and 17. These young, eager and loyal teenage samurai were grouped into six squads of 40 each, or a total of a little over 200, which came to be called "White Tigers." On August 22, 1868, the Satsuma-Choshu forces encountered the White Tiger Squad and engaged them in a hand-to-hand pitched battle. Despite their valour and loyalty, however, the White Tigers were no match against the seasoned adult soldiers. Out of this battle, only 20 survived. Sixteen of them climbed a mountain in Aizu-Wakamatsu, bowed together towards their fallen castle and then committed collective *seppuku*. Shortly after this incident, the remaining four White Tigers straggled onto the mountain and, upon seeing the tragic sight, promptly joined their 16 comrades by slitting their bellies. Out of these 20, only one, Sadakichi Iinuma, survived because some surviving wives of the samurai from the castle happened to pass by and rescued him.

Finally, in the midst of chaos and confusion towards the end of the Tokugawa period, there happened one incident involving French sailors, which was instrumental in making *hara-kiri* a household word in all European languages. This incident took place in Sakai, near Osaka, in 1868 when 13 French sailors were injured by samurai when they tried to land without permission. France demanded a summary investigation and punishment for the culprits and the Japanese obliged by ordering twenty samurai to commit *seppuku*.

On the day of the *seppuku* ceremony, representatives of the shogunate and France were invited to witness the event. After an immaculate preparation, the samurai then went about disembowelling themselves, calmly and serenely, much to the astonishment and disgust of the foreign representatives present. By the time the first samurai, the squad leader, proceeded with his belly-slitting, the Frenchmen turned pale, begged to take leave, and left the scene immediately. Outside the compound, they vomited and ran back to the French battleship. Upon the departure of the French delegation, the *seppuku* ceremony was ordered stopped immediately, sparing the remaining nineteen samurai. After this incident, the word *hara-kiri* (or belly-slitting in Japanese) became a household word among Europeans, North Americans and all foreigners.[13] A typical *seppuku* ceremony, published in 1867 in Britain, illustrates the general set-up of the ceremony as shown in Figure 1.

The resignation of the last shogun began the colourful Meiji period (1868-1912) that transformed Japan into a modern nation. The country under the able Emperor Meiji (1852-1912) set out to accomplish the task of "catching up" with the advanced countries of the West. Importing Western knowledge and technology, the Meiji government initiated a series of reform and changes in Japan, one of which was the official abolition of *seppuku* in 1874. As one of the eloquent opponents of *seppuku* argued, "it is a practice unheard of in the civilized West, and it is also an obstacle to social justice. If someone wants to prove his innocence, he should do so at the court of law...."[14] Thus, in 1874, *seppuku* was officially removed from the list of penalties. After all, the retention of *seppuku* was meaningless now that the samurai class was officially abolished under the Meiji regime and the wearing of swords forbidden. Even though it was officially abolished, *seppuku* continued unofficially as an "honourable private act." For example, on October 24, 1876, more than 170 Shinto priests and ex-samurai committed group *seppuku* after losing a rebellion against the central government (known

Figure 1:   *Seppuku* Ceremony

Source: J.M.W. Silver, *Sketches of Japanese Manners and Customs* (London: Day & Son Ltd., 1867), by the courtesy of Professor D. Waterhouse, Department of East Asian Studies, University of Toronto.

as the Shinpuren Incident in Japan). Probably the most famous *seppuku* was that of Takamori Saigo, a legendary leader in Meiji Japan, who killed himself by *seppuku* after he lost the battle in a civil war against government troops in 1878. No less celebrated was the *junshi* (*oibara*) of General Maresuke Nogi, who committed *seppuku* together with his wife after the death of their benefactor, Emperor Meiji, under whom he served as a soldier.[15] As mentioned earlier, the war in the Pacific was full of *seppuku* incidents by the Japanese, both military and civilian. On August 22, 1945, ten super-patriots, including some women, committed *seppuku* at Atagoya in Tokyo; on the following day, 12 men and women followed suit by disembowelling themselves near the moat of the Imperial Palace; on August 25, 14 young men from an ultra-rightist organization called *Daitojuku* (Greater East Asia Academy) collectively committed *seppuku* as an apology to the Emperor. The romantic aura of *seppuku* was kept alive further by the quixotic *seppuku* of Yukio Mishima, a well-known writer and a rightist, after his botched *coup d'état* in 1970.

ITS TYPES AND METHODS

Seppuku may be classified into two large categories with many subtypes in terms of the presence or absence of the freedom of choice—whether it was a voluntary or forced act. The voluntary *seppuku* came to be called *jijin* or "self-inflicted death with one's own sword." The other kind was called *tsumebara* or "forced *seppuku*" and was a type of self-disembowelment forced on a samurai by the authorities regardless of his own wish or volition. In the first category of *seppuku*, *jijin* (voluntary, self-inflicted disembowelment), there are six basic subtypes. (See Figure 2)

The first subtype of *jijin* is called *jiketsu*, which literally means "self-determination," revealing one's own decision to die. It was a very common type of *seppuku* among the samurai following defeat in battle. Before the Tokugawa period this type of *seppuku* was most frequently committed by warriors and was recorded in military chronicles and historical documents as an example of samurai conduct to be emulated by all. Also, all *seppuku* committed by Japanese military officers during World War II were called *jiketsu* as well, being in the same spirit and tradition.

The next type, *inseki*, literally means "assuming one's responsibility" for mistakes, blunders, wrongdoings and military defeats. This type of *seppuku*, so common during feudal times, was committed by the samurai who was thought responsible by both himself and others for mistakes

Type	Motives	Body Position	Mode of Disembowelment
Jijin (voluntary self-destruction by disembowelment)			
1. *Jiketsu*	defeat in battle	1. *Tachibara* (*seppuku* committed while standing up)	1. *Ichimonji-bara*, single-line belly-slitting sideways
2. *Inseki*	assuming responsibility for mistakes		2. *Nimonji-bara*, double-line belly-slitting sideways
3. *Gisei*	to save one's own group	2. *Suwaribara* (*seppuku* committed while sitting)	3. *Sanmonji-bara*, three-line belly-slitting sideways
4. *Kanshi*	to protest against misconduct		4. *Jumonji-bara*, belly-slitting sideways and vertically
5. *Memboku*	to prove one's innocence		
6. *Junshi*			
a) *Sakibara*	to precede one's lord or someone else in death		
b) *Atobara*	to follow someone else shortly after or later		
c) *Oibara*	to follow someone else immediately after		
i) *Gibara*	committed because of *giri* (indebtedness to one's lord)		
ii) *Ronbara*	to save one's face		
iii) *Shobara*	for the future benefits of one's posterity		
Tsumebara (forced *seppuku* for punishment)			
1. *Munenbara*	mortified suicide for unfulfilled objectives		
2. *Funbara*	assuming responsibility legally and morally for someone else		
3. *Keishi*	legal punishment for crime		

Figure 2: Classification of *Seppuku*

and defeats as well as bungled jobs assigned to him. The samurai's superiors also committed this type of suicide to assume full responsibility for the failures of subordinates. The example given earlier of 53 samurai involved in a flood control project is a case in point. Another example is the aforementioned *seppuku* of military officers and ultra-rightist civilians who killed themselves in front of the Imperial Palace immediately after Japan's defeat in 1945 as an apology to the Emperor for having lost the war. It is to be remembered, as will be explained later, that the *inseki* or "assuming one's responsibility for one's own failures and for those of one's subordinates" has been a powerful motive for suicide in contemporary Japan as well.

Sacrifice *seppuku* is a type of self-disembowelment that took place frequently during the feudal wars. Some defeated generals or warlords offered to commit *seppuku* in front of the victorious enemy with a plea that their own families and men be spared as a result of their sacrifice. At times, however, a line of distinction between the aforementioned *inseki* and sacrifice *seppuku* is rather thin. For example, a head of a samurai household would commit *seppuku* as an apology to his lord for the wrongs committed by him or by a member of his family—*inseki*—as well as for the purpose of sparing his family from any further punishment—sacrifice.

The fourth subtype is called *kanshi*, usually committed as a remonstration or protest against the wrong and immoral conduct of one's lord. When a feudal lord or one's superior continued his wrongful conduct, his chief retainer would sometimes commit this type of *seppuku* in order to force the lord to rectify his misconduct.

Memboku refers to a type of *seppuku* committed when a samurai was wrongly and unfairly accused of a crime or misconduct of which he insisted he was innocent. It was committed, therefore, to prove one's innocence with death and save one's honour and "face." One's honour-saving and face-saving is the overriding motive in this subtype.

The sixth and one of the best known types of *seppuku* is called *junshi*. It was committed in order to follow the death of one's lord to the grave (to become a *shide no michizure* or a travelling companion for the lord on the journey to the next world). This type of *seppuku* became extremely common during the Tokugawa period, which had brought 250 years of unprecedented peace and tranquillity to Japan. In peacetime the samurai were deprived of opportunities to demonstrate their martial valour and loyalty to their lords in battle. Despite prohibitions by the shogunate against it, *junshi* was widely practised by the samurai. In *junshi*, there are some further subtypes in terms of the timing. *Sakibara*, meaning "*seppuku in advance*," takes place when a samurai anticipates his lord's death, either a natural death or a death by *seppuku*, so he proceeds with his own *seppuku* and dies, "preparing for the journey of death" of his lord. *Atobara* or "delayed *seppuku*" is committed not immediately after the lord's death but after some lapse of time. The *seppuku* of General Nogi and his wife on the day of the official funeral of the Emperor Meiji is a case in point. *Oibara* or "follow-up *seppuku*" occurs when a samurai follows his master immediately after his or her death. As such, *oibara* has three further subcategories in terms of different motives and intentions: *gibara*, a type of follow-up *seppuku* committed as an expression of one's deep sense of indebtedness to the deceased lord (i.e., *giri* to one's lord); *ronbara*, a type of follow-up *seppuku* committed because of the suicide of one's peers and colleagues who followed the death of the lord by committing *seppuku* themselves—it might be called a conformist *seppuku* in terms of maintaining one's social standing among the peers; *shobara*, literally means "commercial *seppuku*" or "calculating *seppuku*." It is a type of *oibara* that is calculated to bring future benefits to one's family by showing one's loyalty to the deceased lord. It is analogous to a type of suicide committed to bring life insurance benefits to one's surviving family members in today's society.

The second major group of *seppuku*, *tsumebara*, was forced on the samurai who were accused and convicted of certain legal and moral offences, and it became a common practice during the Tokugawa period. Because of their venerated position in society, the samurai class considered it the worst insult and indignity to be beheaded or executed by the authorities "like common criminals." In a rigid, caste-like society such as Tokugawa Japan, *seppuku* was granted as the last privilege to members of the aristocratic warrior class to preserve their honour. In this category of forced *seppuku* there are three subtypes in terms of the emotional reactions of the individual to the punishment. *Munenbara* is the first subtype in which *seppuku* was forced on a samurai on trumped-up charges or false accusations. The person who was forced to commit this type of *seppuku* dies with a profound sense of rancour, chagrin and mortification for not having been given a chance to refute the charges or accusations. The forced *seppuku* of the Lord Asano of the 47 ronin discussed earlier is a good example. The second type is called *funbara*, meaning "belly-slitting in rage," referring to *seppuku* in which a samurai dies with unrepentance and hateful spite. The third subtype, *keishi*, refers to *seppuku* meted out for the samurai as a penalty for proven legal and criminal offences. It is a just punishment for a crime and is given to a samurai as a formality and consideration to spare him the indignity and embarrassment of being beheaded. Typically, in *keishi*, a short *seppuku* sword would be placed on a little wooden stand in front of a samurai, or at times just a fan in lieu of the sword. The samurai picks up the sword or the fan on the wooden stand, and immediately his second would decapitate him with one masterly stroke. The foregoing discussion summarizes most of the types and subtypes of *seppuku* that emerged during the Tokugawa period as a result of institutionalization and ritualization.[16]

Of all types and forms of suicide, *seppuku* is considered to be one of the most painful. Since the lower abdomen has heavy muscle linings and thick fats, it is not easy even for the sharpest blade to pierce and slit across the belly. It is said that the deepest thrust of the sharpest blade could not reach more than seven centimetres deep. A samurai committing *seppuku* is expected to stab the left side of his abdomen first and then slit open and across to the right sideways. In the process he will also cut and slit the internal organs, thereby causing excruciating pain. Because of such pain, it was not uncommon for some men to faint shortly after the act of disemboweling. Without the timely intervention of the second to decapitate him, it takes usually hours before one finally expires, thereby prolonging the pain. Thus, *seppuku* requires a superhuman ability to bear pain as well as perseverance. It is certainly easy to understand, then, that this form of self-disembowelment had become a way of dying and a badge of personal valour for the proud warrior class in Japan.[17] Thus, the methods of disembowelment are classified in terms of the position (sitting or standing) and the number and manner of slitting the belly. The first and the most common method of disembowelment is called *ichimonji-bara* or single-stroke belly-slitting. In this method, one holds the sword in his right hand, thrusts the blade into the left side of the abdomen several centimetres below the rib cage and then cuts the belly sideways all the way to the right. He bleeds a great deal by the time he pulls the blade all the way to the right, and the blade usually pierces the duodenum but seldom does this piercing and slitting lead to immediate death. If he has no second to assist his death by prompt beheading, he may take the sword out of the abdomen and slash his throat or stab the heart in order to quicken the death. This single-line (*ichimonji*), sideways slitting of the belly was the most common form of *seppuku* among the samurai.

As for the variations of this method of *seppuku*, there are *nimonji-bara* (double-line *seppuku*), *sanmonji-bara*, (triple-line *seppuku*) etc. *Jumonji-bara*, on the other hand, refers to "cross-forming *seppuku*," in which one follows the aforementioned *ichimonji* (single-line) sideway slitting with another vertically cutting this time, thereby forming a cross. You slit the belly sideways and then bring the blade from the upper centre of the rib cage straight up to the throat or down to below the navel. Such "cross-*seppuku*" was rather common among many warriors in the battlefield. At times, both *ichimonji* and *jumonji seppuku* involved taking out one's intestines and other internal organs. It goes without saying that the *jumonji-bara* or the cross-*seppuku* required much greater fortitude and physical stamina to perform than some other methods. But the *jumonji-bara* had gone out of style by the beginning of the seventeenth century as *seppuku* became more and more institutionalized and ritualized in every detail, especially during the Tokugawa period. It became unnecessary to demonstrate this much strength as the introduction of the second spared any unnecessary agony and pain. As mentioned earlier, as soon as the blade pierced the belly and cut across, the second beheaded the samurai. In terms of the position, the type of *seppuku* committed while in the standing position came to be called *tachibara*. Likewise, when *seppuku* was done in a sitting position, as was the case in most *seppuku* outside the battlefield, it came to be called *suwaribara*. The former was the typical way of disembowelling in the battlefield, and the latter always in the *seppuku* ceremony during the Tokugawa period.

In terms of the ritualization and institutionalization of *seppuku*, one of the most important aspects of the *seppuku* ceremony is the emergence of the second, a skilled swordsman who beheads the man in order to spare him any further pain and agony and thus keeps any ugly sights from observers and witnesses. The selection of the second was arranged in compliance with the rank and status of the samurai committing *seppuku*. It was customary for a samurai, therefore, to choose and designate as a second someone renowned for his swordsmanship. It was common at the *seppuku* ceremony that a samurai about to commit *seppuku* and the second exchange a few words before the act and let each other know their names, status and the second's school of martial arts in which he had been trained. It had the effect of personalizing the relationship as well as giving meaning to the act itself and easing the possible anxiety and doubt. By the middle of the Tokugawa period it had become commonplace for the second to behead the man the moment he started stabbing his abdomen, with the aim of sparing him any prolonged and unnecessary pain.

As for the attire, the white kimono was preferred as the traditional and official "death robe." A samurai would sit in the yard for an *official seppuku* ceremony, but in a private ceremony, either in his own house or in the house of the official detainer, he would choose a room set off and detached from the rest of the house. A small sword with the blade of about 20 centimetres long was usually placed on a little wooden stand in front of him. Before committing *seppuku*, the samurai might want to read his last poem (called *"jisei"*) to his family, relatives, close friends or even his lord, might sip a cup of tea or saké for the last time and then prepare for the final act with calmness, serenity and dignity. He would thank the second for the trouble of assisting him in the ceremony, exchange a few words with the swordsman and ascertain the make of the sword used by the second. Finally he would take out a batch of white rice-paper tissue from inside his kimono, pick up the sword placed in front of him, wrap the blade with the tissue paper at least twenty-eight times but with the tip of the blade bared, take it in his right hand and stab his abdomen and bring it below the right-hand rib cage, and then slit the abdomen sideways. At this precise moment, the second standing right behind the samurai would bring his sword swiftly down and behead the man with a powerful single stroke. If *seppuku* had been committed privately in his own house or the detainer's, the samurai would usually ask his best friend or a relative to serve as the second. In an official ceremony in public places such as temple courtyards, as shown in Figure 1, there were always a number of witnesses including the relatives, friends, provincial representatives and official coroners. Then, finally, the disembowelment would be observed and examined by the government inspectors and officially so registered. The majority of *seppuku* were committed privately with only the second present.

It was previously mentioned that *seppuku* was often called *"ishi"* or the "honourable conferred death"—the death "conferred" upon the samurai by one's lord or the authorities as a special consideration for the samurai's aristocratic status and special standing in the community. As such, it was "conferred" on the samurai in lieu of the death penalty, which took the form of public beheading. If a samurai was convicted of a serious crime, he was usually met with the stripping of his samurai status and title, the confiscation of his swords (which were always considered the visible symbol of the samurai status as well as the spiritual symbol of the samurai's inner soul), either an exile or death penalty, the confiscation of the estate and, above all else, the abolition of the family name and title. In order to be spared such humiliation and disgrace, the samurai pleaded for and then obtained the privilege of the said "conferred death" in lieu of the death penalty. The ritual details of *seppuku* were clearly outlined in such samurai codes of conduct as the "Ceremony of Ill Luck" (*Kyorei* in Japanese) and in the "Protocol of *Seppuku*" (*Seppuku Mokuroku*), which was formally codified in 1759. It is said that many samurai were carrying at least one of these documents at all times in their kimono pockets. In the "Protocol of *Seppuku*," there are minute details about the manner, etiquette and requirements of *seppuku*, some of which are listed below for the benefit of the non-Japanese reader:[18]

> Specifications of the swords to be used for the ceremony
> Specifications of the attire
> Specifications of the hair-do and meals to be taken
> Specifications for official inspectors, seconds and custodians
> Specifications for the surviving family and relatives
> Specifications for the seconds (for beheading)
> Specifications for the attire of the seconds
> Specifications for changing the swords, if the need arises
> Specifications for attendants to the ceremony
> Specifications for the chief inspector (for the death certificate)
> Specifications for inspection of the decapitated head
> Specifications for storing the decapitated head
> Specifications for the temple site for *seppuku* ceremony
> Specifications for reception and send-off of inspectors
> Specifications for roping the corpse

According to available historical documents, the only samurai who refused the honour of such "conferred death" and willingly submitted himself to the indignity and humiliation of beheading was a celebrated Christian warrior, Yukinaga Konishi. After the defeat in the Battle of Sekigahara at the turn of the seventeenth century (the battle that transferred the political and military power exclusively to the Tokugawa family, ushering in the 250-year reign of the Tokugawa shogunate),

Konishi believed that being beheaded at the hand of the enemy would be infinitely preferable in terms of his Christian faith to an act of suicide, which in the eyes of Konishi *seppuku* certainly was.[19]

SEPPUKU: DEATH ORIENTATION, PHILOSOPHY AND AESTHETICS

Central to *seppuku* is a highly developed philosophy and aesthetics of death derived from and nurtured by Japan's traditional religious values and ethico-moral system such as *bushido* (or the Way of the Warrior), all of which reveal certain death orientation in the psyche of the Japanese in general and the samurai in particular.

The religious culture in Japan has always been positively oriented towards death: hence, suicide has neither been a mortal sin in religious teachings nor a crime in the legal concepts as has been the case in the West. Moreover, death orientation has been a powerful psychic force in Japanese consciousness for centuries. Over the centuries such death orientation in Japan's religio-moral values has been transformed into a powerful philosophy and aesthetics of death. As such it has played an important role in the development and institutionalization of *seppuku* as a ritual for the samurai as well as in the moulding of the attitudes of Japanese officers during World War II. Yet such a general orientation towards death has not been limited to the ancient samurai class or modern *kamikaze* pilots: it seems to lurk in the consciousness of the average Japanese in modern industrial Japan as well. According to one survey, for instance, 30-60% of Japanese in all walks of life have entertained the idea of committing suicide at least once; in another survey of high school students it was found that 39% of them had thought of committing suicide—suicide ideation—at least once, and 27% had a vague but occasional idea of committing suicide, whereas only 37% had never entertained such an idea. Another survey indicates that 39% had thought "it is no fun to be alive in this world" often, and another 50% said they had felt like that at one time or another.[20]

Another cross-ethnic and cross-cultural survey taken by a Western thanatologist echoes the same point. According to his survey, natural causes were chosen fewer times by the Japanese as the least tragic way to die—the Japanese 64%, blacks 76% and Anglo-Americans 87%—and many more Japanese picked suicide as the least tragic cause of death— the Japanese 26%, blacks 14% and Anglo-Americans only 7%.[21]

It was also mentioned earlier that *inseki* (assuming legal-moral responsibility for one's failure in performing and fulfilling one's job) was a powerful motive for committing *seppuku* in Japan. Suicide in modern Japan is at least partly motivated by such strongly felt sense of responsibility for failure to fulfil and perform one's job. Such an inordinate degree of obsession with one's performance in an assigned social role is called "role narcissism," and it may explain much of Japan's suicide behaviour including *seppuku*. Table 1 illustrates episodes of suicide in modern Japan that powerfully imply the continuation of the *inseki* motive in inducing some Japanese towards suicide as an apology for having failed in fulfilling the alleged mandate of the job. According to the theory of "role narcissism," suicide is a response to a sudden frustration about the continual need for social recognition resulting from a narcissistic preoccupation with the self in respect to status and social role. Many Japanese tend to become excessively involved with their social role, which has become the ultimate meaning in life. Such individuals are often vulnerable to social disturbances or personal mistakes and failures that may bring about a change in role definition, driving individuals to a major crisis, which in extreme cases leads to suicide.[22]

Central to such subjectively felt sense of responsibility is a strong moral sense of shame and guilt, separate from a legal sense, in the individual's own eyes as well as in the eyes of others. Such a mind-set, rather peculiar and unique to Japan, accounts for some suicides during and immediately following major political, economic and social scandals involving government officials, incumbents of political parties, executives and employees of major corporations. Table 1 is a partial compilation of major scandals that have rocked Japan since the end of World War II and the suicides that were committed by individuals involved either directly or indirectly.

In North America, if not in Europe, there has been a definite separation between legal and moral responsibility for the individual. In the face of any infraction of the law, therefore, one is primarily concerned, if convicted, with fulfilling one's legal responsibilities and obligations—restitution and/or serving time in prison. Once legal obligations are fulfilled, however, one is released from any legal debts to society: one is a free citizen again able to get on with life. It is remarkable indeed to watch, for example, the presidential pardon and eventual rehabilitation of Richard Nixon and other Watergate culprits once their legal responsibilities were fulfilled by serving time in jail (except Nixon, who did not even serve any time in jail). For the Japanese, however, legal and moral responsibility have usually been fused and not separated in the eyes of the ego, the public and society. Mere fulfilment of legal obligations, therefore, does not automatically lead to moral exoneration. Hence, legal and financial compensation to the surviving families of the crash victims on the part of Japan Air Lines was a fulfilment of legal but not moral responsibility in the form of an apology to the surviving families and to the deceased. Hence, one of the executives for customer relations took his own life as an apology for the anguish and suffering caused by the plane crash of 1985, the worst in Japan's aviation history. His suicide was followed by a vice president in charge of maintenance and repairs because it was disclosed that the particular aircraft involved in the crash was not properly repaired. A litany of such *inseki* suicide presents other similar cases as enumerated in Table 1, suggesting the powerful mechanism of the fusion of moral and legal responsibility in Japan.

Japanese dedication to one's group is a widely known and legendary trait that requires no explanation. The welfare, integrity, survival and continuity of the group to which one belongs have been considered *sine qua non* in Japanese social values and behaviour. When an aspersion is cast on the reputation of the group, or the very survival of the group is threatened, it has been common in Japan to produce a sacrificial lamb— another legacy of a *seppuku* suicide in which the lord sacrificed his life by slitting his belly in front of his victorious enemy in order to save his own men and their families. Such an extraordinary premium placed on the importance of the group in Japan's social system and value structure has been one of the major reasons for altruistic suicide throughout Japan's history. It has often been common in Japan for some individuals to commit "sacrificial suicide" in order to save the reputation and continuity of their group, especially in times of major scandals.

How does one understand such a powerful orientation towards death, especially as revealed in *seppuku*? A useful tool in understanding Japan's suicide behaviour comes from the role theory mentioned earlier—"role narcissism"—but also from the social action theory discussed in the previous chapter, which may assist the reader to better understand Japan's religio-moral values deeply embedded in Buddhism, *bushido* and the aesthetics of death.

Thus, an appreciation of the concept of life and death and their meaning to the samurai is an important clue to understanding the inner psyche and attitudes of the Japanese in general. Much of one's social behaviour is underlined by a set of cultural symbols and ethico-moral

Table 1:	Scandal and *Inseki* Suicide in Postwar Japan: A Partial List

Scandal	Suicide
1. Shipbuilding industry scandal (March–April 1954)	A ministry of transportation official (age 42) jumps off a building
2. Zen-koren (Consumer Association) scandal (April 1957)	An association official commits suicide by overdose (age 53)
3. Defence Ministry scandal of leaked classified information (March 1968)	A high-ranking officer commits suicide by drowning (age 53)
4. Nittsu Co. transportation industry scandal (April 1968)	A manager at its Saitama branch office jumps off the building (age 47)
5. Ministry of Post, Tokyo branch scandal (October 1968)	The president of an electric company involved in the scandal jumps onto the tracks (age 53)
6. A pharmaceutical company scandal (March 1969)	A Ministry of Health official jumps off a building (age 49)
7. Osaka Board of Education scandal (April 1974)	Superintendent of Board jumps off a building (age 56)
8. Agricultural cooperative scandal (April 1974)	An official jumps off a building (age 59)
9. Gifu Perfecture Water Resources Development Corporation scandal (September 1975)	An official hangs himself (age 49)
10. Lockheed scandal (August 1976)	Private secretary for Prime Minister dies by carbon monoxide poisoning in his own vehicle (age 42)
11. Tax evasion scandal, Ito-Chu Trading Co. (May 1977)	An official in charge of tuna import dies by drug overdose (age 42)

12. City of Kawasaki water pollution scandal (November 1977)	A sewage construction official dies by jumping off a building (age 51); his wife follows him by drowning (age 40); president of a construction firm jumps off a building (age 47)
13. Yamagata Perfecture school construction scandal (June 1978)	A municipal official hangs himself (age 50)
14. Nissho-Iwai trading firm aircraft scandal (February 1978)	A Nissho-Iwai executive jumps off a building (age 56)
15. Nikko Stock & Share Co., scandal (February 1979)	An official hangs himself (age 53)
16. Daiko-Sogin Bank loan scandal (June 1979)	An executive hangs himself (age 49)
17. Tokyo Sewage Office scandal (July 1979)	An official hangs himself (age 43)
18. KDD (telephone-telegram) smuggling scandal (January 1980)	The secretary to the president hangs himself (age 39)
19. Waseda University examination leak (April 1980)	Administrative vice-president hangs himself (age 50)
20. KDD smuggling scandal (February 1980)	Corporation counsel jumps onto tracks (age 62)
21. Osaka Metro Police pinball machine scandal (November 1982)	Superintendent of police (age 52) and police academy principal (age 50) both commit suicide
22. (In the above scandal) (November 1982)	A police sergeant shoots himself (age 35) avowing his innocence

Table 1:	Scandal and *Inseki* Suicide in Postwar Japan: A Partial List
23. School bus accident (September 1985)	Driver of the bus hangs himself (age 45)
24. Japan Air Lines crash near Mt. Fuji (September 1985)	Customer relations executive (age 52) and director of maintenance (age 59) commit suicide
25. Hyogo Prefectural Police failure to capture "Masquerade" bandit (August 1985)	Police superintendent (age 55) shoots himself on his last day of duty as an apology
26. Recruit scandal (April 1988)	Secretary to Prime Minister hangs himself (age 58)

Source: For items 1 through 20, from: Fusé, Toyomasa, *Suicide and Culture, op. cit.*, pp.208-210. The rest, 21-26, were culled from newspaper accounts. Dates indicate the time of suicide, not the occurrence of the scandal or incident.

values that properly interpret and give social meanings to human behaviour. Religio-moral values have always given structure, meaning and purpose to human existence in any culture.

A perusal of Japan's history indicates that the emergence and ascendancy of Buddhism and the development of a warrior code of ethics, *bushido*, had fundamentally altered the *Weltanschauung* of the Japanese. The Japanese philosophy of life began to be replaced by a powerful affirmation of death following the introduction of Buddhism. Likewise, *bushido* had also injected a new twist into the philosophy of life and death—the meaning of life was to be understood in terms of one's ability to find the right time and place to die. As a matter of fact, *Hagakure*, a book generally considered to be the bible for the samurai, unequivocally stated that the Way of the Warrior (*bushido*) is to die.[23]

Such strong death orientation, however, was a radical contrast to the traditional concept of life in Japan prior to the introduction of Buddhism in the seventh century. One of the characteristics of the pre-Buddhist philosophy of life and death, as revealed in *Kojiki* (*Records of*

Ancient Matters), *Nihon Shoki* (*Chronicle of Ancient Japan*) and *Manyoshu* (*Myriad Leaves*), was a powerful affirmation of life and this-worldliness, with emphasis on the importance of human sentiments and emotions, positive appreciation of sensual pleasures and aesthetic immersion in nature.

In Japan's early mythology, as chronicled in *Kojiki* and *Nihon Shoki*, the after-life was always referred to as *yomi no kuni* (or, a dark defiled world). In sharp contrast to this dark defiled world was the "heavenly high mountain" of *Takamagahara*—an equivalent of Paradise in Christianity and the Pure Land in the later Jodo sect of Buddhism where ancient Japanese gods had allegedly resided and reigned over the country. It is fascinating to note that "Heavenly Abode" or *Takamagahara* was considered by the ancient Japanese as coterminous with the world of humans, thus within the reach of human efforts and capacity. Such this-worldliness and affirmation of life were best reflected in the following poems from *Manyoshu*, an anthology of ancient Japanese poems:[24]

> So pleasant is this worldly life
> that I'd rather be born
> even as a bird or worm
> and come back to this world
> > (by Otomo no Tabito)

> All living things are to die
> so one must enjoy this life fully
> while being alive
> > (by the same author)

Such this-worldly affirmation of life is in sharp contrast to the Jewish poems in the Old Testament characterized by lamentation on collective human suffering, hardships and socio-political persecution, and an anticipation of the saviour and the better world to come. Such themes of lament and sorrow are absent in such Japanese writings as *Manyoshu* in pre-Buddhist times. Instead, throughout this anthology one finds expressions of natural human sentiments and emotions such as strong longing for loved ones, an appreciation of nature and its glory, full enjoyment of life, heart pains of separation from the dear ones, agonies and the bitter-sweet fragrance of love.[25]

Buddhism, introduced to Japan in the sixth century, gradually replaced life-affirming and this-worldly orientations with a more pessimistic and other-worldly orientation. Central to the core teachings of Buddhism is the belief that human existence in this "floating," ephemeral world is characterized by incessant suffering and that life is transitory and impermanent; to believe otherwise is the very cause of human illusion, ignorance and suffering. Clinging to and craving for life and longevity, therefore, is the essence of human illusion on earth and the very source of continuous human suffering. Thus, abnegation of life and the extinction of the illusory Self is one of the first steps towards enlightenment and Nirvana or the ultimate liberation.[26] In the early Buddhist scriptures human existence was interpreted in terms of its ultimate termination in death. Thus, "the starting point of Buddhism is death. All doctrines in Buddhism are derived from this inevitable fact of death in human existence...."[27] The ancient value system of Japan and its Shintoism (i.e., Japan's pre-Buddhist, native faith centred around shamanistic and animistic beliefs and the divine origin of the Japanese people and the Japanese archipelago) was geared to life-affirmation, whereas Buddhism is centred around abnegation of life and death-affirmation. One still finds the carry-over of such world views in the religious orientation of the Japanese today: the Japanese invite Shinto priests for ground-breaking ceremonies, weddings and anniversaries, whereas they conduct their funeral and memorial services in Buddhist temples.

The other-worldly orientation in Buddhism gained momentum in Japan when a noted Japanese monk E-on returned from China in 640 A.D. after 30 years studying Buddhism in China. Upon his return to Japan, he gave a series of lectures at the Imperial Court and introduced a rather pessimistic and other-worldly theology known as *Jodo-shu* (Pure Land sect). It did not gain much popularity at the time because Buddhism itself was accepted in Japan at that time in a this-worldly context, clearly a misunderstanding by the Japanese who had not been accustomed to such other-worldly orientations in their indigenous religious life. Thus the so-called Buddhist converts of the day prayed for one's health, long life and for security of the country, much in the same way as they practised their Shinto faith.

In the Heian period (794-1185) an important Buddhist priest by the name of Genshin (982-1017) emerged in Japan who transformed Buddhism from a religion of the rich and the nobility into a faith of the masses by teaching the way to salvation through recitation of a sutra. It is important to note that Genshin separated life on earth from life after death. He taught that this world would be abhorred as impure and defiled and that one must seek the Pure Land instead in one's afterlife. In addition to the concept of *onri edo* ("wish to leave this defiled world"), Pure Land Buddhism also introduced such concepts as *gongu jodo* ("wish for the Pure Land") and *shashin ohjo* ("attainment of salvation by throwing one's life away"). Such concepts were certainly conducive to encouraging suicide, certainly by default if not by design. For example, the concept of *shashin ohjo* drove many nuns to commit suicide in order to leave this defiled world of suffering and seek comfort and salvation in the Pure Land. As recorded in the Yoro Edict, some nuns resorted to self-immolation and other forms of suicide. According to another document, some 30 Buddhists committed such religiously motivated suicide on August 15, in the latter part of the Heian period, followed by eight others on August 16, and more again on August 17.[28]

Thus some zealots found an encouragement and invitation for departing from this defiled world for a better one. It is reported, however, that Honen, the official founder of the Pure Land sect, strictly forbade any form of suicide, including *seppuku*, as antithetical to his teaching.[29] But it cannot be denied that the latent function of such a teaching was a tacit and unwitting encouragement of suicide reinforced by an extremely pessimistic view of life on earth. Thus, since the founding of the Pure Land sect, there had been a rash of religiously motivated suicide such as self-immolation, self-drowning, fasting to death and even *seppuku* by some samurai who disembowelled themselves while chanting a sutra, "*Nam Amida Butsu*" ("Oh, Hail Lord Buddha, Have Mercy Upon Me"). One example is the story of Miura Takanori who, facing West towards the seat of the Great Buddha, committed *seppuku* with his men. They all kept chanting the sutra in order to be received by the Lord Buddha sitting on the lotus flowers in Pure Land.[30]

The Pure Land sect may have been responsible for other forms of religiously motivated suicide as well. *Hodaraku tokai* ("self-drowning in the sea") was associated with a subset of the Pure Land faith that worshipped Kannon (Goddess of Mercy). According to its beliefs, there was a Pure Land across the sea called Hodaraku Mountain. Reportedly 20 suicides were committed in order to reach the Pure Land of the Hodaraku Mountain. Another recorded type of religiously motivated suicide is *dochu nyujo*. A group of Buddhists developed the concept of *miroku* or "saviour"—a Buddha who would come to the world in about five billion years as a saviour in order to save those who were left out of the bliss of Nirvana. The *miroku* Buddha (saviour) was supposed to be training in the Pure Land but would one day make his advent out of his compassion for this world of suffering. Thus, some religious zealots voluntarily and willingly mummified themselves so that they could encounter the advent of *miroku* when the time came.

From the Kamakura period, the samurai had come under the powerful influence of Zen Buddhism and its aesthetic philosophy, which preached the importance of transcending life and death. The importance of such transcendence was constantly stressed in the teachings of Zen Buddhism, as is evident in the following quote by one of the great ancient masters:[31]

> It is fallacious to think that you simply move from birth to death. Birth from the Buddhist point of view is a temporary point between the preceding and the succeeding; hence it can be called birthlessness. The same holds for death and deathlessness. In life there is nothing more than life, in death nothing more than death; we are born and are dying at every moment.

Such philosophy was quite welcome to the samurai who faced death constantly in the battlefield. Zen's emphasis on transcendence over life and death was instrumental in preparing the samurai for battle and death as well as providing a powerful psychological framework for death orientation. Zen was enthusiastically espoused by the warrior class and was later helpful in developing the Way of the Warrior or *bushido*, in which death was not only affirmed but elevated to an absolute aesthetic experience and ideal.

There are two other theological concepts in Buddhism that have contributed to the formation of the philosophy of death in Japan. One, *mujo*, asserts nothing is permanent in life; hence one must escape from the preoccupation with prolonging life or avoiding death. Man must transcend illusion, which is one of the major causes of human suffering and tribulation. One of the ways to reach Nirvana or "ultimate enlightenment" is to be liberated from such preoccupations through transcendence over life and death. The other concept is the belief of three cycles of life or "three generations of life," and this belief was enthusiastically espoused by the samurai class. Originally this referred to past life, present life and future life, constituting three life cycles with a belief in reincarnation and incessant rebirth (*rinne tensho*) until one attains the ultimate liberation from the karma of birth-death-rebirth. But this belief went through some transmutation from the thirteenth century: it eventually came to mean the relative strength of human bonds and relationships in three types of bonding and their duration—the relationship between parents and children was believed to last just one generation, that of a couple for two generations, but the relationship between the lord and the samurai vassal lasted for three generations. In such transformation of the original concept, the samurai came to believe that the relationship between the lord and the samurai vassal was the deepest, strongest and the longest human bond. Bolstered by a belief in reincarnation, the samurai believed that the lord-vassal bond was so strong that following a samurai's death he would be reincarnated as a samurai to serve the same lord all over again. In such thinking, then, death was robbed of its finality and sting because the samurai involved would be born again to serve the lord and renew the bond.[32] In the philosophy of the samurai, feudal bonding and political values were placed above familial values.[33]

Discussion

The previous discussion explains the development of the Japanese philosophy of death nurtured over the centuries in the matrix of Japan's Buddhism, its derivative *bushido* and other related values. This philosophy constituted the very basis of Japan's time-honoured tradition of ritual self-disembowelment, *seppuku*. Transcendence over life and death in the performance of one's duty and honour to the lord had become a *sine qua non* for the samurai and the Japanese soldier. This powerful death orientation among the Japanese was closely related to one's loyalty to one's superior, country and one's honour. Preservation of one's honour had become (and still is) more important than the preservation of one's life.

This powerful death orientation was not limited to fighting men only: countless Japanese civilians—men, women and children—also committed suicide in the South Pacific in World War II for example. In face of the overwhelming American forces, the Japanese garrisons in Saipan faced a grim choice: surrender or death. On July 6, 1945, Lieutenant-General Nagumo, commander of the island's naval forces, and Lieutenant-General Saito, commander of the island forces, committed *seppuku*. Before taking his life, however, Nagumo had given those under his command the following instructions: "Remaining at a standstill means death, and advancing means death as well.... Let us strike a blow at the enemy and die on Saipan so that it will become a breakwater in the Pacific."[34] Thus on July 7 and 8, 1945, Japanese soldiers and 25,000 civilians made a last ditch charge against the enemy. In the end, most of the civilians killed themselves by detonating hand grenades or by jumping into the sea from high cliffs. According to an American correspondent, one father drowned himself in the sea with his three children in his arms; a group of women who had been calmly combing their hair on the same cliff suddenly jumped off into the sea; and 20 to 30 Japanese, including small children, were throwing hand grenades at each other as if they were warming up for a baseball game. In other words, the civilians on Saipan were also following the Field Service Code of the Japanese Imperial Armed Forces, which demanded, "never live to be humiliated as a prisoner of war." This tragic type of suicide recurred in many Pacific islands throughout World War II.

That such a philosophy of death did not die with the demise of Imperial Japan became clear on November 25, 1970, when Yukio Mishima, an extremely talented and admired young writer of Japan, stunned the world with his *seppuku* suicide. On that fateful day, Mishima and his trusted lieutenants stormed into the headquarters of Japan's self-defence forces and tried to stir up the soldiers into a planned *coup d'état*. Realizing that there was no response to his urgent plea for action but only jeers, he committed *seppuku*. The incident stunned Japan and the world. Mishima gave these reasons for his *seppuku*: he believed that the Japanese soul has been lost by the spirit of consumer society and that the old warrior values of *bushido* must be revived in order to give life and vitality to a moribund Japan. He felt compelled to demonstrate to the entire Japanese nation that there is a value far superior to merely preserving one's life. What is important is the quality and meaning of life rather than a mere existence devoid of meaning. When you are willing to die for a worthy cause, life acquires such quality and meaning.[35]

Mishima dealt with the Buddhist theme of reincarnation in his last novels and plays. When he stormed into army headquarters in Tokyo with his men, Mishima wore a headband that read "*shichisho hokoku*" (or, "to serve the country and the emperor by being reborn seven times over"). The philosophy and aesthetics of death will thus continue to live in the deep inner recess of the Japanese psyche for years to come. Mishima's *seppuku* aroused a massive sympathy among the Japanese, revealing the general admiration for his stated motives and action.

The Japanese seem to believe that even the philosophy of *seppuku* is an act in the affirmation of life. The Japanese would not see anything "aesthetic" in dying of the natural aging process, which involves a loss of memory, senility, infantilism, loss of motor coordination, pervasive body decay, debilitating diseases, absence of consciousness and, worst of all, possible continuation of life in a vegetative state with a life-support system. In natural decay and death caused by aging, death will befall the individual regardless; one is the passive and helpless victim of nature's whim. But voluntary, self-inflicted death such as *seppuku* involves elaborate planning as well as psycho-aesthetic preparedness, serenity and presence of mind. In *seppuku* death has a definite meaning as an existential response to a situation. In such a case, then, the individual who commits *seppuku* is the active agent for his own life and death: the person holds total mastery over life and death. In other words, with the exception of *keishi* (forced *seppuku* for a criminal offence), the individual is fully in control in *seppuku*. Unlike natural death in which one is a powerless and passive victim of nature, in *seppuku* the individual is the active agent and master of one's fate who will decide death before one's time. In other words, it is not God's will, fate or the inevitability of aging—agents other than one's own self—that will bring death; it is rather the individual who will hasten or bring about the termination of his or her own life. This is, to some Japanese like the samurai, one of the most powerful ways of affirming one's life. But such an idea is no longer alien to the Western world either as the recent ongoing debate in Euro-American societies on the right to die and dying with dignity movements attests.

Bushido would prefer a life, even if very short, full of meaning to a long vegetative life devoid of quality, dignity, purpose and meaning. The Japanese call it "*ikigai*" or "life worth living for," or "the meaning of life." The following poem by one of Japan's great scholars of the Tokugawa period, Moto-ori Norinaga, best illustrates the point:

> If asked what is the inner soul of Japan
> I will not hesitate to answer
> that it can be found in the cherry blossoms
> fragrant and glistening in the sun

The cherry blossom has long been loved and admired by the Japanese for its beauty, which symbolizes purity, simplicity and innocence. But there is one more attribute of the cherry blossom that has endeared itself to the Japanese: the beauty of the cherry blossom exists for only a short time. When in full bloom, the blossoms are gorgeous, beautiful and fragrant; yet within a week they will fall off and perish. In consideration of this, the Japanese government network, NHK, announces the exact dates of blossoming over the radio and T.V. Cherry-blossom-viewing parties are a national custom, with drinks, box lunches and the recitation of haiku poems. The Japanese pay such extraordinary attention to the cherry blossoms simply because their beauty lasts for only a short while. They love them because in their "fullness of time" they show their very best and they "die," without regrets, rather quickly while being admired and loved for their aesthetic quality. This existentialist orientation has always been a part of the Japanese philosophy and is also compatible with the philosophy of *seppuku*. An infirmed old age is an anathema to many Japanese.

For the Japanese, death does not mean total and complete departure from loved ones in this world. In terms of Buddhist beliefs and practices, the deceased soul is believed to linger on and stay with loved ones for 49 days. Death cannot rob the Japanese of their legendary solidarity and cohesion. The deceased soul will continue to protect the well-being and safety of the surviving members of the family and partake of the daily meals and refreshments offered them in the Buddhist altar, symbolizing the continuous communion between the deceased and survivors. Some Buddhist folk customs commemorate the deceased and renew the communion and fellowship between the living and the dead. The Bon Festival in August, for example, commemorates the annual visit of the deceased to the surviving family. The surviving family members pay a visit to the cemetery and welcome the annual visit of the deceased, bring the deceased home with them, prepare a family dinner and share it with the visiting deceased souls. At the end of the Bon Festival, the deceased is taken to the river and sent back to the other side (*"higan"*). More often than not, the annual reunion between the living and the dead is a festive occasion and one of the most memorable folk customs still practiced, indicating a belief in continuity and the link between life and death.

Buddhism regards this world as ephemeral and a mere way station in the quest to perfecting one's soul through incessant rebirth. Life is perceived as a constant process towards eventual merger with the larger spirit of the cosmos. In this sort of religious philosophy, the earthly life of tribulation and suffering is merely a passing stage to the final and ultimate Nirvana of self-extinction (*gedatsu*). Death is recognized as an ever-present reality in life and ultimately as a release not as a "robber" of life. To the typical Buddhist death is an event at the end of life and is as natural as birth. Death is the ultimate goal in life's temporary journey. In Buddhism it is believed that there is no single permanent unchanging entity or substance which constitutes the self or the soul that endures in a uniform state from lifetime to lifetime. The human self, therefore, is composed of a stream of consciousness, changing from moment to moment, filled with impressions and tendencies created by good and evil actions (Karma), which at death is transformed into a new mode of being, while the imagined and illusory "self" does not survive from one moment to the next. The theology of rebirth in a cycle diminishes the importance of life on earth. In the final sense, death means a departure from the world of suffering and illusions; it is often a liberation from the chain of suffering. One latent function of such death-oriented religious thinking is the ability to take the fact of death naturally and much more calmly than has been the case in Christendom. In fact, many studies seem to attest to this assumption[36] and explain the calmness and dignity with which the samurai carried out their ritual self-disembowelment.

SEPPUKKU AND ITS IMPLICATIONS FOR MODERN SUICIDOLOGY

There has been a discernible tendency in the West to understand suicide behaviour in terms of psychiatric and psychopathological orientations and frameworks: that is to say, suicide has been considered to be a result of emotional disturbance and psychiatric illness. The present study of *seppuku* revealed a deeply nurtured ethico-moral system in which *seppuku* was institutionalized, ritualized and characterized by an absence of emotional illness and disturbance and by the presence of serenity, calmness and dignity. Such considerable forethought and rational preparation cast serious doubts on the appropriateness and validity of Western assumptions of suicide as linked to psychopathology. *Seppuku* has been nurtured in Japan's cultural tradition and religio-moral philosophy as one of the socially and culturally prescribed role-performances in the hierarchical feudal societies and in highly formal and closely knit human groups. As far as *seppuku* is concerned, it must be understood in the context of the intimate relationship between cultural values and human behaviour. As such, *seppuku* is certainly not a psychopathological behaviour. Some types of *seppuku*, as a matter of fact, indicate a highly rational and well-thought-out motivation with long-range goals: e.g., the aforementioned *shobara* as a subtype of *oibara* was committed with a well-calculated thought and wish for bringing benefits to one's family and posterity. Also, all three subtypes of *junshi* had a rational motive: to fulfil one's sense of loyalty or *giri*.[37] Such behaviour is certainly consonant with the highly valued social ethics and behaviour patterns of the times. A study of *seppuku* such as this one stresses the importance of understanding the intimate and inseparable relationship between suicide and culture. It questions some of the widely assumed Western biases on suicide in terms of its cross-cultural applicability. For this reason alone, then, a study of *seppuku* is imperative for any student of suicidology—East or West.

Notes and References

[1]   The only incident of a similar act took place several years ago when the Lockheed scandal rocked Japan. The real manipulator behind the scene was Yoshio Kodama, a notorious power broker in Japan's politics with ties to ultra-rightist organizations and ideology. Shortly after the disclosure of the nature of the scandal, an irate citizen, reportedly deranged mentally, rented a single-engine aircraft and plunged the plane and himself in a *kamikaze* style into the living compound of the Kodama residence. Kodama was not hurt physically by this *kamikaze* attack. To the best knowledge of the present author, this is the only known incident of any *kamikaze* attack by a Japanese involving a pilot and an aircraft after the end of World War II.

[2]   Kurosawa, Hisashi, "Emergency Medicine and Some Problems of Suicide Attempters in Japan," *Japan Medical Newsletter* (*Nippon Iji Shimpoh*), No.3295, June 20, 1989, pp.28-32. Kurosawa, a pioneer in emergency medicine and liaison psychiatry in Japan, especially for treatment of suicide attempters at the Nippon Medical College Hospital in Tokyo, reports that *seppuku* is still one of the methods sometimes used by suicide attempters. His paper was presented by his assistant, Dr. H. Iwasaki, at the special seminar, Crisis Intervention Unit, Department of Psychiatry, Toronto East General Hospital, Toronto, Ontario, under the title "Liaison Psychiatry and Suicide in a University Hospital in Metropolitan Tokyo," on August 12, 1989.

[3]   Schweder, R., in Kleinman, A. and Good, B. (eds), *Culture and Depression* (Berkeley, Calif.: University of California Press, 1985), p.23.

[4]   Ohsumi, Miyoshi, *Seppuku no Rekishi* (History of Seppuku), (Tokyo: Yusankaku, 1973), pp. 7-9.

[5]   *Ibid.*

[6]   Nakayasu, Hiromichi, "Seppuku no Enkaku" (History of Seppuku), in Kenshiro Ohara (ed), *Jisatsugaku: Jisatsuto Bunka* (Suicide and Culture), (Tokyo: Shibundo, 1975), Vol. 5, pp. 87-88.

[7]   *Ibid.*, pp.87-120.

[8]   A major Buddhist denomination in Japan, founded by a priest known as Shinran, it advocated salvation by repentance alone, considerably similar to the doctrine

of "Salvation by Faith Alone" advocated by Martin Luther in sixteenth century Germany. Thus, this denomination discredited the effort of good deeds; its vision of Paradise (the Pure Land, hence the name of the denomination) became a powerful symbol of yearning for many devout believers and unwittingly spurred the rush for Paradise through religiously motivated suicide.

9   Chiba, Tokuya, *Seppuku no Hanashi* (A Story of *Seppuku*), (Tokyo: Kodansha Ltd., 1983), pp.3-32.

10 Yamana, Shotaro, *Sekai Jisatuko* (Treatise on the Comparative Study of Suicide), (Tokyo: Sekkasha Ltd., 1974), pp.92-96.

11 Ohara, Kenshiro, *Jisatsuron* (Treatise on Suicide), (Tokyo: Taiyo Shuppan Ltd., 1978), pp.53-71.

12 Abé, Makoto et al., *Nyomun Nipponshi* (Introduction to Japanese History), (Tokyo: Yoshikawa Kobunkan Ltd., 1980), pp.131-138.

13 Yamana, Shotaro, *Sekai Jisatsuko, op. cit.*, pp.104-105.

14 Ohsumi, Miyoshi, *Seppuku no Rekishi, op. cit.*, p.225. It was Ohno Seigoro who advocated the abolition in Japan's Diet (parliament) continually from March, 1869.

15 For a detailed account of the biography as well as socio-psychological autopsy of the *seppuku* of General Maresuke Nogi and his wife, see: Fusé, Toyomasa, *Profiles of Death..., op. cit.*, pp.195-226, 255-256.

16 For the details of the foregoing discussion, the present author has benefited much from the following sources: Tagiri, Tomeo, *Seppuku Ronko* (Treatise on *Seppuku*), (Tokyo: Chuo Koronsha, Ltd., 1960); L. Seward, *Hara-Kiri* (Tokyo: Charles E. Tuttle, 1968); Nakai, Isao, *Seppuku* (Tokyo: Nohberu Shobo Co., 1960); Ohsumi, Miyoshi, *Seppuku no Rekishi* (History of *Seppuku*), *op. cit.*; Wada, Katsunori, *Seppuku no Tetsugaku* (Philosophy of *Seppuku*), (Tokyo: Rakubunsha Ltd., 1927); Hagiwara, Shinsei, *Bushido Sangé* (Essence of *Bushido*), (Tokyo: Maki Publishers, 1942); Nakayasu, Hiromichi, *Seppuku: Hisobi no Sekai* (The World of *Seppuku*), (Kyoto: Sannin Kai, 1960); Yamana, Shotaro, *Sekai Jisatsuko* (Treatise on the Comparative Study of Suicide), *op. cit.*; Uno, Koichiro, *Kenran taru Ankoku* (Splendoured Darkness), (Tokyo: Shinchosha Ltd., 1972); Ohara, Kenshiro, *Jisatsuron* (Treatise on Suicide), *op. cit.*; Chiba, Tokuji, *Seppuku no Hanashi* (A Story of *Seppuku*), *op. cit.*; Ohsumi, Miyoshi, *Seppuku no Rekishi* (History of *Seppuku*), *op. cit.*

17 All the documents investigated by the author indicate that it took from eight hours all the way to seventy-two hours to die of the *seppuku* wounds. Yet, by the *bushido* code, no one was expected to render first aid or any treatment whatsoever in order to respect the original intention of the dying samurai.

18 Yamana, Shotaro, *Treatise on Seppuku, op. cit.*, pp.94-96.

19 *Ibid.*, p.96.

20 Ohara, Kenshiro (ed), *Jisatsugaku* (Suicidology), *op. cit.*

21 Kalish, R.A. and Reynolds, D.K., *Death of Ethnicity: A Psycho-Cultural Study* (Los Angeles: The University of Southern California Press, 1976) p.146.

22 DeVos, George, *Socialization for Achievement* (Berkeley: University of California Press, 1973), pp.438-485.

23 Yamamoto, Tsunetomo, *Hagakure* (Hiding Behind Leaves). He was a dedicated and highly disciplined samurai in the eighteenth century Tokugawa period. He outlined the virtues of *bushido* and stressed the importance of the aesthetics of death.

24 Yuasa, Yasuo, "*Kodai Nipponjin no Sei to Shi*" ("Life and Death among the Ancient Japanese"), in Tamura Yoshiro and Minamoto Ryo-en (eds), *Nippon ni okeru Seito Shino Shiso* (Concept of Life and Death in Japan), (Tokyo: Yuhikau Ltd., 1977), p.108.

25 Keene, Donald, *Japanese Literature* (New York: Grove Press, 1965), pp.22-46; Hisamatsu, Sen-ichi, *Manyoshu* (Myriad of Leaves), (Tokyo: The Kodansha International Ltd., 1976).

26 *The Teaching of Buddha* (Tokyo: Kenkyusha Ltd., 1965); Japan Buddhist Association, *Gendai Bukkyo Seiten* (Modern Buddhist Scriptures), (Tokyo: Japan Buddhist Association, 1977), Vol.I and II.

27 Tamura, Yoshiro, "*Seishi Jo-jyu no Tetsugaku*" ("Philosophy of Universality of Life and Death") in Tamura Y. and Minamoto Ryo-en (eds), *Nippon ni Okeru Sei to Shi no Shiso* (Thoughts on Life and Death in Japan), (Tokyo: Yuhikaku, 1972), *op. cit.*,pp.66-67.

28 Ishida, Mizumaro, "*Jigoku to Jodo no Shiso*" ("Concept of Hell and Pure Land") in Tamura, Y., and Minamoto, R., *ibid.*, pp.54-60.

29 Tamai, Isamu, "*Bukkyo to Jisatsu*" ("Buddhism and Suicide") in Ohara, Kenshiro (ed), *Suicidology, op. cit.*, Vol.4, pp.51-53. Of course, some scholars in Japan dispute that Buddhism was that pessimistic and other-worldly. They point out that a careful examination of Prince Shotoku's writings in the eighth century reveals that Buddhism stressed the importance of the presence of Buddha here and now. They argue furthermore that such evidence of this-worldliness in Japan's Buddhism is very much evident in the lifestyle of all known Buddhists in Japan who do not avoid eating meat, do marry and engage in all secular life avidly with zest. Such "profane lifestyle" of the clergy in Japan's Buddhism makes a sharp contrast to that of the Buddhists in Sri Lanka, Burma, Thailand and Vietnam. But they seem to be arguing on the point of *explicit* behaviour rather than *inner* beliefs and attitudes. Also, in its early

development in India, Buddhism might have condemned suicide as a "sinful" act, but what is important here is the fact of moral metamorphosis of such an injunction when it was introduced to Japan. Suicide has never been morally or religiously condemned in Japan. See: Tamura, Encho, *Honen: Ohjo Daiyosho*, (Honen: Great Treatise on Dying), (Tokyo: Yoshikawa Kobunkan, 1960).

30 Zoku-Gun Shoruiju Kanseikai, *Bichu Heiranki*, Vol.22, 1958, cited by Tamai, I., *"Bukkyo to Jisatsu"* (Buddhism and Suicide") *op. cit.*, p.56.

31 Kapleau, Philip (ed), *The Wheels of Death: Writings from Zen Buddhism and Other Sources* (London: George Allen and Unwin, Ltd., 1972), p.9.

32 Nishimoto, Sosuké, *"Nipponjin no Kako oyobi Gendai no Seishin Seikatsu to Jisatsutono Kankei"* ("Relationship between Suicide and the Spiritual Life of the Japanese, Past and Present") in Takasaka, Masa-aki and Nishio Usui (eds), *Nipponjin no Jisatsu* (Suicide of the Japanese), (Tokyo: Sogensha Ltd., 1966), pp.333-355.

33 Saliency of polity over the family is one of the main cultural differences between Japan and pre-Communist China. A sense of loyalty to one's superior, suprafamilial in nature, did exist in Japan, whereas in China loyalty to one's family superseded all, thereby preventing the emergence of a strong centralized state. See: Fusé, Toyomasa, (ed), *Modernization and Stress in Japan*, Chapter 2 ("Japan's Modernization Experience"), (Leiden: the Netherlands: Brill Publishers, 1975).

34 Ishikawa, Takashi, "The Last Stage of the Pacific War," *The East*, 1980: XVI, 9, September, p.35.

35 Fusé, Toyomasa, *Profiles of Death...*, *op. cit.*, pp.113-130.

36 Kalish, R.A. and Reynolds, K.D., *Death of Ethnicity..., op. cit.*; Kalish, R.A., and Reynolds, K.D., "Anticipation of Futurity as a Function of Ethnicity and Age," *Journal of Gerontology*, Vol.29, No.2, 1974, pp.224-231.

37 *"Giri"* is a felt sense of obligation to another person in a non-legal, moral sense. Though it is not a legal obligation, it has a powerful grip on the ethico-moral sense of duty among every Japanese even today. For details, see: Fusé, Toyomasa, "Cultural Values and Social Behaviour of the Japanese: A Comparative Analysis," *Cultures et Développement: Revue Internationale des Sciences du Développement*, 1982: Vol.XIV, 2-3, pp.238-252.

CHAPTER 6

Continuities in Suicidology Research— Physician Suicide

A t the personal level suicide is a painful tragedy affecting surviving family members and relatives, close friends and colleagues; at the social and economic level, it is an enormous loss to community and society in terms of human resources. When suicide involves a self-inflicted death of a physician, the social impact and implications are profound. The physician, especially as perceived in North America, is a highly esteemed professional whose training and certification require long years of study, specialized skill and knowledge. As such, the physician has been placed on a pedestal, distinguished by prestige, public trust, admiration and high income.

The modern age worships science and technology. Before the twentieth century, the church had occupied an important place in the life of the average individual. At least in Christendom, one was likely to be baptized in the church, would live a life usually guided by priests or ministers and then be buried in the church. Today, however, one is born in a hospital, raised in a doctor's care from infancy (Dr. Spock's book has been revered as a "Bible of Child Care" by parents in North America for decades) and will likely die in the hospital. In other words, the hospital has replaced the church as a new "cathedral," and religious practitioners have been replaced by physicians who have emerged as the new "high priests" in the age of technology. Thus, it is understandable that the typical physician has become an object of public adoration and the symbol of omniscience and omnipotence. Public opinion surveys on occupational prestige have invariably placed physicians among the top five of more than 100 occupations.[1] The prestige and public trust of the physician is further evident in the fact that, together with clergy and university professors, the medical doctor is one of the officially designated professional persons authorized by the government as a guarantor for the passport application forms for Canadian citizens. It is quite understandable, therefore, that when a physician does commit suicide, the public is usually stunned and the medical community is alarmed. It is usually against the backdrop of such a widely held image of the physician as the omnipotent healer that a doctor's suicide is evaluated.

Recent data, obtained through several means by a project on physician deaths, revealed that 225 physician deaths between 1980 and 1984 in the United States were suicide, or an average of over 56 suicides among doctors annually.[2] Another, more up-to-date study on physician suicide by Holmes and Rich indicates that more than 100 doctors commit suicide every year in the United States and that "3% of all male physicians and 6.5% of all female physician deaths in the United States are accounted for by suicide; moreover, suicide is responsible for 35% of premature deaths among all physicians."[3] If the latter figure of more than 100 physician suicides every year is accurate, then it means that each year the entire output of one medical school is needed to replace the loss caused by physician suicide. Since underreporting has always been a distinct possibility vis-à-vis physician death by suicide, the real loss may be even greater than the annual output of just one medical school. The magnitude of such a loss is not limited to the United States alone as a number of similar studies in European countries indicates. A Canadian medical researcher, for instance, laments the loss of 62 physicians in three years in England and Wales alone and points out that these men and women were in the prime of their lives and represent a loss, the replacement of which requires many years' investment in money and human resources.[4]

In some studies, physicians appear to have been especially vulnerable to suicide, depression, substance abuse and marital discord. Concern with so-called impaired physicians, as revealed by the extent to which such problems have been discussed openly in the medical literature, has dramatically increased in the last 20 years or so. The growing concern about problems among physicians, including suicide, has been attributed by some within the profession to increased compassion for colleagues and concern for the quality of patient care. It may also reflect major structural and ideological shifts in North American society such as major social change since Vietnam and the resultant social anomie, the 1960s "drug scene," the grass-roots movement, the mushrooming self-help groups of the 1970s and 1980s, the dramatic social transformation of medicine and the medical consumer movement of the 1980s.[5]

One of the earliest comments on the phenomenon of physician suicide was presented in a study by the London Statistical Society, subsequently published in the 1886 *Lancet* in Britain, which showed that the physician suicide rate was very high.[6] Such allegedly high suicide rates among physicians continued to be reported in Britain at least in the first half of the twentieth century.[7]

In 1903, the editors of the *Journal of the American Medical Association* (*JAMA*) began to comment on the need for the study of physician suicide in the United States in response to the impetus given by the 1886 study published in *Lancet*.[8] Since then a number of studies have been conducted on the topic of physician suicide, mainly in the United States but also in Europe.

What is the real situation? Do physicians demonstrate higher suicide rates than other groups or the general population? A review of the literature reveals contradictory and equivocal results: some studies argue that doctors do indeed kill themselves at a higher rate, whereas other studies seem to refute such contention and insist that their rate of suicide is either comparable to that of the general population or slightly higher but only in terms of gender. A careful and detailed review of some of these studies will be presented and evaluated.

STUDIES INDICATING HIGHER RATES FOR PHYSICIANS

The first part of the discussion suggests that physicians do kill themselves at rates higher than the general population, or the general population of the comparable age groups and/or than other similar professional groups. Some studies stress higher rates of suicide among physicians in general, and especially for psychiatrists. The following are, therefore, some of the representative studies that reveal higher rates of physician suicide.

(1) Blachly, Osterud and Josslin examined suicide among professional groups in Tulsa, Oklahoma between 1950 and 1961. They found very high rates for physicians, dentists and attorneys vis-à-vis the general population.

They noted further that seven out of eight physicians (or 88%) who committed suicide were under 50 years old and "destroying themselves at an age when they would be expected to be most socially productive."[9] It is to be noted that this study compared the suicide rates of various professional groups in the United States, marking some of the high-risk professional groups in modern industrial society.

(2) Greatly stimulated by this research, an editorial in the *British Medical Journal* reported that between 1949 and 1953 there were 61 suicides among male doctors between 25 and 64 years of age and another 13 among older doctors in England and Wales. It revealed that the rate was two and one-quarter times higher than for all males, and the suicides were committed by comparatively young men. More than one in every 50 male physicians takes his own life, the editorial argued, and 6% of all doctors' deaths under the age of 65 were from suicide—the same as from lung cancer. On the basis of this information, the journal warned the British medical community that "this month and every month a doctor in Great Britain, on the average, will kill himself."[10] Such warning was further reinforced by the tacit understanding that, in view of the fact that these reports were based on death certification, they probably underestimated the true extent of suicide, as many cases were not declared as such. The report did not include the suicide rate of female physicians, but it did point out a "disproportionate number of suicides (among psychiatrists)," and concluded that "the explanation may lie in the choosing of the (speciality) rather than its demands, for some who take up psychiatry probably do so for morbid reasons."[11] This report is significant in that it is probably one of the first to suggest higher frequencies of suicide among psychiatrists.

(3) Another study, presented in 1967, examined the obituary columns of the *Journal of the American Medical Association* (*JAMA*) since 1895 supplemented by official death certificates. The American Medical Association (AMA) keeps a lifelong record of every graduate of every medical school in the United States as well as keeping track of the graduates of foreign medical schools who are known to have returned or immigrated to the United States. The AMA recorded the names, dates, places of birth, education, names and location of the medical schools, dates of graduation and the degrees awarded of each physician. The physician record station and the death editor (who is in charge of the obituary column) learn of physician deaths from newspaper clippings. The death editor then writes to the next of kin, attending physician, local medical association and the vital statistical repository for copies of the death certificate and further

information about the cause of death. The cause of death on the death certificate, if available, is published in the *Journal of the American Medical Association*, regardless of other evidence. The death editor assumes that the AMA publishes obituaries on 90% of actual physician deaths. Thus, a certification of suicide on the death certification by the attending physicians was automatically counted as a suicide. A certification by letter from the deceased physician's personal doctor, colleague or family member testifying to the effect that "the death was a suicide" was also counted as such. In the absence of other information, a written statement from the next of kin or executor that the doctor had killed himself was sufficient for classification as a suicide. Finally, if enough information was available to justifiably call the death a suicide, then it was classified as such even though the death certificate and medical report indicated otherwise.

Under such methodology, then, Freeman examined physician death by suicide and came to the conclusion that medical doctors are more prone to suicide than are men in other professions, and that psychiatrists appear to be at the top of the list. The total number of suicides by psychiatrists was found to be 203. Freeman noted two aspects in the suicide of 203 psychiatrists as cause for serious concern. One is that in the most recent five-year period in his study, 54 killed themselves, more than had done so in any previous decade. The other is that 81, or nearly one out of three, did so before the age of forty. In his sample, nearly half of the 203 psychiatrists killed themselves with poisons and 58 with firearms.

Freeman observed that the development of depression in middle life was a probable factor for suicide, which the psychiatrist was too involved to recognize or for which he was too proud to seek help. Some psychiatrists have had instances of depression among their close relatives, hinting at possible biochemical and genetic inheritance.[12]

(4) Another highly controversial study was presented at the annual meeting of the American Psychiatric Association in May of 1967. It was subsequently published in the *International Journal of Social Psychiatry*, reporting that a check of physician deaths as reported in the obituary columns of the *Journal of American Medical Association* from May, 1965 to February, 1967 revealed a suicide rate of at least 33 per 100,000 among male physicians in the United States—double that of white American males in the same period. For psychiatrists, the suicide rate was found to be at least 70 per 100,000, or at least four times as high as the rate of the general population. The study further suggested that some medical

students and physicians choose psychiatry as a possible aid for their own emotional conflicts and problems. According to this report, some young physicians who turn to psychiatry as a speciality find that the intense emotional experience in undergoing psychiatric experience and training may induce in themselves a crisis of insight that may prove unbearable. The respective suicide rate by different medical speciality as reported in this study is shown in Table 1.[13] According to this report, suicide accounted for 26% of deaths occurring among physicians between 25 and 39 years of age, compared with 9% for white males of the general population.[14]

(5) Sakinofsky's review of studies on physician suicide in England and Wales led him to conclude that the weight of evidence indicated the reality of physicians killing themselves at a rate much higher than that of the general population. Sakinofsky adopted the British method of calculating the Standardized Mortality Ratio (SMR) as a more accurate way of understanding suicide frequency comparisons. The SMR is based upon the percentage ratio of the number of deaths observed over the number of deaths expected from the age-specific death rates:

$$\frac{\text{Observed Number of Deaths}}{\text{Expected Number of Deaths}} \times 100 = SMR$$

His examination of doctors' deaths compared with selected occupational groups lends support to a high physician suicide ratio, together with pharmacists and unskilled labourers (whose SMR actually exceeded that of the physicians), followed by male nurses, entertainers and dentists, in that order (see Table 2 below).[15] Thus, the SMR of suicide for doctors under 65 years of age is 335, which is three times the risk for the general population, six times that of university academics and the clergy and 10 times that of cabinet ministers. His review study also revealed that the male physicians who killed themselves (a total number of 55) during 1970-1972 were overrepresented by unmarried and/or divorced doctors in the age group 35-54. Twice as many doctors among the suicides have remained unmarried longer than their living colleagues.

The comparable SMR among unmarried female physicians who killed themselves was 257, a lower figure than that of male doctors but still two and one-half times greater than the general population of unmarried women. This rate was found comparable to other female professional groups such as lawyers, scientists, writers, physiotherapists and nurses. However, the

Table 1:	Physician Suicide Rate by Speciality (May 1965–February 1967), U.S.	

Speciality	Suicide Rate per 100,000
1. Psychiatrist	70
2. Opthamologist	56
3. Anesthesiologist	43
4. General Practitioner	30
5. Obstetrician-Gynaecologist	19
6. Pediatrician	19
7. Radiologist	12

De Sole, E.E., Singer, P., Aronson, B., "Suicide and Role Strain among Physicians," *International Journal of Social Psychiatry*, 1969: 15, pp. 294-301.

SMRs for female pharmacists and unskilled labourers were 763 and 623 respectively.[16]

The special knowledge that doctors have of drugs and surface anatomy may suggest that physicians' suicide attempts are usually fatal whereas more survive in the general population, as attested by the extraordinarily high suicide risk of pharmacists in the abovementioned study. In addition to ready availability and good knowledge of lethal drugs, Sakinofsky mentions as other suicide-inducing factors stress and overwork, heavy dependence on individual performance, obsession with prestige and internal rivalry with other physicians, a high rate of substance abuse and depression, financial problems and unstable marital relationships.

(6) Rose and Rosow reviewed all death certificates (a total of 406,498) filed in the State of California during the three-year period from January 1, 1959 to December 31, 1961. Death records in California include information on age, sex, race, residence, marital status, occupation and cause of death. Information on suicides by physicians and other selected groups was obtained and suicide rates were calculated on the basis of population figures in the 1960 census. Thus, there were a total of 7471 deaths by suicide in California during the three-year period. They were able to classify 7351 deceased individuals out of 7471 according to occupational

Table 2: Male Physician Deaths Compared with Selected Occupational Groups (England and Wales, 1970-72)	All Causes	Suicide		Cirrhosis		All accidents, poisoning, violence§	
	15-64 (SMR)	15-64 (SMR)	65-74 (PMR)*	15-64 (SMR)	65-74 (PMR)	15-64 (SMR)	65-74 (PMR)
Doctors	81	335(55)	155(4)	311(4)	254(4)	80(115)	103(11)
Dentists	78	206(4)	123(1)	199(2)	—(0)	103(16)	86(3)
Government†	61	34(5)	98(3)	58(3)	156(3)	35(19)	61(8)
Lawyers††	93	102(11)	185(3)	143(4)	309(3)	85(40)	153(10)
Clergy	76	51(6)	138(4)	148(6)	114(2)	74(33)	101(12)
Pharmacists	116	464(22)	238(4)	60(1)	490(5)	188(35)	202(14)
University Teachers	49	56(4)	515(2)	135(2)	853(2)	63(18)	190(3)
School Teachers	66	82(48)	129(7)	87(13)	61(2)	54(135)	91(20)
Scientists†††	76	163(14)	—(0)	—(0)	267(1)	107(39)	119(3)
Writers	94	155(19)	328(5)	314(10)	756(7)	130(68)	207(13)
Entertainers††††	124	218(17)	167(3)	239(4)	546(6)	194(69)	121(9)

Table 2: Male Physician Deaths Compared with Selected Occupational Groups (England and Wales, 1970-72) (continued)

| | All Causes | Suicide | | Cirrhosis | | All accidents, poisoning, violence§ | |
	15-64 (SMR)	15-64 (SMR)	65-74 (PMR)*	15-64 (SMR)	65-74 (PMR)	15-64 (SMR)	65-74 (PMR)
Male Nurses	112	297(34)	—(0)	65(2)	131(2)	147(76)	107(11)
Plumbers	101	76(30)	109(7)	43(4)	26(1)	89(175)	96(25)
Bricklayers	108	75(35)	101(10)	67(9)	102(6)	88(177)	113(45)
Unskilled Labourers†††††	201	70(483)	48(107)	171(71)	66(29)	377(2203)	148(436)

Sakinofsky, I., "Suicide in Doctors and Wives of Doctors," *Canadian Family Physicians*, 1980: 26, June, p. 839.

§ The PMR is the percentage ratio of the number of deaths observed in the group from a particular cause, over the number expected from the age-specific proportions of total deaths attributed to that cause, i.e., it is independent of the population "at risk." In either case, both for SMR and PMR, the standard indicating the general risk is 100.

* Inclusive of suicides.

† Ministers of the Crown, MPs and senior government officials (Occupational Unit 173)

†† Judges, barristers, advocates and solicitors (Occupational Unit 214)

††† Physical and biological scientists (Occupational Unit 205)

†††† Stage managers, actors, entertainers, musicians (Occupational Unit 207)

††††† Labourers and unskilled workers in all industries not elsewhere classified (Occupational Unit 114)

background. Fifty-one physicians killed themselves during this period for an annual suicide rate of 69 per 100,000. Table 3 shows the age-adjusted suicide rates of physicians in comparison to professional-technical workers and the general population. Physicians are almost twice as prone to kill themselves as either of the two other groups.

In terms of the comparison of the age-specific suicide rates for white male physicians and the general population, it appears that doctors age 65 and over have the highest suicide rate, while the age group 45 to 54 shows the single greatest number of suicides, many of which occur during the peak periods in a person's life. Their study also suggests that both physicians and the general population show increasing suicide rates with increasing age, but the rate of increase for the physicians is much greater than the rate for the general population.

They also found that, in terms of marital status, confirming the original insight of Durkheim, married men seem to be the least prone to suicide, followed by the single and the widowed, while the divorced are most inclined to take their own lives. In this study it was revealed that while the divorced in the general population are three times as prone to suicide as married men, divorced physicians are 13 times more likely to take their own lives than married physicians. Likewise, Rose and Rosow concluded that their study corresponded to previous studies showing doctors with a higher incidence of suicide by drug ingestion as compared with the general population.[17]

(7) Epstein et al. identified the problems involved when attempting to develop a predictive scale in efforts to diagnose potential suicidal tendencies among doctors. Their major question, therefore, was to determine if there are specific, identifiable psychological characteristics among future physicians who later commit suicide. Thus, this study has two main stated purposes: first, to determine whether a psychiatrist can distinguish medical students who later commit suicide from the control group of medical students who did not kill themselves; second, if so, to define the features that make the task of identifying such individuals possible.

For this study, 33 graduates were used as subjects. Of the 33, nine had committed suicide some time after graduating from medical school. For each suicidal victim this study included two control students who were matched to the suicidal victim by age, sex, marital status, class in medical school and the results of psychological tests. The psychiatrist reviewing the information was only informed that there were 33 records for

Table 3:	Age-adjusted Suicide Rates for Selected White Men, 24 and Older in California		
Group	Suicides 1959 to 1961	Population April 1960	Annual Rate no/100,000/yrs
Physicians	48	22,290	77
Prof. Tech.	553	462,730	36
General Pop.	4606	40,008,763	38

Source: Rose and Rosow, "Physicians Who Kill Themselves", *Archives of General Psychiatry*, 1973: 29, pp.802.

study and that these included at least one committed suicide and suitable controls.

The age of death of the suicides ranged from 27 to 48 years. Of the nine suicides, seven were males and two were females. The mean age at death was 34.7 years. The suicides killed themselves anywhere from one to 18 years after graduation.

Data included each subject's general background such as family history, medical history, physical examination, sleep habits, nervous tension, medical school grades, comments by faculty members and scholarship information. In order to describe and classify each subject, the psychiatrist used a measure of stress in a subject's life up to the time of graduation from medical school; mood scale scores (Lorr Outpatient Mood Scale in the categories of thoughtfulness, anger-hostility and depression as well as scores on the Katz Adjustment Scale for negativism, suspiciousness, verbal expansiveness, dependency and impulsivity); and clinical characterization.

After reviewing each subject's file and using the scales identified above, the psychiatrist was able to correctly identify all nine suicide victims. With the single exception of one who was rated as being suicidal, all other controls were judged as "little suicidal" or "not at all suicidal," suggesting the psychiatrist's ability to differentiate medical students who later committed suicide from a control group who did not. The suicides showed much higher degrees of depression, hostile-aggressive behaviour and other self-destructive tendencies.[18]

(8) There are a couple of interesting studies on physician stress as a possible correlation to physician impairment including suicide. In the first of these, Vincent argued in his 1983 study that in researching stress in the medical profession one may focus either on the very real stresses inherent in the practice of medicine or on personal vulnerability. In short, both of these factors—one an environmental variable and the other an individual psychological factor—may determine how each physician responds to those stresses. Vincent found that those physicians who had arrived at medical school with the least stable childhood and adolescent environments were most likely to have difficulty. In other words, insecurity in these developmental years may predispose an individual to insecurity in adulthood. Vincent's study is based upon his work as the chief psychiatrist and clinician examining and treating impaired physicians and their spouses at the Homewood Sanitarium in Guelph, Ontario, over a 22-year period. According to Vincent, then, the typical insecure physician has an excessive need to be appreciated, loved and accepted. Based upon his clinical experience, Vincent concludes that it is the insecure physician who is most vulnerable to occupational hazards including suicide.[19]

Another study by Krakowski argues that role strain does not necessarily lead to a breakdown among physicians. Rather, there seems to be a pre-existing degree of neuroticism among doctors leading to self-defeating patterns of behaviour such as compulsive overwork. Krakowski points out a higher mortality rate from coronary-artery disease among many general practitioners due to a preponderance of Type A personality among physicians. According to Krakowski, people with Type A personality traits tend to be impatient, aggressive, competitive and always filled with a sense of urgency. When confronted with a stressful situation in which they feel they have lost control, Type A persons struggle to reassert the control they think they have lost. Thus, they work harder, faster and become more aggressive. Type A people would appear more prone to overload themselves and thereby use up their much-needed adaptation energies (in Selye's sense) and thus exhaustion would result. The exhaustion phase of Hans Selye's theory of stress could include a sense of hopelessness, loss of motivation, intense fatigue, depression and even suicide.[20] It must be noted, however, these two studies are primarily theoretical rather than empirical.

(9) Ross notes two important factors, among many, in physicians who commit suicide: medical and psychiatric conditions and certain personality patterns. Ross asserts that all persons who commit suicide are

psychiatrically ill, citing a study by Blachly which indicated that none of the physicians who killed themselves were considered to be in good mental health at the time. Moreover, less than half of these suicidal physicians enjoyed good physical health, and all doctors who committed suicide suffered from health problems of varying severity. Hence, Ross argues that there is a high incidence of psychiatric morbidity, alcoholism and drug addiction among physicians who killed themselves.

In addition to the above medical conditions, Ross gives a composite picture of the "type of physician" in North America generally considered to be a high risk for suicide. He arrives at such a composite picture after reviewing pertinent literature on physician suicide over the past 75 years. According to Ross, the type of physician who is a good candidate for suicide is characterized as self-seeking and self-indulgent, versatile and resourceful; his or her perceived lack of control of the situation often leads him or her to hasty, impulsive or immature behaviour including suicide. The physician often develops an exaggerated sense of duty and obligation in attending to the demands of patients and their families. Such sense of duty and obligation often arises out of a long-standing relationship to patients, exposing doctors to additional anxieties. Thus, coping with patients' anxieties becomes part of their everyday work; but some find it very difficult and even impossible to cope, and they finally endanger their own mental health, eventually leading to the act of self-destruction.

In terms of medical specialities, Ross echoes the work of Freeman and De Sole et al. cited earlier (see p. 257)by listing psychiatry, ophthalmology and anesthesiology as the leading medical areas for high suicide rates. Pediatrics, dermatology, surgery and pathology were characterized by Ross as low suicide-rate specialities. According to Ross, such low-rate areas have in common a generally short-term and less intense emotional relationship to the patient.

A fundamental question is whether the Type A personality traits of physicians or role strain predisposes a doctor to suicide. For this question, Ross gives a tentative conclusion that the overachieving, perhaps insecure, physician who exhibits personality characteristics similar to the Type A individual may, as a result of these aggressive, achievement-oriented ways, bring additional role strain via overwork. On the other hand, demanding role-strain may induce a need in certain physicians to go at their work too intensely in attempts to overcome or "win out" over the role pressures. Either way, the result may be prolonged and intense stress leading to exhaustion.[21]

(10) Based upon cross-cultural data on physician suicide in the United States, Bavaria and the Federal Republic of Germany, Simon maintained that the suicide rate of physicians seems to be in excess of the general population.[22] In the United States, the suicide rate of physicians has been reported as two times the rate for all white American males, and in female physicians four times that of the general population. As for Britain, Simon reported the physician suicide rate to be 1.76 times that of the general population, while all health-care workers such as dentists, nurses and physiotherapists were two times more likely to commit suicide than other professionals. On the basis of studies originally conducted in Bavaria by medical researchers (i.e., Bamayr and Feuerlein), Simon reports that in the 16-year period from 1963 to 1978, 67 male and 27 female physician suicides were recorded. The physician suicide rates were then compared to those for the general population over 25 years of age. Simon reported that the study found that the suicide rate for males in the general population over age 25 was 39 per 100,000 as compared to the rate for male physicians of 61.7 per 100,000; the average age of death was 48.9 years for male doctors. The suicide rate for females over 25 was 23 per 100,000 in the general population, but the rate for female physicians was 68 per 100,000; the average age at death was found to be 52.6 for female physicians. It is interesting to note that during the last week of their lives, over one-half of the doctors who killed themselves had contact with another physician, usually as patients. Although suicidal tendencies were noticed in some cases, no steps were taken to hospitalize these physicians in distress.[23]

After reviewing these studies, Simon noted that there were not only higher suicide rates among these physicians but also higher levels of alcohol and drug abuse, marital problems and a higher incidence of emotional distress, other psychological impairment and depression. Simon found, for instance, that 55% of male physicians and 70% of the female doctors who committed suicide had reported a dependency on certain types of drugs. Simon believes that the physicians were taking antidepressants in the hope of treating and/or helping themselves, thereby becoming dependent on them.

(11) A ten-year longitudinal study in Sweden compared physician suicide to suicide among academics and the general population. The researchers used people included in the 1960 national census. Occupations were classified according to the standards developed by the International Labour Organisation. Academics included people with three or more years of post-secondary school education.

Table 4:	Physician Suicide Compared to:			
	Other Academics		General Population	
	Male	Female	Male	Female
SMR	1.9	4.5	1.2	5.7

Adapted from Allander et al., "Suicide Patterns among Physicians Related to Other Academics as well as to the General Population," *Acta Psychiatrica Scandinavica,* 1987: 75, p.141.

All suicides in the 1961-1970 period were classified according to the WHO revision of the International Classification of Diseases and International Lists of Diseases and Causes of Death. Comparisons of suicide rates were based on Standardized Mortality Ratios (SMR), which are the ratios of observed to expected deaths with 90% confidence intervals. The 3.7 million males in the 1960 census included 5962 physicians and 210,000 academics. Of these male physicians, 32 committed suicide and 569 academics killed themselves. The researchers subsequently found that male physicians have an increased suicide rate only when compared to male academics but not to the general population. It is noteworthy that male academics were found to have a lower suicide rate than men in the general population.

A total of 3.8 million females were registered in the 1960 Swedish national census, including 900 female physicians and 43,000 academics. There were ten female physician suicides and 78 academic suicides. The Standardized Mortality Ratios for suicide of female doctors were considerably higher than for female academics and for females in the general population as illustrated in Table 4.[24]

(12) Similar results were obtained in other countries. Thus, in England and Wales, researchers found higher Standardized Mortality Ratios for suicide among both male and female physicians under age 40, with a significantly higher rate for female doctors.[25] Likewise, a study in Finland also reported that their male doctors' suicide rate was 1.3 times higher than that for the general population.[26]

In all these studies, the physician suicide rate was higher than the rate for the comparable general population over 25 and, without exception, the suicide rate for female doctors was higher than that of the male counterpart and the general population, echoing similar studies done in North America.

STUDIES THAT EITHER MODIFY OR QUESTION THE HIGH SUICIDE RATES OF PHYSICIANS

In contrast to the foregoing discussions, which emphasized higher physician rates, there are a number of research findings that either contradict such arguments or qualify the nature of the previous findings, especially on the question of gender and medical speciality. Some of them, for instance, strenuously caution against too hasty a conclusion on physician suicide on methodological grounds (e.g., too small a sample, inadequate sampling procedures, etc.). Others contend that the higher rates revealed in the previous studies need to be qualified by gender. They argue that the rates of suicide among male doctors are not appreciably higher than but comparable to those of the general population over 25, whereas female doctors do seem to show considerably higher rates. Another bone of contention is the question of the suicide rate among psychiatrists: some of the findings to be introduced here vehemently argue against the said higher rates among psychiatrists. Such counter arguments on this latter point are usually advanced by psychiatrists themselves.

(1) Craig and Pitts examined the death information of the American Medical Association (AMA) for the two-year period from May 17, 1965 to May 15, 1967. From their findings, Craig and Pitts classified physician deaths into three categories: definite suicide, probable suicide and possible suicide. A suicide was considered definite if the attending physician labelled it as such in the death certificate. It was also termed a definite suicide if there was a letter from the personal physician, colleague or from the next of kin of the deceased to that effect. When the above criteria were not met but there was sufficient evidence available to suggest that the deceased physician had been ill psychiatrically and had died under suspicious circumstances, the death was labelled a probable suicide. Finally, when suicide could not be ruled out but there was not sufficient information that the deceased physician had been psychiatrically ill, the death was then classified as a possible suicide.

The researchers found that in the two-year period there was a total of 8372 physicians deaths (8075 males, 297 females); of this total, 2.72% were due to death by suicide. The age at which physician suicide occurred ranged throughout the years of productive professional life; the median age for physician suicide was 48 for males and 41 for females. Firearms were the most often employed means of suicide for males, whereas 82.4% of females used drugs to kill themselves. This pattern certainly corresponds with the basic trends in the general population in North America.

Before 1968, most of the previously published reports suggested that the doctors' suicide rate was consistently higher than that of the general population, as well as in comparison to that of the members of other occupational groups of similar socio-economic levels. But Craig and Pitts came up with the following rates: 38.3 per 100,000 for men and 40.5 per 100,000 for women doctors, or an overall rate of 38.4 per 100,000 for both sexes. In other words, their argument was that the rate calculated for male physicians was not much different from that by Dublin and Spiegelman in their 1947 study. Dublin and Spiegelman examined the longevity and mortality of American male physicians for the period 1938 to 1942 and found that a crude suicide rate for male doctors was 38.7 per 100,000 per annum suggesting that it was not higher than that of the general male population over 25.[27] However, a major and important difference was found in the female physician rate. The female rate of 40.5 per 100,000 found by Craig and Pitts was much greater than the general population figure (over 25 years of age) of 11.4 per 100,000.[28]

(2) Mausner and Steppacher studied physician deaths from March 1965 to August 1970 using the same methodology as the previous studies of culling from the obituary section of the *Journal of the American Medical Association (JAMA)*. Questionable cases of suicide were investigated through the files of the American Medical Association. Mausner and Steppacher thus identified 530 physician suicides (486 males and 41 females). Physician suicide rates were then compared by gender to the general white population through the Standardized Mortality Ratios (SMR). These researchers found the male physician rate to be 30.9 per 100,000 or 1.15 times higher than the general population. For female doctors the rate of suicide was found to be 33.6 per 100,000 or 3.2 times the risk compared to the general population.

The age distribution of the victims differed markedly. A much higher proportion of the suicides in women doctors occurred at a younger age; for instance, almost 40% of the suicides in female physicians but less than 20% of those in men occurred in persons under age 40. Twelve of the 41 suicides for women doctors (or 29%) occurred during medical training as an intern, resident or fellow; by comparison, it was true of only 37 of the 489 male physician suicides (or less than 10%).

Male physicians in the study most often chose violent methods of suicide; by comparison, female doctors predominantly chose drugs. The pattern was identical to other studies.

As for the marital status of the female physicians who killed themselves, a higher proportion of single female doctors committed suicide than those who were married at one time in their lives. Thus, the study indicated that while male physicians' suicide rate was about the same as that of the general population, female doctors committed suicide more often than females in the general white population, and that their suicides occurred more frequently during the training period of a medical education. Finally, Mausner and Steppacher suggested that these findings might be related to the possible recruitment of suicide-prone women to the profession as well as to the tension and strain of training and practice or a combination of the two.[29]

(3) Pitts et al. conducted a study of suicide among American female doctors in the period from May 22, 1967 to May 30, 1972 in order to determine if the results of female physician suicide rates as found by Craig and Pitts in the previous study would remain constant or vary. They followed the same methodology as the other studies by using the AMA records of death. In the five-year period studied, there were 18,730 physician deaths (17,979 males and 751 females). Of the 751 female physicians' deaths, 49 were suicides; the crude annual suicide rate for female doctors was 40.7 per 100,000 as compared to 11.4 per 100,000 for white women over 25 years of age in the general population. Thus, it appears that the rate of suicide among American women doctors in this study did not differ much from that found by Craig and Pitts; for, once again, it was found that female physicians commit suicide almost four times more often than women in the general population over 25 years of age.

The age at which female physicians commit suicide ranged from 27 to 79 years and the median age was 47, thereby differing from the Craig and Pitts study which placed the median age at 41. The type of medical practice or speciality with which the female doctors were associated at the time of their suicide is shown in Table 5. Thus, 15 of the female physician suicides were involved in family practice, followed by those who were in residency training, in internal medicine, then pediatrics, psychiatry, etc.[30]

This study supports the research done by Craig and Pitts by demonstrating that the female physician rate was constant from one period to the next. The sample size of this study was larger (49 of 751, or 6.52%) than that of Craig and Pitts (17 of 297, or 5.72%). Pitts et al. proposed a further study of the role strain and possible high levels of affective disorders for female physicians. From the known morbid risk for suicide among females with primary affective disorders, Pitts et al. assumed that a very high percentage (65%) of American female physicians suffered from diagnosable affective disorders. On the assumption that there is an association between affective disorder and the selection of a medical career by certain types of women, they proposed that future research into female physicians' suicides involve systematic studies using structured interviews and specific diagnostic criteria, which would be compared to other groups of professional women. But they cautioned against speculations about role strain or the need for an examination of the mental state of the physician who may commit suicide.[31]

(4) Role strain, stress and affective disorders that face highly trained professional women have been discussed by a number of studies. One such study by Welner et al. examined psychiatric disorders among professional women in the United States. It starts with the premise that high levels of education and social achievement are often associated with depression and that a majority of women who commit suicide are afflicted with psychiatric disorders such as depression. Therefore, one would expect to find an increase in the prevalence of affective disorders in female physicians, a group shown to be especially prone to suicide. The purpose of this study was to determine whether there is in fact a high prevalence of affective disorders among female physicians and whether it is related to high educational levels and social status.

For such a study, a group of 111 female physicians and 103 women with doctoral degrees were selected from the general community and studied for the presence of psychiatric illness and primary affective disorder. A list of all female physicians in the St. Louis area was obtained from telephone directories, local, state and national medical directories, and lists of staff members for all St. Louis area hospitals. Then, a comparable list of women with doctoral degrees was compiled by obtaining names of staff members from each college in the St. Louis area, several large St. Louis industries, a number of local school systems and state and local welfare agencies. Each female physician was contacted by a trained interviewer, told the purpose and scope of the study and was systematically interviewed. During the interview data about education, area of speciality, work history, marital status and history, obstetric history, experience of prejudice in training and practice, social history and psychopathology in the subjects and their families was obtained. Those with doctoral degrees were selected to match the physicians for age, marital status and race. The data were analyzed to determine the prevalence of affective and other psychiatric disorders in each group and whether in groups of highly educated women such factors as prejudice, marriage and childbearing, training and employment were associated with the presence of psychopathology, particularly depression.

The study found that 51% of the physicians and 32% of the Ph.D.s were diagnosed as having primary affective disorder (p<0.01); that other psychiatric disorders were found in less than 10% of each group; and that depression among the psychiatrists was significantly more common (74%) than among the other physicians (46%). In addition, it was found that more than 50% of all women professionals reported prejudice in training or employment, and depressed subjects reported prejudice more often than the non-depressed subjects; that the presence of children and depression was shown to disrupt a woman's professional career; and that a high prevalence of affective disorder among female physicians is consistent with the reported excessive risk for this particular group. Such a depression rate among female physicians appears to be unusually high when compared to the general female population, which is in the range of 3% to 25%. Thus, the higher prevalence of depression in physicians than in Ph.D.s can be largely accounted for by the excessively high rate of depression among psychiatrists.[32] It seems, moreover, that the presence of depression in female doctors is often independent of (rather than secondary to) the stresses of medicine, and that whatever legitimately unique stressors women face from the practice of medicine may have little to do with the reason why their suicide rate is so high.[33] In fact, the study showed how depressed physicians and Ph.D.s had significantly higher numbers of first-degree family members with a history of an affective disorder than the comparable non-depressed group. Moreover, it appears that depressive illness in female physicians is not only more frequent but tends to be more severe than in Ph.D.s. Such a high rate of depression among female physicians might be explained by a number of assumed factors: the presence of a predisposition to depressive illness among those who choose the medical profession; certain character and personality traits such as obsessive-compulsive disorder; family pressure on individuals to enter the medical profession as well as the presence of excessive medical illness and psychopathology in the family members of these individuals; and the prolonged period of rigorous study and training required under adverse conditions, in the case of female physicians, such as prejudice, career disruption and the potentially stressful factor of clinical responsibility.

Table 5:   Suicide among Female Physicians: By Medical
           Speciality

	Practice Prefered
Family Practice	15
Residency Training	8
Internal Medicine	5
Pediatrics	4
Psychiatry	4
Pathology	3
Preventive Medicine	2
Anesthesiology	1
Obstetrics-Gynaecology	1
Opthalmology	1
Radiology	1
	45

Source: Pitts, F.N., et al., "Suicide among U.S. Women Physicians, 1967-1972,"
   American Journal of Psychiatry, Volume 136, (May), 1979, pp.694-696.

As for the onset of the illness, in 17 (28%) of the depressed physicians it occurred before entering medical school. All of these subjects had subsequent depressive episodes: five in training, four in practice and eight in both. In the remaining 18, the onset of depression occurred during training in medical school or residency. Of these, seven had subsequent episodes during practice and 11 had all their depressive episodes during training. In addition, more than 50% of all women physicians in this study reported prejudice in training or employment.

The last point mentioned in this study was about the reluctance to seek help on the part of physicians in general. Doctors tend to be secretive about their psychiatric illness for fear of losing their patients and their standing. In the study to be cited next, it was found that a greater percentage of women in medical student populations sought psychiatric counselling than men. It is important to note that despite the greater number of female physicians seeking help more female physicians commit suicide, raising some questions about the efficacy of such help.

(5) It was found that in all previously cited work on physician suicide the rate of suicide was significantly higher in female doctors. In order to answer the question of "What is so different for women doctors?", two female physicians wrote an article and discussed the problems involving female doctors.

Based upon a limited amount of data on female physicians, Nadelson and Notman relied on a review of clinical reports and inferences from medical students and other women professionals. They attribute some of the major problems facing female doctors to their isolation as a minority group (at the time of their writing, women comprised only 10% of all physicians) and their undergoing a different and more stressful psychological experience than men. The fact that after the age of 45 the female physicians' suicide rate drops may mean that the female doctor is more established in her career through contact with other female physicians and hence does not feel so isolated. Nadelson and Notman noted that medical school dropout rates for male and female students were similar as far as academic reasons were concerned. Of those leaving the medical school for non-academic reasons, however, 8% were female and 3% were male. As for divorce, some crucial gender differences were observed. The divorce rate for male professionals including physicians is lower than that in the general population; the divorce rate for female doctors, however, is higher than for male physicians and higher than the divorce rate in the general female population.

Nadelson and Notman then focused their attention on another important factor for female physician suicide—high female doctors' suicide rate during the medical training days. They argued that the demands and consequences of medical training were such that they exceeded that of other graduate and professional training. The length, rigidity and intensity of demands from the beginning of medical school through residency is unparalleled in other professional or graduate programmes. Although the same number of years may be required, the inflexible commitment of time and energy as well as the responsibility demanded of medicine is certainly unique. During medical school training, for instance, the following goals must be accomplished: the consolidation and integration of personal identity and separation from family, the acquisition of a large body of knowledge that must be attained through training, the development of skills related to the medical practice, the development of a professional identity and the formation and implementation of career and life goals.[34]

There are other problems for female doctors. In their training days they certainly lack role models because faculty members are predominantly male. Hence, while the male student can maintain a consistency with his own masculine identification, the female student generally cannot. Another problem for the significantly high rate of suicide among female physicians may be the reasons for choosing medicine as a career. Students who apply to medical school are usually high achievers. Achievement and competition are often conflicting issues for women. Women internalize socially reinforced values concerning achievement and success and may project or externalize their conflicts about activity versus passivity—i.e., they may feel that they should not be active and aggressive and may suppress these traits. For some female doctors, the choice of medicine may look like a deviant choice. Medicine involves caretaking and nurturing. It allows for the expression of these needs in men while still reinforcing achievement needs, but the situation is different for women. Although nurturant qualities have been considered traditionally "feminine," medicine has been seen as an achievement-oriented, "masculine" field. Thus, for some female physicians, conflicts concerning achievement and nurturance may be of major importance. Though anecdotal in nature, this study poses some important considerations for any study of female physicians.

At any rate, it seems undeniable that female doctors' suicide rates are uniformly higher in both Europe and the United States; the annual rate for female physicians has been about three to four times the rate for white women over age 25 in the general population.

(6) Carlson and Miller reviewed previous studies on physician suicide and pointed out the following salient characteristics: female physicians commit suicide three to four times more often than females in the general population, the rates were higher among single female doctors, the rates were higher during the medical training period and suicide occurred most frequently among those female physicians in family practice.

After such a review, these two female researchers raised some problematic methodological issues. First, the number of physicians in the age group 25-64 in the general population was significantly different for the two genders: 0.65% of men were medical doctors as compared to

0.04% for females in the general population over 25 years of age. Carlson and Miller argued, furthermore, that the actual numbers of suicides among female physicians are much too small (nine to ten per year, for instance) to warrant comparisons and general conclusions. Nor is it advisable to compare females who are doctors with females in the general population because the differences between these two population samples are too complex to allow a simple, unicausal explanation for differing suicide rates. They also pointed out the often cited correlations between high I.Q. scores and suicide; but male physicians, who have equally high I.Q. scores, do not commit suicide more often than the men in the general population.

As for affective disorders and suicide for female physicians, their onset between 25 and 45 years of age and their role in the etiology of suicide for female physicians seem to coincide with the general pattern of the same gender—at exactly such ages (25-44) most women actually kill themselves. Just as the greatest risk for depressive episodes for women occurs between 25 and 44 years of age, for female doctors the maximal amount of psychosocial stressors such as medical training, career choice and role conflict occurs at the same period in their lives. Carlson and Miller suggested that a combination of these events can and do trigger suicidal actions for some female doctors:[35]

> Those with the highest levels of perturbation either because of stress, loss, family psychopathology, psychiatric disorder, or all of those factors, develop the knowledge to commit a successful suicide and have at immediate hand a successful way of killing themselves, and their suicide rate will unfortunately increase.

They strongly suggest, therefore, that a mandatory analysis of medical training be done in the near future.

(7) In response to questioning by researchers, the majority of physicians and nurses responded that the quality of their work had suffered as a result of being personally involved with such significant others as parents, children, spouses and lovers who are chemically dependent. They cited reduced cognitive ability such as less capacity for concentration, errors, poor judgment and absenteeism as well as a decline of such important functions as patient care and increasing personal deterioration including depression, attempted suicide, personal chemical dependency and lowered

self-esteem. Although few differences were found between physicians and nurses, nurses and female doctors were found to be more likely to have chemically dependent parents, a higher incidence of depression, personal chemical dependence and suicidal tendencies.[36]

(8) Depression and substance abuse are the major contributors to suicide in physicians and in the general population. In one study it was found that 17% of alcoholic physicians were psychiatrists, as compared to the AMA estimates of 6% of all American physicians who are psychiatrists, suggesting that alcoholic psychiatrists are overrepresented in terms of their ratio in the medical profession. Likewise, 22% of alcoholic female physicians were psychiatrists, compared to the AMA estimate of 9.5% of the women doctors in the United States. This fact suggests that substance abuse might play a major role in the high rate of suicide by psychiatrists as well as women physicians.[37]

(9) Dr. Saul Cohen, chairperson of the Alcoholism Commission of the Saskatchewan Medical Association in Canada, suggested that affective disorders such as depression and substance abuse play a major role in physician suicide. While male physicians have about the same suicide rate as other age-matched men in the general population, the rate for female doctors is three to four times greater than for other women in the general population. Women doctors are more likely to kill themselves during their medical training, and most commit suicide in their middle age. He further pointed out that 54% of these addicted doctors were in the upper third of their graduating class.[38] The Donwood Institute in Toronto, an Ontario programme for rehabilitation of addicted physicians which was started in 1977, includes physicians, registered nurses, dentists and pharmacists as well as their spouses. Of the 200 doctors treated in the programme, 12 were on welfare and one pediatrician had been working for three years on construction jobs. The Ontario Medical Association now makes interest-free loans available for those doctors in treatment. Two hospitals in the Toronto area also have a programme whereby a recovering physician can be a second assistant in the operating room. This way he or she can continue to make some money and can also develop and prepare for a quiet re-entry to the profession.[39] Moreover, a review of existing studies by Krakowski indicates that physicians compare favourably with the general population in mortality rates from physical illnesses but unfavourably with regard to mental and emotional illnesses such as affective disorders, substance abuse and suicide.[40]

On the question of physician suicide, no other aspect of the studies cited aroused more passion, denial and *ad hominem* arguments than the thorny issue of suicide among psychiatrists. One of the early studies that stirred such feverish reactions and controversies in medical circles was a study by Freeman entitled "Psychiatrists Who Kill Themselves: A Study in Suicide," in a "Brief Communications" section of the *American Journal of Psychiatry* in 1967, which followed his presentation on that subject at the annual meeting of the American Psychiatric Association that year. In his study, Freeman stated that physicians were more prone to suicide than were men in other occupations and, furthermore, that psychiatrists appeared to be at the top of the list, as cited earlier in this section.[41] Likewise, a very high incidence of suicide among psychiatrists was raised in a leading article in the *British Medical Journal*, which linked the phenomenon to attracting the "wrong" type of person to psychiatry.[42] Freeman suggests probable "counter-aggression" may be experienced by some psychiatrists in dealing with emotionally disturbed patients' tongue lashings, which may lower the self-esteem of the psychiatrist to the level of contempt expressed by the patient and heightened guilt for it. The process of psychotherapy imposes a considerable strain upon the therapist who is not supposed to relieve his or her own anxiety about the patient by taking responsibility for the patient's difficulties away from him or her.

In a highly reputable and well-known study by Rich and Pitts it was found that of the 18,730 deaths of American physicians from 1967 to 1972, 593 were attributed to suicide (544 males and 59 females). The data showed that psychiatrists commit suicide regularly, year by year, at rates about twice those expected statistically, and the differences between theirs and other physicians' rates were statistically significant.[43] Pitts and his associates reported that male psychiatrists have twice the suicide rate and suggested that the rate of depression among psychiatrists was two to three times greater than in the general population.[44] All in all, such researchers as Freeman, Blachly, De Sole et al., Sakinofsky, Holmes and Rich all reported a very high suicide rate among psychiatrists, from 58 to 70 per 100,000.

It is useful to recall that in their study of psychiatric disorders among female physicians and Ph.D.s cited earlier, Welner et al. reported that psychiatric disorders such as depression were found in 74% of female psychiatrists, which was significant at 0.01 level—a percentage considerably higher than the general female population. This presence of depression, moreover, was found to be independent of the strain of practice; a significant number of these depressed doctors, especially psychiatrists, had a history of affective disorders among first-degree family members.[45]

Surveys of selected postgraduate medical trainees have found that psychiatric and anethesiology residents have a higher frequency of diagnosable psychiatric disorders.[46]

In all these studies that examined the suicide of physicians in relation to speciality, the rate ranged from 10 per 100,000 among pediatricians to 70 in psychiatrists; after psychiatrists, high suicide rates were also observed in ophthalmologists, otolaryngologists and anesthesiologists. Psychiatrists in all these studies occupy either the highest rate or close to the top: psychiatrists commit suicide at about twice the rate of general surgeons. Yet, some studies have questioned the validity of such high suicide rates among psychiatrists. One of the major problems seems to be the very small size of the study sample. For instance, in their 1967 report, Blachly et al. concluded that psychiatrists indeed had very high suicide rates, but their study was based upon the calculation of crude suicide rate on the very small samples in each speciality examined. The same problem plagued the study by Russell, Pasnau and Taintor who came up with an astonishing suicide rate of 106 per 100,000 in their sample of 91.5% of the psychiatric residents in training from July 1971 through June 1972. This incredibly high suicide rate, however, was based on only four suicides! This finding, therefore, cannot be taken as an accurate indicator of the psychiatrist's suicide rate.[47]

Another study by Bergman examined published studies on the suicide of psychiatrists and concluded that when extraneous variables such as age, sex and marital status are controlled, when sample sizes are large and when the data used are from a reliable source psychiatrists are not at a greater risk for suicide compared to the general population. He also insisted that there is no evidence of any medical speciality being at greater risk for suicide.[48]

Rose and Rosow's study, cited earlier, reviewed all the death certificates filed in California from January 1959 to December 1961. They identified 51 physician suicides, but none was a psychiatrist. They concluded that there is no evidence that propensity to self-destruction and one's medical speciality areas are particularly related.[49]

An extensive study on the suicide rates of various medical specialists was undertaken in Scandinavia by Allander, Arnetz, Hedberg, Hörte, Malker and Theorell in 1987. The researchers identified all the physicians who had died in Sweden from 1969 to 1983 using the files of the National Board of Health and Welfare. A comparison of suicide rates was made between the four major speciality groups of general practice, general surgery, internal medicine and general psychiatry and a reference group of six other specialist groups (pediatrics, cardiology, obstetrics and gynaecology, radiology, ophthalmology and otolaryngology). The four major specialist groups comprised 30% of all specialists while the reference group comprised 48% of all specialists. These researchers identified 66 male and five female specialist suicides. The number of female specialists was very low in each group, hence it was not meaningful to calculate risk ratios for them. Risk ratios were calculated for the male specialists, however, and the results were significant within a 90% confidence level. General surgeons were found to have the greatest risk of suicide among the four specialist groups with a risk ratio of 1.8, followed by general practitioners with a risk ratio of 1.5, psychiatrists with a risk ratio of 1.4 and internal medicine specialists with a risk ratio of 1.3. This study does not support previous findings of an increased suicide risk among psychiatrists.[50]

Another study that questions the greater risk of psychiatrists is the one by German researchers, Bamayr and Feuerlein of the Max Planck Institute for Psychiatry in Munich, cited by Simon. In this study of physician suicide from 1963 to 1978, it was found that male psychiatrists had lower suicide rates than the age-matched male general population.[51]

Such studies notwithstanding, there are some important and reputable studies that strongly indicate that psychiatrists are likely to be at a greater risk of suicide than others.

As briefly mentioned earlier, Craig and Pitts reported in 1968 the results of their study on physician suicide during a 24-month period from 1965 to 1967. They found that psychiatrists killed themselves at rates twice that expected, but concluded that the number of suicides by psychiatrists was much too small to warrant a demonstration of statistical significance.

Pitts and Rich replicated this study in 1980 in a five-year period from May 22, 1967 to May 30, 1972 in order to ascertain whether or not psychiatrists do indeed kill themselves at rates higher than expected. This is probably the most comprehensive (and generally considered to be the conclusive) study on the subject. Suicide was the reported cause of death for 3.17% of those physicians studied. The suicide rates of psychiatrists and of speciality board certified physicians were then compared to the base population of American physicians for December 31, 1970, the midpoint of the study. The researchers found that psychiatrists represented 7.0% of physicians by practice preference but 11.8% of suicides. More importantly, psychiatrists represented 8.1% of board certified physicians but 16.5% of suicides by board certified doctors. No other speciality by certified group committed suicide at rates higher than expected.[52]

In total, studies by Freeman (1967), Blachly et al. (1968), De Sole et al. (1969), Sakinofsky (1980), Rich and Pitts (1980) and Holmes and Rich (1991) all suggest that psychiatrists kill themselves at least at twice the rate of other physicians. They hypothesize that either the demands of psychiatry are greater than those of other medical specialities (causing greater role strain) or that suicide-prone individuals are drawn to psychiatry.

Rich and Pitts believe, however, that psychiatrists lead lives less stressful then those of other physicians. (As a matter of fact, a leading psychiatrist and suicidologist in Japan echoes such a viewpoint and argues that those medical students who choose psychiatry as their specialty do so partly because they do dislike seeing so much blood and "mayhem.")[53] Pitts and Craig further propose that high rates of suicide in psychiatrists are due to the fact that physicians with affective disorders may choose psychiatry as a speciality. A study conducted in Switzerland lends support to this assumption. This Swiss study by Willi revealed an increased rate of psychiatric disorder in 19-year-old conscripts in Switzerland who later chose psychiatry as a medical speciality as compared to those who chose general medicine and surgery prior to obtaining their medical degrees. Willi concluded his study by saying that the nature of the emotional impairment determined the choice of medical speciality rather than the speciality training determining the disorder.[54]

A perusal of letters to the editor and the vehemence of rebuttals and denials from practitioners of this particular speciality, and the replication of studies thus far cited, reveal rather consistently high suicide rates in this medical speciality. In the latest and probably most comprehensive review in a highly regarded study on suicide among psychiatrists, Holmes and Rich, the two psychiatrists who authored the study, conclude that the psychiatrists probably constitute a high-risk group for suicide. A quote from their study illustrates the point:[55]

> The other identified major high-risk group for physician suicide are psychiatrists. It seems likely that depression

and/or substance abuse are important contributing factors. However, other evidence supports the conclusion that high-risk individuals may choose psychiatry as a speciality. This conclusion deserves further debate and further systematic study. The psychiatric community should not ignore this potential problem out of concern for their professional image. For example, radiologists are wearing lead aprons now because they were willing to admit that more of them were dying of leukaemia than should have been.

THE QUESTION OF MEDICAL STUDENTS

One of the ways of understanding suicide among physicians is to examine the type of students who come to medical schools as well as their degree of stress and the impact of their educational and training process. One of the underlying assumptions about physicians is that medical schools attract certain types of individuals.

In terms of the requirements for admission into medical school, the following criteria are currently used by many schools to base judgment for admission: grade point average, an aptitude test, letters of recommendation, personal interview, application data and health questionnaires, with an emphasis on the first two criteria. Such heavy stress on grade point average and one's score on the aptitude test suggests that medical schools value cognitive skills.

(1) There is a study that examined aptitude for abstract reasoning and spatial perception among first-year medical students at the University of Toronto, as well as other faculties from that university and others across North America and Britain. These researchers did their study over a five-year period, 1967-1972, using the Raben's Advanced Progressive Matrices for testing cognitive skills and a short version of the Jackson Personality Research Form Manual for non-cognitive skills. They found that scores steadily increased for the first four years and then levelled off for all faculties studied. Medical students differed, however, from other populations significantly ($p=0.001$) on seven of 14 personality measures on the Jackson Personality Research Form Manual. Overall, medical students were found to be more achievement-oriented, less impulsive (in the sense of not being "rash," "impetuous" and "spontaneous") as well as more disciplined, to mention a few. Generally speaking, in other words,

medical students were found to be very sober, purposeful and disciplined as well as scoring higher on the need for achievement and endurance. All these traits were consistent with the grade-oriented selection criteria discussed above. The nurturance subscale yielded the greatest divergence between medical students and their counterparts in other faculties. Consistent with their goals, medical students were more sympathetic, assisting and consoling.[56] Contrary to their career goals, however, medical students scored lower than other faculties on a measure of flexibility or adaptiveness (change) as well as on the ability to tolerate uncertainty. Their lower scores on these two measures are ironic in that they are entering a field which is continuously changing.

(2) In another study, Thomas examined the number of premature deaths (before age 60) and reasons for dropping out of medical school. The sample for this study was fairly large—1337. From this total, 89 dropped out of medical school and 49 died prematurely. Although suicide did not account for a large proportion of the drop-outs, it was the main cause of premature deaths: 17 of the 49 premature deaths (or 35%) were suicides. Furthermore, two of the premature deaths were alcohol-related deaths and many more had a history of having been hospitalized for alcoholism and/or drug addiction. Addiction to alcohol or drugs may be seen as a chronic form of suicide. Thomas then separated the subjects by academic standing. What emerged from this was a bi-modal distribution, with the cases of suicide and alcohol-related deaths being over-represented in the top and bottom portions of the academic standings, while they were under-represented in the middle. It is to be noted that those who died accidentally did not exhibit this pattern (i.e., they were evenly distributed throughout the class standings).[57] In accordance with this finding, Vincent, whose study was cited earlier, stated that insecurity in childhood among medical students predisposes one to various difficulties in adulthood such as the excessive need to achieve. An insecure person, therefore, may place a great deal of emphasis on the grades the person receives, whereas a more secure person may be well-rounded enough to be comfortable with average grades. At the other end of the spectrum, low marks may be an indication of one's inability to meet the demands of medical school so their future goals may begin to seem bleak.

(3) In yet another study, three researchers surveyed all medical schools in the United States in order to ascertain the frequency of attempted suicide and completed suicide among medical students. The intention of this study was to provide data on the parameters of medical students on the basis of a national survey of all 116 medical schools in the United States.

The researchers sent a brief questionnaire to the deans of student affairs of the 116 U.S. medical schools listed in the December 26, 1977 issue of the *Journal of the American Medical Association.* The deans were then asked to report the number of completed suicides and attempted suicides for classes graduating or classes expected to graduate between 1974 and 1981. They also requested the number of students in each class by gender, other demographic data and the number of those who had received psychiatric treatment.

Responses were received from 96 of the 116 medical schools (82%) in the country. Eight of the 96 responding said that data were not available; of the 88 remaining schools there was a total of 52 medical student suicides. These suicides occurred between September 1, 1970 and March 1, 1978. Of these 52 suicides, 34 were males and nine were females. Of the suicides, 39 (or 75%) were single.

It was found that the overall annual rate of suicide among medical students was 18.4 per 100,000 per annum; in terms of gender, the annual rate for men was 15.6 per 100,000 and 18.9 for women. The annual rate of suicide for young physicians in California was 20 per 100,000 and the range of other student populations was between 18 to 21 per 100,000 per year. The age distribution of students entering medical school was as follows: 20 years old and under, 3.9%; 21 to 23, 71.1%; 24 to 27, 18.6%; 28 and older, 6.4%; the mean age at admission was 23.0.

The mean suicide rate for male medical students (15.6 per 100,000) is below that of their age group in the national population. The rate for female medical students (18.9) is two to three times the rate for their age group. Hence, the previous researchers' findings that women physicians have a suicide rate higher than non-physician women can now be extended to include the medical school training period as well.

With respect to the academic year and standing of the student suicides, only 25 of the 52 suicides were reported on: of these 25 suicides reported, three were committed during the first year, 12 during the second year, seven during the third year and three were committed in the fourth and final year. This is significant because it showed a clustering of suicides in the second and third years of medical school. Fifty-four cases of suicide attempts were reported. The usual rate of attempts to completion is said to be seven or eight to one, and the attempt rate in the under-35 in the general population is well over 100 attempts per 100,000 per annum and as high as 600 in some age-sex subgroups. Clearly, either there is a substantial under-reporting of suicide attempts among medical students or as medical students they do not make attempted suicides as much as their age cohorts in the general populations.

It is interesting to note that a number of schools reported that none of their students received psychiatric treatment during the period of study and, at the other end, several schools reported 39-43% of their students received psychiatric treatment. The researchers concluded that some of the medical schools seem to systematically underserve the mental health needs of their student bodies.[58]

(4) Literature on physician suicide highlighted the fact that suicide rates were consistently higher for female physicians than for females in the general population. What about the support systems for female medical students? The following is a study that addressed this very important question. It describes a study of a support programme for first-year female medical students at the University of North Carolina. One of the aims of such a support programme was to provide an opportunity for female students to share problems and concerns; it provides an opportunity for individuals to listen to the problems and dilemmas as well as the opportunity to air out their feelings and to ease the potential tension and stress of their medical training. The researchers reviewed the process of forming a support group and presented an evaluation of the support programme by means of faculty assessment of the group process and a year-end student critique of the programme.

Firstly, a letter was sent to all women entering medical school in the summer as part of their orientation packet. Those who were interested were then invited to attend an informal first meeting. The group who met discussed several issues: e.g., the scarcity of female role models in medical school, the stereotypical view of women physicians, sex role biases by males, family and career role conflicts and the definition of medicine as a "masculine" field. From this first meeting, those who were still interested were then invited to meet on a regular basis. When asked why the females chose medicine as a career, many believed they were supposed to emulate the stereotypic, cold, rational male with a medical career. Some of them even defined themselves as "deviant females" because of professional aspirations. The majority of women also were resentful of the fact that their male peers regarded them only as buddies or laboratory partners rather than as women and equal professionals. Other issues that came out as important and significant were the sense of feeling isolated in medical school, anxiety about course demands and anger over sex discrimination.

The students then assessed whether the support group provided a needed constructive setting within which explorations of personal and professional concerns could occur. It allowed individuals to be heard and helped make all individuals aware that they are not alone. Others concur that such support systems should be made available to all medical students, male or female.[59]

DISCUSSION

Probably no other study of a suicide risk group has provoked such microscopic re-examination, replication, vehement reaction and confusion as that of research findings on physician suicide. It seems that some physicians have taken such studies as an attempt to drive a wedge in the edifice of their exalted profession. Fuel was added to the burning flame of controversy when some studies pointed out the alleged high rates of suicide among psychiatrists who are, in the eyes of the public and colleagues, supposed to be engaged in handling and treating emotional and psychiatric problems as well as suicide attempts and ideation. As evident from the letters to the editor of *JAMA*, some psychiatrists made hostile and aggressive reactions to such studies, especially to the inflammatory editorial of *JAMA* which stated, "Manifestly, the admonition Physician, heal thyself', has been heeded. Shouldn't there be a special one: Psychiatrist mind thy psyche' for the suicide-prone healer of the mind?"[60]

Whichever arguments and research findings may satisfy the reader, a careful and dispassionate review of the preceding discussion highlights the following points.

(1) In reviewing all the studies on this question, one serious issue yet to be resolved is the methodological one. In the past 100 years or so, the national rate of suicide for doctors has averaged between 35 to 40 in most studies reviewed. When one compares this to the entire national population, this is about three times the rate for the general population in the United States, but it is about the same as that for white males over age 25, to which physician suicide rates must be compared, not to the rates of the entire population. Thus, when the comparison is made between physicians and the national population over 25 years of age it suggests that, in general, physicians in America have not been at greater risk for suicide than the general population. Likewise, in other countries, as has been reviewed earlier in this chapter, the Scandinavian research found that male physicians have an increased suicide rate only when compared

to other academics but not when compared to the general population. The Bavarian findings concluded that the male physician suicide rate was only slightly higher than that of the male general population. Sakinofsky's review of the British study and some other studies cited found, however, that the male doctor's suicide rate was much higher than that of the general male population over 25 and higher than that of many other occupational groups. The picture is rather opaque and the issue contradictory; in most North American studies, age-specific rates were used, whereas in British studies SMR was the instrument of measurement. Future and continuous research is certainly in order with definitive, larger samples and key variables well controlled.

(2) What has been observed in many studies reviewed in this chapter, both from North America and from Europe, is the higher rate of suicide among female physicians when compared to the general population over 25. Whereas the rate of suicide for male physicians has been found to be more or less similar to that of the general male population, female doctors seem to kill themselves at least at two to three times the rate of their age cohorts in the general population. Consistently cited factors for suicide involving both male and female physicians, but more frequently mentioned vis-à-vis female physician suicide, are mood disorders such as depression and substance abuse.

(3) In terms of physician suicide by medical speciality, some of the studies mentioned in this chapter—e.g., those of Freeman, Blachly et al., De Sole et al., Rich and Holmes—cited high suicide rates among psychiatrists (ranging from 58 to 70 per 100,000). No such trends were observed by Craig and Pitts or Simon. A number of reputable studies discussed earlier in this chapter, however, lend support to an assumption that psychiatrists do indeed constitute a high-risk group. Even some physicians who question the reported high suicide rate for doctors in general seem to acknowledge that psychiatrists are inclined to kill themselves at a rate higher than that for the general population.[61] Some physicians even put the "teachings of psychiatry" in question until psychiatry can attain the lowest rate of suicide of any professional group.[62] Some go so far as to suggest that medical students should be made aware of possible conceptual errors in psychiatrists' knowledge of mental illness because quite a few young physicians choose psychiatry as their speciality on account of their unconscious needs and conflicts and as an attempt to seek solutions to their own unconscious problems.[63] The bottom line seems to be: "Does the strain and stress of the practice of psychiatry as a

speciality somehow predispose an individual to suicide or does the discipline of psychiatry attract more suicide-prone individuals?" Since there seems to be no irrefutable evidence to support the contention that psychiatry, or medicine in general for that matter, is more stressful than many other occupations (such as air-traffic controllers and police officers), one of the answers must be sought in the type of people drawn to this field. It seems quite appropriate and timely to look into the question of whether or not psychiatry may attract individuals to medicine who are saddled with emotional problems and a propensity to suicide. Some of the important research findings cited in this chapter seem to indicate the presence of greater degrees of problems and disorders among psychiatric students and practitioners, especially for females.

(4) In terms of the profile of the "physician at risk," the following composite picture seems to emerge. As mentioned by Ross earlier, the physician at risk seems to be characterized as excessively active, aggressive, ambitious, competitive, compulsive and self-oriented rather than group-oriented. He or she also exhibits an excessive need for achievement and recognition, an inability to comfortably tolerate delay in gratification and an exaggerated sense of duty and obligation to the demands of patients and their families. Epstein et al. mentioned a "blind test" in which a psychiatrist correctly identified all of the medical students who later killed themselves. From their successful results, the following features were identified as factors for eventual suicide, which differentiated the suicides from the control group: the suicide group scored significantly higher on thoughtfulness, anger-hostility and depression, negativism, suspiciousness, verbal expansiveness, excessive emotional dependency and impulsivity. Rimpela argued that physicians at risk are characterized by a grandiose self-image as well as a highly idealized parent image. Thus, according to this postulate, choosing a career in medicine is one way of achieving the need for others to depend on the person and maintain self-grandiosity. Thus, physicians develop a need for patients emotionally as well as professionally. Physicians who have not been able to develop a normal sense of self-esteem will be constantly dependent on others mirroring their grandiosity and may become dependent on their patients who experience the doctor as omnipotent.[64] The retention of the sense of grandiosity requires the repression of those parts of the personality or internal world that might take the doctor away from those who continually mirror the sense of the self. This may contribute to the difficulty in forming close emotional attachments, thus creating interpersonal and marital dissatisfaction and greater levels of depression due to the absence of a

social support system, which usually serves as a buffer against depression.[65]

(5) Suicide is a phenomenon not uncommon to highly successful people. Such seemingly successful people may project the outward persona of confidence, competence, control and regard for excellence; emotionally, however, there can be deep, masked insecurity and the looming sense that one is really a fraud, unworthy of being in a position of public trust and influence (known as the imposter syndrome). For such people, then, there is the constant fear that other people will unmask them and expose them as imposters. When and if such a public persona is threatened or there is some threat of embarrassment or humiliation, the ego finds it intolerable to bear the pressure of the feared loss. The individual becomes despondent, depressed and in extreme cases may even choose self-inflicted death.

(6) Another factor, often mentioned in some of the research findings cited in this chapter, is the alleged prevalence of Type A personalities among physicians, predisposing them to the experience of extreme stress and even suicide. In their earlier study between 1938 and 1942, Dublin and Spiegelman found that cardiovascular disorders among physicians were higher than the general population. They also found that coronary-artery disease was the highest for all medical specialities except for internists and pediatrics. Krakowski and Ross confirmed the same trends today and proposed that the higher mortality rate due to coronary-artery disease may be coincidental with the greater frequency of Type A personality traits among physicians who in general represent a sizeable population of compulsive-obsessive personalities when compared with other professions. They tend to be impatient, aggressive, competitive and filled with a sense of urgency; when confronted with a stressful situation, they feel they have lost control, struggle to reassert the control they think they have lost, work harder and faster and become very aggressive.

(7) Vincent outlined the patterns of distress that physicians tend to go through after graduating from medical school. Following the end of one's medical training, the young doctor usually goes into practice. It is well known that doctors are worried about developing a large enough practice to pay off their debts and make a comfortable income. Usually they work very hard to build their practice. Those physicians who have the desire to be needed, valued and appreciated are usually those who are working the hardest and have difficulty in refusing patients even if they are already overloaded. These physicians usually face extremely long hours to the point where there is no time left for outside interests. Eventually

there is insufficient time left for friends, spouse, family or any personal interests. Unfortunately, the new doctor is often not prepared for the workload and problems that may now arise; at times, these physicians are driven to sedatives and tranquillizers. As has been pointed out by many studies, the so-called "three Ds" (drink, drugs and depression) are the main contributors to deepening personal problems and distress, ultimately leading to self-inflicted death.[66]

(8) Even though some studies refuted the role-strain of the job contributing to suicide propensity, there is a report that lends some support to the assumption of a peril inherent in the job of the physician who deals with suicidals. The assumption that experience in psychiatry may induce an unbearable crisis to the practitioner has been pointed out by a team of psychiatrists from the psychiatric clinic at the University of Luebeck in Germany. Dr. Riemer reported that 100 physicians of different specializations, all employed at the University Hospital, were given a questionnaire. All of these physicians were charged with caring for suicidal patients. Riemer pointed out that suicidal patients often aroused vehement emotional reactions in the physicians involved in caring for them. Yet, the vast majority of these doctors felt that in facing possible suicide-inducing situations no external help could be expected and that the main help must come from their own efforts. In seeking external help, these doctors were fearful of a possible devaluation of their status and sense of omnipotence in the eyes of others. The suicidal patient represents an obvious emotional danger and threat; refusing the possible help, physicians would feel insecure, reactivating their own narcissistic problems, potential depressive tendencies and aggressive impulses.[67]

Such potential problems for caregivers, in their roles as physicians, psychiatrists, psychologists, counsellors, social workers, nurses and mental health workers, are often that they are the overlooked survivors of suicide. Caregivers also grieve and need support and understanding as much as other survivors. It is often forgotten that the relationship of therapist and patient is more than just a clinical interaction. A client's or patient's suicide often affects their caregiver both professionally and personally. Reactions may include disbelief, shock, feelings of failure, loss of self-esteem, a sense of inadequacy, feelings of being marked and exposed, fear of professional consequences, anger, guilt and intrusive thoughts. One study reveals that 57% of the psychiatrists reported experiencing post traumatic stress disorder syndrome (PTSD) similar to familial survivors. Thus, patient suicide poses a real occupational hazard for caregivers such as psychiatrists who work with suicidal people, and many of them may feel ill-prepared to deal with the aftermath.[68] These reports from the University of Luebeck and the *SIEC ALERT* published by Alberta's Suicide Information and Education Centre both emphasize the peril and risk of psychiatric caregivers in relation to their job and the potential strain involved. This may have some important implications for "helping the helpers."

(9) Narcissism and an exaggerated sense of grandiosity may enhance proneness to depression, especially when and if these needs are not satisfied or are barely compensated for through intellectual and professional accomplishment. Also, the length of time involved in study and training for the physician, the consequent and unusually long delay in achieving independence as well as the binding and extended ties to institutions may be seen as an abnormal prolongation of adolescence.[69] Moreover, from being familiar with birth and death and often functioning to interfere in those processes, depressed physicians may be less in awe of death and find it easy to see death as a real and acceptable way of solving problems. To make the matter worse, when an impaired physician, "a doctor in distress," does see a therapist, special difficulties arise on the therapist's side: i.e., problems of identification may interfere with true compassion and give rise to either overprotective action or unrealistic hesitation to hospitalize a colleague or potential friend.[70]

(10) What can be done, then, to either prevent or reduce the incidence of physician suicide? Sakinofsky suggests intensive career counselling prior to medical school, careful screening of candidates in order to make certain of the individual's ability to function in a small-group learning and training-oriented setting, early detection of the "three Ds" (drink, drugs and depression), refusal to cover up for colleagues who become impaired and the willingness to help those in distress and impairment. As Sakinofsky says: "If we are to prevent suicide among doctors at all, we have to act boldly, act early, and confront our own attitudinal ambiguities."[71] Yet, some medical researchers caution against such a screening process on the basis of factors that are frequently associated with suicide on the grounds that a large number of people with these risk factors will never commit suicide.[72] Even in the highest risk group of psychiatrists, only a very small number actually kill themselves. Any prematurely devised screening process may lead to the loss of potentially great contributions to medicine if entry to medical school or particular specialities was based on these "risk factors" with low specificity and reliability for predicting which individual will eventually commit suicide.[73]

(11) Another problem is that very few physicians have a primary-care doctor of their own. Even if they do, they seem to migrate to one who does not see alcoholism, chemical use or dependency as a problem. All doctors should be encouraged, therefore, to have a primary-care physician of their own choice—someone they can trust, feel comfortable with and talk to in confidence.

Another obstacle to physician welfare has been a great resistance and refusal to seek help. It is hard for most physicians to accept the fact that they need help; at the same time, they often do not know where to find it. Being self-employed, they must worry about a source of income when they go into treatment, and finally they must face the fear that their impairment may cost them their patients when they come back to the practice. Most of these fears are legitimate and must be taken into account.

One way of helping "physicians in trouble" is to set up a help line for doctors by volunteer physicians after the model of the lay telephone crisis line. In the mid-1980s, 115 physicians volunteered in Canada as "physician advocates" to provide a friendly, accessible ear to addicted physicians and/or doctors in emotional crisis. It is certainly possible that such a volunteer programme can be extended to impaired doctors in suicidal crises. The physicians in distress would not feel as hesitant to seek help anonymously from fellow doctors who are willing to extend a helping hand to peers in crisis. The benefits are evident from the experiment at the medical school in North Carolina as well as in the small-group discussion groups organized by medical students at McMaster University in Canada.

A 1993 Canada-wide survey of 3352 physicians revealed that female doctors are more likely than males to feel stress and are less happy in their marriages, sex lives and with the way their children are growing up; 46% of all physicians surveyed responded that they suspected they were suffering from clinical depression and 9% of them have admitted suicide ideation.[74]

Part of the physician's unwillingness to seek help is due to the unrealistic and excessive adoration of the medical practitioner on the part of the public, the fact of which makes it difficult for physicians to feel like "normal human beings." Society seems to force them into a posture of omnipotence and omniscience. For the genuine welfare of the physician, however, such exaggerated and unrealistic adoration must be tempered with the full appreciation of the physician's humanity. There have been some discernible trends in recent years in North America in which patients increasingly take charge of their health management and physicians serve as expert partners. In the same spirit, the public must learn to readjust their view of the physician and put the image in the right perspective. Only then is it possible for physicians to feel comfortable enough to reach out for help in time of crisis, and society and the public are the ultimate beneficiaries together with the physician in crisis.

NOTES AND REFERENCES

1   Cuneo, C.J., "Class, Stratification and Mobility," in Robert Hagedorn (ed), *Sociology* (Toronto: Holt, Rinehart and Winston, 1983), pp.256-258.
2   Brown, R., "Life Events and Their Effect on Suicide: A Test among Physicians," *Advances in Medical Sociology*, 1990: 1, pp.171-188.
3   Holmes, V.F. and Rich, C.L., "Suicide among Physicians," in Blumenthal, S.J., and Kupfer, D.J., (eds), *Suicide over Life Cycle*, (Washington, D.C.; 1991), p.599.
4   Sakinofsky, I., "Suicide in Doctors and Wives of Doctors," *Canadian Family Physicians*, 1980: 26, June, pp.837-844.
5   Johnson, T.M., "Physician Impairment: Social Origins of a Medical Concern," *Medical Anthropology Quarterly*, 1982: 2, 1, March, pp.17-33.
6   Motto, J.A., "Suicide and Suggestibility—The Role of the Press," *American Journal of Psychiatry*, 1967, 124, 2, p.252.
7   Registrar-General, Decennial Supplement—England and Wales, 1951, *Occupational Mortality*, Part 2, Vols. I and II (London: H.M.S.O.).
8   *Journal of the American Medical Association* (JAMA), Editorial, 1903: 41, p.263.
9   Blachly, P.H., Osterud, H.T. and Josslin, R., "Suicide among Professional Groups." *New England Journal of Medicine*, 1963: 268, pp.1278-1282.
10 *British Medical Journal*, "Suicide among Doctors," Editorial Article, 1964: March, No.5386, p.789.
11 *Ibid.*
12 Freeman, W., "Psychiatrists Who Kill Themselves: A Study in Suicide," Brief Communications, *American Journal of Psychiatry*, 1967: 124, pp.846-847.
13 DeSole, E.E., Singer, P. and Aronson, S., "Suicide and Role Strain among Physicians," *International Journal of Social Psychiatry*, 1969: 15, pp. 294-301.
14 *Ibid.* p.17.
15 Sakinofsky, I., "Suicide in Doctors and Wives of Doctors," *op. cit.*
16 Sakinofsky, I. "Correspondence," *British Medical Journal*, 1980: 2, August, p.386.

17 Rose, K.D. and Rosow, I., "Physicians Who Kill Themselves," *Archives of General Psychiatry*, 1973: 29, pp.800-805.

18 Epstein, L.C., Thomas, C.B., Shaffer, J.W. and Perlin, S., "Clinical Prediction of Physician Suicide Based on Medical Student Data," *Journal of Nervous and Mental Diseases*, 1973: 156, pp.19-26.

19 Vincent, M.O., "Some Sequelae of Stress in Physicians," *The Psychiatric Journal of the University of Ottawa*, 1983: 8,3, pp.120-124.

20 Krakowski, A.J., "Stress and the Practice of Medicine—The Myth and Reality," *Journal of Psychosomatic Research*, 1982: 26, 1, pp.91-98.

21 Ross, M., "Suicide among Physicians," *Diseases of the Nervous System*, 1973: 34, 3, pp.145-150.

22 Simon, W., "Suicide among Physicians: Prevention and Postvention," *Crisis*, 1986: 7, (1), pp.1-13.

23 *Ibid.*

24 Arnetz, B.B., Hörte, L.G., Hedberg, A., Theorell, T., Allander, E. and Malker, H., "Suicide Patterns among Physicians Related to Other Academics as well as to the General Population: Results from a National Long-Term Prospective Study and a Retrospective Study," *Acta Psychiatrica Scandinavica*, 1987: 75, 2, February, pp.139-143.

25 Rickings, J.C., Khara, G.S. and McDowell, M., "Suicide in Young Doctors," *British Journal of Psychiatry*, 1986: 149, pp.475-478.

26 Rimpela, A.H., Nurminen, M.M., Pulkkinen, P.O. et al., "Mortality of Doctors: Do Doctors Benefit from Their Medical Knowledge?", *Lancet*, 1987: 1, pp.84-86.

27 Dublin, L.I. and Spiegelman, M., "Longevity and Mortality of American Physicians," *Journal of the American Medical Association*, 1947: 134, pp.1211-1215.

28 Craig, A.G. and Pitts, F.N., "Suicide by Physicians," *Diseases of the Nervous System*, 1968: 29, pp.763-772.

29 Mausner, J.S. and Steppacher, R.C., "Suicide in Male and Female Physicians," *Journal of the American Medical Association*, 1974: 228, 3, pp.323-328.

30 Pitts, F.N., et al., "Suicide among U.S. Women Physicians, 1967-1972," *American Journal of Psychiatry*, 1979: 136, 5, May, pp.694-696.

31 *Ibid.*

32 Welner, A., Marten, S., Wochnick, E. et al., "Psychiatric Disorders among Professional Women," *Archives of General Psychiatry*, 1979: 36, pp.169-173.

33 Holmes, V.F. and Rich, C.L., "Suicide among Physicians," *op. cit.*

34 Nadelson, C. and Notman, M., "What is Different for Women Physicians," from Schreiber, S.C., and Doyle, B.B. (eds), *The Impaired Physician* (New York: Plenum Medical Book, 1983), pp.11-26.

35 Carlson, G.A. and Miller, D.C., "Suicide, Affective Disorder, and Women Physicians," *American Journal of Psychiatry*, 1981: 138, pp.1330-1335.

36 Williams, E., Bissell, L., Sullivan, E., "The Effects of Co-Dependence on Physicians and Nurses," *British Journal of Addiction,* 1991: 86, 1, January, pp.37-42.

37 Bissell, L. and Jones, R.W., "The Alcoholic Physician," *American Journal of Psychiatry*, 1976: 133, pp.1142-1146.

38 *The Journal*, Ontario Addiction Foundation, October 1984, p.7.

39 *Ibid.*

40 Krakowski, A.J., "Stress and the Practice of Medicine—The Myth and Reality," *op. cit.*, pp.98.

41 Freeman, W., "Psychiatrists Who Kill Themselves...," *op. cit.*

42 *British Medical Journal,* "Suicide among Doctors,"*op. cit.*

43 Rich, C.L. and Pitts, F.N., "Suicide by Psychiatrists: A Study of Medical Specialists among 18,730 Consecutive Physician Deaths during a Five-Year Period, 1967-1972," *Journal of Clinical Psychiatry,* 1980: 41, 8, August, pp.261-263.

44 Pitts, F.N. et al., "Letters to the Editor," *American Journal of Psychiatry*, 1979: 136, 12, p.1608.

45 Welner et al., *op. cit.*

46 Russell, A.T. et al., "Emotional Problems of Residents in Psychiatry," *American Journal of Psychiatry*, 1975: 132, pp.263-267; Ward, C.F. et al., "Drug Abuse in Anesthesia Training Programme: A Survey 1970-1980," *Journal of the American Medical Association,* 1983: 250, pp.922-925.

47 Russell, A.T., Pasnau, R.O. and Taintor, Z.C., "Emotional Problems of Residents in Psychiatry," *American Journal of Psychiatry*, 1975: 132, pp.263-267.

48 Bergman, J., "The Suicide Rate among Psychiatrists Revisited," *Suicide and Life-Threatening Behavior*, 1979: 9, 4, pp.219-226.

49 Rose and Rosow, *op. cit.*

50 Allander, E., Arnetz, B.B., Hedberg, A., Hörte, L.G., Malker, H., Theorell, T., *op. cit.*

51 Simon, W., "Suicide among Physicians: Prevention and Postvention," *Crisis*, 1986: 7, (1) pp.1-13.

52 Rich and Pitts, *op. cit.*

53 Kurosawa, H., *Dialogue and Handshake for Suicide Prevention* (Tokyo: Kobundo, 1988).

54 Willi, J., "Higher Incidence of Physical and Mental Ailments in Future Psychiatrists as Compared with Future Surgeons and Internal Medicine Specialists at Military Conscription," *Social Psychiatry*, 1983: 18, pp.69-72.

55 Holmes and Rich, *op. cit.*, p.615.

56 Parlow, J. and Rothman, A.I., "Personality Traits of First Year Medical Students: Trends over a Five Year Period," in Short, S.E., (ed), *Psychiatric Illness in Physicians* (Springfield, Illinois: Charles C. Thomas, 1982), pp.211-219.

57 Thomas, C.B., "What Becomes of Medical Students: The Dark Side," *Johns Hopkins Medical Journal*, 1976: 138, pp.185-195.

58 Pepitone-Arreola-Rockwell, F., Rockwell, D. and Core N., "Fifty-two Medical Student Suicides," *American Journal of Psychiatry*, 1981: 138, pp.198-201.

59 Hilbertman, E., Konanc, J., Perez-Reyes, M., Hunter, R., Scagnelli, J. and Sanders, S., "Support Groups for Women in Medical School: A First-Year Program," in Short, S.E., (ed), *Psychiatric Illness in Physicians, op. cit.*, pp.305-315.

60 "Physician Heals Himself," *Editorial, Journal of the American Association*, 1971: 218, pp.1823.

61 "Mental Disturbance in Doctors," Editorial, *British Medical Journal*, 1969: 4, p.448, *op. cit.*

62 Ellerbrook, W.C., "Suicide in Psychiatrists," *Journal of the American Medical Association,* 1972: 222: p.364.

63 Braun, M., "Suicide in Psychiatrists," *Journal of the American Medical Association*, 1973: 223, p.81.

64 Rimpela et al., "Mortality of Doctors...," *op. cit.*

65 Johnson, E., "Predisposition to Emotional Distress and Psychiatric Illness among Doctors: The Role of Unconscious and Experiential Factors," *British Journal of Medical Psychology,* 1994: 64, 4, pp.317-329.

66 Sakinofsky, *op. cit.*

67 Riemer, C., "Problems of Interaction with Suicidals," presented at the 11th World Congress of Suicide Prevention, Paris, 1981.

68 SIEC ALERT, "When a Patient or Client Commits Suicide," (Calgary, Alberta: Suicide Information and Education Centre, 1996) February, 1996, p.2.

69 Mendeewicz, J. and Wilmotte, J., "Letters to the Editor," *American Journal of Psychiatry,* 1971: 128, pp.364-365.

70 *Ibid.*

71 Sakinofsky, *op. cit.*, p.843.

72 Pokorny, A.D., "Predictions of Suicide in Psychiatric Patients: Report of a Prospective Study," *Archives of General Psychiatry*, 1983: 40, pp.249-259.

73 For a fuller discussion of preventive measures for physician suicide, see, Holmes and Rich, *op. cit.*, pp.611-615.

74 *The Toronto Star*, October 29, 1993, A.15.

CHAPTER 7

Suicide as Crisis:
Prevention, Intervention and Postvention

S uicide is understandably the extreme end of a continuum involving a crisis in life; as such, it has received serious attention from social, behavioural and medical scientists as well as concerned and trained lay persons. In this chapter, then, discussion will focus on the various aspects of suicide as crisis, including various issues of prevention, intervention and postvention. There is a division of labour in such crisis management: prevention has been largely, but not exclusively, the area of concern and activity of lay people such as the volunteers at the crisis telephone line; intervention has been handled mainly by medical and mental health professionals as well as trained lay persons on the crisis help line; and postvention has mainly been the domain of the caring and skilled staff and trained volunteers of a self-help group for survivors.

This last chapter, therefore, will be useful for those who are currently involved in prevention, intervention and postvention of suicide, and for those who are interested in going into such areas either as volunteers or professionals. With such aims in mind, the present chapter has been organized to present both theoretical and practical information for the management of suicidal crisis. It may be mentioned parenthetically that the discussion in this chapter incorporates both findings by clinicians and personal input of the present author as a former volunteer at one of the telephone crisis lines in Toronto.

PREVENTION

Crisis

In life one sometimes encounters an event or a situation for which no previous experience is of much use, and one's coping and problem-solving abilities are diminished or in some instances severely impaired. In such a case one is said to be in crisis.

The experience of crisis has subjective and objective dimensions. Just as beauty may be in the eye of the beholder, crisis is in the subjective experiences and feelings of the individual involved. It means, therefore, that one person's experience of an event or a situation is probably different from that of another. What may be experienced as devastating or traumatic by one person could be shrugged off as "just bad luck" by another individual.

What is the definition of the term and concept of "crisis"? One dictionary defines crisis as the turning point (as in a disease) towards life or death as well as a point or a deciding event at which a change must come either for the better or the worse.[1] In Chapter 1 we explored the implications of the etymology of "suicide," etymology being the science of probing the root of given words in a language. In the same vein, a cross-cultural examination of the word "crisis" also reveals a rich wisdom of different cultures both in the East and West. The word "crisis" is derived from *krisis* in Greek meaning "decision" and a "turning point." It is *crisis* in English, *crise* in French, *crisi* in Italian, *crisis* in Spanish, and *Krise* in German. All these European words suggest a common origin in Greek and common meaning—"decision" and "turning point." That is to say, in facing a serious and hazardous event, one must face the "turning point" of deciding how to handle it and in which direction one must move. It is a well-known fact among people engaged in crisis intervention that individuals in crisis are much more willing to slough off defences and thereby become more open to suggestions and to gaining new insights and coping skills. In short, crisis serves for some as a turning point by assisting individuals to make decisions that may hopefully lead to self-empowerment.

In Japanese, the word "crisis" is a composite word made up of *danger* and *opportunity*, as shown in Figure 1. In other words, a crisis is a situation or an event in one's life in which an individual faces danger

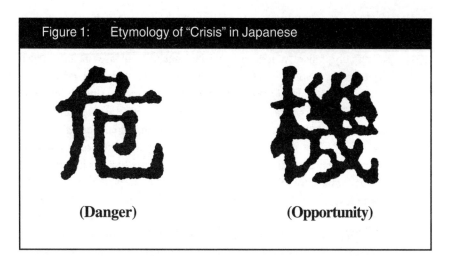

(Danger)   (Opportunity)

but uses it as an opportunity for self-growth, development and learning.[2] It is interesting to note that the etymology of crisis both in the East and West assumes that there is latent human capacity for limitless growth, development and learning even in the most severe, adverse circumstances (such as divorce, serious physical illness, etc.), and that crisis basically is temporary and self-limiting in nature and can be arrested and even turned around to one's advantage. There is tremendous wisdom involved in such implications: to interpret crisis as "illness" after the medical disease model may suggest treatment or medicalization, whereas understanding it as opportunity for self-growth can and does imply a positive, self-directed response to the crisis.

In this book, crisis is understood as an "acute emotional upset arising from situational, developmental (i.e., life-stage transitions) or social sources, which may result in a temporary reduction in one's usual problem-solving skills."[3]

There are two types of crisis: maturational-developmental and accidental-situational. The former refers to those life events and processes every human being is bound to encounter and experience and, hence, cannot avoid in the course of life—illness, growing old, death, etc.[4] In maturational-developmental crisis the individual can, to a large extent, anticipate that during each stage of life the individual will be subjected to a unique stress, natural changes in roles and physical functions, which creates internal turmoil and high levels of anxiety and stress. By contrast, in the latter type of crisis, such a hazardous event or situation is not expected and thus the individual is thrown off balance with little time to effectively prepare for it. Such accidental, unexpected crises include sudden death, rape, divorce, etc. It is possible, however, that some preparatory knowledge may reduce the shock, severity and profundity of stress and psychic pain as well as aid in the cultivation of specific problem-solving skills and emotional strength with which to withstand the crisis.

In terms of duration, acute crisis is usually temporary and self-limiting. Hence, the time-limiting nature of the crisis makes it possible for support and short-term therapies to work as opposed to long-term therapies such as psychoanalysis that require a much longer period for effective treatment.

One other major feature of crisis is that it often reduces the individual's self-defence mechanisms and thereby enlarges one's capacity for learning and growth. For some people crisis may have the devastating and traumatic effect of crushing the individual involved, but for others it may offer an opportunity to learn new coping skills and accelerate growth and development by providing profound insight as well as lowering the defensiveness that has stunted growth in the past. Crisis workers are often amazed at the openness and willingness of the individual in crisis to gain new insights into the nature and resolution of their problem(s). People in crisis have the genuine and intense desire to get out of their unbearable pain and suffering. Their capacity for growth is usually enhanced with timely help from such personal and social resources as close friends, family, neighbours, trained crisis workers and mental health professionals. Conversely, failure to receive such timely assistance, when urgently needed, can result in diminished growth, impaired or collapsed coping ability and disastrous crisis resolution in the form of self-inflicted death or injury to others. The crucial factors seem to be the presence and strength of the personal desire for resolving the crisis and self-empowerment as well as the timely availability of help from others, all of which will influence the outcome of crisis in a favourable direction.

To summarize, the fundamental question to be asked is not "Will I encounter distress or crisis in life?"(no one can avoid some kind of crisis in one's life anyway), but rather "How does one understand crisis and deal with it?" and "How can one use crisis as an opportunity for growth and empowerment?"

Theory of Crisis

One of the most crucial studies of crisis was conducted by Lindemann, a psychiatrist at the Massachusetts General Hospital, in 1944. In conjunction with a project in the regional mental health programme, he investigated the horrible effects of a fire that gutted the Coconut Grove Melody Lounge, a nightclub in Boston, a fire which killed 492 persons. He interviewed surviving family members who had lost their dear ones to the fire and revealed that there were some common physiological and psychological manifestations: physiologically, there were unmistakable signs of numbness, deep sighing, heart palpitation, shortness of breath, tension in the throat, dryness in the mouth, fullness in the stomach and loss of appetite, muscular weakness, motor retardation and disoriented behaviour; cognitively, there was a drastic decline in power of concentration and memory; psychologically, such symptoms as strong death ideation, despair and hopelessness, guilt and self-blame, rage and aggression that had not been vented or displaced emerged. Lindemann found that these survivor-victims of the disaster developed serious psychopathologies and were unable to go through the normal grieving process. Later Lindemann expanded his research by including other people who experienced a sudden and unexpected loss such as death in war and/or death in hospital. He concluded that the aforementioned symptoms were commonly observed among most people who were subjected to a serious, sudden and unexpected loss.[5]

According to Lindemann, in each of these situations emotional strain would be generated, stress would be experienced and a series of adaptive mechanisms would take place that could lead either to mastery of the new situation or to failure to function. It is true that people usually experience stress when exposed to severe, sudden and unexpected loss, "[which] become crises for those individuals who by personality, previous experience or other factors in the present situation are especially vulnerable to this stress and whose emotional resources are taxed beyond their usual adaptive resources."[6] Hence, Lindemann stressed the importance of encouraging people to allow themselves to go through the normal grieving process and subsequently prevent negative outcomes of crises due to loss.

Another important figure in the theory of crisis, who ranks as importantly as Lindemann, is G. Caplan. Also a psychiatrist at Harvard Medical School, Caplan conducted joint research with Lindemann, did extensive research in Israel, participated in the regional mental health programme of Harvard University and made important contributions to the field of preventive psychiatry.

His theory is based upon the mechanistic model and concept of equilibrium and assumes that people in disequilibrium are out of balance in respect to both their personality and the social system. According to Caplan, the individual tries to solve problems that occur in human environments and tries to maintain constant equilibrium in physical and emotional conditions. This equilibrium is usually maintained with an optimal amount of internal tension and external stimuli without, however, wasting energy. When such balance is broken, restorative mechanisms go into operation and bring back the original balance. Crisis happens when restoration of the equilibrium cannot be achieved with the help of previous problem-solving skills and experience. According to his theory, however, a crisis does not occur instantaneously. Rather, there are identifiable phases of development (primarily psychosocial in character) that lead to an active crisis stage.

Caplan described four phases in the development of extreme anxiety and crisis, occurring in a gradual process from less catastrophic stressors. In Phase 1, a person encounters a traumatic event which raises one's level of anxiety to such an extent and degree that the person feels quite uncomfortable and tries to reduce or eliminate the stress, discomfort and the resulting and mounting anxiety. At this stage, however, the person's encounter with the traumatic event has not yet escalated it into a crisis. In Phase 2, with the failure of the person's problem-solving skills, the tension and anxiety remain unabated and generate confusion and a mounting sense of powerlessness. In Phase 3, with the ever-rising tension and anxiety, the individual's latent coping ability would now be mobilized, employing new or unusual means to solve the problem. Yet, despite all this, the person fails to reduce the level of anxiety and tension. Finally, in Phase 4, the person is now in the full grip of crisis with the physical and emotional tension rising to an unbearable limit; one's own inner resources and coping skills are either extremely diminished or near the collapsing point in the absence of support. Preventive psychiatry, therefore, should enable people in crisis to at least return to their precrisis state by restoring equilibrium; help people in crisis to grow and become stronger as a result of learning from the crisis and acquiring new ways of problem-solving (empowerment); and it should learn to discern the danger signals. As a pioneer in preventive psychiatry, Caplan introduced the three stages of preventive psychiatry: the primary stage of preventing the occurrence of mental and emotional disorder, the secondary stage of shortening the period of affliction after the occurrence, and the tertiary stage of reducing the effects of psychiatric disorder.[7]

More recently, Brockopp and Lester maintained that crisis does not exist in the traumatic event itself but rather in the way the person perceives it and responds to it. The question of how a person responds to the crisis event or situation is dependent on the following factors: the individual's personality structure and way of living, the quality and nature of the situations the person has encountered in the past, the degree of social support and the presence of a support system and a coping ability that can withstand the crisis without being crushed.[8]

The Telephone Crisis Line

The Origin of the Telephone Helpline

One well-known suicide prevention measure has been the volunteer-based activities of the telephone crisis line. How did the crisis hotline come about and develop? What do they do, and how effective are they?

In the history of mental health, there have been three major "revolutions." The first of these occurred during the turbulent years of the French Revolution towards the end of the 18th century. Throughout the centuries in Europe the psychiatrically ill were called "insane" and were invariably chained to their chairs and shackled in insane asylums. Confinement of the mentally ill began in earnest in the fifteenth and sixteenth centuries, and these asylum conditions were truly deplorable. The prevailing ideology in Europe since the Middle Ages held that the psychiatrically ill were "possessed by the devil," and treatment largely consisted of bloodletting, purging, baking, dunking in cold water and whirling in beds. Most European hospitals for the mentally ill were little more than prisons for keeping patients off the streets. The situation began to change dramatically with the intervention of a young French physician who introduced a new type of humane treatment of the mentally ill shortly after the French Revolution.

Philippe Pinel (1754-1826) obtained the permission of the revolutionary Paris Commune in 1793 to release about a dozen of the more docile asylum patients and studied their reactions for several days. He then had more patients released after ascertaining and proving that they are usually harmless to the public. He even designed new hospital rooms; kept records of the patients' diagnoses, treatments and outcomes; and tried to understand the patients' troubles rather than simply locking them up in a hospital. Many who had been excitable and completely unmanageable became calm and much easier to handle; they strolled through the hospital grounds with no inclination to create disturbances or to harm anyone. Some who had been incarcerated in the asylum for years were soon restored to health and were eventually discharged from the hospital. Pinel thus started the first major revolution in mental health by freeing these patients from chains, shackles and dungeons as well as by emancipating medical treatment of psychiatric patients from the domains of witchcraft and demonology.[9]

The second revolution was the introduction of psychotropic drugs—especially antidepressants—that have, since the late 1950s, made it possible for many psychiatric patients to be released from psychiatric wards and treated as "outpatients" and to resume normal routines at home and at work. Moreover, thanks to such drugs, seriously depressed patients who had previously been impervious to any psychotherapy have been able to respond to psychotherapy and other therapeutic measures.

The third mental health revolution has been the massive participation of lay volunteers in many aspects of mental health programmes, suicide prevention and intervention tasks. Probably the most dramatic undertaking of suicide prevention are the telephonic emergency services, which are operated by trained lay volunteers. These services provide active listening and befriending to those anonymous callers who may be lonely, distressed, in crisis or at times suicidal.

Today the telephone has become an indispensable item in every person's daily life. It is literally a "lifeline:" the emergency number (911 in Canada and the United States and 110 in Japan) enables a person to seek help in emergency situations such as fire, crime, sudden illness, accident and suicide. It is common knowledge that a special red "hot line" has been installed in the offices of the presidents of the United States and of Russia in order to prevent any accidental triggering of disastrous nuclear war. The role of the telephone in saving human lives cannot be exaggerated.

The world's first suicide prevention activities by phone and by lay persons were initiated by an Anglican priest in a small parish church in London in 1954. The catalyst for the Rev. Chad Varah's initiative was the suicide of a 14-year-old girl who had been receiving counselling from Varah. Due to inadequate knowledge, this young girl mistook her menstrual bleeding as signs of venereal disease and committed suicide. Shaken by the incident, Varah and his secretary installed a telephone in the basement of the church, advertised its number in London's daily newspapers and made appeals to all those in distress or contemplating suicide to call. This was the beginning of the world's first telephone befriending and emergency service, and the phone has been ringing ever since. Eventually, Chad Varah's initiative led to the formation of a volunteer group that came to be known as "Samaritans," to symbolize the unconditional neighbourly love to strangers as described in the Bible. Today the Samaritans boast a network of more than 200 crisis centres all over the British Isles, in addition to 275 branches worldwide. The Samaritans' services include lay volunteers befriending on the phone around the clock as well as face-to-face counselling. They do not trace calls or take any unrequested action. Central to their philosophy is a dedication to active and befriending listening to those in distress. Almost all of the branches of the Samaritans in the British Isles have outreach programmes, and they have been actively involved in the schools, speaking to students, holding workshops for parents and educators as well as befriending survivors of families after a suicide has taken place. The Samaritans also serve the hearing-impaired: some centres have mechanical phone aids so hearing-impaired individuals can communicate. The Samaritans also help the prison population by speaking with the inmates and training some of them to help others in the prison.[10]

Telephone crisis lines around the world are roughly divided into three major groups: Befrienders International, Lifeline International and International Federation of Telephonic Emergency Services (IFOTES). Samaritans belong to Befrienders International. The second group, Lifeline International, was started in 1963 by a Protestant minister in Australia, Allan Walker, after he received a jarring, anonymous phone call announcing suicide. Walker's group in Australia performs such functions as answering all incoming calls, arranging interviews with mental health professionals and lawyers, arranging lodging and on occasion, dispatching a deputation team to the caller (with the caller's consent, of course). In contrast to the Samaritans who recruit volunteers widely regardless of race, creed or colour, Walker's Lifeline accepts volunteers, in principle at least in its inception, from the established evangelical churches. Lifeline is called Contact in the United States and Telecare in Canada. The third group, the International Federation of Telephonic Emergency Services (IFOTES), is primarily based in Europe with crisis telephone centres for all the countries that are not part of either Samaritans or Lifeline International. Its international stature and scope increased when Japan's INOCHI-NO-DENWA (Lifeline) joined the IFOTES officially at the conclusion of its annual meeting in Jerusalem in the summer of 1994.

The present author has had the pleasure of visiting many kinds of telephone help lines and crisis centres in 45 countries around the world. Many have adopted their own name and logo: the service is called Samaritans in Britain, SOS-Amitié in France, Telefonseelsorge in Germany, La Main Tendue and Die Dagebotene Hand in Switzerland, Distress Centre and Telecare in Canada, Contact and Crisis Center in the United States, Lifeline in Australia, Elet in Hungary, La Esperanza in Spain, La Voce d'Amica in Italy, INOCHI-NO-DENWA in Japan and ERAN in Israel.

Despite some differences in the founding principles and methods of recruiting volunteers, all telephone helplines are basically united in their common purpose: in the spirit of active listening, unconditional acceptance and befriending will be offered immediately to any caller by a trained lay person without judgment and without prejudice to the caller's situation. In short, every telephone helpline tries to offer empathy and nonjudgmental listening and support to the caller. In this regard, helplines differ from the role of the therapist whose attitude may typically be "I am going to do such and such for your benefit," with the concommitant clinical judgment, evaluation and professional detachment. Herein lie the unique features and strengths of lay-oriented crisis centres, which at times can surpass the ability of professionals to reach out to those in distress and crisis. Robert Litman, a former medical examiner and an associate director of the Los Angeles Suicide Prevention Center, has aptly summarized the potential effectiveness of the volunteer in what has come to be known as "Litman's Law": "the more severe and acute the suicidal crisis is, the less one needs to be professionally trained to manage it effectively."[11] This belief was echoed by two well-known psychiatrists in Europe who, after years of distinguished psychiatric practice and research in suicide behaviour, concluded that psychosocial crises are resolved today in 70 to 80% of cases by self-help, family resources and neighbourly help. It is assumed that only the remaining 20% may need professional intervention.[12]

A comparative study of 65 lay volunteers and 27 professionals in terms of empathy, warmth, sincerity and therapeutic effect on helplines revealed that lay volunteers scored higher than the professionals for empathy, warmth and overall atmosphere; only on standards of therapeutic effect did the professionals score slightly higher.[13] Furthermore, people in distress and crisis generally have the intense desire to be free of the unbearable pain and suffering, and have proven to be capable of helping themselves to repair and restore their problem-solving and coping skills. Their capacity for recovery and growth from the crisis experience is usually enhanced with timely help from available social resources such as friends, family, neighbours, trained lay crisis workers and mental health professionals. Conversely, failure to receive such help, when urgently needed, may result in inadequate recovery, diminished growth and disastrous crisis resolution in the form of suicide or assault on others. The strength of an individual's desire for re-empowerment, along with timely availability of help from others, may influence the outcome of crisis in a favourable direction.

What is most desired and required for the volunteers on the helpline is neither professional knowledge nor skill in dealing with a particular crisis but rather the ability to be a good and compassionate listener. Hence, the crisis centre treasures human attributes such as warmth, the ability to listen, empathize and accept others unconditionally and without moral judgment as well as the capacity to form a bond with another human being who is lonely, in distress or in crisis.[14]

There are a number of distinct advantages and merits in the lay-oriented helpline. By its very nature, there is little restriction by either location or time; one can place a call anytime, anywhere, as often as one wishes. There is complete freedom to say anything one wishes without any constraint because all callers are free to remain anonymous. In addition, the initiative lies entirely on the caller from start to finish whether to continue or terminate the call without consultation or permission. Such freedom would be extremely difficult in face-to-face counselling with a professional. There is also a complete sense of equality between the caller and the volunteer; by contrast, the relationship between the professional therapist and client/patient is bound to be unequal and hence vertical. The typical volunteer on the helpline is a non-professional lay person who may have gone through similar life situations and is completely free to admit this to the caller. Such equality enables the caller and volunteer to establish an immediate rapport and a feeling of emotional proximity, mutuality and identification. For better or worse, open and frank self-disclosure and revelation is quite rare, if not impossible, between a professional therapist and client/patient in face-to-face relationship. There is the additional advantage of immediacy: the helpline service is available

Inochi No Denwa

(Life Telephone)

Federation of Inochi No Denwa

Affiliated with the International Association for Suicide Prevention

5-3-1 Ibori Kokurakita-ku
Kitakyushu-shi, Fukuoka-ken, JAPAN
Tel.: 093-651-6595,   Fax: 093-651-6595

Courtesy of Japan's INOCHI-NO-DENWA

Courtesy of Japan's INOCHI-NO-DENWA

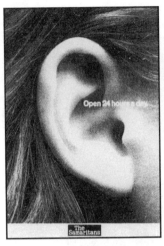

世界の40数か国にいのちの電話があります

Courtesy of Japan's INOCHI-NO-DENWA

immediately, free of charge and is only a phone call away without the necessity of an appointment, which would certainly be necessary in order to see a professional. One does not have to wait before getting help when one is in urgent need of immediate emotional first aid (it is befitting that the ERAN, the Israeli telephone crisis line, means "emotional first aid"). Precisely because of its anonymity, the caller can and does skip any social formality and come straight to the point and confide in the volunteer without fear of judgment or being controlled.[15] As testified by a psychotherapist in the crisis intervention unit in a well-known Toronto hospital, there has been a problem of an unconscious or latent desire to control the behaviour and thinking of a client on the part of professionals, teachers and others in the helping profession.[16] In this regard, the very emphasis of the helpline is actually a positive asset in offering a nonjudgmental, listening ear without trying to control the caller's behaviour or thinking. The crisis line's ethos is primarily centred around active listening rather than therapeutic measures such as trying to modify one's behaviour and thinking. Finally, the helpline is the only service that extends its ear to loneliness. If a person suffering from loneliness tried to book an appointment with a mental health professional in a country with a publicly financed health-care system, he or she would most likely be laughed out of the therapist's office, not treated seriously or dismissed as wasting taxpayer's money. The vast majority of incoming calls to crisis lines in nearly every one of the 45 countries investigated by the present author are such "loneliness" calls. The role and function of the telephone helpline in dealing with loneliness ought to be noted and appreciated. Upon discovering that a vast majority of calls at crisis centres around the world are about loneliness, the present author tried to locate a bibliography on loneliness. Surprisingly, there is actually very little work done on the subject of loneliness by sociologists, psychiatrists and psychologists. As a matter of fact, what little has been written about loneliness is by religious thinkers, theologians and novelists. Yet loneliness, if and when it reaches an unbearable point, may lead to serious despair, hopelessness and self-destructive acts. At present, the telephone helpline seems to be one of the few helping organizations that treats loneliness seriously and deals with it.

Be that as it may, the telephone helpline is fundamentally different from the various forms of advice offered in newspapers, magazines and radio programmes. The "life advice" vehicles usually have a well-known personality or media savvy professional answering problems and giving one-sided advice, yet their effectiveness has never been investigated or verified. From the standpoint of mental health and psychotherapy, general agreement among professionals is that these methods are probably not very effective in dealing with human distress and crisis.[17] The fundamental purpose of the helpline is not problem-oriented but rather person-oriented: that is to say, it is not meant to deal with specific issues or problems like professionals so much as trying to reach out to people in distress by helping them to vent their feelings and find their own way of solving problems through active listening, empathy and emotional support. Herein lies the essence of telephonic befriending. Probably the Japanese (and Chinese) character for "listening" best describes and represents the spirit of active listening practiced by telephone crisis lines the world over. As shown in Figure 2, the Japanese character for "listening" is composed of four subcharacters: ear, eye, undivided attention and heart. In Japan, listening to someone means you lend your ears, eyes and heart in undivided attention. Thus, the etymology of words for both "crisis" and "listening" reveals a rich human wisdom, East or West.

Befriending on the phone, however, requires more than empathy, acceptance and support. The volunteer training includes special skills in active listening as well as evaluative skills in dealing with each call. Each volunteer is required to write and turn in an evaluation sheet after the call, and at the end of his or her shift submits all the call sheets to the staff for further evaluation and comment. Examples of such call sheets from the world-renowned Los Angeles Suicide Prevention Center Telephone Service and the Ontario Distress Centre are given in figures 3 and 4.

According to the Ontario Association of Distress Centres (OADC) there were 150,844 calls from 17 distress centres in Ontario between January and December 1992. The following trends were observed: in terms of age, 47.9% of the callers were between 25-44 years of age, with the smallest percentage of calls from the aged (despite the fact that they constitute one of the highest risk groups for suicidality); as for gender, 57% of the calls were from females, compared to 42.6% from males. A majority of callers (49.4%) are single, followed by the divorced (13.7%), the married (10.6%), the separated (6.5%) and the widowed (4.7%). As for living arrangements, half (50%) live alone and 32.5% live with others. Almost half of the callers (48.1%) are what the distress centre calls

Figure 2: The Japanese Characters that Make up the Verb "To Listen" Tell us Something Significant about this Skill

Figure 2: The Japanese Characters that Make up the Verb "To Listen" Tell us Something Significant about this Skill

Ear
Eye
Undivided Attention
Heart

"repeat callers," as compared to 19.2% of the new callers, suggesting that there may be a sort of support relationship in formation through the centre's befriending. For the vast majority of calls (almost 90%), active listening and befriending were given, and only 0.27% of the calls required intervention, suggesting that secondary and tertiary prevention does not occur very often. In terms of the major problems of the callers, the highest percentage of calls (37.7%) were about interpersonal problems, followed by health concerns (32.6%) and only 2.7% of the calls were suicide related; an in-depth analysis of the foregoing indicates that for "interpersonal problems," a majority (43.2%) were loneliness calls, followed by relationship problems (28.9%) and marital problems (9.6%). In terms of the "health-related calls," a majority (47.5%) were about mental-health issues, followed by emotional problems (24.0%) and then physical problems of both short- and long-term (6.1% and 7.1% respectively, or 13.2% together). A vast majority of calls were for emotional support and distress reduction (53.7%and 35.8% respectively, or 89.5% together), but only 4.3% of the calls were judged to be "crisis" calls. Finally, of the 2.7% suicide-related calls, a clear majority (64.1%) were calls from people who were threatening to commit suicide or from those who entertained suicide ideation, followed by calls that expressed concerns about the suicide danger of significant others (26.9%); only 2.6% of the calls were from people who had previously attempted suicide.

Figure 3: A Sample of a Call Sheet

LOS ANGELES SUICIDE PREVENTION CENTER - TELEPHONE SERVICE

CALL DATA

Day Of The Week (1)
☐ 1. Sun. ☐ 2. Mon. ☐ 3. Tue. ☐ 4. Wed.
☐ 5. Thu. ☐ 6. Fri. ☐ 7. Sat.

Date (2-6): Month | Date | Year
Time (7-10): Hours | Minutes
Call Duration (11-12): Minutes
Called Before (13): ☐ 1. Yes ☐ 2. No

NAMES

Client
Name_____ First _____ Last
Address_____
Phone_____ Work Phone_____

Third Party Caller (14)
☐ 1. Yes ☐ 2. No
Name_____
Address_____
Phone_____ Work Phone_____
Relationship To Client_____

CLIENT DATA

Age (15-16)_____ Sex (17) ☐ 1. M ☐ 2. F

Marital Status (18)
☐ 1. Single ☐ 2. Married ☐ 3. Divorced ☐ 4. Separated
☐ 5. Widowed ☐ 6. Living Together

Race (19)
☐ 1. White ☐ 2. Black ☐ 3. Spanish ☐ 4. Oriental
☐ 5. Other_____

Employment (20)
☐ 1. Full Time ☐ 2. Part Time ☐ 3. Unemployed
☐ 4. Retired ☐ 5. Disabled ☐ 6. Housewife ☐ 7. Student

CLIENT'S RESOURCES

Living Alone (21)
☐ 1. Yes ☐ 2. No

Social Contact (22)
☐ 0. None ☐ 1. Minimal ☐ 2. Moderate ☐ 3. Frequent

Friends/Relatives (23)   List on other side
☐ 1. Yes ☐ 2. No

Finances (24)
☐ 0 None ☐ 1 Cash
☐ 2 Medi-cal ☐ 3 Insurance
Insurance Co._____

SUBSTANCE ABUSE

Alcohol History (25)
☐ 0. None ☐ 1. Moderate ☐ 2. Severe

Current Alcohol Problem (26)
☐ 0. None ☐ 1. Moderate ☐ 2. Severe

Drinking At Time (27)
☐ 1. Yes ☐ 2. No ☐ 3. Can't Decide

Current Drug Problem (28)
☐ 0. None ☐ 1. Moderate ☐ 2. Severe

SUICIDAL HISTORY

How Long Since First Attempt (29)
☐ 0. None ☐ 1. 3 Mos or Less ☐ 2. 3 Mos - 1 Yr.
☐ 3. 1 - 5 Yrs. ☐ 4. Over 5 Yrs.

How Long Since Last Attempt (30)
☐ 0. None ☐ 1. 3 Mos or Less ☐ 2. 3 Mos - 1 Yr.
☐ 3. 1 - 5 Yrs. ☐ 4. Over 5 Yrs.

Number Of Attempts (31)
☐ 0. None ☐ 1. One ☐ 2. Two
☐ 3. Three ☐ 4. Four or More

Current Behavior (32)
☐ 0. None ☐ 1. Thoughts ☐ 2. Threats
☐ 3. Preparation ☐ 4. Low Risk Attempt
☐ 5. High Risk Attempt

Plan (33)
☐ 0. None ☐ 1. Gun ☐ 2. Pills
☐ 3. Cutting ☐ 4. Jumping ☐ 5. Other_____

TREATMENT

Hospitalization (34)
☐ 1. Yes ☐ 2. No

Therapy (35)
☐ 0. None ☐ 1. Prior ☐ 2. Current

PRESENTING PROBLEMS

Presenting Problems (36-37)   Check One Only
☐ 1 Bizarre/Psychotic ☐ 9 Alcohol
☐ 2 Emotional/Psychological Long Term ☐ 10 Drugs
☐ 3 Emotional/Psychological Short Term ☐ 11 Marital/Family
☐ 4 Interpersonal Loss ☐ 12 Material Needs
☐ 5 Relationships ☐ 13 Violence/Homicide
☐ 6 Depression ☐ 14 Multiple
☐ 7 Medical ☐ 15 Other_____
☐ 8 Urinary

RESOLUTION

Service Provided (38)
☐ 1. Support/Reinforce ☐ 2. Refer to Prof. Help
☐ 3. Refer to Emergency Help
☐ 4. Soc. Called Emergency Help
☐ 5. Service Rejected ☐ 6. No Service

RATES

Suicide Risk (39)
☐ 1. Low ☐ 2. Moderate ☐ 3. High

Emergency Risk (40)
☐ 1. Low ☐ 2. Moderate ☐ 3. High

CALL REPORT FORM

ONTARIO
ASSOCIATION
OF DISTRESS
CENTRES

REPORT # _____

Date ___|___|___
        Y   M   D

Volunteer's
Name _____ # _____ Leader _____ Time _____ to _____
(Alias)   Start   End

Caller's Name _____ **Marital Status**   **Living Alone**

Age _____ Gender _____   1. Single ☐   2. Separated ☐ 3. Widowed ☐   1. Yes ☐
                                                                              2. No ☐
Municipality _____   4. Married ☐ 5. Divorced ☐   6. Unknown ☐   3. U/K ☐

| **Previous Call?** | 1. New ☐ | 2. Previous ☐ | 3. Regular ☐ | 4. Unsure ☐ |

Content of Call:

Volunteer's Comments: (Caller's voice tone, feelings, changes; Volunteer's feelings)

What support did you give this caller?

☐ Emotional support / listening   ☐ Exploration of options   ☐ Crisis support   ☐ Emergency intervention

☐ Information   ☐ Referral to _____   ☐ Other _____ (specify)

Feedback:

These trends somehow reflect similar patterns of telephone crisis centres around the world. This is especially true about the "suicide calls." Despite the widespread belief among the public, the percentage of the so-called "suicide calls" at any telephone helpline usually ranges from a low of less than 1% to a maximum of 4 or 5%.[18] It is important to remember, therefore, that at any crisis centre, anywhere in the world, at any time, the vast majority of the incoming calls are not suicide related. In this regard, it is both possible and probable that the people who are determined to go through with self-destructive acts may not be calling the help line.[19] From worldwide data, it also seems likely that the telephone helpline deals primarily with loneliness and other relationship issues most of the time, together with health-related problems (both physical and mental). Therefore, it is quite possible and desirable that the telephone befriending line could increase its function as a filter or referral system within the health-care system in society.

How Effective is the Helpline in Preventing Suicide?

One of the remarkable facts of Britain's postwar years has been the dramatic change in suicide rates. Those rates were quite high in the early 1930s, reflecting the socio-economic difficulties of the time, but the rates began to drop dramatically, especially among men, as World War II started. The rates returned to the expected levels after the war ended, as had been predicted by Durkheim and as has been the case in all other countries. From 1955, however, there has been a steady and rather consistent decline in overall suicide rates in Britain. The drop thereafter was a remarkably steady decrease of 200 deaths a year until 1972 when the suicide rate reached an all-time low of less than 8.0 per 100,000. The overall decline, which is just over a third, equals almost 2000 fewer deaths by suicide compared to the previous ten years.[20]

Such a dramatic drop is all the more surprising against the backdrop of industrial unrest, rising unemployment and a constant state of economic crises which almost resembles the 1930s. Even during the war years, which predictably lower the suicide rate, the rate never reached that low. This dramatic and sustained decline was certainly unparalleled in other countries. One of the debates advanced to account for this decline, of course, has been the role of the Samaritans in suicide prevention. Advocates of such a view point out that no medical treatment of any mental illness, anywhere and at any time, has been known to lower suicide rates; for instance, effective and increasingly popular treatment of depression, either by drug or electric convulsive therapy (E.C.T.), led to no reduction of suicide rates.[21]

One well-known study in Britain evaluated the role of the Samaritans in dealing with the suicidals. The researcher acknowledged that many people in distress and crisis will come to the Samaritans because they are suspicious or afraid of doctors and other professionals or because, in depressive fashion, they "don't want to bother the doctor." In Britain, the new clients contacting the Samaritan organization every year increased steadily from 12,000 in 1964, when records were first kept, to over 156,000 for 1972 and 1973. This is almost tantamount to one in 300 of the population or to one family in 100.[22] Today the figures would even surpass these estimates. Do the Samaritans really contribute to the reduction in the suicide rate?

Research conducted by Bagley studied the suicide rates before and after the opening of 15 early Samaritan branches and then compared the changes with 15 control towns without a Samaritan service. Bagley did find a decline in the rates.[23] Bagley's original research caused much controversy, stimulating other research projects which either supported or refuted his findings. Thus, Bagley's study was followed by Barraclough who compared British cities with and without Samaritan centres, matching them by ecological similarity, with results that seriously questioned the study by Bagley.[24] These two studies were followed by Jennings who replicated Bagley's findings with methodological improvements, including a wider variety of matches and a larger area. Jennings also found no differences in suicide rate reduction between towns with Samaritans and those without them.[25] However, a statistical study by Varah, the founder of the Samaritans, lent support to a decline in suicide rates in England and Wales from 1959 to 1986.[26] Other researchers pointed out that the drop in the suicide rates was probably due to the national trend, which began to decline in 1964; they argued, therefore, that the alleged decline was probably due to increased and better services available to the mentally ill as well as to the increased awareness on the part of physicians in general practice in dealing with depressed patients.[27] Thus, the controversy still remains unresolved, even though a vast majority of suicidologists in the U.S., including Shneidman, the doyen of American suicide researchers, embrace the reduction hypothesis as a landmark in the history of social science.[28]

A study at the Los Angeles Suicide Prevention Center (LASPC) revealed different results. California has experienced a very high suicide rate for years, and it stands to reason, therefore, to expect that if there is any significant preventive benefit by the suicide helpline in reducing the rate, then Los Angeles ought to witness a decline in the suicide rate. But suicide rates have apparently not gone down anywhere. Fox lists a number of reasons why the Los Angeles Suicide Prevention Center (LASPC) has been less effective than Britain's Samaritans in reducing the suicide rate. Compared to Britain, where about 80% of all Britons know what Samaritans are and said they would contact them if they felt the need, the Los Angeles Suicide Prevention Center is simply not as well known as the Samaritans, probably due to the absence of national news coverage and a nationwide image. A plethora of emergency services in the U.S. (multiplicity of "crisis centres" for rape victims, drug addicts, sexual deviants, the mentally impaired, kids-in-trouble, etc.) may actually confuse potential callers with differing advice and training after ringing many numbers in search of help. The heavy American dependence on the telephone (due to the country's geographical expanse) could be potentially restricting. Volunteers could reduce the interminable metaphysical telephone argument with a caller if they could simply invite a distressed person for a face-to-face chat as has been the case with Samaritans (in the U.S., by contrast, a vast majority of distress/crisis centres do not have a drop-in, face-to-face counselling programme); such face-to-face befriending is a cornerstone of the Samaritans, and in view of the close correlation between suicide and social isolation it seems to reduce suicidal danger. In the U.S. there is a greater danger of police involvement with emergencies (e.g., someone who is overdosing from a phone booth), and the police will likely take the person to hospital and will be on the scene anyway as all ambulance calls go routinely to them as well; it means, therefore, that the caller in crisis is immediately subject to compulsory orders and may be confined to a mental hospital, whereas Samaritans never take action in relation to doctors or police without the express consent of the caller.[29]

There are other studies in the U.S., the results of which, however, are inconclusive either way, and there have not been any recent studies to shed light on this question. Among some studies done earlier, Lester's study examined samples of U.S. cities, controlling for the size of the city, and found no effect on the suicide rate by the establishment of suicide prevention centres or distress centres. He compared suicide rates in eight cities before and after the establishment of such helplines in 1969, together with eight control cities. His study, however, found only small and statistically insignificant differences in favour of the cities with suicide prevention centres.[30] Another study compared the suicide rate in 100 counties in North Carolina with and without suicide prevention centres. It was found that the suicide prevention centres have a minimal effect in reducing the suicide rate.[31] Despite the continued increase in the number of new callers and volunteers, no appreciable decline in the annual suicide rates was observed in some of these studies.

A study by Miller et al. examined suicide rates from 1968 to 1973 (the years of the greatest growth of suicide prevention centres in the U.S.), by comparing the suicide rates in counties that possessed crisis centres with counties that did not. Their studies suggested that these centres had a beneficial impact on the decline of the suicide rate for those who were white, female and younger than 24 years of age.[32]

Yet another study in Alabama gave 3000 university students questionnaires to find out the effectiveness of the local telephone crisis line. Of the 88 students who had called the centre, 66 (75%) placed the calls for personal help and the remaining 22 (25%) phoned for information or a direct referral. Of the 66 who called, 42 (or 64%) were female and 24 (36%) were male, a ratio of about 2:1. It is interesting to note that 80% of all females and 60% of males considered the phone befriending and counselling effective, but between 20% and 33% respectively said it made their problem(s) worse.[33] Interestingly, however, female callers who talked to male volunteers rated their phone counselling and befriending as having a significantly greater positive impact on their problem(s) and life than did females who talked to female volunteers, suggesting the possibility of positive transference on the phone! The volunteers were generally rated as somewhat to extremely intelligent, warm, understanding, honest, caring and helpful, with the highest ratings given to categories of "being honest" and "understanding."[34]

In terms of the effectiveness of the crisis line, some researchers developed an evaluation system in which volunteers assigned code numbers to callers when they recognized certain individuals as previous callers and gave them the same code number assigned during the previous call. When the caller used the crisis line just a few times, they were called "previous callers;" when they called the centre repeatedly and regularly, they were usually referred to as "regular callers." Every centre has a roster of such "regular callers." The volunteers in this study asked the callers if they have called the centre before, and then, if they have called the centre before, asking them to give some indications of the effectiveness of the call. The assumption here is, of course, that the rate of repeat callers is a simple way of evaluating the effectiveness of the crisis line, as these callers are using the line repeatedly because they evidently found the telephone befriending service helpful—they would not call back if they did not find the telephone conversation beneficial.[35] Thus, when one uses the criterion of the frequency and rates of the "repeat callers" as an index of the assumed effectiveness of the telephone help line, then just about every befriending line in the world could be assumed to be "effective" because repeat callers are indeed numerous. (Likewise in Ontario repeat callers constitute almost 68% of all callers!)

To the argument that the "really suicidal people" never contact a crisis line, an important study provides an interesting perspective. With the cooperation of local Samaritan branches in the south of England, researchers found that clients who lapsed from contact with Samaritans were very suicidal for a full year afterwards with a suicide rate many times more than expected, hinting at the potential importance and preventative aspect of the centre for regular callers.[36] Since many suicidals oscillate between wishing to live and wishing to die (ambivalence), they may contact the centre thinking that perhaps these people will and can help them and, if so, they will have another go at life, suggesting the potential effectiveness of the helpline in preventing the suicides of those ambivalent callers. However, it must be cautioned that the high rate of repeat callers may actually indicate a dependency situation, or even addiction, without the caller really learning or acquiring a new coping skill.

Another study focuses on one readily available source of data, specifically the population comprising persons admitted to the inpatient service of a mental health centre due to depressive and/or suicidal states, including suicide attempts, vis-à-vis the role of suicide prevention centres in providing services to this group. A sample of 575 persons who fit the criteria were interviewed and the findings were as follows. Eleven percent had utilized the telephone suicide prevention centre services, with 59% of these experiencing substantial benefit. Twenty percent stated they were unaware of the centre. Eight percent expressed the view that calling the centre would be inappropriate because a suicide attempt was not imminent; and 26% indicated an inclination to call the centre in the event of subsequent difficulties. It was also suggested that response to a crisis (intervention) as well as response to low lethality callers with "everyday problems" (prevention) constitute valid functions of a suicide prevention and crisis centre. The author of this study, however, admonishes the reader not to be preoccupied with such goals as reducing the apparent suicide rate.[37]

In the previous pages, the question of the effectiveness of the crisis helpline has been examined. Some arguments lend support to their effectiveness in dealing with and even preventing potential suicide, others refute such arguments. Caution must be taken that, even in some of the studies that support the positive work of the helpline, short-term, temporary relief from distress is not synonymous with long-term restoration of problem-solving skills. Any serious doubt expressed on the effectiveness of the crisis line must be highly disheartening to the well-intentioned volunteers who literally spend hours on the phone or in mental health centres dealing with myriad numbers of people and suicidal problems. They understandably feel that their work is justified by their own results and may cite individual examples of persons saved from the threshold of suicide by having called a centre or having been seen in a clinic. Robert Litman, a doctor and a longstanding director of the Los Angeles Suicide Prevention Center, is always remembered as a staunch defender of the effectiveness of the volunteer, but this author of the famous and previously cited "Litman's Law" takes a more sober and cautious view of the effectiveness of the crisis line by pointing out that volunteers in crisis lines want to believe that their therapeutic endeavours are not wasted. But Litman warns against such thinking because mental health work in suicide prevention is only now beginning to build the conceptual and methodological tools needed to establish which interventions are effective and which are not.[38]

In addition to the temporary nature of tension relief, there are some built-in problems in the crisis lines. They are not able to offer follow-up programmes, as has been the case with some professional programmes and services. Strict confidentiality, a cornerstone of all such crisis lines, nevertheless prevents volunteers from providing aftercare or forming long-term relations. Limited funding and personnel shortages make it possible to have only two or three phone lines available at any time; hence, they are always busy and callers often cannot get through. Such a situation can be very trying, disheartening or even damaging to someone going through an acute crisis. Feelings of rage and abandonment may amplify the sense of distress and/or crisis. To make matters worse, there is also a limitation of time allowed per call (at most centres, a maximum 15 minutes is recommended for befriending calls and a bit longer for other distress calls). It means, therefore, that once the caller gets through their conversation is timed and their sense of distress may not be effectively dealt with. From the standpoint of the crisis line which must respond to as many calls as possible, logistics require a time limit on the calls. The caller, however, may take it personally and not see the logic behind it. Moreover, there are some problem callers who do not take the help line seriously and use it for their known gratification (such as sex calls, verbally abusive calls, crank calls). This is a universal problem that seems to plague every known crisis centre in existence; these callers are blocking the lines and the callers in real need are unable to get through. Sex calls in particular often lower the morale of many female volunteers, the fact of which may account for the high turnover of female volunteers at many centres.

It is extremely difficult to assess the so-called "effectiveness" of the helplines. For one, it is technically difficult to conduct a controlled study, and the targeted population fluctuates too much to enable any certain conclusions. Be that as it may, the role of the crisis centre cannot be measured in terms of quantifiable scores: its *raison d'être* lies in its readiness to lend an active listening ear to the caller in need through unconditional neighbourly love and compassion for the human condition. The crisis centre may not respond to the so-called suicide calls as often as it is popularly assumed, but it cannot be denied that it may "nip the problem in the bud" when it deals effectively with lonely calls. As mentioned earlier, the crisis line is probably the only place which treats human loneliness head-on and compassionately mitigates its sting before it escalates into a tragedy. The crisis line, therefore, must be understood and appreciated for its unique role as the agent of primary prevention service.

There is a powerful, indirect support to the role of active listening in reducing stress in a series of studies by an American clinical psychologist. His studies lend strong support to the positive effects of encouraging "confiding" and "talking about" one's trauma, distress and crisis.[39] On the basis of available evidence that stress, especially the stress of "bottling up one's feelings" about a traumatic event, hinders the body's ability to fight disease, James Pennebaker underscored the psychological and physiological benefits of "talking about an upsetting event." In this regard, having a good friend to "confide" becomes crucially important, and for many lonely and isolated individuals the active listening offered willingly and freely becomes the needed surrogate friend. The point is that when individuals inhibit their behaviour or don't talk about something that is very important to them, that act of inhibiting is physically stressful and, in the long run, is associated with increased disease levels. Good examples are those people who underwent traumatic sexual experiences before they were seventeen, people likely to be punished if they talked about their feelings. They were found to be more prone to reporting disease.

One of the most traumatic events in anyone's life is the death of a spouse. Pennebaker and his assistants studied people whose spouses had died a year earlier and their health in relation to confiding in others. They found that spouses of suicide victims were more likely to have talked with friends than were spouses of accidental death victims; the more these subjects talked with friends, the fewer were the increases in health problems; the more they thought about the death of their spouses, the greater were the number of health problems; the sudden death of a spouse was associated with increased health problems, regardless of the cause of death; confiding to friends appeared to play a central role in the coping and health process; and, over time, not confiding seemed to place cumulative stress on the body, increasing the long-term probability of stress-related illnesses. To summarize, the more one talked about the event, the less one was obsessed about one's spouse and the healthier one was. For those people in distress who have no friends to confide in, therefore, the befriending telephone line provides the crucial listening ear of a surrogate friend. Parenthetically, what is fascinating in Pennebaker's study is the fact that talking about the death with a professional counsellor was less related to health change! It seems that genuine, non-professional and empathic friends may be potentially more beneficial to individuals in distress than trained professionals whose services are offered for a fee and for a set time-frame.[40]

A final word about the potentially powerful role of the crisis line is in order, suggesting that a little thought could go a long way towards the prevention of suicide. For instance, Mt. Mihara in Japan has been an extremely popular site for suicide among Japan's youths and lovers for decades, but the erection of a pole warning against suicide and a suggestion for serious reflection and second thoughts on self-destruction, have been considered factors in reducing the number of suicides in that particular site. Another example is a famous monument for the war dead in Beer Sheba, Israel, which had been a popular suicide site for some time. Distraught officials and some suicide prevention professionals built a fence around it to prevent people from jumping off, thereby dramatically reducing the number of suicides. Probably the best example of suicide prevention in this vein is the bridge telephone called "Helpline." The bridge phone project, Helpline, represents the first known programme in which dedicated, two-way communication devices have been installed at a public place known for attempted suicides and linked directly to a mental health agency. The Duchess County, New York experiment suggests that such suicide prevention efforts are both feasible and effective. The bridge phone system has already saved lives and, therefore, has more than justified its existence and its relatively low cost. Moreover, the bridge phones provide a legitimate means for a potential suicide to make a "cry for help." This programme could be easily replicated in other settings, and it may be worthwhile for mental health officials in other communities to consider the benefits of installing a suicide prevention helpline in places where a high suicide risk exists.[41]

Myths and Misconceptions about Suicide

Whether one is a concerned lay person or a suicide prevention professional, it is of crucial importance to know the basic facts about suicide. It is unfortunate, however, that there are certain myths and misconceptions about suicide still prevalent in society. Some of the salient fallacies about suicide will be summarized below.[42]

(1) "Suicide occurs without warning." Some coroners' reports attached to the death certificate investigation, postmortem interviews with relatives and thorough psychological autopsies reveal that a majority (60-80%) of suicides show definite clues to suicide. It is very important, therefore, that family members, teachers, friends and professionals remember that suicide seldom occurs in a vacuum without warning, and to learn to discern such clues to suicide.

(2) "Suicidal people are fully intent on dying." It is fortunate for family members and those engaged in suicide prevention work that a suicidal person is usually characterized by ambivalence: the wish to die and the wish to live. It is well known among suicide prevention workers and mental health professionals that many suicidal people are trapped between these two opposing wishes and reach out for helping hands precisely because of such ambivalence. In this light, suicidal gestures are often a "cry for help." It is important to remember that the suicidals

are not fully intent on dying but oscillate between the powerful wish to die in order to escape from acute psychic pain and the need to reach out for assistance and support in order to live. The suicide prevention work must seize "cries for help" as opportunities to vitalize and strengthen the suicidal person's "wish to live."

(3) "Once the suicidal person is hospitalized and under professional care, the danger has passed." Far from being true, the patient in a psychiatric hospital or crisis intervention unit runs a risk of suicide at least several times greater than the general population. It is important, therefore, that special attention and care be provided to those persons who are hospitalized for suicidal danger.

(4) "He or she is not the type to commit suicide." There simply is no such thing as a "suicidal type." Suicide is a human tragedy and phenomenon observed universally, irrespective of race, creed, colour, nationality and social class. Suicide rates may be observed in greater frequencies in certain socio-economic groups, but there is no scientific basis for the existence of a specific type of suicidal individual. As discussed earlier in this book (especially on the theory of suicide by Freud), the death wish (thanatos) as a potential for suicide seems to exist in every human individual.

(5) "Someone who threatens suicide will not do it. It's 'all talk, no action.'" The person who verbalizes the wish to die does so because he or she has a death wish either consciously or subconsciously. Just like the proverb "there is no smoke where there is no fire," the intimation of suicidal threats must be taken seriously as people who threaten suicide are known to run the high risk of translating their threats into action.

(6) "Once suicidal, always suicidal." In fact, suicidal crisis is known to be time-limiting, meaning that for most people suicidal thoughts may come but they usually go away after a while. It is true that while some people repeat suicide attempts (the present author knows somebody who made 16 suicide attempts in four years!), most people usually return to their normal life and routines and do not revert to harmful behaviour once their problems which originally precipitated the suicide are resolved. The author has encountered many individuals who intimated to him in retrospect "how good it is to be alive" and "how lucky that he or she had not gone through with the attempt." Incidentally, this is also powerful evidence for suicide prevention and intervention, for it illustrates that suicide is a permanent solution to a temporary problem.

(7) "Suicidal individuals are always depressed." It is true that suicidal people are often depressed, but it is equally true that not all depressives commit suicide. Many people who take their lives are not depressed. In fact, once the decision for suicide has been reached, some people appear calm, serene and at peace with themselves. Equating obvious depression with imminent suicide sometimes runs the danger of overlooking other important signs of impending self-harm.[43]

(8) "Suicidal persons are mentally ill." It is true that most suicidal individuals are very unhappy, but many appear to be completely rational and in touch with reality. The suicidal individual is often going through many complex, personal and life crises such as the loss of a loved one or important relationship, a chronic or very painful illness, unbearable isolation or exhausted emotional resources on the verge of helplessness. All of these experiences are, however, primarily normal and ever-present in the course of life. When an individual feels trapped in an intolerable situation, hopeless and helpless, when normal coping techniques are diminished or exhausted, suicide may occur as an ultimate kind of coping mechanism. A student of suicide in France, Jean Baeschler, once said that suicide to some people is a logical response to an existential problem.[44] Furthermore, there is no clear-cut scientific basis to support the assumption that suicidals are mentally ill.

(9) "Improvement in suicidal danger suggests lessened risk of suicide." Some people are inclined to think that after timely and needed professional emergency care or hospitalization the suicidal individual may appear to be headed towards recovery and hence out of danger. After regaining the physical and emotional strength and leaving the hospital to return to a normal routine, however, the suicidal individual may find that the original situation which contributed to their suicidal thoughts and action has not really changed. With renewed and regained energy levels, as well as renewed emotional distress, the individual now has the strength and energy to make another attempt. The first three months after the recovery, therefore, are considered still a potentially dangerous period for another suicidal act, especially when the situation that precipitated the act in the first place has not really changed.[45]

(10) "Suicide is always a solitary event." Though suicidal thoughts originate in an individual's head, suicide is not a solitary event in the sense that it is often deeply immersed in and related to a frustrating and painful relationship with another person. Suicide is seldom a "solitary

event," but it is a result of a chain of events and relationships that involve another individual.

(11) "One should not talk about suicide because it might encourage people to actually do it—frank talk is dangerous." In fact, talking about suicide provides an opportunity for the suicidal individual to air his or her suicidal feelings and intent, thereby defusing the sense of crisis as well as providing a chance to share one's problems and difficulties and explore alternatives to suicide. Helping the other person to air pent-up feelings (called "ventilation") is quite therapeutic. The suicidal person is usually blocked in ventilating bottled-up feelings and resentments. This technique of assisting the other party to ventilate feelings has been a mainstay of every crisis centre. Blocked communication and bottled-up feelings often contribute to suicide by denying the person an outlet for deep sentiments. A recent cross-cultural study of depression, hopelessness and suicide ideation among students in Canada and Japan—students in liberal arts classes and students in suicidology—revealed that students in a year-long course in suicidology (in which every aspect of suicide ideation and behaviour, risk factors and self-assessed feelings are being openly discussed in a small, intimate seminar class) had the lowest depression and hopelessness scores. There has been a high rate of suicidology students seeking help from professionals, the fact of which might account for the low degrees of depression, hopelessness and poor coping skills. All in all, the exposure to suicide topics seems to have helped the students to talk about suicide by externalizing and ventilating bottled up feelings and to explore the options and modalities of therapies.[46]

"How Informative are Textbooks on Suicide for Health-care Professionals?"*

The acquisition of detailed and up-to-date information about suicide is not only expected but also indispensable for front-line professionals such as psychiatrists, psychologists and nurses who usually deal with the suicidals. The type of information these professionals come to possess is likely to be influenced by traditional teaching, the literature on the subject and clinical experience. Education and training are of the

---

* The discussion in this section has been written in cooperation with Heather Johnson, Department of Social Work, Atkinson College, York University. The author expresses his gratitude to her for co-authoring this section.

utmost importance as they offer vital information by linking theories and facts with regard to suicide.

Most health-care professionals, as well as the public, usually consider psychiatrists, psychologists and psychiatric nurses as professionals with highly specialized and extensive expertise in suicide information, care and management. A legitimate question arises as to the kind and extent of information these professionals receive through textbooks used in their education and training that enables them to understand, respond to and deal with suicidal behaviour effectively and quickly.

In a study which surveyed psychologists, physicians and psychiatrists about "what MDs ought to know about psychiatry," suicide was mentioned in the top ten of the 21 topics assessed.[47] It stands to reason, then, to expect the subject of suicide to occupy an important share and focus in any textbook for mental health professionals who deal with suicidal patients. In one such textbook reviewed, it is confidently stated that mental health professionals are very thoroughly trained in detecting suicide ideation and behaviour.[48] Is this a safe and reasonable assumption to make?

A study in Japan by a well-known suicidologist in the medical profession suggests that a vast majority of medical students in Japan have never been exposed to any formal education or training concerning suicide during their medical student days.[49] This professor of psychiatry examined seven representative textbooks on psychiatry used in his medical college (department of psychiatry) and found, much to his dismay, that five of them did not have any discussions on suicide, and only two texts spared a few pages for the subject. The author of this study, himself a psychiatrist and professor of medicine, questions if psychiatrists could possibly be considered, under such conditions, "experts" on suicide behaviour.

The following discussion is a much more systematic follow-up on this study in order to learn about the type and extensiveness of information about suicide as contained in selected textbooks in psychiatry, nursing and clinical psychology in North America—the three disciplines which usually and traditionally deal with the suicidals in the medical and clinical setting.

Method

Twenty-one textbooks were examined: 11 texts in psychiatry, five in psychiatric nursing and another five in clinical psychology. For the content analysis[50] of each textbook the following criteria were used: information on the prevention of suicide; information on intervention and treatment therapies (i.e., types of pharmaco- and psychotherapy prescribed); information on postvention and dealing with families after a completed suicide or an attempt; information on causes of suicide; reference to particular theories; referencing to previous studies; and information on assessment and diagnosis. Likewise, the following aspects were measured quantitatively: total number of pages written on suicide as verified in the general index; their percentages in terms of the total number of the pages in the text; the number of pages in specific sections or chapters dealing with suicide, if any; and the sources and nature of specific information, which allow the reader to refer to other materials. Finally, averages were calculated for each of the three types of textbooks (psychiatry, nursing and psychology) to determine which contained the most information on each of the criteria.

Results

Overall, 13 of the 21 textbooks (or 61.9%) reviewed had separate chapters dealing with suicide. Seven of the 11 psychiatry texts (or 63.6%) had separate chapters on the subject; on the other hand, only one of the five texts in clinical psychology (20%) had a separate chapter; five of the five nursing texts (or 100%) had chapters on suicide (see Figure 5).

In the percentage of pages devoted to suicide in the entire textbook, psychiatric textbooks had an average of 3.3% of the total pages dealing with suicide (or an average of seven pages). There was an average of 2.7% in psychology texts (or an average of 6.6 pages) and, finally, nursing texts had an average of 3.5% (or an average of 14.2 pages), as shown in Figure 6.

As for referencing, in psychiatry and nursing texts, 81.8% and 80% respectively referenced the information, whereas all five of the psychology texts (100%) referenced it.

When the content analyses of the seven criteria were examined there were some variances among the three disciplines (see Table 1). Assessment was the one criterion mentioned most often in the psychiatry texts (81.8%), whereas intervention was mentioned most frequently in the nursing texts (100%). Clinical psychology texts, on the other hand, stressed prevention (80%), etiology of suicide (80%) as well as reference to previous studies (80%). It is to be noted that prevention is one of the criteria mentioned least often in psychiatric and nursing texts—the two disciplines in the frontline of traditional medicine (45.5% and 40%

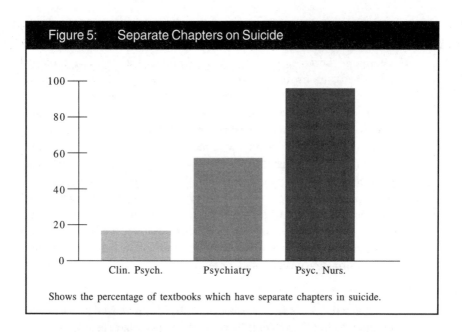

Figure 5: Separate Chapters on Suicide

Shows the percentage of textbooks which have separate chapters in suicide.

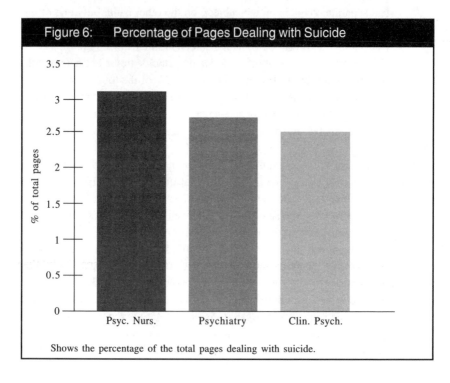

Figure 6: Percentage of Pages Dealing with Suicide

Shows the percentage of the total pages dealing with suicide.

	Psychiatric	Psychiatric Nursing	Clinical Psychology
Table 1: Amount of Information Contained in Textbooks			
Prevention	45.5% *	40%	80%
Intervention	63.6%	100%	80%
Postvention	27.3%	40%	40%
Causes	63.6%	60%	80%
Theories	27.3%	80%	40%
Prev. Studies	63.6%	60%	80%
Assessment	81.8%	80%	20%

* This shows that 45.5% of the psychiatric textbooks examined contained information of prevention.

respectively). Likewise, postvention and information on the theories of suicide are mentioned very little in the psychiatric and clinical psychology textbooks, as shown in Table 1.

Overall, results indicate that nursing and psychology textbooks had more of the criteria discussed than the psychiatry textbooks in each of the seven criteria with the single exception of assessment. Psychiatry textbooks had an average of 3.7 items out of the seven discussed (or 53%); an average of 4.6 items (or 66%) appeared in nursing texts, and 4.2 items in psychology (or 60%). Nursing texts had certainly the best coverage of the three disciplines examined, followed by clinical psychology and psychiatry texts in terms of information on the subject of suicide.

Discussion

Nursing textbooks came out on top in many of the categories examined. On average, the nursing textbooks had more pages discussing suicide (3.5%), had more information on intervention (100%) as well as references to theories and postvention (80% and 40% respectively) than did the psychiatry and psychology counterparts. In fact, it turned out that the only criterion in which psychiatry texts excelled over others was assessment, but this was only 1.8% more than the nursing textbooks. The nursing textbooks had even more of the seven criteria discussed than the other two types of textbook. They had an average of 66% of the criteria covered as compared to 53% and 60% for the psychiatric and clinical psychology textbooks respectively. Though this may not appear to be a great difference, the psychiatric nursing texts often contained more practical information than did the psychiatry or psychology counterparts. This would likely help a nurse feel more prepared to deal with a suicidal patient.

Though all helping professions should be aware of the importance of suicide education, the nurse may be more directly involved with the care of the patient. Whereas the psychiatrist or psychologist may see the patient for an initial interview and assessment, and for perhaps an hour at a time, it is the nurse who cares for the patient during hospitalization. It is also the nurse who is responsible for the patient and must be able to act quickly should an emergency arise. All these factors may explain the degree and nature of information and coverage in their textbooks.

The clinical psychology textbooks came out ahead of the psychiatry texts in many of the criteria looked at as well. On average, they had more information on prevention (80%) and postvention (40%) than did the other two disciplines. They had also referred to previous studies (80%) more than the other two disciplines, and all of the psychology textbooks fully referenced their information. At the least, psychology texts certainly came ahead of the psychiatry ones, lending support to earlier findings by Burstein that psychology students outperformed psychiatry residents in the area of evaluating suicidal potential.[51]

The quality of information seems to be rather inadequate in many of the textbooks reviewed. Much of the information given is too elementary. There may be some information for a brief overview of suicide, but, for those health-care professionals who will be in direct contact with suicidal patients, much more practical information should be included. Many of the textbooks do not contain separate chapters on suicide, and any information on the topic is scattered throughout the entire text. For a complete understanding each text needs separate chapters to summarize the main points of suicidology.

One especially informative book (an edited reader), *Suicide over the Life Cycle,* contains over 700 pages of information on the topic of suicide for professionals. The final chapter of 37 pages is an overview of the entire book. Certainly many textbooks would benefit from this example. The chapter touches on each important aspect in the area of suicide: i.e., the epidemiology of suicide, theories of suicide, risk factors of suicide, assessment and treatment are examined in detail and refer the reader to other chapters in the book. Though this last chapter claims to be only a brief overview, the information here is much more in depth, compact and useful than the majority of textbooks examined. It is certainly beneficial to heed the recommendation of this textbook that "it is crucial that curricula in health and mental health care professional training and in continuing education programmes contain information about diagnoses and treatment of psychiatric disorders and complex human behaviours such as suicide."[52]

As for the contemporaneity of the information provided, more current studies need to be introduced and discussed. Many of the texts rely on dated material instead of focusing on the current information in this area. By relying on dated material misconceptions surrounding suicide are often perpetuated. For instance, when suicide is mentioned with other disorders, it is most often found in the section on depression. Though depression is usually an accompaniment of suicide, not all depressives commit suicide.[53] Moreover, from the results of general population studies and from clinical reports, hopelessness and schizophrenia are much more predictable variables among patients who kill themselves while attending a psychiatrist.[54] More importantly, the absence of close and stable interpersonal relationships, rejection and recent object loss, isolation and social withdrawal are noted to be better indicators of suicide than either depression or suicide ideation.[55]

The fact that psychiatry textbooks lag behind the texts in psychology and nursing is a cause for concern. Epidemiologically speaking, suicide is fortunately a relatively rare event, even in the experience of individual psychiatrists in practice. Studies indicate that the mean contact experience with suicidal patients in Ontario, for instance, is 0.12 suicides per psychiatrist per year per practice, or, a psychiatrist in Ontario can expect to see one suicide for every eight years of practice. Furthermore, one-third of psychiatrists have been found to have no patients who committed suicide or who had suicide ideation.[56] These results are quite comparable to a national survey conducted in the United States.[57] Similar results were obtained in Japan, where psychiatrists' contact experience with suicide was reported to be 0.25 persons per year per practice or one suicide every four years.[58] Though it must be remembered that completed suicide may not be a common occurrence, for every suicide there are probably ten to 20 attempted suicides.[59]

If the contact experience of the psychiatrist is limited, it is all the more imperative that the textbooks used in education and training for front-line health-care professionals provide up-to-date, pertinent and sufficient information on suicide prevention, intervention and postvention. The limited amount of literature in this field suggests that physicians in general lack the education, training and expertise necessary for dealing with suicide[60] and that even psychiatry residents receive insufficient training and possess no systematic and comprehensive information for dealing with suicidal patients.[61] It has been suggested that physicians in general lack the education, training and experience necessary for dealing with suicide[62] and that they possess no systematic and comprehensive approach for dealing with suicidal patients.[63] It was even suggested that psychiatry students and trainees often report feeling ill-prepared for the eventuality of a patient's suicide because the training and education do not seem to have well-established protocols for helping these residents and other trainees deal with various aspects of suicidal behaviour.[64] It was also pointed out that 49% of graduates from medical schools across the United States and Canada "felt that the course content [in their education and training] did not adequately prepare them to deal with psychological problems encountered in medical practice."[65] Even though senior clinicians and professionals hopefully learn to deal with suicidals, many of the techniques and information used are considered by suicide experts as inadequate and out-of-date.[66] The present study of textbooks used in psychiatry, nursing and psychology reinforces this concern and reality. It is certainly hoped that such findings would trigger an enhanced and expanded coverage and quality of information on suicide for health-care professionals in the future.

INTERVENTION

Sometimes an event presents a serious threat to an individual's daily functioning, and the person in such a state does not know how to deal with it; they feel they cannot wait for its solution until the following day. Such a sense of "crisis" can be developmental in the sense that it can occur anywhere along the developmental sequence from childhood through adolescence and into adulthood and old age. Or, it can be situational in the sense of losing a loved one through separation, divorce or death, loss of health, wealth, role change or loss of public standing. As such, crisis is usually acute rather than chronic and requires immediate attention. Hence, the aim of crisis intervention is to offer the immediate help and support the person in crisis desperately needs, thereby helping him or her to re-establish emotional equilibrium, to rebuild significant relationships and finally to learn new coping skills for the present and future. Of the many crises mentioned in earlier sections, suicide is certainly the most extreme and lethal.

The principal purpose of intervention is to assess the degree and extent of psychic pain, sense of hopelessness and helplessness and the seriousness of suicide intent. Secondly, it is to establish appropriate modalities of aid and therapeutic measures in order to diminish these symptoms of distress and crisis. Thirdly, it hopes to assist the individual in restoring his or her problem-solving abilities as well as in learning new coping mechanisms for the future (empowerment).

Assessment

One of the essential ingredients of crisis intervention for suicidality is assessment. Assessment can be either subjective or objective. When an individual fills out a questionnaire, in which one expresses one's feelings in self-reporting fashion, or answers specific questions in the interview and reveals one's feelings, it is called "subjective reporting method." By contrast, when a clinician or a mental health worker observes the person in crisis and evaluates the nature and degree of crisis, it is an "objective method," even though the clinician must by necessity use subjective judgment in the evaluation. In reality, both assessment techniques are often used in combination.

The best example of an objective assessment would be taking an inventory, either by an interview or by a questionnaire, of pertinent demographic information (age, gender, occupation, marital status, family background, religion, income, education, ethnic and racial background, medical history, etc.). In assessing such sociological-demographic data, as well as probing the inner subjective feelings of the interviewees, caution must be taken against the ecological fallacy. One such error would be the extrapolation of certain socio-demographic characteristics of suicide risk in certain high-risk populations (group traits) to specific individuals. Be that as it may, such socio-demographic factors are useful indices that have been found to correlate with increased risk. Such information is indispensable in identifying high-risk populations in terms of some salient group attributes and characteristics. The second ecological fallacy is that risk factors and clinical features thus observed and identified may be different for different sample universes: e.g., suicide attempters, completers and suicide ideators. In assessing the risk factors, therefore, one must constantly be aware of whether the risk factors identified apply to all cases or only to some specific sub-populations.

By far the most reliable assessment modality is the individual case method: assessment of the individual's feelings, anxieties, resentments, thoughts, death ideation, general mental state and idiosyncratic meanings. Thus, the clinician who is well informed of the socio-demographic background as well as the subjective inner states of people who committed suicide is likely to be in as close to an optimal position as one can be to assess suicide risk.

Figure 7 summarizes some of the warning signs and clues to suicide in verbal, cognitive, affective and behavioural dimensions. Most people do communicate clues about their suicidal intentions; hence, these warning signs constitute useful "clues to suicide," and may be interpreted as "cries for help." In assessment, then, it is important to train caregivers in discerning these warning signs when they are being communicated, and to learn to evaluate how close the person at risk is to suicidal behaviour.

In assessment, Shneidman has emphasized the clinical usefulness of evaluating the excessive psychic pain (called "perturbation") and considering suicide as the only option in alleviating the perturbation (called "lethality" by Shneidman), which often leads to tunnel vision or constricted vision. Perturbation is usually experienced as subjective psychic pain with emotional upsets, tension, anguish, turmoil, dread, hopelessness, helplessness or disturbance. It is an important ingredient of suicidality. Precisely because this acute psychological pain is so subjective and private, assessment of perturbation is extremely difficult. The person may be reluctant or unable to talk about feeling suicidal due to psychic pain, at least in its initial stage.[67] Some clinicians recommend, therefore, going beyond the verbal and obvious level to the understanding of such non-verbal clues as mannerisms, physical appearance, complexion, agitation and any other signs of underlying perturbation.[68]

Lethality is more dangerous than perturbation. After all, no one has ever died of elevated perturbation alone, but elevated lethality does enhance the probability of serious self-harm because it leads the individual to think that suicide is a desirable option. In its milder form,

Figure 7:	Some Clues to Suicide (Warning Signs)

VERBAL	– "I want to die..."
	– "I don't want to be around anymore"
	– "I can't take it anymore"
	– "It would be better all around if I weren't here"
	– "Nobody cares about me anymore"
	– "I have nothing else to live for"
COGNITIVE	– dichotomous thinking (either/or)
	– inability to see alternatives
	– egocentric and narcissistic thinking
	– tunnel vision, inability to think of any other alternatives than suicide
	– confusion, inability to decide
	– incoherence and circular thinking
AFFECTIVE	– emotional dysphoria (depression)
	– felt sense of failure
	– felt sense of loss
	– low self-esteem and self-pity
	– felt sense of powerlessness and helplessness
	– felt sense of hopelessness and despair
	– sense of guilt and self-blame
	– sense of isolation and rejection
BEHAVIOURAL	– withdrawal
	– sudden change in behaviour
	– eating disorder (overeating or loss of appetite)
	– sleeping disorder (oversleeping or insomnia)
	– fatigue and sense of unwellness
	– substance abuse
	– writing a will and giving away items
	– hoarding of drugs, gun, ropes, etc.
	– farewell visits and phone calls

lethality leads to thoughts of suicide (suicide ideation). Quite often these suicidal thoughts are not clear even to the suicidal person. It is important, therefore, to ask directly if a person is thinking about suicide. Such questions could take the following forms: "I think I've heard you mention suicide, right? Is this something you are thinking about?" "Are you thinking about killing yourself right now?" "So, you are really feeling down. Sometimes when people feel like this, they have thoughts of suicide. Are you thinking of suicide?" "So, you have just experienced a devastating loss—your lover has just left you right? In such situations, some people think life isn't worth living. Are you having thoughts like that—thoughts of killing yourself?"[69]

With regards to lethality, it is necessary to assess its degree by evaluating the deadliness of the suicide plan, as well as questions of *how*, *where*, and *when* suicide would be attempted. One of the easiest scales to use has been devised by a crisis specialist for use in crisis centres in the United States. Figure 8 presents a lethality assessment scale.

A number of clinically important indicators or predictors of impending danger of suicide must be determined: the seriousness of the current suicide plan; degree and extent of preparedness of the plan including availability and accessibility of lethal methods and means (firearms, drugs); a history of prior self-harm behaviour; inadequate or absent social support resources; and hopelessness. It is important to elaborate on these indicators a bit further.[70]

Seriousness. It must be remembered that people at risk may not know about the firmness of their plans. They are usually too caught up in feelings of pain and loss as well as in the desperate wish to escape from such unbearable psychic pain (perturbation). The caregiver must ascertain the firmness of such suicide plans. A skilled caregiver often gently prods those at risk about the suicide plan. It will help both the caregiver and those contemplating suicide to know how serious they are about suicide.

Preparedness. Since serious planning suggests serious intent, it is important to find out as much detailed information as possible about availability, accessibility, specific methods and means of self-harm. Such information helps in assessing how close the plans are to actually being carried out. Every crisis centre manual, therefore, usually contains instructions on how to prod the suicidal caller into divulging how he or she plans to do it, with what means, how accessible such means are and when he or she wants to carry the plan into action. Figure 9 is a suicide intent scale which has been used at many crisis intervention centres and

Key to Scale	Danger to Self	Typical Indicators
1	No predictable risk of immediate suicide	Has no notion of suicide or history of attempts, has satisfactory social support network and is in close contact with significant others
2	Low risk of immediate suicide	Person has considered suicide with low lethal method; no history of attempts or recent serious loss; has satisfactory support network; no alcohol problems; basically wants to live
3	Moderate risk of immediate suicide	Has considered suicide with high lethal method but no specific plan or threats; or, has plan with low lethal method, history of low lethal attempts, with tumultuous family history and reliance on Valium or other drugs for stress relief; is weighing the odds between life and death
4	High risk of immediate suicide	Has current high lethal plan, obtainable means, history of previous attempts, has a close friend but is unable to communicate with him or her; has a drinking problem; is depressed and wants to die
5	Very high risk of immediate suicide	Has current high lethal plan with available means, history of high lethal suicide attempts, is cut off from resources; is depressed and uses alcohol to excess, and is threatened with a serious loss such as unemployment or divorce or failure in school

Source: Hoff, L.A., *People in Crisis* (New York: Addison Wesley, 1988), p.209.

hospital units for suicide attempters and/or ideators. It is very easy to use and based upon the Likert Scale. One of the reasons why it is so important to assess the seriousness of intent is that medical seriousness is not a reliable indicator of the degree of despair or perturbation experienced by the injured person. For some people, a minor self-inflicted injury may precede death by suicide. By the same token, an attempter's own account of the seriousness of his or her intention is not a good indicator of the level of distress or crisis. Sometimes a person may deny or minimize any personal problem soon after an attempt and may say, for example, that he or she took an overdose of medication just for a good night's sleep.

In Figure 9, if a person scores a total of 4 or more points on the scale the suicide attempt may reflect a serious intent to die, regardless of what the person says or how serious the physical injury. This level of risk indicates that it is advisable for the person to be seen by a mental health professional for a more thorough examination.

Prior suicide attempt. It is important to find out the person's previous self-harm behaviour in view of the fact that previous attempters run a statistically much higher risk of another attempt, especially when the last attempt is recent. For some people self-harm behaviour has become an acceptable means of coping with stressful life events. Because of the possibility that previous attempters may not be willing to divulge their prior history of self-harm, it is important for caregivers to ask about such previous attempts in detail.

Absence or inadequate degree of social support resources. The person most at risk usually feels quite alone and isolated. For such a person in serious crisis, his or her own inner resources and coping skills have either greatly diminished or, in the extreme, collapsed. A socially and interpersonally isolated person, without any or inadequate support systems or resources, has no one to fall back upon in time of extreme distress. Usually such support resources come from family, close friends and colleagues, satisfying job, economic security, availability and easy access to professional and medical care, and church or other social groups. The accessibility to social support resources usually minimizes the sense of isolation and loneliness (which are often preconditions for distress and crisis) and feelings of helplessness. The presence of a good support system increases the likelihood of rescue if a person at risk does make an attempt.

Hopelessness. Another important and proven predictor is hopelessness. A high level of hopelessness, whether rated on a scale or assessed clinically, is among the best evaluators of suicide potential.

Circle one score for each item: **Score**

1 **Isolation at the time of self-harm**

   Somebody present 0

   Somebody nearby or in contact 1

   No one nearby or in contact 2

2 **Timing**

   Timed so that intervention by another person is:

   Probable 0

   Not likely 1

   Highly unlikely 2

3 **Precautions against discovery or intervention**

   None 0

   Passive precautions 0

   Active precautions (e.g., locked door) 2

4 **Acting to gain help during or after the act**

   Notified potential helper regarding the attempt 0

   Contacted but did not specifically notify potential helper 1

   Did not contact or notify potential helper 2

5 **Final acts in anticipation of death**

   None 0

   Made some arrangements or thought about them 1

   Definite acts (e.g., making a will and taking life insurance)............... 2

6 **Degree of planning**

   No preparation 0

   Minimal or moderate preparation 1

   Extensive preparation 2

7 **Suicidal note**

   No note 0

   Note written but torn up or not thought about................................ 1

   Presence of note 2

Total Score:_____

Source: Courtesy of S.H.A.R.E., Toronto General Hospital, 1989.

Precipitating circumstances for hopelessness have been: situations that plunge the person into despair and extremely low self-esteem; thwarting of goals that are extremely important to the person or emergence of an insoluble dilemma; single stressor of overwhelming magnitude, or several stressors occurring in a series all at once; physical disease or abnormality that activates ideas of deterioration or death without much hope of improvement; and profound pessimism that the present condition will not improve in the foreseeable future. Depressed individuals become more motivated to attempt suicide if their levels of hopelessness have been rated very high. A study of hospitalized patients with suicidal ideation found that after a five to ten-year follow-up period, 14 of the 207 patients in the study committed suicide. Only the results of Beck's Hopelessness Scale and the pessimism item of Beck's Depression Inventory correctly identified 91% of the completed suicides, lending strong support to the contention that the degree of hopelessness is an effective indicator of long-term suicidal risk.[71]

If no tests are given to assess the degree and seriousness of the crisis and suicidality, then the foregoing indicators must be kept in mind by a crisis intervention worker and a caregiver in interviews and caregiving. All caregivers must be assured quite clearly and firmly that direct inquiry does not plant ideas of suicide into the person in distress or crisis.

Finally, with regards to the assessment, it is also important to determine whether the person at risk faces an emergency risk or a long-term risk. As a general rule of thumb, an emergency rating may be defined as the estimated potential of the person for suicide within the next 24 to 48 hours; the rating of the long-term risk may be based upon the likelihood that a person at risk will commit suicide probably within the next two years. Ratings of most suicidal individuals fall somewhere between such a broad range. Admittedly such a rating is highly subjective and at times arbitrary; it is advisable, therefore, that the rating be considered in combination with the aforementioned scales and the enumerated predictors, certainly in conjunction with interviews and clinical observation.

It must be cautioned, however, that at this stage of development in suicidology (and in psychometry), it is not possible to really predict who will ultimately commit suicide for a number of reasons. First, being deemed a high risk by a variety of assessments and observations does not guarantee predictability of suicide. One well-known study identified 803 out of 4800 psychiatric admissions (or about 15%) to a U.S. veteran's hospital to be at high risk. The study identified far too many high-risk individuals to be of any practical value in long-term or intensive follow-up for preventive purposes. The author's conclusion was that it was impossible to identify to a useful degree the particular persons who will commit suicide.[72] Another more recent study examined a statistical model for the prediction of suicide, which was based upon an investigation of 1906 inpatients with affective disorders. There were eventually 46 cases of suicide, none of which were predicted by the model. The authors of the study concluded that it would be unrealistic for the general public or the legal system to expect that health professionals would be able to predict suicide in specific patients on the basis of the present level of knowledge.[73] Secondly, prediction is also difficult because of the often transitory nature of suicidality. In most cases, the high risk of suicide probably exists for only hours or a few days at most; suicidal intent is not constant in the individual over time and the suicidal crisis will probably pass. Thirdly, conclusions drawn from the risk factors, lifestyles and statistics of suicide attempters should not automatically be transferred to completers, as they often represent two different populations. There are many differences between suicide attempters and completers and caution must be taken when comparing the two groups. For example, most attempters tend to be young, female, use less lethal means and have less severe mental disorders. The completers, on the other hand, tend to be older, male, use more lethal means, have an alcohol problem and often have more serious psychiatric disorders. Fourthly, the so-called high-risk factors are so many and common that recognition of these factors is of little proven value in predicting which individuals will go on to kill themselves. For example, depression is an often-mentioned risk factor for suicide, but it is also a fact that not all depressives go on to commit suicide. It is unfortunately safe to conclude, therefore, that identification of high-risk factors strengthens the possibilities of suicide but does not predict the probabilities of self-destruction.

Basic Principles of Intervention

Psychological autopsies of 11 well-known individuals in Europe, North America and Japan, as conducted by the present author, revealed basic commonalities of crisis leading up to the suicide act, despite obvious socio-cultural differences. They are: acute and unbearable psychic pain on account of a significant loss; cognitive disturbance (the inability to concentrate, remember and think or to render rational decisions, a state of confusion and panic); collapsed or severely diminished coping skills;

severe depression, hopelessness and helplessness; extremely low self-esteem, guilt and self-devaluation; strong need to escape from the intolerable psychic pain; and powerful death intent ready to translate into suicide action. In other words, when a person experiences what he or she believes to be a severe stress in life and is unable to effectively deal with the problem, then he or she distorts the situation and thus becomes hopeless about the future possibility of solving the problem. Under such circumstances, death may appear preferable to living.[74]

Suicidal thoughts (cognition), suicidal feelings (affect) and suicide intent are all considered to be expressions of a crisis situation in an individual's life, all of which may lead to the final stage of an initiated suicide attempt. This process from thought to action is well demonstrated in a pamphlet distributed by a crisis centre in Toronto, Canada, as shown in Figure 10. It also gives good examples of how to deal with such suicidal thoughts and feelings as well as with serious suicide intent and an already initiated act.

By its very nature and urgency, crisis intervention usually requires immediate attention and assistance. The degree, extent and share of the health-care professional's participation in crisis intervention and management is, therefore, much greater than is the case with prevention, which has usually been handled by trained volunteers at crisis centres and other volunteer-based facilities. Crisis intervention centres can be based either on the medical or non-medical model. Medically based crisis centres are usually located in the crisis unit of a hospital within the department of emergency medicine or in the department of psychiatry; or such centres may be situated outside the hospital but staffed with well-trained medical or mental health professionals.

Toronto's Self-Harm Assessment, Research and Education (SHARE) is a hospital-based crisis unit located inside Toronto Hospital. Created in 1979 as an outpatient clinic with a three-bed facility and funding from the provincial Ministry of Health, it was expanded to six beds in 1981. In the late 1980s, emphasis shifted back to outpatient assessment and brief intervention with patients in crisis; today, the funding and interest has been moving from institutional settings to community-based mental health programmes. As such, SHARE clinic is based inside the Toronto Hospital (currently at the Western Division) with an office in the psychiatry unit. Staff include one psychiatrist, one nurse, a half-time research assistant and one secretary all devoting their time exclusively to the SHARE programme. Their programme offers prompt, direct service counselling

Figure 10: From Thought to Action

SUICIDAL THOUGHTS	SUICIDAL FEELINGS	SUICIDAL ACTIONS	INITIATED SUICIDE
"Everyone will be better off without me."	*"I feel like killing myself."*	*"I am going to kill myself."*	*"I have taken enough pills to kill myself."*
Nothing matters anymore.	*Death would be better than living this way."*	*I have tried before, and I feel that way again."*	*"I have a gun, it's loaded and I know how to use it on myself…"*
I just can't go on facing all these problems."			
Most of us have had suicidal thoughts. It can be frightening because we wonder if such a thought might lead us to act on it. This anxiety is unfounded, because it is relatively normal to get trapped or overwhelmed by the events of our lives at times. Thinking about suicide is a long way from action.	Feeling suicidal is not uncommon. Usually, such feelings are temporary. For some people, however, the death wish is a more persistent feeling. Talking about suicide almost always dissipates the feelings. Being emotionally supportive allows the person to feel secure and safe. Suicidal feelings usually ease quickly.	Assess the risk. The more specific the person, the higher the risk of suicide. Ask, *"Have you though about how you might take your life?"* If the person is vague as to means, there is less risk than if s/he has pills or a gun. In a high risk situation, be ready to get someone to help you in getting Poison Control information, in tracing the call, or in calling an ambulance. If dealing by telephone, ask if anyone else is there.	ACT. Press the person to accept help. An ambulance can be sent. Hospital emergency rooms are 99% effective in saving people who arrive, even severely overdosed. If it is a telephone call where the person is drugged and vague, trace the call if at all possible. I feel that the suicidal person's call to me or contact with me in these circumstances is adequate permission for me to take charge.
A person is usually relieved when you respond to his suicidal thought by reassuring him that it is normal to have such thoughts on occasion. Be direct: *"Are you thinking of suicide?"* This puts the issue on the table and assures the person that you are willing and able to understand. Encourage the person to talk about the circumstances and help to find some small positive steps that can be taken to start to change the situation.	Help the person identify some action that can be taken to help change the situation. This further eases the suicidal feelings.	Be as emotionally close as possible and encourage the person to get help. Suicidal people are ambivalent. They want to die but at the same time they want to live. We can help them want to live by trying to understand how painful life is for them just now. Being cared about is a positive life support for all of us.	While you are pushing for action, continue to be as emotionally supportive, caring and sensitive as possible.

Courtesy Distress Centre I, Toronto, 1989.

and intervention, thereby avoiding unnecessary hospitalization, if at all possible. It is an operation based upon the medical model entirely.

Then there is the synthetic model in which crisis intervention is offered and managed by medical staff and well-trained lay personnel such as the Crisis Intervention Unit at the Toronto East General Hospital. This crisis unit is unique in that the medically trained staff and lay volunteers work together with mutual respect and almost equal responsibility. In this hospital, the patient is seen by a triage nurse who assigns the patients to the appropriate departments for the type of care required as well as evaluates the nature and urgency of the problem(s). The crisis intervention unit volunteer does not interview anyone who has not been medically cleared first because some psychological symptoms may be caused by physiological disorders—such "panic" syndromes as racing pulse, palpitation, chest pain and nausea may be signs of a mild coronary disturbance. Once medically cleared, most patients requiring emergency psychiatric care are interviewed by the crisis intervention volunteer. In the interview, the volunteer collects all necessary information such as the outward appearance and presentation style of the interviewee, past history of hospitalization, medication history and compliance, assessment of suicidality, any history of previous self-harm, involvement with the police and other law-enforcement agencies and absence or degree of support systems. After the interview, the volunteer confers with other members in the back-up team who are full-time workers of the crisis intervention unit. Contact and consultation with a back-up team is mandatory after each interview. The volunteer and the professional back-up team members then decide on the most appropriate measures for the patient. The recruitment of volunteers is done on a bi-annual basis. The potential resourcefulness of these volunteers is implied by the fact that in 1994, for instance, 90% of selected applicants had previous experience in the helping professions.

And finally, there is another modality based primarily on the non-medical model such as the Gerstein House in Toronto, which is located in a Victorian house in downtown Toronto, offering clients greater flexibility and autonomy. It is a community mental health centre, offered as an alternative to the traditional medical model of crisis intervention. Its staff include two co-directors, 20 crisis workers working in a team of four per shift and two crisis worker trainees (one of whom is a former user of the Gerstein House services and the other is recruited from the multicultural community, both for one-year contracts). Ideally, staff and clients work in partnership at all levels as much as possible so that the staff continue to be sensitive to the expressed needs and wishes of the user group. The client could stay at Gerstein House for up to five days (the centre has ten beds). Alternatively, a mobile crisis intervention team may offer support to an individual at their home or at a location in the community mutually agreed upon—restaurants, parks, public buildings. A deputation team may spend one to three hours with a client, at which time some clients may be encouraged to utilize the centre's short-term beds. Gerstein House accepts both self-referral and referrals from a second party. Since its founding, Gerstein House has attained much fame, visibility and community respect for its unique offer of respect for privacy, dignity and autonomy of the client/user. There is no waiting time between the telephone inquiry and the availability of service: the mobile unit comes to the client where he or she is and wants to be. Only time will tell if such a non-medical model proves to be as useful and effective in dealing with crisis.[75]

Whether it is professional-oriented or lay-centred, crisis intervention is based upon the following six principles: to render immediately the desperately needed "emotional first aid" to the person in crisis (principle of immediacy); to identify as well as to assist the person to recognize the nature and core of the problem (principle of identification); to assist the person to ventilate pent-up feelings (principle of ventilation and tension management); to establish and maintain rapport, trust and emotional bond with the person in crisis (principle of support); to assist the person to learn and institute new coping mechanisms for the present and for the future (principle of empowerment); to anchor the person in crisis with appropriate social support resources such as mental health professionals, friends, colleagues and school counsellors (principle of anchoring).[76]

Crisis intervention is *ipso facto* short-term, well focused, reality-based and task-oriented. Some of the practical steps for crisis intervention will be introduced next.

Some Practical Steps to Crisis Intervention and Management

The following steps are recommended by some crisis intervention specialists:[77]

1. Try to calm the person, relieve their anxiety, stress and panic; try to limit the extent of their sense of disorganization.
2. Remove the person from the crisis situation where possible, and

exclude disturbing persons, at least temporarily.

3. Communicate calmness, strength and confidence in yourself.
4. Make contact on both a feeling and a factual level.
5. Accept what they have to say and do not be judgmental.
6. Complete the picture of the precipitating event.
7. Find out how much of their daily functioning has been disrupted.
8. Try to identify all present stresses; get the person in crisis to be concrete and specific as much as possible.
9. Focus, because focussing will actually help the person to avoid further confusion and deterioration.
10. Find out if others are affected by the person's crisis.
11. Help them ventilate their feelings and gain relief.
12. Keep clarifying for the person and yourself, so you can both agree on the main elements of the problem.
13. Help the person gain an intellectual understanding and grasp of the problem as well as a sense of structure by defining the problem(s), thereby reducing the sense of chaos.
14. Begin to build in your own mind, and theirs, a logical connection among events.
15. Develop a sense of how to look at the problem realistically.
16. Move towards focussed problem-solving and steer the person away from maladaptive coping and towards adaptive coping strategies.
17. Help them to face up to problems and help them to see how such problems happened.
18. Agree on a specific problem to focus on, this should be the one causing the most pain and also the one that is most amenable to change.
19. Examine and explore the supports the person has and what other supports can be drawn upon.
20. Don't argue! Just point out there are many ways of looking at the situation as well as many other options for solving the problem.
21. Try to help the person set reasonable goals.
22. Contract an agreement on a plan (and a handshake, if appropriate).
23. Reinforce newly acquired coping skills.
24. Review success in a follow-up.

These useful pointers are for those people who are actually involved in the crisis intervention centre. What about other people who know little about the principles and techniques of crisis intervention and suicide management? For such people who may also encounter friends or relatives who may be suicidal, here is a list of dos and don'ts for concerned lay persons who wish to be helpful to someone who is threatening suicide:

1. Be direct. Ask if the person is thinking about suicide. Talk openly and freely about suicide.
2. Be willing to listen and keep the spotlight on the other party.
3. Try to ask questions which will help the person to explore further (e.g., "What do you think are the causes of your difficulty?", "What have you done so far to improve the situation?", "What do you think is standing in the way of working things out?", "Do you have someone to whom you can take your problems?").
4. Always tell the truth when answering questions.
5. Don't debate whether suicide is right or wrong or if feelings are good or bad. Don't lecture on the value of life.
6. Don't dare the person to do it.
7. Don't give advice by making decisions for someone else or telling him or her to behave differently.
8. Don't ask "why." This encourages defensiveness.
9. Don't be shocked; this will put distance between you.
10. Don't be sworn to secrecy. Don't promise not to tell anyone (Saving someone else's life may be more important than a promise to secrecy).
11. Point out some other alternatives that are available, but do not offer glib reassurance because the person can see right through such phony reassurances.
12. Take action. Get help from persons or agencies specializing in suicide prevention and management.

Before moving on to the discussion of crisis intervention and management by the medical model, it may be useful and informative to the reader to have some idea of crisis intervention and suicide management by the non-medical model—by volunteers at a telephone crisis centre. The following is a real case of dealing with an initiated suicide and its profound impact on the volunteer:

The Initiated Suicide*
by Anita, Volunteer #144

"I feel dizzy. I've taken some pills to make me sleep."

With those few words the call began. I asked quietly, "How long did you want to sleep? A few hours or forever?" The reply came back, "Forever."

An hour and ten minutes later, when the call ended, I put my head down and cried. John was going to live.

Since then I have replayed that call inside my head to analyze what happened, and I wanted to share my thoughts on caring for the troubled person who has begun the dying process before he calls.

It is initially frightening to know that the person on the other end of the phone is dying. Very few of us have talked to a person during the last moments of life so we don't have a lot of personal or learned resources to fall back on. But the initial fear has to be overcome or there is a great danger of treating that anguished other person as an object to be manipulated. The tendency is to overlook the pain that brought on the suicide attempt and to concentrate on tearing information from the caller. "Who are you? Where are you? What is your phone number?"

And that doesn't seem to be what the caller wants. It is not what John wanted. He wanted to tell me about himself. About what had gone wrong. And most of all, he wanted me to understand how it felt to be "dead inside." Like a film in slow motion, his life revealed itself and I listened carefully and shared with him his feelings of pain and gave him back the only resource I had, myself. The life story came in short sentences, punctuated by long pauses, and when it seemed appropriate I would ask quietly, "John, will you tell me where you are?" He didn't want to and I could understand that.

There were some bizarre moments as the call progressed. John would keep saying, "I can't understand it. One Valium usually knocks me out and here I've taken 45 and nothing is happening. Do you think the chocolate milk I mixed with them and the cheese I ate slowed down the process?" And then we'd talk awhile in quite a matter-of-fact way about how the acid in the pills and the calcium in the milk and cheese might have slowed down the absorption of the drug. He had been planning his death for months and had bought the milk and cheese especially to take with the pills. He thought his stomach would hold down the drug if it was soothed with milk and cheese. John had mixed 450 milligrams of Valium with chocolate milk in his blender.

So we talked. And he told me about his work. He hadn't done with his life what he thought he should have. And his voice became slow and his thinking a little disjointed. Then he would pick up, and when I suggested he might have been trying to live up to some kind of competitive standard, which our society seems to value, he was able to argue that this was not so and to tell me what his values were. And the minutes ticked by. The alert was on in the phone room. Poison Control has advised that John should be taken to hospital immediately. I told him this and he brushed it aside as if the knowledge were of no importance.

Going to sleep should have been easy. Dying should have been a release from his hurts.

"John, will you tell me where you are? I promise not to send anyone without your permission, but if you go unconscious suddenly, I'll have to make a decision about sending help. Please."

"...and I've been asked to be the best man at a friend's wedding next Friday...."

We continued to talk. Then, when he knew he could trust me and that I cared enough to let him choose to live or die, he gave me his address and his last name. But not permission to send the ambulance.

An hour after the call began, I asked again if I could send help. John's voice had begun to blur and his feet and hands to go numb. He was frightened then. Dying was not going to be a blissful sleep but a terrifying slowing down of his whole body. As we spoke at the end, his breathing became rapid. He said I could send help. The ambulance was called and within minutes had reached John's apartment and he was taken to hospital, where his stomach was washed out and he was admitted into psychiatric care.

The dying caller needs to be treated with grace. Your compassion must be apparent to him. Having made the decision to die and begun the awful process of self-destruction, the will to live suddenly reasserts itself. It is this ambivalence which can be confusing. The dilemma can be looked at in two ways. Since the cry for help is genuine, might it not be better to hustle the caller into accepting immediate help? Or should we listen to the cry for help because the dignity of a human being is at stake? This innermost part of his being, the "I," the hurting soul can shrink back even further into itself if the utmost care is not taken. To become angry and say, "Why did you call if you don't want me to do anything..." and to try and make the caller react to the seriousness of his situation will only increase his anguish and guilt.

The human body can take a lot of abuse. It will not give up easily on life. Even a massive overdose of drugs takes a while to cause death. In almost all cases there is time to spend in quiet talk. There is time to allow trust to develop; for deep and concerned caring to reach out and embrace the caller. "Let me die peacefully and please try to understand" is the message. And if you can reconcile yourself to being there with the caller and truly understanding his pain, you will give him the precious moments he needs to work out his own destiny.

There are some simple and sensible things to be done with the initiated suicide call. There is the alerting of your volunteer partners that you have a serious crisis and might need help.

Once trust has been established with the caller and an address is given and the feeling of wanting to live begins to change the original message, I always ask the caller to try and unlock the front door of the house or apartment. This saves the terrible embarrassment of having the police break down the door and the neighbours being alerted. A person almost completely unconscious from an overdose can find the will to go to the door if the instructions are given gently, with no panic.

There is, of course, no absolutely right way to deal with the initiated suicide. But it is always right to act with compassion, make no judgments of why the suicide attempt has been made, allow the caller the dignity of telling you about himself, trust the caller to decide if he can go on living and listen with every nerve in your body.

*Source: Courtesy of Distress Centre I, Toronto, Ontario, 1995.

Some Steps for Crisis Intervention and Management (A Medical Model)

For medical practitioners the following aspects of crisis intervention are crucial: first and foremost, the establishment and maintenance of a warm and trusting doctor-patient relationship; liaison with the family in order to remove all lethal objects such as guns, drugs and knives from the person at risk; monitoring of the compliance with prescribed drugs and tests (serum and urine tests); follow-up on missed appointments because suicide often occurs during missed office visits or therapy sessions; and consultation with a liaison-psychiatry colleague.

For the psychiatric model of intervention and management, the following steps are usually recommended and taken: pharmacological intervention to relieve some of the initial suffering such as sleep disturbance, loss of appetite, agitation, depression; the medication to be entrusted to a relative if at all possible, and to prescribe medication only in small quantities to prevent overdose (no more than a five-day supply) and not permitting refills without writing another prescription (such precautions are necessary not only for keeping the suicidal person alive but this also gives the patient the feeling that the clinician cares); and pharmacological therapies such as serotonin reuptake blockers for suicidal and depressed patients, neuroleptics for schizophrenics, borderline personality disorders and psychotic depression.[78]

In addition to somatic treatments and psychotropic medications, physicians and psychiatrists sometimes resort to ECT (electro-convulsive therapy) for alleviating depression. Finally, medical practitioners may employ psychotherapies such as psychodynamic treatments, cognitive therapies which may reduce or diminish the degree of hopelessness (a major component of suicidality) and distorted perception of the situation that often produces such hopelessness associated with suicidal thoughts and behaviour. Complementary to these psychotherapies is the utilization of community resources such as mental health associations, telephone crisis centres and school programmes.

The medical model stresses the importance of early detection of serious affective disorders and other risk factors as the key for prevention and treatment. Table 2 illustrates guidelines for the clinical management of suicidal persons on the part of physicians and other medical professionals.[79]

Thus far, rather detailed guidelines for crisis intervention and management have been presented and discussed both on the medical and the non-medical model. What is crucially important (and the remaining problem in suicide prevention and intervention) is effective liaison and cooperation between the two models. Unfortunately, the two models do not always work well together but on occasion work at cross-purposes as the following example, a real case, (Figure 11) illustrates.

Some Guidelines for Deciding Whether or Not to Hospitalize a Person at Risk

Ideally speaking, a mental status examination that determines the presence or absence of psychiatric illnesses and assesses suicide ideation together with levels of lethality, cognitive constriction and imminent risk to one's own life ought to be taken into account before deciding on the appropriateness of hospitalization. Hospitalization ought to be seriously considered when: the person is uncertain that the suicidal impulse can be resisted and controlled; a serious suicide attempt has just been made, requiring definite medical attention and care; the risk seems high and the person is not well known to the caregiver nor has a supportive relationship

General Points

> Inquire about suicidal thoughts and plans at every visit
> Set up frequent appointments and contact by telephone
> Follow-up missed appointments
> Document positive and negative findings in the chart
> Seek psychiatric consultation when necessary

Psychological Aspects

> Establish therapeutic relationship (alliance)
> Allow expression of painful feelings
> Use a flexible, empathic and supportive therapeutic style
> Provide reassurance and hope
> Rectify cognitive distortions
> Strengthen social supports and interpersonal relationships
> Form a non-suicide contract
> Develop and administer follow-up plan

Medical Components

> Importance of symptomatic relief
> Adequate doses
> No refills
> Supervision by a relative when possible
> Assess patient compliance
> Obtain serum levels when appropriate
> Pay attention to side effects

Environmental Interventions

> Detoxification of the home
> Close supervision
> Family therapy
> Community support
> Work/school interventions

Source: Blumenthal, S.J., and Kupfer, D.J. (Eds.), *Suicide Over the Life Cycle: Risk Factors, Assessment, and Treatment of Suicidal Persons* (Washington, D.C., American Psychiatric Press, 1990), p.714.

METRO'S
MUNICIPALITIES

North York

Scarborough

Etobicoke

York

Toronto

INCORPORATED 1975

COUNCIL ON
SUICIDE
PREVENTION

METROPOLITAN TORONTO

News

Fall 1989

FRONT LINES

Dealing with a suicidal client in a community setting, frequently leaves agency staff feeling confused with and frustrated at the apparent lack of responsiveness of the Mental Health system. An example of such a situation occurred when an agency staff member of a local drop-in accompanied an acutely distressed suicidal client to a downtown hospital emergency room. Nearly four hours elapsed before a doctor assessed the client and suggested that he could go home. Neither the staff member nor the client received any guidance about a plan of action to help him through the crisis!

with others; the suicidal state is related to an organic brain syndrome, such as in alcoholic withdrawal or use of psychedelic drug with subsequent psychosis or delirium; the person is unable to function because of the psychological pathology with which the suicidal behaviour is associated; the suicidal person is an adolescent and is threatening or has just attempted suicide; and at times a hospital must be used simply because no other alternatives are available or the person refuses to accept other options. When these conditions are met, an inpatient psychiatric hospital unit may be the best place to manage the suicidal person and provide around-the-clock psychotherapeutic and psychopharmacological interventions.[80]

On the other hand, alternatives to hospitalization are indicated when: both the person and family are firmly opposed to hospital care; the risk does not seem high, and responsible, caring persons are available for the person at risk; a firm relationship has been established with the person and assurances can be accepted on the basis of trust; the person is primarily seeking a place to be cared for and the suicidal behavioural is consciously or unconsciously serving to request such a place; and use of a psychiatric hospital would impose an insurmountable psychological burden by virtue of the socio-cultural setting in which the person lives.[81]

There are times when the person refuses hospitalization and involuntary measures are not appropriate. Under such circumstances, it may be advisable to settle for less than the ideal: i.e., to inform the person of the serious concern the situation warrants, to offer what help the person will accept, to give assurances of the helper's availability and desire to be of continued assistance, and to ask that if the person's decision about hospitalization changes to let the caregiver (or someone) know.

Naikan as a Buddhist-based Ethnotherapy

The medical model discussed in the previous section recommends pharmacotherapy and psychotherapy of various orientations for people who are deemed to be in crisis or in danger of harming themselves. Every human being is likely to experience some type of crisis at some point in his or her life; at the same time, the manner in which the crisis is handled or managed is often contingent on specific traditions and values of a particular culture. Every culture, East or West, North or South, has developed its own unique way of tension management for individual and group survival.

One example of such culture-specific tension management mechanisms may be the legendary "politeness" of the Japanese. In many animal experiments in North America, it has been known that extreme density of living space contributes to slaughter and injury among the experimental animals; likewise, high urban density among human beings has been known to breed tension, crime, violence and conflict. Tokyo certainly has one of the world's highest population densities (almost half the population of Canada squeezed in a small area). Yet, in fact, Tokyo has managed to keep its rates of human violence low: Tokyo's homicide rate is the lowest of all the industrialized world, and its suicide rate inside Japan has been much lower than sparsely populated areas of that country. How have the

Japanese done it? One explanation offered by a social psychologist in Japan is that "politeness" is an effective tension management technique by which the people create "psychological space" and keep each other at arm's length, thereby minimizing social friction and conflict. Likewise, the legendary group cohesion and emphasis placed on group membership among the Japanese contributes to group identity, support and security, all of which would minimize loneliness and isolation.[82]

Psychotherapy, in Japan or in the West, is directed towards helping people reduce tension, stress and psychic pain as well as helping them to change in order to better adapt to external situations. One cannot, however, "vault across dissimilar cultures and apply the same terminologies [and therapies] in the same way without lapsing into serious, ethnocentric misjudgment."[83] Ideally speaking, psychotherapies are anchored in and harnessed to a specific culture's language, history and common collective experience in order to be maximally effective. Under such optimal conditions, psychotherapies are more effective in providing recovery and empowerment. Thus, when a particular psychological method of self-improvement is the product of a collective learning and common experience rooted in cultural history, it is called "ethnotherapy" by the present author. It stands to reason, then, that in the field of psychotherapies culturally distinct social groups such as the Japanese may develop their own forms of therapies deeply anchored in the long tradition of value systems and religion. In the case of Japan, there have indeed been a number of such indigenous ethnotherapies; two of the best known psychotherapies are Morita therapy and *Naikan* therapy, both of which are originally Buddhist-based.

The former was developed in Japan in the early part of the twentieth century by Professor Shoma Morita of the Jikei University School of Medicine in Tokyo. The principal aim of Morita therapy, largely based upon the tenets of Zen Buddhism, is not to alter symptoms but rather to alter the person's perspective on them by accepting the symptoms as a natural part of themselves—accepting them "as they are." For almost all Western psychotherapists, anxiety, for instance, is an intrusive element like a fever or rash—something to be eliminated. But in Morita therapy, the client is encouraged to see anxiety as part of himself or herself, not as an appended symptom. Rather than trying to change existing realities, the client alters his or her perspective on those realities and finds purpose or meaning in them, and thus accepts them as they are (*arugamama*, or "as they are" in Japanese).[84] In Western approaches, like psychodynamic orientation, for instance, the emphasis is placed on the control, mastery and resolution of the symptoms as evident in Freud's dictum: "the patient shall no longer be suffering from his symptoms and shall have overcome his anxieties and his inhibitions."[85] For behavioural and cognitive therapy in the West, altering symptoms or behavioural problems or the perceptions and interpretations of the problem(s) has been a central objective rather than accepting such symptoms as they are. As such, Morita therapy has been used primarily for neurotic symptoms in Japan by therapists.

The other ethnotherapy in Japan, *Naikan*, will now be discussed in more detail as this therapy has been effectively used for suicide attempters and for those who have suicidal thoughts more frequently than Morita therapy.

Origin of *Naikan*

Naikan in Japanese is a composite word with "*nai*" ("inside" or "within") and "*kan*" ("looking"), meaning "observing the inner self" or "self-introspection." It is both a form of meditational spiritual training and a psychotherapy. When this method is applied to one's own spiritual development and exploration without any therapeutic aims, it is called *Naikan-Ho* ("Naikan Approach"); but when it is used as a psychotherapy, it is referred to as *Naikan-Ryoho* ("Naikan Therapy"). This method in contemporary Japan was developed by a devout Buddhist businessman and lay practitioner, Ishin Yoshimoto (1916-1988), more than 50 years ago. Yoshimoto attained enlightenment through a practice known as *mishirabé* ("self-examination") in the tradition of the Jodo Shinshu Sect of Buddhism, in which the practitioners were isolated and, without eating or sleeping, would reflect on their past towards the goal of enlightenment. This original and highly ascetic practice of *mishirabé* that had been practiced in Jodo Shinshu Sect circles for centuries, underwent considerable modification under Yoshimoto and came to be known as *Naikan*. The entire programme is based upon meditation in the form of recollecting and reflecting on one's past.

Morita therapy is based upon the Zen Buddhist tradition of "accepting things as they are;" *Naikan*, by contrast and in accordance with Jodo Shinshu theology, emphasizes the crucial role of a sense of gratitude and contrition for inner transformation. *Naikan* therapy is a guided meditation and self-introspection aimed at attitude and behaviour change. It is not related to any professional psychotherapeutic form, either in the East or the West, and for a long time it was practiced inside penal institutions and other correctional facilities. In its earlier days, *Naikan* was known for its helpfulness with alcoholics, hardened criminals and juvenile delinquents. It is claimed that 80% of alcoholics who went through the *Naikan* programme were recovered or greatly improved. Another study found that in several prisons where *Naikan* has been used, prisoners had impressive reductions in recidivism. In some prisons, those who had gone through *Naikan* therapy were later convicted of new crime at a quarter the rate of those who did not get it.[86]

In the past 20 years or so, *Naikan* has become widely known not only in Japan but around the world, and a number of counsellors have been treating people in medical and educational settings in addition to correctional institutions. Now 15 *Naikan* centres are in operation throughout the Japanese Isles, and *Naikan* training or therapy sessions are being held twice or three times monthly. As it became better known beyond Japan, many centres opened abroad: in the United States in 1980s, in the suburbs of Vienna in 1986, in northern Germany in 1987, in the suburbs of Munich in southern Germany in 1988 and in Great Britain in 1989, to name only a few.

Basic Tenets of *Naikan*[87]

The fundamental assumption of *Naikan* is that human beings are essentially self-centred, therefore they cause numerous problems in life. A person's relationships with others in society are strongly influenced by the development of one's relationship with one's parents, particularly with the mother. In any culture the fundamental social relationship is that between mother and child, hence within such a relationship lies the fundamental spring for guilt and gratitude. In the process of growing up, however, one learns what may be taken from others; thus, one accepts kindness and benevolence without acknowledging, appreciating or extending them (either in return, to the giver, or along to others). Others are often seen as tools useful for satisfying one's own needs. When feelings of guilt and acknowledged appreciation of the benevolence of others towards one's own self occur, they can dramatically change one's attitudes towards other people. "The time of self-acceptance emerges when the guilt is balanced by the recognition that one has been loved and taken care of by others in spite of one's own imperfection."[88] *Naikan's* guided introspection ideally provokes an emotionally intense rearrangement and restructuring of the client's self-image and current social relationships; the resultant sense of gratitude to others through inner introspection and a strong desire to repay others who have given love and caring, generates profound joy, new purpose and new meaning in life. Thus, the client's attitude towards his or her own past and towards others is profoundly changed. In this process, changes in behaviour problems are merely circumstantial by-products. *Naikan* is fundamentally concerned with achieving a positive readaptation to persons both in the past and present life of the client.

The Procedure

Naikan's procedure involves continuous, carefully structured, solitary meditation, initially in a small enclosed space, from early morning until late at night.

The *Naikan* method proceeds in a purposeful sequence, reviewing the central interpersonal relationships in one's life, beginning with childhood experiences and proceeding chronologically through the client's life. This guided introspection begins with the person's relationship with his or her mother—this particular relationship is given special attention and is reviewed carefully with perhaps 25 to 35 hours of an approximately 100-hour meditational, one-week period. Relationships with the client's father, siblings, marital partner, teachers, employers, employees and friends are subsequently reviewed in a chronological sequence during the week. It is expected that through such concentration the client will recall experiences that are not usually available to the daily consciousness.

The guide, called "*sensei*" in Japanese, comes to the client eight to ten times at intervals of from one or two hours during the day. The guide tries to gently and quietly direct the client to meditate on two central themes of *Naikan*: the rediscovery of personal guilt for having been ungrateful and irresponsible towards people in the past and the discovery (or rediscovery) of gratitude towards those persons who have extended kindness, love and acts of kindness to the client. In order to achieve such goals, therefore, the client will be instructed to reflect on three specific items: what he or she received from that person (in terms of objects, services and acts of kindness), what he or she returned to that person; and the troubles, inconveniences, deceit and pettiness for which he or she may have been responsible in relation to that person. It is usually the case that the client will report having received a great deal from others but having returned little and having caused a great deal of trouble and inconvenience to the person.

Many clients pass through a number of stages as the week progresses. The following quote by one of the best known proponents of *Naikan* in North America summarizes such experiences:[89]

> Initial difficulties in concentration and a rather bitter view toward other significant persons are replaced by the 'emergence of the real self' with accompanying regrets, guilt and sorrow over the way the client has treated loved ones. The client may want to die and may even voice thoughts of suicide. The next stage is prompted by the guide's reminder that in spite of his insensitivity and unkindness to others, they [still] loved and cared for him. When he recognizes this, the client feels repentance, along with a strong desire to serve and repay others from the well springs of gratitude that have their source in his recognition of others' sacrifices for him and kindness to him. Then comes joy . . . the client alternately compares *his* deeds and attitudes with his perceptions of *others'* deeds and attitudes, and finds himself relatively wanting in human virtue. This results in a *self-directed* depressive response from which the only escape is seen to be other-directed acts of service.

Discussion: *Naikan* as an Ethnotherapy

Deep emotions are evoked by this process and tears are common, inducing a genuine discharge of feelings in connection with these recollections involving other persons who played parts in the client's life.[90] In *Naikan*, intellectual understanding or "insight" is considered to be incomplete unless it has been accompanied by a catharsis through genuine repentance and contrition leading to a sense of gratitude to others. In *Naikan* only through the recognition and confession of one's self-centredness can one be free of the pain and worry caused by this behaviour and can experience feelings of gratitude.

Likewise, feelings of guilt and appreciation can dramatically change one's attitudes towards other people. Self-acceptance emerges in *Naikan* when the guilt is balanced by the awareness and recognition that one has been loved and taken care of by others in spite of imperfections and ingratitude.

In *Naikan*, life is perceived to be one of dependence on the unmerited benevolence, love and support of others from infancy onwards. *Naikan*, therefore, understands psychological health as not only a matter of improving relationships but as a matter of recognizing helplessness in the self and acknowledging the assistance of others who are even now willing to help.

In order to fully appreciate the importance of "repaying others for what they have done for you," a word of explanation is in order for the non-Japanese reader. Japan's religio-ethical values believe that one is constantly blessed by nature and by other people (called "*On*" in Japanese); hence, it is the obligation of the recipient to make return for these various blessings (called "*Ho-on*" or repayment of such blessings). The idea of "*Ho-on*" is Buddhist in origin: stress is placed on indebtedness or returning kindness. In the Buddhist scriptures, the Buddha is said to have preached on four debts which the Buddhist owes: to one's parents, fellow human beings, one's sovereign and the three holy treasures of Buddhism (i.e., the Law, the Church and the Buddha). The theory assumes that human beings can never fully repay "*On*"—they always stand in debt. Hence, the implicit assumption in Japanese life is an awareness of unmerited natural blessing and benevolence such as sunshine, soil, rain and crops. One must also become aware of other human blessings such as love and nurturing which one receives from one's parents (especially from one's mother), siblings, relatives, friends and teachers. "*Ho-on*" is directed to all sorts of benefactors: when it is directed to one's parents, it is called "*Ko*" (or filial piety); when it is expressed to one's ruler or superior ("*Chu*," etc.).[91] This is the historical and ethico-moral background for *Naikan's* enormous stress on becoming aware of one's blessings as well as the importance of repaying such blessings.

Western psychotherapy has not been accepted well in Japan. The Japanese are inclined to consider the North American preoccupation with one's personal problems as an outcome of American individualism and narcissism. For the Japanese, relationships and social obligations matter more than the individual ego. The bond between a dependent child and a loving, indulgent mother, for instance, is duplicated in primary social relationships throughout Japanese society such as employer-employee, teacher-student, elder colleague-younger colleague, and so on. Herein lies *Naikan's* enormous emphasis on the restoration of warm, benevolent relationships through appreciation and gratitude. Gratitude is considered to be an antidote to the narcissism and alienation of the American ethic of self-made success. Furthermore, gratitude to others, especially to one's parents, may be a good antidote to the resentment against one's parents that is so often evoked in the course of psychotherapy in the West.

Naikan as a type of psychotherapy has a few common grounds to share with mainstream Western psychotherapy: the presence of a therapist to guide the client (the therapist is called a "guide" or "*sensei*"), the intensive use and review of the client's past history, the anticipation of successful social and psychological rehabilitation, the resolution or diminution of problems in the client's life and the effective employment of catharsis as a therapeutic means of ventilating the client's feelings. These similarities notwithstanding, there are a number of crucial differences as well.

(1) In comparison to client-centred therapy in North America, the *Naikan* guide is perceived literally as a guide to actively direct the client's meditation and self-examination. Moreover, the relationship between the guide and the client in *Naikan* is simpler and more goal-directed than most Western psychotherapies.[92]

(2) The Western concept of "self" usually implies a freestanding, independent and separate individual, forming and regulating social relationships according to his or her will. The Japanese concept of "*jibun*" (self), by contrast, encompasses a slightly different emphasis. The Japanese "self" is, in a sense, the sum total of one's relationship with the people around oneself. The person in Japan is inherently dependent on the reference one has towards others, one's attitude towards them and one's position among them in social interaction. In Japan, one's self-definition is always social and relational: the person is always the parent of somebody, the employee of somebody, or the teacher or student of somebody. The Japanese, therefore, attach much value to the preservation of harmony in the group to which the person belongs and try to avoid and/or resolve relational conflicts in a person's life.

(3) The importance of relationships in the group is not too difficult to understand sociologically. In a society such as Japan, where natural resources are scarce, group survival becomes *sine qua non*—certainly far more important than in a society of abundance such as the United States. In a densely populated and overcrowded country like Japan, highly intricate and well-developed behaviours regulate the daily life of a hierarchical society and minimize friction and conflict. In a vertically oriented society like Japan, everyone is unequal but everyone belongs, whereas in North America, everyone is hierarchically equal but everyone is alone. In Japan, harmony in the group is highly appreciated and

rewarded, individual wishes and desires are often placed on the back seat; in North America, success is to be sought, found, attained and then judged by the self alone. *Naikan's* extraordinary emphasis on the assumption of personal guilt and the restoration of positive gratitude towards significant others must be understood and appreciated in this context of preserving or restoring the individual's reintegration into one's primary group in a society where one's belonging in the group is extremely important.

(4) The North American approach to psychotherapy is aimed at maximizing the individual's autonomy and individuation, which may unwittingly foster excessive self-absorption at the expense of a collective, be it a social group or society. Erich Fromm pointed out a long time ago that, in addition to the danger of narcissism, excessive individuation may lead to alienation and loneliness.[93] Fromm argued that the post-Renaissance emphasis on individual freedom in the West led to increasing levels of autonomy and individuation. The process of such individuation, however, encourages the cutting off of the primary bond and emotional "umbilical cord" which have offered belonging, security and social anchoring. Severing such primary ties, through increasing individuation, fosters a spiritual and emotional vacuum and creates negative freedom (what Fromm called "freedom-from"). The single-minded pursuit of freedom from control and dependence may lead to satisfying one's wishes at the expense of the needs of a group. If one of the primary aims of North American psychotherapy is personal restoration and re-empowerment apart from a group of which a person is a part, Japanese ethnotherapy such as *Naikan*, by comparison, is aimed at readjustment, readaptation and re-integration of the individual in social terms with corollary individual improvement as a by-product.

(5) Traditional psychoanalysis may require a minimum of two years for therapy, and even short-term therapy in recent years still requires up to 12 weeks. By contrast, *Naikan* requires a maximum of four to six days. Such intense concentration, from early in the morning till late in the evening with short intervals for meals, which are prepared and brought by the guide (in the spirit of Zen in which unconditional service is encouraged and practiced regardless of the guest's social status), may result in its maximum effect for those who participate.

(6) In Western psychoanalysis, enormous emphasis is placed on drawing out ambivalent feelings concerning one's parents and significant others as well as one's own self, discovering in the process primal sexual

feelings towards mother and father, which have been subsequently disguised during the Oedipal transition. In *Naikan*, however, positive memories are employed as inducements to rediscovering one's guilt, especially the reaffirmation of gratitude to significant others, which hopefully contributes to the client's inner transformation (emotional, not intellectual) and ultimately to reconciliation in social relationships. Reconciliation in social and relational context is *sine qua non* in *Naikan*. In order to fully and better understand this crucial point in *Naikan*, it is useful to appreciate the Japanese concept of Ajasé complex.

(7) Freud's theory of Oedipus complex was derived from the Greek tragedy of Oedipus as told in Sophocles' *Oedipus Rex*. According to this legend, it was predicted before his birth that Oedipus would kill his father and marry his mother. Despite his conscious efforts to evade the prophecy, Oedipus committed the sins of incest and patricide (by marrying his mother/ queen and killing his father/king). Shaken by the incest, his mother committed suicide, and Oedipus plucked out his eyes and went into exile. According to Freud, the social taboos against these two impulses (incest and patricide) have generated the fear of external punishment in the form of castration. Through such threat and fear, the external social norm becomes the individual's internalized norm, or superego. Castration thus represents the principle of paternal society in which the father represents and wields authority and power. To Freud the Oedipus complex thus generates guilt and fear of punishment (by castration): the paternal authority represented is stern and uncompromisingly judgmental.

By contrast, Japan's Ajasé complex is derived from ancient Buddhist scriptures and emphasizes maternal compassion and forgiveness rather than the judgment and punishment of paternal authority. The concept of Ajasé complex was developed by a pioneer in Japan's psychoanalysis, Professor Heisaku Kosawa (1897-1968), who had chaired the Department of Psychiatry, School of Medicine, Keio University for a long time. He identified the basic structure of the typical, Japanese mother-child experience and called it Ajasé complex in his article entitled "Two Types of Guilt Consciousness-Ajasé Complex."[94] In July 1932, Kosawa visited Freud at his home and presented his original work to Freud for his comments. Unfortunately, Kosawa's paper drew little response from Freud and other Western analysts. In 1978, however, Keigo Okonogi, one of Kosawa's students and a well-known psychoanalyst in contemporary Japan, popularized the essential aspects of Kosawa's theory in Japan and abroad.

Ajasé complex is based upon the story of an Indian prince named Ajasé who was in conflict with his mother. His mother, the queen, tried to conceive a male child in order to retain the fading interest of her wayward king. She killed a holy man in the mountain in the hope that he would be reincarnated as her son. Horrified by her act, however, she tried to abort the child of such a curse in vain. When the son, Ajasé, learned of the circumstances in which he was born, he became consumed with hatred against his mother. Such intense hatred and rage led to a terrible skin disease all over his body emitting an unbearable odour so foul that no one would come near him, much less tend to him. It was his mother the queen, however, who tended to him in the spirit of contrition and repentance and nursed Ajasé back to health. Moved by his mother's untiring care and contrition, Ajasé repented about harbouring such hatred against his mother and forgave her; she in turn forgave her son's hatred. In the end, therefore, the two mutually exchanged contrition, forgave each other and reconciled.

To Kosawa, this story represented the spirit and reality of wrong, immoral deeds, repentance, forgiveness and, ultimately, reconciliation. Ajasé complex represented maternal love—never-ending and unconditional—in Kosawa's theory.

The Ajasé complex and the Oedipus complex share a common element of resentment of parents. The fundamental difference lies in the fact that the Oedipus complex stems from sexual love of the mother and the resultant hatred of the father, whereas the theme of Ajasé complex is the resentment of the mother for not having borne and raised one out of pure love as well as for not having rejoiced unconditionally in one's birth. Another difference is that the Oedipus complex focuses entirely on the child's impulses of sexual desire and the resulting murderous intent, in which the child wishes to intrude on the natural conjugal rights of the parents as man and woman. Ajasé complex, on the other hand, is centred around the child's resentment and the eventual mutual forgiveness leading to reconciliation. Mutual penance and reconciliation symbolizes the restoration of the lost relationship; it is, therefore, the central theme of this theory of Ajasé complex, corresponding to and ringing a harmonious chord in *Naikan* therapy. Figure 12 summarizes the foregoing discussion and illuminates the highlights and differences of these two culturally sensitive concepts.

Naikan's strong emphasis on gratitude to one's mother and reconciliation is certainly understandable in the context of Ajasé complex. Thus, in the words of a prominent Japanese anthropologist, *Naikan* is

Oedipus Complex	**Ajasé Complex**
From Greek Mythology	From Buddhist Scripture
Source of Guilt – Patricide and Incest	Source of Guilt – Attempt for abortion – Revenge
Outcome – Suicide and self-injury – Guilt – Banishment – *Tragedy*	Outcome – Atonement; repentance – Forgiveness – Ultimate reconciliation – *Inner Transformation*

Figure 13:   Oedipus Complex and Ajasé Complex Compared

the type of therapy and character-building which "best elucidates the core values of Japanese culture."[95]

(8) The foregoing discussion undergirds the earlier assertion that a therapy which is well rooted in the collective experience and culture of a given people would probably work best for maximum effect. Available literature strongly indicates that *Naikan* has been extremely effective in preventing recidivism of suicide attempts in Japan. Miki, the successor to Yoshimoto who founded *Naikan* therapy in Japan, reported a remarkable success in dealing with suicide attempters, none of whom has made another attempt. It is believed that a re-awakened sense of gratitude to others, the restoration of interpersonal relations and re-integration into one's primary group contribute to reducing suicide risks. The empirical data, however, are still scarce and anecdotal, and more systematic and controlled study is needed. Be that as it may, this particular branch of ethnotherapy may hold some promise for reducing suicide behaviour in Japan and elsewhere.[96]

POSTVENTION

The term "postvention" was introduced into the lexicon by the founder of modern suicidology, Edwin Shneidman, and it refers to those activities that serve to reduce the after-effects of a traumatic event in the lives of survivors of suicide.[97] As such, postvention is a composite word derived originally from "pasca" in ancient Sanskrit (meaning "after"), which was then incorporated into Latin "post" (also meaning "after"); it has since been used as a prefix to the noun "vention," which comes from medieval French *venir* (to come). Thus, it means what comes after suicide.

It is assumed that for each death by suicide an average of seven to ten people will be intimately affected, including family members, close friends and acquaintances, colleagues, professionals (police officers, ambulance crews, physicians, psychiatrists, etc.) and on occasion even strangers. No death is neutral; it is bound to affect many other people.

Moreover, surviving family members run a greater risk of suicide themselves—perhaps between 80% and 300% higher than the general population.[98] Intimate human relationships offer a sense of belonging, being wanted and appreciated, a purpose and order in one's daily life enabling individuals to cope with life's hardships. The death of a loved one, especially in the family, means the death of an important and very intimate relationship, affecting feelings of trust and security in other relationships as well, often leaving an indelible scar on the survivors and enhancing their own risk of self-harm behaviour.

Coping with death by suicide is extremely difficult because it involves many unanswered questions. It may lead to denial or the wish to hide the event because death by suicide brings forth a sense of rejection, shame, guilt, social embarrassment and stigma. The perceived social stigma attached to suicide often interferes with the grieving process. Some of the issues that arise after the suicide of a family member or a loved one now will be discussed.

Impact on the Family

Since most suicides occur in the home, many survivors will actually discover the body themselves, and the traumatic impact on the survivor may last a lifetime. Suicide involves much more than the destruction of the person who swallows an overdose of pills or pulls the trigger: it very often destroys others in the surviving family, burdening them with guilt, an indelible stigma and destroying the interpersonal relationship that had endured for years. The real victim is not the body in the coffin but often the surviving members of the family. Yet, the surviving family members have been overlooked as "victims of suicide" and are very often forgotten. In some cases, society may even point its accusatory finger at the family.

Contrary to the assumption that a tragedy may bring a family closer together, suicide can and often does tear a family apart. People who normally communicate with each other and trust each other may find themselves unable to do so. When this happens, members of the family do not get the love, help and support they need from one another. Some family survivors may go through a serious denial by never discussing the violence and horror that took the life of a family member, despite the fact that family survivors ought to be allowed to grieve openly, to express their feelings towards the victim and to discuss their own feelings about suicide. Anger, a common reaction in survivors following a suicide, can either be turned inward, or directed externally as aggression towards other survivors in the form of blame and resentment. Either way, however, family relations are disrupted and seriously damaged.[99]

To family members, suicide may appear to have been sudden and unexpected; survivors are left with no time to deal with unfinished business or with the painful memories of an angry farewell. Some surviving family members may feel guilty for not having been there to prevent the act; still others anguish over the thought of the victim dying alone. These feelings of guilt, pain and anguish are made worse by the fact that the behaviour of community members towards suicide survivors differs from other types of bereavement. A group of funeral directors in a survey observed that many of them noticed that "community members did not always know what to do and had difficulty expressing their sympathy to the surviving families."[100]

It seems that spouses have greater problems with grief experiences than other family members. This is not difficult to understand as the death of a spouse is one of the most stressful life events, but a death by suicide is even more difficult to face. Due to the social stigma attached to suicide, the surviving spouse may be discouraged from seeking the support needed to continue with life. Although these experiences are similar for both widowers and widows, widowers have been found to experience a more difficult bereavement and adjustment than widows, perhaps due to the fact that females have long been expected to be the caregivers in a relationship and males the receivers.[101]

As for parents who have lost a child to suicide, grief is usually more severe and long-lasting than if the child had died from natural causes.

With the suicide of a child, the grieving parents experience guilt which arises out of feelings of failure. Precisely because parents are considered to be responsible for the growth and protection of their children, the competency and credibility of the parents is often called into question in face of their child's suicide.

As for children who lost a parent in suicide, they can be greatly affected but will often refuse to share their thoughts or concerns: very often children believe that they caused the parent's suicide because they were bad. Such feelings of "being responsible" for the suicide almost always lead to feelings of guilt. When parents die, children experience such a great feeling of loss that they may attempt or complete suicide, often in the belief that they would rejoin their deceased parent in death.[102]

Anatomy of Grief

Grief is the subjective emotional response to loss including a number of psychological and somatic reactions whereas bereavement refers to the objective situation experienced by an individual who has lost a loved one.[103] Mourning is the actual behavioural manifestation of grief.

Grief includes feelings of abandonment, shock, disbelief, confusion, depression, anger, anxiety, panic, bewilderment, fear, guilt, shame and a sense of failure. The bereaved often feel they are in a state of shock or panic ("going crazy") without knowing how to cope with mixed thoughts and emotions, even though such evoked emotions are quite normal and experienced by most people who lose someone to suicide. As already discussed in the section on the theory of crisis, there are some somatic characteristics in grief as well: numbness, tightness in the chest, nausea, fatigue, loss of appetite or an inability to sleep. When suicide occurs, all these emotional and somatic reactions may overshadow the intense sadness, inhibiting the normal process of grief and causing the bereaved to feel isolated in their search for understanding and consolation.

One of the first to propose a theory of grief was Freud. He stated that there are two types of bereavement—normal and pathological. Freud suggested that after object loss, such as the death of a loved one, both types involve similar grief reactions (i.e., a loss of interest in the outside world, emotional pain, the loss of the capacity to love and some decline in the normal functions of daily routine). In pathological mourning, however, there is an added reaction not involved in the normal bereavement process—a drastic lowering of self-esteem. According to Freud, this leads the pathological mourner into a delusional need for self-punishment. It is this transference of feelings for the lost object to oneself that inhibit the reintegration of oneself into the world and the reincorporation of the lost object into one's memory. Inner rage and inversion of hostility towards oneself and one's ego arises, allowing the continuation of self-punishment which becomes eventually more pleasurable (masochism).[104]

Proposing that bereavement is a homoeostatic process in that it enables the bereaved to recoil, react and adjust to the loss, and then continue on with life, Bowlby and Parks suggested the following stages of grief.[105] In stage one people function mechanically, feeling numb. They may additionally experience anger, confusion or even relief. As a defence mechanism many people keep an emotional detachment from others in order to protect themselves and refuse to discuss the death. This stage lasts up to three months or longer after the death. The second stage is marked by general disorganization, in which many people experience feelings of loneliness, depression and deep sorrow as well as an overwhelming preoccupation with the deceased. They may also go through such somatic symptoms as sleep disturbance, decline in appetite and constant tearfulness. During this stage, it is advisable to reach out to someone for help. This stage may continue for one year after the death. The third stage contains a re-organization, in which feelings of grief become less intense and daily activity becomes easier to manage. Eventually one resumes normal daily life. This stage is displayed about one year after the death.

Another theory was proposed by Fleming and Robinson, involving three processes: typical grief process, chronic grief process and delayed grief process. The first one corresponds to Freud's normal grief in which the survivor experiences feelings of guilt, anger, loneliness, sadness and helplessness in the mourning process due to fear, lack of social support, the type of relationship with the deceased and multiple life stressors.[106]

Are bereavement experiences of survivors of suicide different from the experiences of survivors of other specific forms of death? In a study which compared survivors of suicide with those of accidental death, it was found that the resolution of grief and adjustment to bereavement depend primarily on the interaction of the coping strengths of the individual, cumulative stress experienced during the adjustment period and the social support available and used by the survivor; otherwise, there were no significant differences between the two types of bereaved families.[107] Such studies refute earlier studies that suggested a much more difficult bereavement for survivors of suicide. What is crucial, then, may not be the mode of death, but rather the extent of anticipation of death, the quality of the relationship between the family member and the deceased, the coping ability of individual family members and the availability and use of social support networks.[108]

Survivor Support Programme as a Self-Help Group

It is known that sometimes bereaved families have expressed the strong desire to be seen by a professional person within hours after the death.[109] Unfortunately, this is not always possible; however, a group such as the survivor support programme offers the needed support, sometimes on the spot, helping the survivor to deal with the initial reaction of shock, trauma, confusion and a host of other complex feelings. The survivor support programme focuses its services specifically on the survivors of a suicide, going beyond counselling to self-help and on to empowerment. The services of such a group are extremely useful precisely because the bereaved often feel isolated from family and friends, and expect little help from such sources. Friends often feel uncomfortable talking to the bereaved; it is much easier to avoid the bereaved than to make social mistakes of inappropriate consoling. Friends report that the survivors of suicide are the most difficult to express sympathy to at a funeral.[110]

In other types of bereavement, the church is usually seen as a major source of comfort, support and guidance for the grieving family. Today, however, people who have recently lost a loved one by suicide tend to turn to their family physician because members of the medical profession are assumed to be acquainted with the reality of death.[111] But there may be some basic limitations to what the general practitioner can do other than prescribing medication. In their busy practice, they have neither the time nor the expertise and training to deal with grief after suicide.

Mental health professionals such as clinical psychologists and psychiatrists are usually capable of helping the survivor to work through some of the complex emotions associated with the trauma of suicide bereavement. Professional support can and does help survivors to overcome feelings of guilt and express their thoughts and emotions openly. Unfortunately, however, only a small proportion of survivors seem to make use of such professional help. With this backdrop, then, self-help and mutual support services can be extremely useful and desirable.

Meetings with fellow survivors (since many counsellors in the survivor support programme are survivors themselves) can help surviving families to see themselves in a less negative and isolated manner. Survivors are also helped in a safe setting in which they are able to acknowledge and talk about feelings without the fear of stigmatization.

In Ontario, Canada, for instance, there are four support programmes located in Toronto, Hamilton, Windsor and Ottawa. The survivor support programme in Toronto has been well known for providing counselling, self-help and mutual support services. It has a 24-hour service as well as a mobile team to respond to the survivor at a certain location when immediate services are needed. Support services offered by this Toronto group have three major components. The first component is an initial assessment interview by a member of the programme with a member or members of the family, during which general background information is gathered including scores on the Beck Depression Inventory to assess the degree of depression. On the basis of such information, the programme tries to assess if the client needs immediate professional support and services. The second component consists of arranging family or individual sessions. Thus, the survivor, either individually or with their family, meets with two volunteers from the programme—one a survivor of suicide and the other a non-survivor. Such pairing of the survivor and the non-survivor as a team is extremely useful because the client initially feels more comfortable talking to a person "who has been there." Such sessions last for a total of eight weeks, two hours per session once a week. Meeting at their own home may assist the grieving process. The third component of the programme is a series of group sessions, which usually occur five to six weeks after the second component. In the course of the next 12 weeks, the group meets every other week. This last component acts as a bridge back to the general community.

Support programmes offer a number of goals for the bereaved in order to help them through their grief in a healthy, progressive manner: getting the suicide into perspective, dealing with family problems caused by the suicide, feeling better about themselves, talking about the suicide, obtaining factual information about suicide and its effects, having a safe place to express their feelings without stigmatization, understanding and dealing with other people's reactions to suicide and getting advice on practical and social concerns.[112]

In a study to find out if these stated goals were met at the completion of the programme, survivors ranked the following among the top three:

first, getting the suicide into perspective so that it does not drain all of their energy and emotions; second, having a safe place to air out their feelings without fear of being judged or stigmatized; and third, talking freely about suicide.[113] In a follow-up study of the survivor programme at the Memphis Suicide Prevention and Crisis Intervention Center it was found that most of the participants in the programme said the programme had met their needs in less than ten sessions of one-and-one-half hours each. After they left the group at the completion of the programme, 61% reported that they had been helped, 27% said that the programme could not help them any further and 12% said they were not helped at all.[114]

When a person commits suicide, for the victim life is over, but for the family tragedy has just begun. The unique aspect of support programmes is that they serve to fulfil the three-tiered needs of crisis management: prevention (through public education); intervention (to assist the surviving family shortly after the suicide, often in their own home); and postvention (offering support as well as helping the survivor acquire the necessary coping strategies for empowerment). It is expected, therefore, that the support services and programmes of this nature would only increase and gain saliency in the years to come.

Notes and References

1. *World Book Dictionary* (Chicago: World Book, 1983).

2. Fusé, T., "Suicide and Crisis: Etymology and Its Cultural Implications," *Focus on Listening*, 1993: 2, Spring, pp.1-2.

3. Hoff, L.A., *People in Crisis* (Redwood City, CA.; Addison Wesley, 1990), Third Edition, p.4.

4. In Buddhism, there is a concept known as *shiku-hakku* ("four sufferings and fourfold tribulations"). It includes four basic unavoidable sufferings of birthpain, growing old, illness and death, in addition to other fourfold tribulations such as the fate of separation from loved ones, having to see those one dislikes and detests, not getting what one really wants, and finally the grim awareness that life is full of suffering. These eight constitute the aforementioned *shiku-hakku* in life, and today the word is a synonym for the totality of suffering one experiences in life

5. Lindemann, E., "Symptomatology and Management of Acute Grief," *American Journal of Psychiatry*, 1944: 101, pp.101-148.

6. Aguilera, D.C. and Messick, J.M., *Crisis Intervention: Theory and Methodology* (St. Louis: C.V. Mosby Co., 1985), p.5.

7. Caplan, G., *Principles of Preventive Psychiatry* (New York: Basic Books, 1954).

8. Lester, D. and Brockopp, G.W., *Crisis Intervention and Counselling by Telephone* (Springfield, Illinois: Charles C. Thomas, 1973).

9. Zilboorg, G. and Henry, G.W., *A History of Medical Psychology* (New York: Norton, 1941).

10. Varah, Chad, *The Samaritans: Befriending the Suicidal* (London: Constable and Co. Ltd., 1988).

11. Lester, D. and Brockopp, G.W., *Crisis Intervention and Counselling By Telephone, op. cit.,* p.224.

12. Poldinger, W. and Holsboer-Trachsler, E., "Suicidal Tendencies: Detection and Evaluation," *Crisis*, 1990: 11, 2, pp.11-12.

13. Inamura, H., *Suicidology* (Tokyo: Tokyo University Press, 1979).

14. Kyoto INOCHI-NO-DENWA, *Newsletter,* February 25, 1990.

15. Fusé, T., *Emotional Crisis and Ethnotherapy* (Tokyo: Chuo-Koronsha, 1993), pp.131-137.

16 Crocker, P., "On Power and Helping," *Centrepoint*, Vol.2, No.2, 1988, p.3, Ontario Association of Distress Centres.

17 Japan INOCHI-NO-DENWA (ed), *Telephone Counselling: Theory and Practice* (Tokyo: Gakujutsu Publishing House, Ltd., 1989).

18 Fusé, T., *Introduction to Suicidology in Comparative Perspective, op. cit.,* pp.196-206; Fusé, T., *Emotional Crisis and Ethnotherapy, op. cit.,* pp.102-149.

19 Kurosawa, H., *Dialogue and Handshake - Don't Throw Your Life Away, op. cit.* Kurosawa, a psychiatrist and probably Japan's best known suicidologist, states that of all the suicide patients treated in his Emergency Medicine Department at Nippon Medical College Hospital for an eight-year period, only one did contact the telephone crisis line but the rest never did. It seems clear that there are two kinds of population here: those who phone the centre, and those who never call such centres and just go ahead with their suicide acts.

20 Fusé, T., "Epidemiology of Suicide in Britain," in Fusé, T., *Introduction to Suicidology..., op. cit.,* pp.64-69.

21 Bagley, C., "An Evaluation of Suicide Prevention Agencies," *Suicide and Life-Threatening Behavior,* 1971: 1, 4, pp. 245-239.

22 Fox, R., "The Suicide Drop - Why?" *Journal of the Royal Society of Health,* 1975: 95, 1, February, pp.11-14.

23 Bagley, C., *op. cit.*

24 Barraclough, B.M., "Suicide Prevention by the Samaritans: A Controlled Study of Effectiveness," *Lancet,* 1977: pp.237-239.

25 Jennings, C. et al., "Have the Samaritans Lowered the Suicide Rate? A controlled Study," *Psychological Medicine,* 1978: 8, p.413.

26 Varah, C., *The Samaritans. Befriending the Suicidal* (London: Constable and Company, Ltd., 1988), p.68.

27 Cutler, F., "The Relation of New Samaritan Clients and Volunteers to High risk People in England and Wales, 1965-1977," *Suicide and Life-Threatening Behavior,* 1979: 9, 4, pp.245-250.

28 Fox, R., "The Suicide Drop - Why?", *op. cit.,* p.12.

29 *Ibid.,* pp.12-13.

30 Lester, D., *Can We Prevent Suicide?* (New York: AMS Press, 1989).

31 Bridge, T.P., Potkin, S.G., Zong, W.W. and Soldo, B.J., "Suicide Prevention Centre: An Ecological Study of Effectiveness," *Journal of Nervous and Mental Diseases,* 1977: 16, 1, pp.18-24.

32 Miller, H., Coombs, D. and Leeper, J., "An Analysis of the Effects of Suicide Prevention Facilities on Suicide Rates in the United States," *American Journal of Public Health,* 1984: 74, pp.340-343.

33 King, G., "An Evaluation of the Effectiveness of a Telephone Counselling Centre," *American Journal of Community Psychology,* 1977: 5, 1, pp.75-82.

34 *Ibid.*

35 Aspler, R. and Hoople, H., "An Evaluation of Crisis Intervention Services with Anonymous Clients," *American Journal of Community Psychology,* 1976: 4, 3, pp.298-302.

36 Fox, R., "The Suicide Drop - Why?" *op. cit.,* p.13.

37 Motto, J.A., "Evaluation of a Suicide Prevention Center by Sampling the Population at Risk," *Suicide and Life-Threatening Behavior,"* 1971: 1, 1, pp.19-22.

38 Lester, D., Brockopp, G.W. et al., *Crisis Intervention and Counselling by Telephone, op. cit.,* p.224.

39 Pennebaker, J.W. and O'Heeron, R., "Confiding in Others and Illness Rate among Spouses of Suicide and Accidental Death Victims," *Journal of Abnormal Psychology*, 1984: 93, 4, pp.473-476; Pennbaker, J.W., "Traumatic Experience and Psychomatic Disease: Exploring the Roles of Behavioral Inhibition," *Canadian Psychology*, 1985: 26, 2, pp.82-95.

40 *Ibid.* In addition to confiding to one's friend, Pennebaker points out the beneficial effects of other confiding methods such as "confession through a prayer" and writing in a diary, neither of which requires a visible listener. Pennebaker found these methods effective in reducing stress which is related to illness. His studies are certainly pregnant with implications for beneficial therapeutic measures other than paid mental-health professionals. Fusé also explored the theoretical basis and application of benefits in relation to writing a diary, which he calls "epistotherapy." See: Fusé, *Crisis and Ethnotherapy, op. cit.,* pp.178-192.

41 Glatt, K., "Helpline: Suicide Prevention at a Suicide Site," *Suicide and Life-Threatening Behavior*, 1987: 17, pp.299-309.

42 The following discussion, unless otherwise indicated, is based on the information taken from: Fusé, T., "Suicidology and Crisis Intervention: Theory and Practice," *Mental Care Nursing: Special Issue on Suicide - Its Psychology and Mental Health Approach for Prevention,* 1995, 1, 4, November, (Nagoya: Nissoken), pp.22-28.

43 Shneidman, E., "Suicide," in *Encyclopedia Britannica* (Chicago: Encyclopedia Britannica, 1990), pp.777-782.

44 Jean Baeschler, *Suicides* (New York: The Free Press, 1976).

45 Shneidman, "Suicide," *op. cit.*

46 Heisel, M. and Fusé, T., "Suicide Ideation, Depression and Hopelessness among Students in Liberal Arts, Suicidology, Psychiatry, and Nursing: A Cross-cultural Pilot Study," an unpublished paper, Department of Psychology, York University, Toronto, Canada, 1996.

[47] Johnson, W. and Snibble, J., "The Selection of a Psychiatric Curriculum for Medical Students: Results of a Survey," *American Journal of Psychiatry,* 1975: 132, 5, pp.513-516.

[48] Barlow, D.H. and Durand, V.M. *Abnormal Psychology: An Integrative Approach* (Pacific Grove, Ca.: Brooks/Cole Publishing Co., 1995), p.295.

[49] Kurosawa, H., *Dialogue and Handshake—Strategies for Suicide Prevention* (Tokyo: Kobundo Co., 1989), pp.197-199.

[50] Merton, R.K., *Social Theory and Social Structure* (New York: The Free Press, 1968).

[51] Burstein, A.G. et al., "Assessment of Suicidal Risk by Psychology and Psychiatry Trainees," *Archives of General Psychiatry,* 1973: 29, pp.792-794.

[52] Blumenthal, S.J. and Kupfer, D.J. *Suicide over the Life Cycle* (Washington, D.C.: American Psychiatric Press, 1990), p.722.

[53] National Task Force Report, *Suicide in Canada: Update of the Task Force on Suicide in Canada* (Ottawa: Ministry of Health and Welfare, 1994), p.17.

[54] Iwasaki, Y. "Consultation Liaison Psychiatry in Critical Care Medical Centre," a special lecture given at the Crisis Unit, Department of Psychiatry, East General Hospital, Toronto, Ontario, August 2, 1990; Morrison, J.R. "Suicide in Psychiatric Practice Population," *Journal of Clinical Psychia*try, 1982: 43, pp.348-352.

[55] Fusé, T., *Introduction to Suicidology in Cross-Cultural Perspective* (Tokyo: Seishin Shobo Publishers, 1990), pp.185-195.

[56] O'Reilly, R.L., Traut, G.S., Donaldson, L., "Psychiatrists' Experience of Suicide in their Patients," *Psychiatric Journal of the University of Ottawa,* 1990: 15, 3, pp. 173-176.

[57] Chemtob, C.M., Hamada, R.S., Bauer, G., Kinney, B., Torigoe, R.Y., "Patients' Suicides: Frequency and Impact on Psychiatrists," *American Journal of Psychiatry,* 1988: 145, pp.224-228.

[58] Kurosawa, H., "Psychiatric Care of Attempters," *Emergency Medicine* (Tokyo), 1985: 9,3, p.29, cited in Fusé, T., *Introduction to Suicidology in Cross-Cultural Perspective* (Tokyo: Seishin Shobo Publishers, 1990), pp.211-217.

[59] W.H.O., *Patterns of Suicide - Europe,* Euro Report, (Copenhagen: Regional Office of the World Health Organization, 1988) p.1.

[60] Kurosawa, H., *Dialogue and Handshake, op. cit.,* pp.197-199.

[61] Chemtob et al., *op. cit.,* p.227.

[62] Eynan-Harvey, R. and Stevens, T.V., "Death and Suicide Education in Canadian Medical Schools," unpublished manuscript, Division of Social Science, York University, Toronto, 1993.

[63] Shein, H.M., "Suicide Care: Obstacles in the Education of Psychiatric Residents," *Omega,* 1976: 7, 1, pp.75-81.

[64] Chemtob et al., *op. cit.*, pp.224-228.

[65] Johnson and Snibble, *op. cit.*, p.516.

[66] Light, D., "Professional Problems in Treating Suicidal Persons," *Omega*, 1976: 7, 1, pp.59-67.

[67] Shneidman, E.S., "Suicide as Psychache," *Journal of Nervous and Mental Disease*, 1993: 181, pp.145-147.

[68] Kral, M.J. and Sakinofsky, I., "Clinical Model for Suicide Risk Assessment," *Death Studies*, 1994: 18, pp.311-326.

[69] Ramsay, R.F., Tanney, B.L., Tierney, R.J. and Lang, W.A., *Suicide Intervention Handbook* (Calgary, Alberta, Canada: Living Works Education Inc., 1994), pp.22-24.

[70] *Ibid.*, pp.25-28.

[71] Beck, A.T., Brown, G. and Steer, R.A., "Prediction of Eventual Suicide in Psychiatric Inpatients by Clinical Ratings of Hopelessness," *Journal of Consulting and Clinical Psychology*, 1989: 57, pp.309-310.

[72] Pokorney, A., "Prediction of Suicide in Psychiatric Patients," *Archives of General Psychiatry*, 1983: 40, pp.249-257.

[73] Goldstein, R.B., Black, D.W., Nasralla, A., Winokur, G., "The Prediction of Suicide," *Archives of General Psychiatry*, 1991: 48, pp.418-422.

[74] Fusé, T., "Hopelessness—An Anatomy of Despair and Suicide: Reflections of a Suicidologist," Keynote Address, *Proceedings of the XIII Congress of International Federation of Telephonic Emergency Services* (Jerusalem: ERAN, 1994), pp.66-80; also, Fusé, T., *Profiles of Death - Why Did They Kill Themselves* (Tokyo: Seishin Shobo Publishers, 1991).

[75] The foregoing discussion is partly based upon the information provided by: Dick Butcher, "Different Modalities of Crisis Intervention," an M.A. review paper, Department of Sociology, York University, 1993.

[76] Fusé, T., *Emotional Crisis and Ethnotherapy, op. cit.*, pp.136-137.

[77] *Manual for Crisis Intervention*, Crisis Unit, Department of Psychiatry, Toronto East General Hospital, Toronto, Ontario, Canada. (Modified with the author's own experience as a volunteer at a crisis centre.)

[78] Blumenthal, S.J., "An Overview and Synopsis of Risk Factors, Assessment, and Treatment of Suicidal Patients Over the Life Cycle," in Blumenthal, S.J., Kupfer, D.J., (eds), *Suicide Over the Life Cycle: Risk Factors, Assessment, and Treatment of Suicidal Patients* (Washington, D.C.: American Psychiatric Press, 1990), pp.710-722.

[78] *Ibid.*, p.714.

[80] *Training Manual*, Crisis Intervention Unit, Toronto East General Hospital, *op. cit.;* Ramsey, R.F. et al., *Suicide Intervention Handbook, op. cit.*, pp.30-39.

81   Blumenthal, S.J., "An Overview...," *op. cit.*, pp.710-720.

82   For a detailed discussion on the relationship between cultural values and Japanese social behaviour, see: Fusé, T., "Cultural Values and Social Behaviour of the Japanese: A Comparative Analysis," *Cultures et Développement*, 1982: XIV, 2-3, pp.227-257.

83   Murase, T. and Johnson, F., "Naikan, Morita, and Western Psychotherapy; A Comparison," *Archives of General Psychiatry*, 1974: 31, July, p.127.

84   *Ibid.*

85   Freud, S., *Introductory Lecture on Psychoanalysis* (Part III), in Strachey, J. (ed), *The Standard Edition of the Complete Psychological Works of Sigmund Freud*, Vol. 16 (London: The Hogarth Press, 1963), p.454.

86   Reynolds, D.K., *Flowing Bridges, Quiet Waters* (Albany, N.Y.: State University of New York, 1989).

87   The ensuing discussion has been based upon information from the following sources: Fusé, T., *Emotional Crisis and Ethnotherapy, op. cit.,* pp.169-179; Yoshimoto, I., *Invitation to Naikan* (fourth edition) (Osaka: Toki Publishers, 1990); Ito, R., (ed), *A Handbook on Psychotherapy* (Tokyo: Fukumura Publishers, 1989), pp.393-416; Reynolds, D.K., *Naikan Psychotherapy* (Chicago: The University of Chicago Press, 1983); Miki, Y., *Introduction to Naikan: A Japanese Way of Self-Exploration* (Osaka: Sogensha, 1984).

88   Makino, R., "Naikan Psychotherapy in the West: A Survey of Naikan Participants," *Psychologica* (Kyoto, Japan), 1996. Interestingly, this theme in Naikan corresponds intriguingly to the theological concept of grace in Christianity.

89   Reynolds, D.K., *The Quiet Therapies: Japanese Pathways to Personal Growth* (Honolulu: The University of Hawaii Press, 1980), p.12 (italics, author's).

90   The author wishes to express his gratitude to Professor Miki at the Nara Naikan Institute in allowing him to participate in a Naikan session for three days in 1989. The experience has deepened the author's belief in ethnotherapy.

91   Fusé, T., "Cultural Values and Social Behaviour of the Japanese...," *op. cit.,* pp.235-240.

92   Noon, J.M. and Lewis, J.R., "Therapeutic Strategies and Outcome: Perspectives from Different Cultures," *British Journal of Medical Psychology*, 1992: 65, pp.107-117.

93   Fromm, E., *Escape from Freedom* (New York: Holt, Rinehart and Winston, 1941).

94   Kosawa, H., "Two Types of Guilt Consciousness - Ajasé Complex," *Research on Psychoanalysis*, 1950, 1, 1, cited by Okonogi, K., "The Ajasé Complex of the Japanese," *Japan Echo*, 1978: 4, pp.88-105.

95 Lebra, T.S., *Japanese Patterns of Behavior* (Honolulu: University of Hawaii Press, 1976), p.223.

96 Miki, Y., *op. cit.,* 1984.

97 Shneidman, E., *Deaths of Man* (New York: The New York Times Book Co., 1973).

98 Presentation by Karen Letofsky, Director, Survivor Support Programme in Toronto, February 25, 1995, York University, Toronto, Canada.

99 Lukas, C. and Seidman, H., *Silent Grief: Living in the Wake of a Suicide* (New York: Charles Scribners and Sons, 1987), p.171.

100 McIntosh, J. and Wrobleski, A., "Grief Reactions among Suicide Survivors: An Exploratory Comparison of Relationships," *Death Studies*, 1988: 12, pp.21-39.

101 Wertheimer, A., *A Special Scar* (London: Routledge, 1991), pp.10-45.

102 Lukas and Seidman, *op. cit.*

103 Stroebe, W. and Stroebe, M.S., *Bereavement and Health: The Psychological and Physical Consequences of Partner Loss* (New York: Cambridge, 1989), p.9.

104 Freud, S., "Mourning and Melancholia," *op. cit.*

105 McIntosh, J., "Survivor Family Relationship: Literature Review," in Dunne, E.J. et al. (eds), *Suicide and Its Aftermath* (New York: W.W. Noerton, 1987), pp.57-70.

106 Fleming, S.J. and Robinson, P.J., "The Application of Cognitive Therapy to the Bereaved," in Vallis, T.M., and Howes, J.L., (eds), *The Challenge of Cognitive Therapy: Applications to Non-traditional Populations* (New York: Plenum, 1991), pp.135-158.

107 Barret, T. and Scott, T., "Development of the Grief Experience Questionnaire," *Suicide and Life-Threatening Behavior*, 1989: 19, 2, pp.201-215.

108 McNeil, D.E., Hatcher, C. and Reuben, R., "Family Survivors of Suicide and Accindental Death: Consequences for Widows," *Suicide and Life-Threatening Behavior,* 1988: 18, 2, pp.137-148.

108 Hatton, L.C. and Valente, S.M. (eds.), *Suicide: Assessment and Intervention*, (Norwalk, Conn.: Appleton-Century-Crofts, 1989), *op. cit.,* p.145.

110 Wagner, K.G. and Calhoun, L.G., "Perceptions of Social Support by Suicide Survivors and Their Social Networks," *Omega: Journal of Death and Dying*, 1991-92: 24, 1,

111 Wertheimer, *op. cit.,* p.144.

112 Rogers, J. et al., "Help for Families of Suicide: Survivor Support Program," *Canadian Journal of Psychiatry*, 1982: 27, p.144.

113 *Ibid.*

114 Battle, A.O., "Group Therapy for Survivors of Suicide," *International Journal of Suicide and Crisis Studies*, 1984: pp.45-58.

Epilogue

There is one issue that must be discussed sooner or later by suicidology in the twenty-first century—the thorny question of euthanasia, especially in the form of physician-assisted suicide. Unfortunately, there is no space left in the present volume to ponder in detail on this important and highly controversial subject, which must be conceded to another occasion in the near future.

As this book goes to press, the highest court in Australia has upheld the euthanasia law in one of its territories; in the Netherlands, there has been *de facto* and highly liberal practice of euthanasia (including physician-assisted suicide) for some time now. In the United States, some states have accepted the so-called Living Will and the "right to die with dignity," while some others have been putting the question of euthanasia on referendum. In fact, euthanasia was recently rejected by a referendum in the state of Washington by a very slim margin. A former pathologist in Michigan (Dr. Kevorkian) has already assisted almost 30 suicides who had been suffering from painful, terminal illness. *Final Exit*, written by Derek Humphrey of the Los Angeles Hemlock Society, shot up to the best-seller list within a few months of its publication in the early 1990s. In both Britain and France, how-to manuals on euthanasia (*Exit* and *Suicide— Mode d'Emploi* respectively) became run-away sellers in the late 1980s. Half way around the world, a book entitled *Kanzen Jisatsu Manyuaru* (*A*

Complete Manual for Suicide) has been one of the unexpected best sellers in Japan since 1994. It appears as if the basic world trend is steadily moving towards affirmation of "dying with dignity" (including physician-assisted suicide) for those who are terminally ill and in unbearable pain.

Those who are committed to euthanasia (which means "good death" in Greek) believe that it is one of the fundamental human rights of the free individual in a free society. Public opinion polls in North America, Europe, Japan and elsewhere have been inching towards the favourable approval of euthanasia. In this day and age, then, on what grounds is one justified in preventing and intervening with suicide, which, after all, may be the result of an exercise of one's basic human right?

The present author was born and raised in a country that has always been tolerant of and even hospitable to death in general and suicide in particular. Moreover, he has been raised amidst the folklore and aesthetics of death such as *seppuku* and *kamikaze*; he had been more tolerant of the arguments for self-inflicted death and euthanasia. However, his involvement with years of research, many and long interviews with individuals who have survived their suicide attempts, exposure to various aspects of crisis intervention in many different countries of the world and, finally, active involvement in the "active listening" of the crisis line as a volunteer—all these experiences have considerably modified his attitude towards the "right to suicide."

Such changing and evolving views were further reinforced by the writing of a monograph on the biographical and psychological autopsies of 11 personalities from four different countries as mentioned in the present book. That work convinced the author rather compellingly that, despite obvious differences in gender, sex, age, religion and nationality, there are certain discernible factors common to all these suicidal individuals. These include unbearable psychic pain because of a deeply felt sense of loss, increasing despair and hopelessness about the present and the future, intense desire to escape such pain even at the expense of one's own life. Furthermore, there was sufficient evidence to suggest that they were reaching out for help. If timely help had been given in whatever form, all, or at least some, of them might have been saved.

It is perhaps appropriate to conclude with a highly personal and subjective note on the very difficult and admittedly controversial question of the rationale for the prevention and intervention of suicide. First, when someone is physically and visibly hurt and in great pain, immediate help and empathy is usually extended and ought to be rendered. Likewise,

when a person is emotionally hurting and in great psychic pain such an individual also deserves help from family members, friends and the public. Secondly, in the course of the author's research in suicidology for over a quarter of a century, he has been privileged to talk to many individuals who have made suicide attempts yet survived. They all intimated to the author, without exception, how fortunate they were to have survived. This interview experience and encounters with suicidals on crisis lines, suggests that such suicidal feelings are often transient and time-limiting, and that *suicide, therefore, is a permanent solution to a temporary problem*! Thirdly, it is good to remember what the historian Arnold Toynbee once said: "there are always two parties to a death: the person who dies, and the survivors who are bereaved." (Turner and Porter Funeral Home, "Helping a Suicide Survivor Heal," Toronto, Ontario). No death is neutral. Suicide may take the life of one person in a physical and biological sense, but it also kills a part of everyone who has had a close relationship with the individual who committed suicide. Friends and family members must now contend as survivors with the emotional pain that will surface as a result of the recent loss. They must come to terms with intense feelings due to a sense of loss and possibly guilt or rage, shock, deep sorrow, and shame. As such, suicide is far from being a solitary act but one with a devastating impact on those who were close to the individual. Surviving family members of suicide run a much greater risk of suicide themselves. An individual may have a right to suicide, but others also have a right to lead a life unstained by suicide.

In human existence, which is merely a brief span of life on earth, one's joy and sorrow are always related to that of others. No human being is free from existential problems, pain and death. This common humanity generates a deep sense of relatedness in every individual. The point is poignantly driven home by the great English poet and thinker John Donne (1572-1631):

> No man is an island, entire
> of itself; every man is a piece
> of the continent, a part of
> the main.

Index

Baeschler, Jean, xvi-xvii, 30, 61, 104-09, 132, 151, 326
Bagley, C., 317
Bamayr, [name], 264, 278
Bangalore, 190
banzai charge, 4
Barkey, K., 91
Barraclough, B. M., 30, 64, 317
Basel, 191
Battle of Sekigahara, 230
Bavaria, 264, 285
Beck, Aaron, xvi, 30, 133-35, 148-49, 152, 175, 179, 182-83, 190
Beck's Depression Inventory, 342, 373
Beck's Hopelessness Scale, 135, 342
Beer Sheba, 323-24
Befrienders International, 305
Beiser, M. F., 193
Belgium, 40-41, 46, 66
Benin, 189
Bergman, J., 277
Berlin, 190
Biathanatos (Donne), 17, 19-20
Bible, 14-16. *See also* Old Testament
Bille-Brahe, U., 92
Biller, O. A., 90
Binitie, A., 192
biochemistry, 6, 136-39, 142-49
biology, xv, 76
Birtchell, J., 123
Blachly, P. H., 253, 263, 276-77, 279, 285
blacks, 48-49
Blake, J. A., 89
Bon Festival, 244
boshi-shinju, 2-3
Boston, 301
Boutroux, Emile, 77
Bowlby, [name], 371
Breault, K. D., 91
Breuer, Joseph, 111-12
British Columbia, 52
British Columbia Supreme Court, 23
British Isles, 305. *See also* Great Britain; United Kingdom
British Medical Journal, 254, 276
Brockopp, G. W., 303
Brown, E. P., 108
Browne, Sir Thomas, 2

Buddha, 239, 249n, 362
Buddhism, 233, 236-42, 244-45, 249-50n, 358, 362, 375n. *See also* Pure Land sect; Zen Buddhism
Bulgaria, 46
Bulletin of Suicidology, The, 4
burial, 4, 18, 22
Burma, 249n
Burstein, A. G., 332
Burton, Richard, 24
bushido, 217-18, 231, 233, 236, 240-43, 248-49nn
Byakkotai (White Tiger Squad), 220

California, 62, 257, 261, 277, 282, 317-18
Canada, 23, 41-43, 45-46, 48, 52, 65-66, 93, 96, 120, 135, 170, 190-91, 193-94, 203, 252, 290, 304-06, 327, 334
Canary Islands, 63
cancer, 64-65
Canterbury Suicide Project, 167
Caplan, G., 301-03
Carlson, G. A., 273-74
Catholic Church, 12, 16-21, 84
Catholics and Catholicism, 27, 41, 43, 50, 81, 83-84, 90, 98. *See also* Catholic Church
Cato, 14, 24
Central Statistical Office (Finland), 92
Central Statistical Office (Paris), 54
cerebrospinal fluid (CSF), 137-39, 143-45, 187
"Ceremony of Ill Luck" (*Kyorei*), 230
Chad, 108
Charcot, Jean, 111-12
Chatterton, Thomas, 21
Cheyne, George, 24
Chicago, 89
Chile, 46
China, 189-90, 216, 238, 250n
Chiyoda Castle, 219
Christians and Christianity, 16-17, 196-97, 245, 251. *See also* Catholic Church and specific denominational groups
Chu, 362
Cicero, 13-14
Clarke Institute of Psychiatry, 168
Clues to Suicide (Shneidman), 29

Duchess County (New York), 324
Durkheim, Emile, 30, 59
  biographical background of, 76-79
  theories and findings of, xiv-xv, 26-27, 36,
    46, 49-50, 76, 79-105, 119-20, 150-51,
    260, 316
  works of, 6, 25-26, 77-78, 94
  Du Suicide et la Folie Suicide (de Boismont),
    25

East Germany, 40-41. *See also* Germany
Ecclesiastical History (Eusebius), 17
École Normale Superieure, 77
Ecuador, 63
Edo, 218-19
*Éducation et Sociologie (Education and
  Sociology)* (Durkheim), 78
Egeland, J. A., 140
ego, 27, 113-15, 117-18, 127-28, 233, 287,
  371
Egypt, 43
Elet, 306
empowerment, 8-9, 298, 300, 307, 335, 347,
  357, 364, 372, 374
England. *See* England and Wales
England and Wales, 46, 51, 53, 61, 64-65,
  67, 107, 189, 252, 254, 256, 258-59,
  265, 317, 320
E-on, 238
Epicureans, 14
epidemiology
  definition of, 35
  nature of, 35-36
Epstein, L. C., 260, 286
ERAN, 7, 306, 311
Erikson, Erik, 178
eros, xiii, 113-15, 117, 127
Escape from Freedom (Fromm), 89
Esquirol, Jean-Étienne, 24-25, 60
Ethics Committee (Japan Medical
  Association), 23
ethnotherapy, definition of, 357
etymology, definition of, 1-2
Europe, 39-40, 168, 171, 232, 253, 273,
  285, 303, 305, 343, 384
Eusebius, 17
euthanasia, 12, 22-23, 383-84
Exit, 22, 383
Exodus, 18

Falret, J. P., 24
family risk studies, xvi, 139-40, 183-86
Farberow, Norman, xvi, 29-30, 131-33, 152
Fatality Inquiries Act, 1976 (Alberta), 52
Federal Republic of Germany. *See* West
  Germany
Feuerlein, [name], 264, 278
Field Service Code (Japanese Imperial Armed
  Forces), 242
Final Exit (Humphrey), 22, 383
Finland, 40-41, 45, 92, 142, 168, 265
Fisher, S., 119
5-HIAA (5-hydroxyindoleacetic acid),
  136-39, 142-47
Fleming, S. J., 371
Flint (Michigan), 91-92
47 ronin, incident of the, 219, 226
France, 22, 24, 27, 40-41, 45-46, 48, 54-56,
  201, 221, 306, 383
Frankl, Victor, 181
Freeman, W., 255, 263, 276, 279, 285
French Revolution, 22, 303
Freud, Sigmund, 358
  biographical background of, 111-12
  theories and findings of, xiii-xiv, xvi,
    27-28, 36, 110-28, 130, 152, 176-77,
    182, 325, 365, 370-71
  works of, 28, 111-12, 114-16, 176-77
Fromm, Erich, 89, 364
funbara, 224, 226-27
Fusé, Toyomasa, 109, 135, 190, 193
fushi-shinju, 2-3
Fustel de Coulanges, [name], 77

Galton, Francis, 199
Garland, Judy, 109
gedatsu, 244
genetics, xvi, 6, 29, 76, 136, 139-47, 149,
  176, 183-87, 255
Genji Clan, 216
Genshin, 238-39
Georgianna, S., 90
Germany, 27, 46, 188, 192, 201, 306, 359.
  See also East
Germany; West Germany
Gerstein House, 346-47
Gestalt theory, 77
gibara, 224, 226

mental disorder, definition of, 173
mental illness, 165-172
    problems of assessment, 197-204
Metropolitan Toronto Police Force, 54, 58
Mexico, 43, 65
Meynert, Theodore, 111
Michigan, 383
Middle East, 40
Miki, Y., 367
Miller, D. C., 273-74
Miller, H., 319
Minnesota Multiphasic Personality Inventory (MMPI), 193
miroku Buddha, 239-40
Mishima, Yukio, 109, 215, 223, 242
mishirabé, 358
Miura Takanori, 239
MMPI (Minnesota Multiphasic Personality Inventory), 193
Mochiuji Ashikaga, 218
Mongols, 217
Monroe, Marilyn, 97, 109
Montaigne, Michel de, 19
Montesquieu, 21, 32n
Montreal, 119-20, 191
Mood Disorder Clinic (University of Pennsylvania), 134, 146
More, Sir Thomas, 19
Morita, Shoma, 357
Morita therapy, 357-58
Morselli, Henry, 26, 48, 60
Motohashi, Y., 121
Moto-ori Norinaga, 243
"Mourning and Melancholia" (Freud), 28, 114-15, 176
Mt. Mihara, 323
mujo, 240
munenbara, 217, 224, 226
Munich, 359
Murphy, H., 191
Murray, Henry, 108
Myers, I., 122

Nadelson, C., 272
Nagasaki, 191
Nagumo, Lieutenant-General, 241-42
Naikan, xix, 356-67
Naikan-Ho, 358

Naikan-Ryoho, 358
Nakatoki Hojo, 217
Nancy B., 23
Nara, 215
Nara period, 216
National Board of Health and Welfare (Sweden), 278
National Center for Health Statistics (United States), 62, 92
National Institute of Mental Health (United States), 145
National Task Force on Suicide in Canada, 36, 52, 127, 198, 203
natives (North American), 93, 96. *See also* Indians; Inuit
Navajo Indians, 168
neo-Platonists, 12, 17
Nero, 13
Netherlands, 22-23, 40, 46, 383
neurasthenia, 190
neurobiology, xvi, 29
neurochemistry, 76
neuropharmacology, 149
neuropsychiatry, 149
neurotransmitters, 6, 136-38, 147, 183, 187. *See also* serotonin
Newfoundland and Labrador, 52, 65-66, 143
New Hampshire, 124
New Haven (Connecticut), 122
Newslink (AAS), 29
New Testament, 16. *See also* Bible
New York City, 48, 50
New York University, 125
New Zealand, 40-42, 167
NHK, 244
Nigeria, 189, 192
Nihon Shoki (Chronicle of Ancient Japan), 237
nimonji-bara, 224, 228
Nippon Medical College Hospital, 169, 247n, 376n
Nixon, Richard, 232
Nogi, Maresuke, 109, 226
North America, 38-40, 51, 171, 203, 232, 253, 266, 280, 285, 290, 328, 343, 363-64, 384
North Carolina, 319
Northern Ireland, 53
Norway, 40, 46, 51, 65, 121

Rimpela, A. H., 286
Rio de Janeiro, 191
Ripley, H., 123
Robinson, P. J., 371
Robinson, Svend, 23
Rochester (New York), 142-43
Rodriguez, Sue, 23
role narcissism, 232-33
Roman, Jo, 109
Romans, 13-14
ronbara, 224, 226
Rose, K. D., 257, 260, 277
Rosenhan, D. L., 202
Rosow, I., 257, 260, 277
Ross, M., 262-63, 286-87
Ross, O., 64
Roy, Alec, 140-41, 144-45
Russell, A. T., 277
Russell, Gail, 97
Russia, 40
Ruzika, L. T., 60

Sadakichi Iinuma, 220
SADD (Standardized Assessment of Depressive Disorders), 191, 194
Sainsbury, P., 30, 64-65
Saipan, 101, 241-42
Saito, Lieutenant-General, 241
Sakai, 221
sakibara, 224, 226
Sakinofsky, I., 256-57, 276, 279, 285, 289
Samaritans (telephone crisis line organization), 7, 305-06, 316-18, 320
Samson, 14
samurai, 2, 86, 109, 214, 216-21, 223, 225-31, 233, 239-41, 243, 245, 248n
Sanders, George, 97
sanmonji-bara, 224, 228
Santiago, 191
Sara Nar, 108
Satsuma Province, 220
Saul, 14
Scandinavia, 53
schizophrenia, 141, 146, 166, 168-69, 171, 173, 184, 186-87, 333
Schutz, Alfred, 105
Scotland, 53, 64
Seattle, 191
Seberg, Jean, 98, 109

Second Gujarat Suicide Inquiry Commission, 192
Self-Harm Assessment, Research and Education (SHARE), 168, 344, 346
Self-Rating Depression Scale, 190
Seligman, M., 180-81, 183
Selye, Hans, 262
Seneca, 13, 21
Senegal, 193-94
seppuku
  definition of, 2-3
  as a form of altruistic suicide, 86
  history of, xvii, 4, 109, 213-23, 225-33, 239, 241-42, 247-48nn
  implications for modern suicidology of, xvii, 109, 192-93, 214, 245-46
  and Japanese philosophy and aesthetics of death, 214, 231-45, 384
  and misconceptions about suicide rates in Japan, 41
  as a socially meaningful act, 104, 109
  types and methods of, 213, 216-18, 220-31, 248n
serotonin, xvi, 136-39, 142-44, 146-48, 155, 183, 187, 353
Shanghai, 191
SHARE (Self-Harm Assessment, Research and Education), 168, 344, 346
shashin ohjo, 239
shiku-hakku, 375n
Shinpuren Incident, 223
Shinran, 247n
Shintoism, 238
Shneidman, Edwin, xvi, 4-5, 28-30, 108, 129-32, 147, 152, 317, 336, 367
shobara, 224, 226, 246
Shogun (television drama), 215
shoshin, 2-3
Shotoku, Prince, 249n
SIEC (Suicide Information and Education Centre), 28, 289
SIEC Alert, 289
Simon, W., 264, 278, 285
Simpson, M. E., 91
Singapore, 41, 46
Snow, John, 35-36
social action theory, 101-10, 151, 233

Ten Commandments, 196
terrorism, 100-101
Tertullian, 16
Thailand, 249n
thanatos, xiii-xiv, 113-17, 127, 325
Theorell, T., 278
Thomas, C. B., 281
three cycles of life (Buddhist concept), 240-41
Three Essays on the Theory of Sexuality (Freud), 112
Todd, R. E., 62
Tokugawa period, 218, 221, 223, 225-29, 243
Tokyo, 44, 218, 356-57
Tokyo Metropolitan Medical Examiner's Office, 44, 129-30
Toronto, 142-43, 168, 275, 297, 344, 346, 373
toshin, 2-3
Toynbee, Arnold, 385
Trovato, F., 120
tsumebara, 218, 223-24, 226
Tsunetomo Yamamoto, 249n
Tulsa, 253
Turner and Porter Funeral Home, 385
twin studies, xvi, 139-41, 144-45, 183-86
Type A personalities, 262-63, 287

U.N. (United Nations), 91
United Kingdom, 40, 42, 45, 48, 53. *See also* British Isles; Great Britain
United Nations (U.N.), 91
United States, 23, 27, 29, 41-42, 45-46, 48-50, 60, 64-65, 90, 92, 120-21, 142, 189-91, 198, 201-02, 252-55, 264, 267-69, 273, 281-82, 284, 304-06, 318-19, 333-34, 338, 359, 363, 383
University of Bordeaux, 78
University of Kyoto, 125, 171
University of Luebeck, 288-89
University of Munich, 199
University of North Carolina, 283, 290
University of Pennsylvania, 134, 146, 183
University of Toronto, 280
University of Vienna, 111
Uruguay, 43, 46
Utopia (More), 19

Van Praag, Herman, 136, 142
Varah, Chad, 304-05, 317
Venezuela, 46
Verona, 191
Verstehende Soziologie, 102
Vicious, Sid, 97
Vienna, 359
Vietnam, 249n
Vincent, M. O., 262, 281
Voltaire, 24

Wales. *See* England and Wales
Walker, Allan, 305
Washington (state), 383
Watergate, 232
Weber, Max, xvi, 101-04, 107, 109, 151, 196
Weishaar, [name], 190
Welner, A., 269, 276
Wender, P. H., 186
Wenz, F. V., 91-92
Werther effect, 30
West Germany, 45, 48, 65, 264. *See also* Germany
Wetzell, R. D., 135
whites, 48-49, 96
WHO. *See* World Health Organization
Willi, J., 279
Windsor (Ontario), 373
Woolf, Virginia, 109
World Health Organization (WHO), 38-39, 51, 53, 59, 63-64, 69, 70n, 89-90, 166, 168, 190-91, 194, 201, 203, 265
World War II, 4, 86, 100-101, 213-15, 223, 225, 231, 241-42, 316
Wundt, Wilhelm, 77

Yasusuke Fujiwara, 215
yomi no kuni, 237
Yorimoto Minamoto, 216-17
Yoro Edict, 239
Yoshitsune Minamoto, 217
Young, Gig, 97
Yugoslavia, 70n
Yukinaga Konishi, 230-31

Zen Buddhism, 217, 240, 357, 364
Zimri, 14